A Bloody Day at Gaines' Mill

A Bloody Day
at Gaines' Mill

*The Battlefield Debut of the Army
of Northern Virginia, June 27, 1862*

Elmer R. Woodard, III

McFarland & Company, Inc., Publishers
Jefferson, North Carolina

LIBRARY OF CONGRESS CATALOGUING-IN-PUBLICATION DATA

Names: Woodard, Elmer R., 1961– author.
Title: A bloody day at Gaines' Mill : the battlefield debut of the Army
of Northern Virginia, June 27, 1862 / Elmer R. Woodard III.
Description: Jefferson, North Carolina : McFarland & Company, Inc.,
Publishers, 2019 | Includes bibliographical references and index.
Identifiers: LCCN 2018053094 | ISBN 9781476673578
(softcover : acid free paper) ∞
Subjects: LCSH: Gaines' Mill, Battle of, Va., 1862. | Confederate States
of America. Army of Northern Virginia—History.
Classification: LCC E473.68 .W66 2019 | DDC 973.7/455—dc23
LC record available at https://lccn.loc.gov/2018053094

BRITISH LIBRARY CATALOGUING DATA ARE AVAILABLE

ISBN (print) 978-1-4766-7357-8
ISBN (ebook) 978-1-4766-3342-8

The front cover painting is of the *5th U.S. Cavalry Charge* (courtesy of the
U.S. Cavalry Museum, U.S. Army Center of Military History)

Printed in the United States of America

McFarland & Company, Inc., Publishers
Box 611, Jefferson, North Carolina 28640
www.mcfarlandpub.com

To Mrs. Linda Woodard

Acknowledgments

This book would not have been possible without the assistance of many others, including, in no particular order, the following.

Major Kyle and Captain Cate Duffer, who brainstormed the logistics of the march from the Valley. Major Duffer was also instrumental in sleuthing many odd occurrences and in calculating march rates, road space, and many other details, especially divining why a commander would or would not do something. Colonel Guy Gormley (ret.), sponsor of VMI Reenacting cadets, researched the Beaver Dam Depot to Ashland march route. Petty Officer Zachary Lowe, United States Navy, patiently listened to endless hours of arcane Gaines' Mill trivia. J. Patterson Rogers, Esquire, Danville, Virginia, performed valuable research and excellent emergency proofreading that materially improved the manuscript. The Hon. George A. Jones, Chatham, Virginia, ably proofread and encouraged, as did the Hon. Brian A. Turpin, Chatham, Virginia, who offered friendly motivational abuse when my enthusiasm started to wane. Terry Reimer, director of research, National Museum of Civil War Medicine, went out of her way to find obscure information. Rosa Santos at the Collections Registrar at the Texas Heritage Museum, Hill College, Hillsboro, Texas, also went out of her way to look for a missing map of a key portion of the battlefield.

There were many others.

Table of Contents

Preface

This book is a detailed account of the Battle of Gaines' Mill, June 27, 1862, and the events leading up to it. Gaines' Mill was the first large battle designed by Robert E. Lee, and was the Army of Northern Virginia's first battle. At the time, it was the bloodiest battle in the Eastern Theater, and the second bloodiest of the war to that point, behind Shiloh. During the whole war, only Gettysburg and Antietam had higher single-day casualties. Just the Union or Confederate casualties alone were higher than the single-day rates at Okinawa (246; U.S.), Iwo Jima (743; U.S.), Verdun (1,806; French) Stalingrad (2,453; German), the Argonne (2,597; U.S.), and the Battle of the Bulge (4,304; U.S.). The U.S. Army lost more field artillery here than almost any other battle, over 20 guns. It was the first occurrence of real-time imagery in the form of the sketches of Alfred Waud. The Rebels had about 42,000 men on the field, and the Yankees about 29,000 men, yet for 139 years, the most detailed discussion of the battle was approximately 48 pages long.[1]

In 1995, some friends of mine and I met at the Richmond National Battlefield Park to visit the Gaines' Mill battlefield. We drove about a mile from New Cold Harbor to the Watt House unit of the Richmond National Battlefield Park, on the road called the NPS (National Park Service) Road. As we stood there, behind a 40-foot-deep ravine, we wondered how anyone with 20,000 men and boatloads of artillery could possibly be driven from the position. Since the battle was fought 99 years to the day before I was born, I decided to look into it further.

As I read more, it seemed as if different authors were telling the same story, with a slightly different seasoning of poignant quotations. Even worse, nothing made sense. Powell Hill sent two brigades down one road through the federal lines, but he did not send any down the other road, now the NPS Road, to the heart of the federal position. Why not? The Federals had at least 12 guns covering all of the other roads, but only two on the NPS Road to the Watt House. This was odd. Further reading made even less sense of the situation. There was not one mention of the road to the Watt House by anyone. I began to pore through all of the Civil War map books. They all showed a road from New Cold Harbor to the Watt House.

One day, J.P. Rogers, Esquire, called me at work. His arguments to the Virginia Supreme Court had not been as successful, nor as lengthy, as he had hoped, so he had decided to visit the Museum of the Confederacy before coming home to Danville. He had found a map dated August 1862, and it showed the area around Gaines' Mill. The road to the Watt House was not on it. I asked him to make a copy of it, and we pored over it with a magnifying glass the next day after court. He was right: the Watt House

Road was not there. This prompted us to research more maps. We found that none of the maps before 1864 had the Watt House Road, but all of the ones after 1864 did. These were not just military maps, but even those in *Battles and Leaders*, and every other post-war publication. No wonder nothing made sense. Since 1872, everyone had been viewing the battle using the wrong map!

This has contributed to a wealth of absurd history. A condensed, yet not exaggerated, postwar version is: Major General Porter, with 20,000 United States regulars and 500 guns,[2] was deeply entrenched on a hill 400 feet high,[3] without reinforcements. Stonewall Jackson, and only Stonewall Jackson, who was late, attacked Porter with 90,000 men.

Since the entire Union army had been only 15,000 men strong a year before, and there are few hills 400 feet high near Richmond, suspicions arose about the veracity of these accounts. If they all had the map wrong, what else did they get wrong? I went back to all of the Seven Days books, which still made no sense, but were, again, the same story with different quotations. I finally found the source, which was 48 pages in Douglas Southall Freeman's *Lee's Lieutenants*. Here, the postwar story changed: General Porter, with thousands of regulars and many guns, was fully and completely entrenched, and without substantial reinforcement. The dull, exhausted, and befuddled Stonewall Jackson, who was late, attacked late with his Valley Army, which Jackson's dullness, exhaustion, and befuddlement had caused to be late.

This "Gospel According to Freeman" has been regurgitated, in about 48 pages, ever since. For example, on page 506, Freeman asserts, "Some of the troops left for the long summer's day march with no water," when Jackson's Valley Army reached Ashland on June 26. In fact, Ashland, 12 miles from Richmond, was a mineral spring resort and had been a water stop on the Richmond, Fredericksburg & Potomac Railroad since the 1840s; it had been refilling 10,000-gallon locomotive water tenders at least daily for 20 years, and was still doing so in 1942. In 1861, it had been a camp of instruction for infantry and cavalry, each horse of which drank about 4 gallons of water *per day*. Nevertheless, Uzal Ent, in his excellent 2014 book on the Pennsylvania Reserves, parrots this alleged Ashland water shortage. Reading the source material makes it clear that the original author, the Rev. Major Dabney, of Stonewall Jackson's own staff, commented on the inexperienced nature of the troops, not on some water shortage.

This book seeks to chronicle accurate information as to the events leading up to the battle and those of battle itself. In doing so, it also seeks to drive a stake through the heart of over 100 years of myths about the battle. It is not a general history of the Seven Days Campaign, the later battles of which have already been covered. See, e.g., Ent, *History of the Pennsylvania Reserves* as to Beaver Dam Creek; also Crenshaw, *The Battle of Glendale*. It is not a biography of any the 71,000 men involved, nor an analysis of leadership. Little worthwhile analysis can be done when no one knows what happened.

The research was difficult because the eyewitness accounts were scattered in regimental histories, diaries, and letters organized by people and regiments rather than battles. No one has ever gathered the information exclusively on Gaines' Mill. The research has been made more difficult by of the immense corpus of misleading information. This begins virtually with the name of the battle. Half of the Confederate army and most of the Union forces called it Gaines' Mill, but many on both sides knew it as Cold Harbor. This is not surprising, because the mill belonging to Dr. Gaines is near Cold Harbor, which itself is about a mile and a quarter from Burnett's Tavern, which is at Old Cold

Harbor. Equally confusing is that "Cold Harbor" is the name of another battle in June of 1864, which was fought between Cold Harbor and Old Cold Harbor.

Adding to this maelstrom is that the 1864 battle was one of immense entrenchments, which altered the 1862 battlefield, in some places permanently. Since the victors write the history books, there is much more contemporaneous information on the 1864 Union victory at Cold Harbor than on the 1862 loss at Cold Harbor, which was behind the Confederate lines until 1865. With a correct 1862 map, the eyewitness accounts begin to make sense. They tell who did what, but not precisely where or when. For example, the Gospel According to Freeman says that Powell Hill started the battle at 2:30 p.m., but Hill's subordinates unanimously say that it actually started about 4:00 p.m. Without some appreciation of what it takes to move 10,000 men on foot from marching column into battle line, one might easily believe that Hill could do so in just half an hour. This is where my 30 years of reenacting experience comes in.

Another source of difficulty was that at one point, Colonel Lee of Branch's Brigade, Hill's Division was fighting across Boatswain's Branch against the enterprising Col. James T. Kirk, while half a mile away, a different General Hill's artillery was ordered by General Jackson open fire on Colonel Jackson. A final source of difficulty is the utter inability of anyone on that field to accurately designate the regiments around them. Almost universally, they get the state or the regimental number correct, but not both. This is how an eyewitness to this battle can describe the glorious charge, under a galling fire, of the 15th North Carolina, which was actually *in* North Carolina at the time.

In addition to the first-person accounts, I used the greatest single source of information, the *Official Record of the War of the Rebellion*, but its utility is limited; the writers had careers and reputations to protect. The first-person accounts from letters and diaries reveal what the professionals won't. Neither are eager to document the writer's own cowardice or incompetence, but they are quick to detail the faults of others. For example, Reynolds' Brigade of the Pennsylvania Reserves spent approximately two hours out of ammunition within sight of the main Union ammunition dump, a fact which is not mentioned anywhere but in other units' accounts.

Research for this book was done in two phases, analog and digital. When it started, the Internet was new and provided little information; many dusty old books were copied from the U.S. Army Military History Institute in Carlisle, Pennsylvania, the Library of Virginia, and the University of North Carolina. This included hundreds of pages from the *Official Record of the War of the Rebellion*, the Southern Historical Society Papers, and *Confederate Veteran*. Sadly, the Grand Army of the Republic did not publish a veterans' magazine, and so Union information was difficult to find. To find this arcane information, I turned to Civil War reenactors, who have a wealth of information on their own units. Much of the information on the Michigan regiments comes from such a source. By 2016, a great many sources were on the Internet and many more accessible. The bibliography contains over 450 separate sources.

Other works on the subject simply do not exist. E.A. Pollard's *Seven Days* was written in 1862, before General Lee had even submitted his report. Freeman's *Lee's Lieutenants* spends only 48 pages on the subject. Clifford Dowdey, a pulp fiction writer, omitted any citations in his *Seven Days: The Emergence of Lee*; his section on this battle is an example of regurgitation, as are the works of Catton, Foote, Sears, and others. Brian K. Burton's *Extraordinary Circumstances* (2001) devoted about 100 pages to the subject, still woefully insufficient for any full understanding of a battle involving 71,000 men, 200 guns, and a charge half again as large as Pickett's pitiful performance in Pennsylvania. Henry W. Pfantz wrote 1,648 pages on two days at Gettysburg, 829 pages per day.

All of these authors were "egg-heads," to purloin a phrase originated by Jefferson Davis Futch, Ph.D., of Washington and Lee University. Those who have never bitten a cartridge, executed "By Company into Line" at the double quick step in the Pennsylvania heat, nor been overrun by a whole *brigade*, cannot possibly understand the dynamics of a Civil War battle sufficiently to figure it out from scratch. Freeman agreed; the title of his chapter on Gaines' Mill is "Jackson Marches to a Confusing Field." As set forth below, Jackson was less confused than later historians, because *he* started with an accurate map.

Because of the difficulties, this book uses some unconventional devices to promote clarity. The organization of a Civil War army and its weapons are utterly alien to many now, and so some explanation of them is necessary in order to help the modern reader understand the more complex information later. Almost all of the brigades fragmented and fought as subformations. To keep track of them, I designate them as Battle Groups, borrowing from World War II scholarship. I have read many Civil War books, and have attempted to remedy some of their faults, often at the expense of convention. In using place names, I have attempted to make them unique and consistent. For example, the dwelling house of Dr. Gaines is Dr. Gaines' Mansion, not the Gaines' house, nor "Powhite." When mentioning artillery batteries, it seems pointless to me to expect the reader to keep track of what battery had which guns, so almost all mentions of artillery specify their armament. I have breached convention to simplify, as far as possible, the confusing mishmash of names. Some of the personages in this battle are Generals A.P. Hill, D.H. Hill, J.R. Anderson, G.B. Anderson and R.H. Anderson; General Ambrose Powell Hill's Division was right next to General Daniel Harvey Hill's Division, and each contained a Brigadier Anderson. Accordingly, this work will refer to General Powell Hill, General Harvey Hill, and Brigadiers J.R., G.B., and R.H. Anderson. In *A Bridge Too Far*, Cornelius Ryan referred to Gerald "Legs" Lathbury, of the British 1st Parachute Brigade, as "Brigadier Lathbury." There is no reason why this use should be forbidden to this work; it saves words and promotes clarity. References to strengths and casualties are calculated using the figures in the two Orders of Battle in the Appendices.

Finally, this work attempts to describe contemporaneous events in several different places. To do so, a short heading alerts the reader to a change. Misspellings and grammar shortcomings in first-person accounts have been retained. Maps are amply supplied to assist; please use them.

Brigadier Porter did not have 20,000 United States regulars nor 500 guns, was not entrenched on any hill, and was generously reinforced twice. To find out more about Mrs. Tinsley's adventure, Stonewall Jackson's punctuality, the African Pioneers, machine guns, and Yankee spies, read on!

Prologue:
When the Yankees Came

Summer Hill Plantation

The Yankees came at the beginning of May. There was, to say the least, great anxiety around Richmond. Thomas McNiven, an abolitionist Scotsman, was said to be a member of the "Waldeness Society," an enigmatic group of abolitionist Scots. Henry David Thoreau, writer of *Walden*, was a rabid abolitionist, a conductor on the Underground Railroad, and a staunch supporter of John Brown, calling him "an angel of light."[1] Before the war, McNiven illegally ran escaped slaves from Bowling Green, Virginia, to Port Royal, Virginia (southeast of Fredericksburg on the Rappahannock River), in a wagon with a false bottom. At the war's outbreak, McNiven suddenly moved to Richmond using funds from the Society, acquired a code name, "Quaker," and opened a bakery at 811 North 5th Street. One of his clients was Jefferson Davis, president of the Confederate States of America.[2]

Mary Brockenbrough Newton lived at Summer Hill, a plantation about ten miles north of Richmond. Her father founded the Washington and Lee University Law School. She was at church when the Yankees came. By that afternoon her husband, former Congressman Willoughby Newton, and some of her sons, all in the 4th Virginia Cavalry, came to visit, and the Yankees were just a few miles south at Old Church. The next day, the "cut throat looking fellows" of the 6th Pennsylvania Cavalry, Col. Rush's Lancers,[3] surrounded Summer Hill at dawn, and demanded three hundred pounds of bacon.[4] The Yankees then stole a horse and all its trappings.

A few days later, the Yankees returned, but this time it was the 5th New York Zouaves, "the most dreadful looking creatures I ever beheld, with red caps and trousers." They burned a nearby bridge. At least one of them claimed that there would soon be a battle nearby, so Mrs. Newton sent her son William to the Confederates with this vital intelligence. Without warning, a stranger arrived at Summer Hill, "an abolitionist of the deepest dye." Despite his insults, the ladies held their tongues for fear the boy's mission would be discovered, but William returned safely. Within a few days, Captain Newton was accused of slipping the Yankee plans to the Confederates. Mary commented that "they little know what women and children can do!" The days became full of the roar of artillery, and soldiers' campfires were seen every night.

One day, the Yankees filled their wagons with corn from her brother's barn. They gave him a receipt, which would only be paid if he took an oath of loyalty. She wrote, "God forgive me for my feelings towards them; but when I see insolent fellows riding around and around our dwellings, seeking what they can devour, every evil feeling of my heart is kindled against them and their whole nation." The next day, the Lancers returned, tearing the boards off the corn crib to get at the feed for their horses. Then the officers ransacked the house, stealing damask towels, a cooked ham, and even a plate of rolls from the pantry. Several days later, a lieutenant sought to buy butter, chickens and eggs. Mrs. Newton informed him that his men had looted the poultry yard the night before. So the young officer shot a servant's hog and took it. A few days later, a Rebel lieutenant arrived with a corpse. This was his brother, the 20-year-old Captain Latane, shot in four places. The ladies buried him at Summer Hill.

Hearing that the mails were operating again, the ladies sent letters to their husbands. The Yankees captured them and published them in the New York newspapers. By mid–June, Summer Hill had a 25-man guard stationed there, regular soldiers from Sykes' Division, who were "more decent men than the volunteers." When the wheat was ready to harvest, the regulars told the servants that they did not have to work for white people any more. But they did not offer to share their rations. A week later, Mrs. Newton was able to receive smuggled newspapers, and read of General J.E.B. Stuart's Great Raid, and how Captain Latane had come to be killed. The Yankees became more insulting after these newspaper accounts, and began taking what little grain was left, with a guard of Rush's Lancers with the wagons. Mrs. Newton could not understand why such a distinguished and accomplished man as Rush would be so cruel. "We hope and believe that the Quaker element is at the foundation of their ill will."[5]

Sydnor's Farm, Near Mechanicsville, Just North of Richmond

Henry Clinton Sydnor was 11 years old when the Yankees came. He lived about a mile east of Mechanicsville, on a bluff overlooking the Chickahominy River. He was too young to enlist, but his six brothers all went to fight for Virginia. One day the family physician stopped by and said that the Yankees were approaching Richmond, and that Henry's father, W.B. Sydnor, should send his daughters away. Henry remembered how sad the old servants were when the girls left, but entertained himself by organizing the servant children into his own little army and had a "big time" having battles with stick guns.

Soon the last of the Confederates left. Shortly after that, Mrs. Sydnor made Henry a money belt which contained the family's gold. Confederate money was used for buying items; gold was too precious when the Yankees were coming.

Uncle Tom was a servant who, being long in the tooth, took care of the Sydnors' carriage and went to town on marketing days. "He had a consequential air, dressed well, and bossed it over the other Negroes." He always occupied the front seat in the gallery at church. (Another servant, Uncle Americus, was over 100 years old, and regaled the children with tales of the Revolutionary War. Henry viewed him with awe and admiration.) One day, Uncle Tom came running in and breathlessly said "Marse William, dey is come fir sure. My God marster, de woods is full of dem Yankees! Well Marster, I wants to tell you right now; all de young niggers am going to leab you, but you is been a good marster to me and you can count on dis nigger stayin wit you till dis war am over."

A few days later, Yankees rode up to the house, and asked if there were any Rebels around. Precocious Henry corrected him on a fine legal point; they were Confederates, not rebels. Then the rest of the Yankees came, with wagons and mules by the thousands, putting up tents, and stringing telegraph wires through the trees. The officers assured Mr. Sydnor that his property would be respected, but he could not show any lights, nor leave the vicinage. The soldiers camped in the orchard, and occupied the barn as a guard shack. Henry milked the cows and sold the milk to the soldiers. He took sugar and real coffee in return. Again, a working relationship was struck, and the Yankee officers would gather on the porch to discuss the war with Mr. Sydnor. Henry especially remembered Major Boyd.[6]

Mr. Sydnor asked a Union officer for some small favor. The next day, that officer replied that he would grant the request, if Mr. Sydnor took the loyalty oath. After reading it, Mr. Sydnor "handed it back to him and with a voice full of fire and emotion and trembling in pointing toward the Confederate line his whole frame quaking: I have six sons on yonder hill! If I sign this, it will deny me the right to welcome them home; if I sign this, it will deny me the right to feed them; if I sign this, it will deny me the right to show them my love and affection when with God's help I will meet them again. Never! Never! How can you ask it?"

Yankee artillery horses grazed in the Sydnors' clover field. Some Yankees stole most of Henry's pet geese, including his favorite, "Major." Uncle Tom and Uncle Moses found the culprits plucking them behind the barn, and came to Henry. Henry broke down and went crying to the officer of the guard. The officer exclaimed, "We are here to take Richmond, not make war on geese; they shall have to pay you for them," and took Henry behind the barn. On seeing Major dead and ready for the pot, Henry broke down again. The officer took Henry in his arms and made the men pay fifty cents each for the geese. Uncle Tom and Uncle Moses buried Major near the house.[7]

"Powhite," Dr. Gaines' Mansion, Six Miles East of Mechanicsville

Fannie Gaines Tinsley was newly married and had just had her first child, Hattie. Mr. Tinsley had a job with the Confederate Treasury Department. She was staying with her parents, Dr. and Mrs. Gaines, at their home, "Powhite."

The day after the Yankees came, an officer put a 30-man guard around Dr. Gaines' Mansion to protect it, but they moved in, too. The carriage house became a hospital, and the doctors moved into the schoolhouse. Still, they were polite; the officers never came into the house, the guards at the three gates would not even let privates into the yard, and another private guarded each door to the house. Dr. Gaines, Mrs. Gaines, their daughter Fannie Tinsley, and their granddaughter Hattie were reasonably safe.

Soon they established a working relationship with the Yankees. Hattie was just a baby, and needed milk from the cows. A deal was made whereby the guards would drive the cows into the yard for milking. Mrs. Gaines sent milk to the sick and the surgeons, and sold the excess to the soldiers for .25 (silver only) per canteen full. One guard could not abide army rations, so the Gaines fed him three meals a day. The daily officer of the guard also ate with the family. Another guard was stationed at the garden. Mrs. Gaines had given the garden to Toler, one of the house servants. Since he maintained it, he also

Powhite, the ancestral home of Dr. Gaines and his family (Library of Congress).

had the excess of the family's needs. He would load up a cart and sell the vegetables in the Yankee camp at a handsome profit. General Porter, the "quartermaster of the army," would bring Dr. Gaines the latest newspapers every day. Brigadier General Fitz John Porter was in fact commander of the whole Union Fifth Corps.

All was not idyllic, however. As soon as they arrived, the Yankees established a camp for their newfangled balloons on Powhite Creek, between the mansion and Dr. Gaines' mill.[8] Sometimes, Mr. Tinsley would ride out of Richmond and to the banks of the Chickahominy River, just south of the Mansion, hoping to catch a glimpse of his wife and daughter. Fannie would go search for him almost every day. On June 23, Brigadier Porter asked the Gaines to leave, as he was building a fort near the overseer's house, and the family might get hurt. The family went to Dr. Curtis' house, about two miles away. Toler the servant stayed at the mansion and brought the Gaines vegetables every day.

At the Watt House, Half a Mile East of Dr. Gaines' Mansion

Mary Jane Haw was ten years old and remembered the August visits to her grandmother. In August, the roses were in their second bloom, the fields high with corn, and the orchards groaning from the weight of their fruit. As they neared grandmother's, they could smell the apples and peaches. The servants would greet them first, and then grandmother in her gingham dress and cap. The first place the children would go was the cellar, where watermelons and musk melons cooled. Next they would visit the china cupboard and be reminded of Aunt Sarah, who had died 30 years ago, at the age of only five. Soon, Uncle Peter and the field hands would come in for dinner at a well-furnished

Top: **Union balloon *Intrepid* and its hydrogen gas generator wagons at the balloon camp just north of Dr. Gaines' Mansion (Library of Congress).** *Bottom:* **The Hugh and Sarah Watt House (Library of Congress).**

table. Afterwards, Uncle Peter would carve a watermelon and serve it out to all. One diversion for the children was Parson's Spring. The water at grandmother's was not very cold, so the children would cross Boson [Boatswain] Creek, which was not even knee deep.[9] Following the path through the woods, they would go to a spring near the Parsons House, drink their fill, and then play "Snake in the Gully" (tag) along the creek. As Mary Jane grew older, grandmother's became rather dull.

The last visit to grandmother was in the spring of 1862; the Yankees were coming. Mary Jane was sent to stay with grandmother, now 78 years old. They could see the camp-fires of the 15th Virginia across the river, where Mary Jane's three brothers were defending Richmond. Uncle Peter reported that the Confederate rear guard had disappeared, and that the Yankees would come by the next morning. And they did. They asked to buy eatables, and did not seek to enter the house. Nevertheless, the house rocked with the concussion of cannon during the day. So far the Yankees did not steal anything, and the servants had not run off, despite the Yankees' entreating them to do so. One day, the cannon fire was more rapid, and musketry was heard. Aunt Betsy, the cook, ran into the yard and said: "Where is Mars Peter? Somebody go find Mars Peter! Ef they don't stop this foolishness, somebody is gwine to get hurt presently!"[10] Grandmother was Sarah Watt, and the house is now part of the Richmond National Battlefield Park.

CHAPTER 1

Operation Chickahominy

In early June of 1862, Robert E. Lee, the newly appointed commander in chief of the Confederate army, had many concerns, the most important of which was that the new nation's capital was under attack. Lee immediately stopped the practice of civilians visiting his army by requiring passes. Said the clerk who was responsible for issuing passes, "No man without a passport from Gen. Winder, or from his Provost Marshal, can pass the pickets of Gen. Lee's Army."[1]

Union Major General George B. McClellan was a few miles away[2] and was every day inching closer. McClellan's 100,000 men only threatened Richmond's southeast quadrant; any siege would ultimately fail without closing off the other three quadrants. That would presumably take another 300,000 men, which the Yankees did not have now, but might have sometime in the future. However, wars are not won by delaying sieges, so McClellan's would have to be lifted. The recent carnage at Shiloh in April of 1862 and at Seven Pines in June indicated that attacking the besiegers was hardly worth the cost in men, especially when you have fewer of them.[3] The weak point of a besieging army was that it had to be fed.

McClellan's whole army was supplied through Lee's son's[4] property at White House Landing on the Pamunkey River, which flows into the York River, and thence to Hampton Roads and the well-supplied northern ports. White House Landing had a dedicated supply fleet of over 400 vessels. The Rebels had destroyed the Richmond and York River Railroad yards, so the Yankees just brought in a whole new one, with ties, rails, five locomotives and eighty cars.[5] The rails moved immense amounts of supplies from White House to the front. Over a 3-week period, the transports moved 3,600 wagons, 700 ambulances, 300 pieces of artillery, 2,500 beef cattle, and 25,000 draft animals.[6] In addition, the quartermasters moved 500 tons of food and another 100 tons *per day*, over 18,000 tons per month.

Other items also came into White House for sale to the men: "Their sutlers' shops were on the most elaborate scale—quantities of barrels of sugar, lemons by the millions, cases of wine, beer and other liquors of every description, confectionary, canned meats, and fruits and vegetables, and great quantities of ice, all still in excellent condition. The eggs were packed in barrels of salt."[7]

George Alfred Townshend described life at White House Landing:

So far as I could observe and learn, the authorities at White House carried high heads, and covetous hands. In brief, they lived like princes and behaved like knaves. There was one— whose conduct has never been investigated—who furnished one of the deserted mansions nearby, and brought a lady from the North to keep it in order. He drove a [carriage] that rivalled anything in Broadway, and his

White House Landing, 1862. Note the sprawling tent city in the background (Library of Congress).

wines were luscious…. My impression is that everybody at White House robbed the Government, and in the end to cover their delinquencies, these scoundrels set fire to an immense quantity of stores, and squared their accounts thus: Burned on the Pamunkey….[8]

White House Landing, despite its millions of lemons and cases of wine, was McClellan's weakest point. Its capture would be catastrophic. How, then, could "Little Mac" be separated from his sole source of supplies?

Lee's initial idea was to cut the rail line from White House Landing with an ironclad railroad gun.[9] He gave orders that day for its construction.[10]

At the same time, he would reinforce Jackson's Valley Army and send it into Pennsylvania, threaten Washington, and force the Yankees to withdraw everything they had in the South to protect the capital.[11] Lee also ordered a reinforcement of the Valley Army, General Lawton's Georgians.[12] Yet something changed his mind. The notoriously difficult Chickahominy River flowed between White House Landing and the Union Army. On the south side of the Chickahominy, the Yankees were besieging, but not so much on the north side. Perhaps the north side was more lightly defended than the south side. By June 8, Lee had decided that the Valley Army would come to Richmond rather than rampage alone to Washington.[13]

On the night of June 8, Lee sent his cavalry commander, Brigadier General J.E.B. Stuart, into no-man's land to see just how strongly defended White House Landing was. The next night, Stuart sent Pvt. John S. Mosby to gather more information. Mosby discovered that "six to eight miles of McClellan's front was a mere shroud of cavalry pickets." White House Landing was only ten miles away. Stuart met with Lee on June 10.[14] On June 11, Lee ordered his cavalry commander to reconnoiter:

HEADQUARTERS, Dabb's Farm, Va., June 11, 1862.
Brig. Gen. J.E.B. STUART,
Commanding Cavalry:

GENERAL: You are desired to make a secret movement to the rear of the enemy, now posted on Chickahominy, with a view of gaining intelligence of his operations, communications, &c., of driving in his foraging parties, and securing such grain, cattle, &c., for ourselves as you can make arrangements to have driven in. Another object is to destroy his wagon trains, said to be daily passing from the Piping Tree road to his camp on the Chickahominy. The utmost vigilance on your part will be necessary to prevent any surprise to yourself, and the greatest caution must be practiced in keeping well in your front and flanks reliable scouts to give you information.

You will return as soon as the object of your expedition is accomplished, and you must bear constantly in mind, while endeavoring to execute the general purpose of your mission, not to hazard unnecessarily your command or to attempt what your judgment may not approve but be content to accomplish all the good you can without feeling it necessary to obtain all that might be desired. I recommend that you only take such men and horses as can stand the expedition, and that you take every means in your power to save and cherish those you do take. You must leave sufficient cavalry here for the service of this army, and remember that one of the chief objects of your expedition is to gain intelligence for the guidance of future operations.

Information received last evening, the points of which I sent you, lead me to infer that there is a stronger force on the enemy's right than was previously reported. A large body of infantry, as well as cavalry, was reported near the Central Railroad. Should you find upon investigation that the enemy is moving to his right, or is so strongly posted as to render your expedition inopportune—as its success, in my opinion, depends upon its secrecy—you will, after gaining all the information you can, resume your former position.

I am, with great respect, your obedient servant,
R.E. LEE,
General.[15]

Brigadier J.E.B. Stuart did all that Lee ordered, and more. On June 12, his raid penetrated to Old Church, 10 miles away from White House Landing. On the 13th, he had penetrated to within 4 miles. On the 14th, caught between pursuing Yankees and a raging river, Stuart made sure to send a courier, Benjamin Turner Doswell (4th Virginia Cavalry) on a harrowing ride through the lines to General Lee. Doswell reached Lee on the night of the 14th,[16] with the information that the way was open to White House Landing. After evading the Yankees, Stuart himself abandoned his men, snuck through the Federal lines at night, and rode directly to Lee's headquarters.[17] Stuart's report of July 14, 1862, a month later, reveals what was not in his June 17 report:

It is proper to remark here that the commanding general had, on the occasion of my late expedition to the Pamunkey, imparted to me his design of bringing Jackson down upon the enemy's right flank and rear, and directed that I should examine the country with reference to its practicability for such a move. I therefore had studied the features of the country very thoroughly, and knew exactly how to conform my movements to Jackson's route. As that part of my former mission was confidential I made no mention of it in my former report, but it is not, I presume, out of place to remark here that the information obtained then and reported to him verbally convinced the commanding general that the enemy had no defensive works with reference to attack from that direction, the right bank of the Totopotomoy being unoccupied; that his forces were not disposed so as successfully to meet such an attack, and that the natural features of the country were favorable to such a descent.

General Jackson was placed in possession of all these facts....

Though Stuart could raid White House Landing, it would take a much larger effort to take it and hold it while McClellan's Army ran out of ammunition or starved. Any large movement of troops near Richmond in daylight could easily be seen by the Yankees' accursed balloons,[18] or discovered by cavalry or spies.

Just two days earlier, Lt. General Thomas "Stonewall" Jackson had finally finished driving two small Union armies out of the Shenandoah Valley. While the Valley was important, Richmond was more important. It was only about 100 miles from Staunton to Ashland down the Virginia Central Railroad. Ashland was only 22 miles north of Richmond, and 20 miles west of White House Landing.[19]

If the Valley Army materialized in Ashland, the Yankees' choices would become very limited. They could bring General McDowell's 40,000 men down from Fredericks-burg, 40 miles away, but the Valley Army would be there to meet them. Since McClellan had taken over three months[20] to move the 65 miles from Fort Monroe to Richmond, such a lightning thrust by McDowell was improbable. Major General Fremont's Yankees in the Shenandoah Valley could surge back into it, but Winchester to Staunton is 85 miles, and at McClellan's 20 miles per month pace, that would take four months. Lee could have the Valley Army back in the Valley in two weeks. Moreover, with McClellan defeated, he could strike at Washington, threatening *their* capital, and requiring them to consolidate *their* armies for its defense. This might neutralize the threat in the Valley, and liberate Fredericksburg.

To be safe, it would probably be a good idea to crush Fremont while the Valley Army was still in the Valley. Lee had already sent Lawton's Georgians to the Valley.[21] He still had unoccupied troops in Richmond, so on June 10, he sweetened the pot by sending General Chase Whiting's Division, another 4,000 men, to reinforce the Valley Army.[22] With Lawton and Whiting in the Valley, Jackson's command went from 7,000 men and 24 guns to about 15,000 men with 32 guns. Its basic load of ammunition was 150 tons, and for a ten-day operation it would need 150 tons of food and fodder,[23] requiring 400 wagons and thousands of draft animals to move. Would Jackson's tactics in defeating three Union armies at the same time work with twice as much of everything? Despite the risk, Richmond was still more important than the Valley.

On June 11, Lee asked the Secretary of War, George W. Randolph, to strong-arm the press from reporting any of these troop movements, curiously using a telegram.[24]

That same day, he wrote to Jackson:

> To Brigadier General THOMAS J. JACKSON, Commanding Valley District:
> Your recent successes have been the cause of the liveliest joy in this army as well as in the country. The admiration excited by your skill and boldness has been constantly mingled with solicitude for your situation. The practicability of re-enforcing you has been the subject of earnest consideration. It has been determined to do so at the expense of weakening this army. Brigadier-General Lawton with six regiments from Georgia is on the way to you, and Brigadier-General Whiting with eight veteran regiments leaves here to-day. The object is to enable you to crush the forces opposed to you. Leave your enfeebled troops to watch the country and guard the passes covered by your cavalry and artillery, and with your main body, including Ewell's division and Lawton's and Whiting's commands, move rapidly to Ashland by rail or otherwise, as you may find most advantageous, and sweep down between the Chickahominy and Pamunkey, cutting up the enemy's communications, &c., while this army attacks General McClellan in front. He will thus, I think, be forced to come out of his entrench-ments, where he is strongly posted on the Chickahominy, and apparently preparing to move by gradual approaches on Richmond. Keep me advised of your movements, and, if practicable, precede your troops, that we may confer and arrange for simultaneous attack.
> I am, with, great respect, your obedient servant,
> R.E. LEE,
> General."[25]

General Jackson replied two days later:

Headquarters Valley District
Near Mount Meridian
June 13, 1862

Your letter of the 8th [*sic*] instant was not received until this morning…. [C]ircumstances greatly favor moving to Richmond in accordance with your plan….

I remain your obdt sert.

T.J. Jackson
Maj. Gen.

General Lee updated Jackson two days later:

Headquarters Near Richmond, Virginia
June 16, 1862

General: I have received your letter…. McClellan is being strengthened, Burnside is with him and some of McDowell's troops are also reported to have joined him…

The present therefore seems to be favorable for a junction of your army and this. If you are with me the sooner you can make arrangements to do so the better. In moving your troops you could let it be understood that it was to pursue the enemy in your front. Dispose them to hold the Valley so as to deceive the enemy keeping your cavalry well in their front and at the proper time descending upon the Pamunkey. To be efficacious the movement must be secret. Let me know the force you can bring and be careful to guard from friends and foes your purposes and your intention of personally leaving the Valley. The country is full of spies and our plans are immediately carried to the enemy…. Unless McClellan can be driven out of his entrenchments he will move by positions under cover of his heavy guns within shelling distance of Richmond. I know of no surer way of thwarting him than the proposed. I should like to have the advantage of your views and be able to confer with you. Will meet you at some point on your approach to the Chickahominy….

I am with great respect your obt servant
R.E. Lee General

Published here for the first time, on June 18, Jackson's quartermaster asked that the Virginia Central Railroad place all of its rolling stock at General Jackson's disposal.[26] The Virginia Central delivered more than twenty locomotives and most or all of its 183 cars to Staunton on June 19. The Virginia Central would bill the government for moving 496 carloads of men and material 9,244 miles.[27]

Jackson left staff officers to move the Valley Army and was himself on the way to Richmond by midday on June 19.[28] Everyone was expressly admonished to keep their mouths shut about everything.[29] He arrived at Lee's headquarters at the Dabbs house about 3:00 on June 23[30]; Lee's division commanders joined them soon thereafter. General Harvey Hill[31] arrived first, followed by General James Longstreet[32] and then General Powell Hill.[33] Someone at the meeting, probably a staff officer, wrote a memorandum[34]:

Maj. Gen Jackson to be in position on Wednesday night on the Hanover Ct. Ho. Road, or near that road, about halfway between Half Sink Bridge, and Hanover Ct. Ho. He will communicate to Maj. Gen A.P. Hill, through Brig. Gen. Branch, who will immediately move himself.

Gen Jackson will commence his movement, precisely at 3 o'clock Thursday Morning, and the moment he moves, send messengers to Gen Branch in duplicate, to inform Gen Branch, who will immediately move himself.

Gen Jackson to move from his position down the second road from the Chickahominy, parallel to the first road, and near to it. Major Gen. A.P. Hill, as soon as the movement of Jackson or Branch is shown on the other side of the Chickahominy, will push his columns across the Chickahominy at Meadow Bridge, turn to the right and move on Mechanicsville. Maj Gen Jackson will endeavor to come into the Mechanicsville Turnpike in rear of Mechanicsville.

Maj Gen Jackson and Hill will unite here, and taking different roads bear down towards Coal Harbor, and on to York R.R. Maj Gen Longstreet to support Maj Gen A.P. Hill, and Maj Gen D.H. Hill to support Maj Gen Jackson. If practicable, it will be best for the supporting columns to take different roads from, but near to the main columns.[35] [errors in original]

The reference to the first and second roads indicates that the meeting involved some sort of map. Jeremy Francis Gilmer was an engineer in the U.S. Army, resigning at the beginning of hostilities and becoming an engineer for General Albert Sidney Johnston. Gilmer was wounded at Shiloh in April of 1862 and after recovering became the chief engineer for the Department of Northern Virginia as a brigadier general. In his papers is an undated map, No. 537, titled "Sketch of area between Chickahominy and Pamunkey Rivers from Cold Harbor south to Hanover Court House." It is hand drawn without topography, and includes a place called "Merry Oaks," but does *not* include any reference to "New Cold Harbor"; only to "Cold Harbor." This map details, in red ink, the road network from Ashland to Gaines' Mill and Cold Harbor, but ends there. More importantly, it also bears the intriguing notation "From Lt. Timberlake's Statement." In his report, General Stuart mentions, "The majority of the Hanover Company (G) Fourth Virginia Cavalry, possessing invaluable merits as guides, were distributed as such among the various Generals. First Lieut. D.A. Timberlake accompanied me...."[36] Gilmer Map 537 will be designated the Timberlake Map, and is probably the master copy of the map used at this conference.[37]

Lee and his subordinates discussed the plan with the Timberlake Map until about 7:00 p.m.[38] Jackson then left to return to his command, meeting them at about 10:00 a.m. on Tuesday, June 24, about 40 miles from Richmond.[39] In the meantime, Lee's staff was working on the official operations order. That order is of crucial importance, and so its pertinent part is reproduced here in full[40]:

GENERAL ORDERS, NO 75
Headquarters, Department of Northern Virginia
June 24, 1862

   I. Genl Jackson's command will proceed tomorrow from Ashland towards the Slash Church to encamp at some convenient point west of the Central Railroad. [General L. O'Bryan] Branch's brigade, of A.P. Hill's Division, will also tomorrow evening take position on the Chickahominy near Half Sink. At 3 o'clock Thursday morning, 26th instant, Genl. Jackson will advance on the road leading to Pole Green Church, communicating his march to Genl. Branch, who will immediately cross the Chickahominy, and take the road leading to Mechanicsville. As soon as the movements of these columns are discovered, Genl A.P. Hill will cross the Chickahominy near Meadow Bridge and move direct upon Mechanicsville. To aid his advance the heavy batteries on the Chickahominy will at the proper time open upon the batteries at Mechanicsville. The enemy being driven from Mechanicsville, and the passage across the bridge opened, Genl. Longstreet with his division and that of Genl D.H. Hill will cross the Chickahominy at or near that point, Genl D.H. Hill moving to the support of Genl Jackson, and Genl Longstreet supporting Genl. A.P. Hill. The four divisions keeping communication with each other, and moving in echelon, on separate roads, if practicable, the left division in advance, with skirmishers and sharpshooters extended in their front, will sweep down the Chickahominy, and endeavor to drive the enemy from his positions above New Bridge, Genl Jackson bearing well to his left, turning Beaver Dam Creek and taking the direction toward Cold Harbor. They will then press forward towards the York River Railroad, closing upon the enemy's rear and forcing him down the Chickahominy. Any advance of the enemy towards Richmond will be prevented by vigorously following his rear and crippling and arresting his progress.

   By command of Genl Lee:
   R.H. Chilton
   A.A.G.

Lee probably included a copy of the Timberlake Map with the copy of General Order 75 sent to each of his five immediate subordinates. Harvey Hill referred to this map after the war: "The map furnished me (and I suppose the six other major-generals had no better) was very full in regards to everything within our own lines, but a red line on the east side of the Chickahominy and nearly parallel to it, without any points marked on it, was our only guide to the route on which our march was to be made."[41] Jackson received his copy of confidential[42] General Order 75 early the next morning.[43] Operation Chickahominy was ready to roll.

Union Army Headquarters, Trent House

George B. McClellan did not get to be a Major General by being a fool. By the same token, he was an engineer and very methodical. He spent most of June bringing up more men and guns. His plan was to put heavy guns (range 4 miles) at Mechanicsville, rake the Confederate works from a position that was out of range of return fire, and unleash his legions in a massive attack that would carry Richmond itself. He kept anticipating making his attack in two days, but kept postponing it.[44]

By June 23, McClellan sensed that something was up:

June 23, 1862

Mary Ellen [McClellan, his wife]

Every poor fellow that is killed or wounded almost haunts me! My only consolation is that I have honestly done my best to save as many lives as possible.

I have had a very anxious day, *the movements of the enemy being mysterious*. I think tomorrow will bring forward *something—what* I do not know. I expect to take a decisive step in advance day after tomorrow and if I succeed will gain a couple of miles toward Richmond. It now looks to me as if the operations would resolve themselves into a series of partial attacks rather than a general battle.

George

The "mysterious movements" were Lee's troops realigning themselves to free half their number for the Chickahominy operation. Thaddeus Lowe, the balloonist, was making daily, and even hourly, reports. Only a blind aeronaut could fail to see this realignment.[45] Moreover, McClellan was also receiving information from his nascent internal intelligence operation, commonly known as "scouts." These intrepid individuals ventured into no man's land seeking information on the enemy.

Judson Knight, 2d New Jersey Infantry, was one of these scouts. There were certainly others.[46] The 1st Pennsylvania Reserves, stationed at Mechanicsville, picked up a deserter with a thick Irish brogue that very rainy night.[47] Further north, just east of Ashland, the cavalry brought in another "deserter." Private Rean, 1st Maryland Cavalry (U.S.), claimed to have been captured by the Rebels and held prisoner in Lynchburg. He further claimed to have escaped, made his way to Ashland, taken a train west, spied on the Confederates, and then gone back to Ashland to make contact with the Yankees. Col. Farnsworth of the 8th Illinois Cavalry thought he was a provocateur, but sent him up to headquarters anyway.

General McClellan believed every word Rean had to say.[48] On June 24, McClellan *knew* something was up, telegraphing the Union Secretary of War, Edwin Stanton:

June 24, 1862

Edwin Stanton

> A very peculiar case of desertion. The party states that he left Jackson, Whiting, and Ewell, 15 brigades at Gordonsville on the 21st. They were moving to attack my rear on the 28th.
>
> G.B. McClellan

Trying to confirm the story, McClellan sent out two Negroes to go along the railroad and investigate, but Stuart's pickets were too vigilant for the Negroes to get past them.[49]

White House Landing

On June 24, 700 vessels were off White House Landing, stuffed with everything a 100,000-man army might need.[50] Despite history's labeling him the Jonah of the Peninsula Campaign, McClellan clearly saw the writing on the wall about White House Landing on June 24. The worst-case scenario was that the rebels would cut him off from it. This presented a logistics nightmare. McClellan's army was so large that it could not be fed in a day. That is, the supply system could only distribute an inadequate amount of rations per day with their 6,000 wagons. Generally, a different third of the army received rations every three days. If those rations were cut off, the whole army would be relying on any local depot cushion in 9 days. Assuming that cushion was another 9 days, the army would be starving in 18 days, which would be July 12, 1862, some three weeks hence. It is no wonder that Jeb Stuart called White House Landing McClellan's "Achilles Heel."[51] Accordingly, on June 24, a Captain Keenan with two companies of cavalry was sent to reconnoiter a route to the James River, up which the 400 vessels of the supply fleet could steam and sail.[52]

McClellan ordered White House to be evacuated with apocalyptic haste on June 26:

> On the same day [June 26] General Van Vliet, chief quartermaster of the army of the Potomac, by my orders, telegraphed to Colonel Ingalls, quartermaster at the White House, as follows: "Run the cars to the last moment, and load them with provisions and ammunition. Load every wagon you have with subsistence, and send them to Savage's station, by way of Bottoms Bridge. If you are obliged to abandon White House burn everything you cannot get off. You must throw all our supplies up the James river as soon as possible, and accompany them yourself with all our force. It will be of vast importance to establish our depots on James river without delay, if we abandon White House. I will keep you advised of every movement so long as the wires work; after that you must exercise your own judgment."

With the Valley Army, Northwest Hanover County, Virginia, Near the Louisa County Line, 40 Miles Northwest of Richmond

Jackson returned to the Valley Army at a stop on the Virginia Central called Beaver Dam Depot[53] about 10:00 a.m. on Monday, June 24, 1862, after a grueling all-night ride. The tracks were torn up to the east, so that was as far as the Valley Army could go by rail.[54] Beaver Dam Depot was named for the nearby Beaver Dam Plantation of Edmund Fontaine, president of the Virginia Central Railroad.[55] Jackson was chagrined to find that only the lead division, Winder's, of the Valley Army was there. It had taken all day for those lead elements to move by rail 20 miles from their last camp, Frederick's Hall, in Louisa County, and the Valley Army itself was strung out all the way to Louisa Courthouse, 15 miles west.[56] Exhausted from his ride, Jackson himself went to sleep at another nearby plantation, that of Howard Carter.[57] When Lt. Henry Kyd Douglas arrived at Carter's, Jackson was still asleep.[58] General Order 75, dated June 24, reached him that night. Then it rained.

It rained as in the Old Testament.[59] Captain Campbell Brown was asleep in the woods near the depot under a waterproof blanket. He was awakened by the rain and found a gallon of water in one of its folds.[60] It also rained in Richmond.[61] Surgeon William Potter, 57th New York Infantry, remarked: "A great thunder shower prevailed all last night, and another came today. I never experienced anything like such severe storms of that character such as we have here. The lightning was so continuous that it was quite light the most of the night, and the electricity came so near the earth as to nearly convulse my extremities, several times."[62]

2

The Tocsin Sounds

Union Army Headquarters, Trent House

By June 25, Operation Chickahominy was becoming clear to the Union high command:

> June 25, 1862
> Edwin Stanton
>   Several contrabands just in give information confirming that Jackson's advance is at Hanover Courthouse. I incline to think that Jackson will attack my flank and rear. This Army will do all in the power of men to hold their position and repulse any attack.

General McClellan had the blessing of several French princes with him as volunteer aides. Henri d'Orleans, Comte de Paris, emphasized that on June 25: "[E]ven while the battle of Oak Grove was being fought, he received positive information of Jackson's approach, the advanced cavalry of the latter having appeared at Hanover Court-house."[1]

The "advanced cavalry ... at Hanover Court-house" is not exactly accurate. While there were Confederate cavalry videttes at Hanover Court House,[2] the Valley Army was not there. The Valley Army was, however, at Ashland at about 4:00. Lt. Col. William T. Martin reported that after Jackson's men started arriving in Ashland, the 8th Illinois Cavalry attacked him *from* the intersection of the Ashcake Road and the Telegraph Road.[3] That intersection is less than a mile from Ashland, and is indeed wooded.[4] Martin's report is a good example of how one must carefully read official reports. Martin does not address the elephant in the room: that Union cavalry probably watched the Valley Army arrive at Ashland, and reported it up the chain of command. The 8th Illinois had unquestionably discovered the whereabouts of the Valley Army.

That day McClellan also got word that the attack was imminent:

> June 25, 1862
> Edwin Stanton
>   Jackson will soon attack our right and rear.
>   G.B. McClellan[5]

McClellan's chief engineer, Brigadier General John G. Barnard, recounted: "[T]he night of the 26th.... It had been known some days previous to this that Jackson's command had reached Frederick's Hall Station on its way from the Shenandoah, and there was presumptive evidence that an attack on our right wing was meditated by the concentrated forces of the enemy, and that, too on the 27th."[6]

Confederate Headquarters, Dabbs House,[7] Behind the Confederate Lines

Lee's plan was coming together nicely. Intelligence from the Valley revealed nothing threatening from Fremont, McDowell was not marching from Fredericksburg, and McClellan was relatively quiet. But those balloons were still up, especially at Dr. Gaines' Mansion, and would surely see the movement of Lee's men to their jumping-off points. Orders to move specified that the respective divisions must march after dark, which was about 7:30 p.m.[8]

Beaver Dam Depot, Northwest Hanover County, 40 Miles from Richmond

Despite the previous night's downpour, the men had a hearty breakfast the next morning: "Having in our haversacks some fat bacon and flour, we mixed the flour on the stumps, with water from our canteens, and this dough we wound around sharpened sticks and held over coals, turning every few minutes until they were done."[9]

Published here for the first time is the Valley Army's route from Beaver Dam Depot to Ashland. The weary Valley Army marched out of the Beaver Dam Depot area early Tuesday morning, into a black hole that has existed for over 150 years. Zion Church is just east of Fontaine's Beaver Dam Plantation and due south of Beaver Dam Depot. The marching portion of the Valley Army left Zion Church on a road heading southeast. The railroad part of the army left Beaver Dam Depot on a different road heading south-southeast. These two roads met at Trinity Church. From there, the column marched southeast, across the Little River Bridge (east of Futcher's Mill). One man summed up the march as "slow progress over bad roads through the forest."[10] The raw recruits of Lawton's Georgians, the trail brigade, had an especially rough time of it: "The roads were so cut up with the wagons and artillery until we could hardly get along. Some of the boys would bog so deep into the mud till when he got out, their shoes would remain often ten and twelve inches below the surface.... Some of the boys had white sheets, and a few I believe had feather pillows. Jackson's old soldiers ... made sport of us. They would ask us what command we were wagonning for, and what train that was. Some of our boys cursed the war, others shed tears (for there were a lot of young boys in the brigade)."[11]

The rain from the night before had pushed the Little River out of its banks.[12] It was too fast and deep to ford, so the whole Valley Army had to stop to rebuild the bridge. Capt. C.R. Mason was widely known in Virginia as "the Napoleon of railroad contractors" for the Virginia Central Railroad before the war. Jackson made him his bridge builder. Mason had his own gang of skilled construction men that he used. Jackson's quartermaster Major Harman called them Mason's "African Pioneers."[13] Thirty-nine of them were hired from June 23 to June 30, 1862, each earning over $5.00 per day when a soldier's pay was only 36 cents per day, $11.00 per month. Mason and his men could apparently build a bridge faster than the army engineers could design it.[14] At New Found River, near

A Civil War bridge. The African Pioneers could build one like this in about two hours (Library of Congress).

Clayton's, they apparently cut two trees down to bridge it; the infantry used this precarious and painfully slow crossing[15] while the African Pioneers[16] built a bridge suitable for artillery and wagons.[17]

Legend has it that at some point on the march, Jackson and his staff stopped for water at a house near the road. The officers handed the water pitcher to the older man, whom the owner soon recognized. To the staff's chagrin, she emptied the pitcher and went into her dwelling house. The officers begged for water, to which she replied, "All right, but no one else shall ever drink from General Jackson's pitcher!"[18]

The column then crossed the New Found River, and moved to Mt. Olivet Church; from there, the column marched east and then due south to Negro Foot[19]; from there, they probably went east and then south again to the area of Mallory's Mill, on the South Anna River. The route from Mallory's Mill toward Ashland is subject to some debate. What is known is that the 10th Virginia (Winder's Division, Valley Army) was at Hughes' Tavern that night.[20] Hughes' Tavern was probably somewhere on the Hughes Road, and (with a certain irony) near the Hanover County Alms House.[21] This is consistent with the Reverend Dabney, Jackson's chief of staff, who says that he was within few miles of Ashland.[22] Brigadier Winder says it was 6 miles.[23] Col. William T. Martin's cavalry was picketing south of Ashland and reported that Jackson's advance guard reached Ashland itself on the afternoon of June 25.[24] Captain Campbell Brown, also of Ewell's division, saw Jackson himself at Ashland.[25] The 58th Virginia of Ewell's Division camped at the racetrack in Ashland.[26] Legend even has it that Jackson's headquarters was at the house of C.W. McMurdo at 713 Railroad Avenue that night.[27] Brigadier Isaac Trimble of Ewell's Division, Valley Army, says that he marched *from* Ashland on the 26th.[28] Who was in Ashland, and who was not?

The answer lies in a concept called "Order of March." The Valley Army had three divisions, those of Winder, Whiting, and Ewell, and one division-sized brigade, under

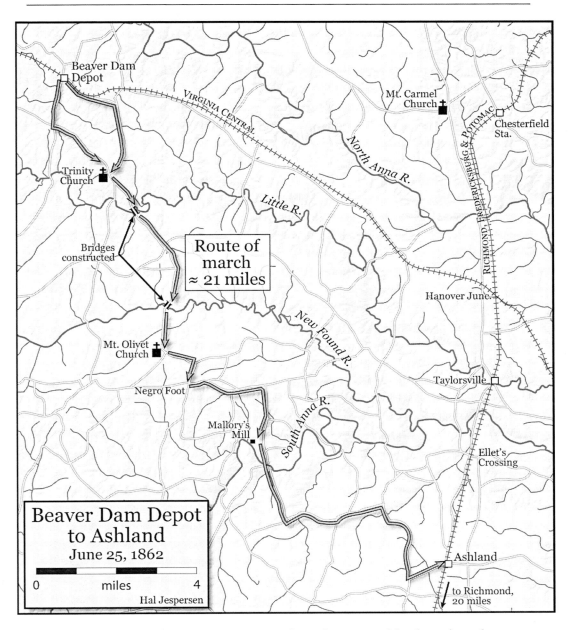

Route of
march
≈ 21 miles

**Beaver Dam Depot
to Ashland**

June 25, 1862

| 0 | miles | 4 |

Hal Jespersen

Brigadier Lawton, each about 4,000 men. These four rotated leading the column, or "walking point" on a 4,000-man scale. In the move from Staunton, today's trail division would be tomorrow's lead division, so today's trail division was put on the cars and taken forward to the next bivouac, giving welcome rest to tired soldiers who would be tomorrow's lead division.[29] This is how Winder's Division came to arrive at Beaver Dam Depot on the railroad.[30] Now on foot, Winder's Division would lead the march towards Ashland. Once almost there, the lead division would stop, and the rest of the army would march past it, the next day's "lead" going the furthest. Jackson himself specifies that Ewell was in the lead on June 27, and that Whiting was in the lead on June 26[31]; this puts Winder (and the 10th Virginia) in the lead on June 25, so he stopped short of Ashland, at Hughes Tavern, while Ewell, Whiting, and Lawton went on to Ashland itself. This is why Lee in his report mentions that Jackson's "whole" force had not made it to Ashland.[32] The Alms House is almost exactly six miles from Ashland.[33]

Ashland was an ideal place to stop for the night. At the beginning of the war, the town hosted Camp Ashland, a very large cavalry and infantry training camp just south of town, at the defunct racetrack.[34] This means that it had space and a good water source for the weary men of the Valley Army.

The Gilmer map reveals that the roads in this area barely deserve the name. Gilmer's map uses red lines for the roads, and the finer the line, the smaller, i.e., worse, the road is. The road from Zion Church to the New Found River Bridge is relatively wide; all of the rest are barely discernible. Further, crossing 4,000 men on two slippery trees is tedious at best. Since Winder had artillery with him, as did the rest of the Valley Army, a bridge would have to be built. Nevertheless, the Valley Army, wearing woolen uniforms in hundred-degree heat, after a rain of biblical proportions, made 18 miles on June 25.[35]

Valley Army Camp, Ashland, Virginia

General Order 75 specified that Jackson was to leave Ashland on Wednesday, June 25, and camp between Ashland and the Virginia Central Railroad in the direction of "Slash Church." On the Gilmer Map 548, the Virginia Central is six miles due east near Lebanon Church. It is also six miles southeast near the Saw Mill. "Slash Church" does not appear on that map. However, it does appear on another period map.[36] Slash Church is just north of a place named Merry Oaks. Merry Oaks does not appear on Gilmer Map 548, but it does appear on Gilmer Map 544, just south of Slash Church. General Order 75 does not say *when* Jackson is supposed to camp at Slash Church/Merry Oaks, other than to say he will leave camp there at 3:00 a.m. on the morning of Thursday the 26th. In any event, General Jackson was just a few miles short of where he was supposed to be. From his headquarters, that point was about 6 miles distant down the Ashcake Road. To make up the difference, he planned to have his men up at 2:30.

Late in the day, Jackson received a communication from Lee[37]:

> In your march tomorrow [June 26] on reaching Merry Oaks, the roads divide. By the map before me, the right hand, called the Ash Cake road, intersects, near Mrs. McKenzies, a road leading by Shady Grove Church to Mechanicsville. If one of your columns followed the road to Shady Grove Church, it would there unite with Branch's Brigade from "Atlee's," and there the rest of Genl. A.P. Hill's division from the Meadow Bridge road. If a second column continued on the Ash Cake road to J Overton, & thence on the road to Pole Green Church, it would strike the road from Shady Grove Church to Old Raleigh, a mile and three quarters east of the Shady Grove Creek. Your two columns would therefore be in close communication, and north of Beaver Dam Creek. You would then be in a position either to take the road across Beaver Dam Creek by Walnut Grove Church and Gain's Mill to Cole Harbor; or to pursue the road by Old Raleigh & Bethesda Church to Cole Harbor either of the latter routes would entirely turn Beaver Dam Creek. Perhaps it would be better for one of your columns to take the road by Walnut Grove Church, and the other road by Bethesda Church, or Old Raleigh, whichever you find most advantageous.[38]

More importantly, Jackson was studying a map when Jeb Stuart arrived about 4:00 p.m.[39] This was undoubtedly the Timberlake Map; Jackson was probably referring to it while reading the Merry Oaks Communiqué.

The Valley troops cheered Stuart's arrival.[40] In his report, Stuart did not mention a word about having to hunt Jackson down; Stuart just rode up the Telegraph Road.[41] The dashing cavalryman made sure to inform Jackson of his previous reconnaissance: "General Jackson was placed in possession of all these facts...."[42]

Lee's communication created a lot of confusion for historians, but none for Stonewall Jackson. Jackson not only had the Timberlake Map, but he also had Stuart, who was intimately familiar with the area, having ridden all over it for the past month, and probably Lt. Timberlake himself. Moreover, a John Henry Timberlake graduated from University of Virginia in 1857, received a master's degree there, and was in the Hanover Light Dragoons, Company G of the 4th Virginia Cavalry. John Henry Timberlake was General Jackson's guide,[43] probably becoming so at Ashland. It makes perfect sense that Lee would send a map with the communication detailing what roads Jackson should take.

Merry Oaks was a tavern.[44] This is where Patrick Henry mustered his company of minutemen in 1774.[45] In this communication, Lee was using it as a synonym for the Slash Church area. Turning right at Merry Oaks, the road runs southeast towards and past Saw Mill, and then to Mrs. Makenzie's/McKenny's. There, a road to the right leads south to Shady Grove Church. Marching straight at Mrs. Makenzie's/McKenny's takes one to Overton's/Dr. Shelton's, and then to Pole Green Church, just as Lee said in both General Order 75 and the June 25 communication.

Lee was clarifying General Order 75 as to where he wanted Jackson to be on the night of the 26th, to wit, at Shady Grove Church and Pole Green Church. Shady Grove Church is two miles and almost due north of Beaver Dam Creek, and Pole Green Church is about three miles north and *east* of the Yankees' Beaver Dam line. Lee wanted Jackson in this position because he wanted Jackson to be able to move east, not to help Powell Hill at Mechanicsville. Longstreet and Harvey Hill, with 20,000 additional men, were at hand if Powell Hill needed any help.[46] From Pole Green Church, the Shady Grove Church Road goes east to Old Raleigh. From Old Raleigh, the road leads further east—to Old Church, and then only 10 miles on to White House Landing. One right-hand turn goes south to Cold Harbor.

Contrary to the claims of 150 years of historians,[47] Lee's communication of June 25 was specific. He wanted Jackson in camp on the night of June 25 east of Ashland and *west* of the Virginia Central, i.e., near Merry Oaks. At Ashland, Jackson was only a few of miles from that point. This was easily made up by (a) starting half an hour early,[48] and (b) having Stuart's cavalry to screen him so that the lead elements did not have to be so cautious, and could move faster.[49] If Jackson had any questions, he could just telegraph Lee. Though the 8th Illinois had cut the wire, Col. Martin had repaired it.[50] In a pinch, Jackson could send a courier south on the Telegraph Road, since Stuart and his men had just ridden it going north.

General Jackson in fact sent word to Lee of the day's events, both to give notice that he was in communication, and to acknowledge Lee's Merry Oaks instructions:

TO: Jefferson Davis, Richmond, Virginia
Headquarters, Dabbs House

June 26, 1862

Sir:

A note just received from General Jackson this morning states that in consequence of the high water and mud, his command only reached Ashland last night. It was his purpose to resume the march at 2.30. I fear from the operations of the enemy yesterday that our plan of operations has been discovered to them. It seemed to be his purpose by his advance on our right yesterday, to discover whether our force on that front had been diminished. General Jackson writes that there was a movement on our extreme left beyond the Chickahominy. The cavalry pickets were driven in that direction, & the telegraph wire near Ashland was cut.

I am most respy, your obt. Servant,
R.E. LEE
Genl

General Order 75 envisioned that the Valley Army would reach Merry Oaks on June 25, and sit there until it marched at 3:00 a.m. June 26. Lee sent Stuart's cavalry to Ashland/Merry Oaks on the afternoon of June 25, to act as an additional screen to prevent its discovery at Merry Oaks. The communication above shows Lee's concern that the operation had been discovered a day early.

McClellan's Headquarters, Trent House

At 6:15 p.m., about the time Col. Farnsworth was cutting the Confederate telegraph wire, General McClellan used the Union line to telegraph Edwin Stanton, Secretary of War: "Several contrabands just in give information confirming supposition that Jackson's advance is at or near Hanover CH…."[51] Despite the slightly erroneous location, whether it was truly contrabands, or the resourceful Col. Farnsworth, the jig was indeed up.

Just North of Richmond, Behind the Confederate Lines

General Order 75 specified that Brigadier General Lawrence O'Bryan Branch's Brigade of Powell Hill's Division would take position at Half Sink by the evening of June 25.[52] Half Sink was the plantation of John Minor Botts, a former U.S. Congressman, vocal Unionist, and accused traitor.[53] Seven miles from Richmond, the Brook Road crossed the Chickahominy (the Bowes/Upper Chickahominy Bridge[54]) near Half Sink. Across that river, a road led south-southeast along the bluffs from Hughes' Store (a different place than Hughes' Tavern) to Atlee's Station (on the Virginia Central Railroad) and then to Widow Crenshaw's house. From there, the road ran southeast to Mechanicsville.[55] More importantly, about a half mile east of Mrs. Crenshaw's were the Virginia Central's tracks, and about 3.5 miles east of that was Pole Green Church, whence the Valley Army was ordered. The road from Merry Oaks/Slash Church to Shady Grove Church parallels the tracks.[56] Brigadier Branch was to follow this route and link up with the Valley Army near Mrs. Crenshaw's. Branch was in position at Half Sink at 4:00 a.m.[57]

In his march to Half Sink, Branch dropped five companies of the 33rd North Carolina off at the Confederate end of the Crenshaw Bridge, on the road to Widow Crenshaw's. They were to cross when they heard Branch engage.[58]

Powell Hill's Division, 5 brigades without that of Brigadier Branch, about 10,000[59] men plus artillery, marched up the Meadow Bridge Road towards the bridge, "entirely concealed,"[60] and bivouacked for the night.[61]

Major General Daniel Harvey[62] Hill had 6 brigades, about 10,000 men, under Brigadiers Roswell Ripley, George Anderson,[63] Alfred Colquitt, Samuel Garland, and

Robert Rodes. At 2:00 a.m. on June 26, he marched his men to the Mechanicsville Bridge, where they bivouacked for the night.[64] The 3rd North Carolina Regiment led Ripley's brigade, which led the whole division. Ripley generated a battalion[65] of skirmishers with a company from each regiment of the brigade, and they crept forward to observe the two bridges crossing the Chickahominy.[66]

Major General James Longstreet's Division marched out an hour after Harvey Hill's Division, and both were in place by 8:00 a.m.[67] He did not bother with skirmishers, as Harvey Hill's Division took care of that.

Midnight, June 25, 1862

Though it had been dicey for a spell, by the night of June 25, Jackson and the Valley Army were mostly where Lee wanted them, as was everyone else. Branch was ready to cross at Half Sink; Powell Hill was ready to go at Meadow Bridge. Longstreet was ready to go at Mechanicsville. June 26 would be another blisteringly hot day.

3

The General and the Private
View a Battle

Dr. Gaines' Mansion

By June 26, even the servants at Dr. Gaines' mansion knew that Jackson was near. "That night Mary, the cook, came up stairs and said 'Miss Jane, did you know that Jackson's men was up here at Mechanicsville?'"[1]

Union Army Headquarters, Trent House

McClellan's information was surprisingly accurate. The Valley Army was indeed at Gordonsville on the 21st, and at Frederick's Hall Station, but on June 22. As of June 24, McClellan's information was only 48 hours old. The Valley Army did indeed include the divisions of Jackson himself,[2] Ewell, and Whiting, and the latter had indeed been recently sent from Richmond. As usual with Union intelligence, the unit strengths were 100 percent off; the Valley Army only had about 15,500 men,[3] but the combined Confederate forces for Operation Chickahominy were about 42,000. Jackson's intent was to threaten McClellan's right and rear[4] at Mechanicsville. That attack was to come on the 28th, and actually came on the 26th. There is every indication that Brigadier Porter, and therefore probably General McClellan, had much better information than he reported to the War Department.

White House Landing

General McClellan's supply officer, Brigadier General Van Vliet, telegraphed Lt. Colonel Ingalls early on June 26: "You will have your whole command in readiness to start at any moment. Please consult with Lt. Nicholson of the Navy to have his vessels placed in such a position that he can protect our depot…. Don't fail to send down into [the York River] all the vessels in the Pamunkey that are not required soon. Three or four days' forage and provisions are all that should be retained afloat at White House. This is a precautionary measure entirely, but must be attended to at once."[5]

War correspondent Joel Cook recorded what he observed:

Servants at the Gaines' Mansion (Library of Congress).

[A] change in the course of transportation caused considerable commotion and speculation.... On the same day General Casey came from the army in front of Richmond and took command of the small land-force, [about] six hundred men, and in the evening was notified to prepare at any moment for the entire evacuation of the post, and the preservation, as far as practicable, of the public property.... [T]hat evening there was a report that a body of Rebels were approaching the Pamunkey. The trains on the railroad were kept running as swiftly as possible, carrying forward nothing but ammunition and munitions of war, with siege and rocket trains and fieldpieces. On Thursday morning it was found that the gun-boats had all taken position in front of the landing, with their ports open and their guns run out. This, and the equally astounding discovery that the trees had been cut down, gave great activity to all the camp-followers congregated at White House. The quartermaster's office was thronged by those anxious to procure transportation to Fortress Monroe, and the population was rapidly depleted.... Throughout the day the greatest vigilance was observed in and around the headquarters of General Casey, who had pitched his tents on the lawn in front of the White House, the building itself being occupied by the Sisters of Charity. The stocks of goods piled on the landings were rapidly diminishing, as the wagons carried them off. The railroad-trains moved steadily forward with ammunition. Cavalry scouts were sent out to different points, and preparations made for obstructing the roads. And at dusk a panic was occasioned by the discovery that bales of hay had been piled over and around the stores still remaining at the wharves—indicating the probability that during the night it might become necessary to apply the torch.... There was also great commotion among the crowds of contrabands employed as laborers. They soon understood that danger was apprehended, but, being assured by Lieutenant Colonel Ingalls that they would not be left behind to meet the vengeance of their masters, they worked with renewed energy. Stores and munitions everywhere disappeared from the landings, and were being packed on the wharf-boats and the vessels contiguous. The wives and children of the contrabands also made their appearance, and, being sent on the canal-boats, were floated out into the stream.... [A]t eleven o'clock a dispatch announced that General Porter had driven the enemy before him, repulsing them three times with terrific slaughter, and was then ordered by General McClellan to fall back. This dispatch was the signal for renewed energy in the work of evacuation, and all the quarter-masters' papers and valuables, and the chests of the paymasters, were taken on board the mail-boat. The household furniture and servants of some officials following, it increased the excitement among the sutlers and campfollowers. Some of the former because so panic-stricken as to sell out their stocks at half price, and hastened on board the boat. Others, however, determined to keep their goods and to take their chances. That there was an intention on the part of General McClellan to evacuate White House as soon as his movement in front should be perfected, there was no doubt, but for what cause, no one there knew.[6]

The new supply base would be at Harrison's Landing on the James River, near Berkley Plantation, first settled in 1619. It rather surprisingly had taken about a year for the first settlers to invent bourbon whiskey.[7] McClellan and his army would wish they had whole hogsheads of it.

White House of the Confederacy, 1201 E. Clay Street, Richmond, Virginia

McNiven's bakery wagon clopped up Clay Street just after dawn and stopped at 1201. As usual, Mary, an intelligent servant, came out to choose the choicest loaves for the president and his family.[8]

Valley Army Camp, Ashland, Virginia

The Valley Army left Ashland before daybreak on June 26. Ewell's Division, in the lead, left about 4:00 a.m.[9] The mission that day was to camp that night at Pole Green Church, some 14 miles away. Jeb Stuart's cavalry was out in front; it did not turn right at Merry Oaks/Slash Church, but continued moving east, turning southeast just beyond Lebanon Church, and moving down to Taliaferro's Mill.[10] Marching with the infantry, Campbell Brown recalled: "The march thro' the 'Slashes of Hanover' began before the day and was a strange & dreary one—simply on account of the flat, swampy, dense nature of the country—with no extended views, almost no population."[11] Richard Taylor's brigade[12] was leading Ewell's Division, and the 1st Maryland Infantry, under Col. Bradley Johnson, was leading the brigade, with orders to "drive away the enemy's pickets when found."[13] At the beginning of the war, the 1st Maryland had no arms. Mrs. Johnson went to Raleigh, North Carolina, and personally lobbied Governor John Ellis for arms. She returned to the regiment with 500 Mississippi rifles.[14] Jackson himself pointed out to Lt. Henry Kyd Douglas the birthplace of Henry Clay near Perrin's Mill.[15] Ewell turned right at Merry Oaks/Slash Church, and crossed the Virginia Central near the Saw Mill[16] at about 9:00 a.m. Pursuant to General Order 75, Jackson sent word to Brigadier Branch that the Valley Army had crossed the Virginia Central Railroad.[17] Whiting's Division crossed it at 10:00 a.m.[18]; about half of the Valley Army was actually behind the Union cavalry outpost at Hughes' Store. At McKenzie's/McKenny's, Ewell's Division took the right fork, which ran south-southwest across Totopotomoy Creek, then to Shady Grove Church. The rest of the Valley Army, with Whiting's Division in the lead, kept straight, marching to J. Overton's/Dr. Shelton's, then Totopotomoy Creek, and ultimately to Pole Green Church. This was in accordance with Lee's Merry Oaks Communiqué of June 25, received at Ashland; the two churches were only about two miles apart. Branch received Jackson's note and marched across the Bowes/Upper Chickahominy Bridge just after 10:00 a.m.[19]

Hughes' Store, Between Half Sink and Merry Oaks

Col. John Farnsworth of the 8th Illinois Cavalry had videttes[20] covering the countryside from Hughes' Store, near Half Sink, to Widow Crenshaw's to Atlee's Station on the Virginia Central to Shady Grove Church,[21] and then nothing for several miles to Hanover Courthouse, northeast of Ashland.[22] About 7:00 a.m., he received word that Hughes Store, northeast of Half Sink, and had been attacked by Rebels. Farnsworth ordered his men to fight a delaying action, falling back after delaying the enemy as long as possible.[23] Little known to him, these were the scouts of the Valley Army.[24] Sometime later, two of his officers were ambushed on their way back from checking on the company at Hanover Courthouse[25]; one survived to tell the tale, but missed the obvious. The whole Valley Army, about 15,500 infantry, was marching though the 10-mile gap between the cavalry companies at Hughes' Store and Hanover Courthouse.

Union Side of the Chickahominy, Near Atlee's Station on the Virginia Central Railroad[26]

Major Roy Stone of the 13th Pennsylvania Reserves[27] had only 6 companies of his regiment. With these, he was required to watch the Rebels along the river west of Mechanicsville. He put two companies[28] at the Meadow Bridge, one covering the road bridge and another covering the Virginia Central Railroad bridge. He had another company spread out[29] from Meadow Bridge southeast to Mechanicsville, and the other three in reserve.[30] At 1:00 p.m., he was ordered to take the three reserve companies to Atlee's Station on the Virginia Central. Stone positioned two of his companies south of Atlee's and sent one forward to that place as skirmishers.[31]

Stone's skirmishers soon ran into skirmishers from Branch's brigade coming southeast from Hughes' Store. These were three companies from the 7th North Carolina.[32] With Branch's whole brigade only a mile behind them,[33] Stone could not hope to do much. According to Stone, his skirmishers' first volley "threw them into confusion,"[34] so he gave them another. At that point, Stone found out that his companies at the bridges had withdrawn by order of another officer.[35] Fearing he would be cut off, he retreated to his two companies at Widow Crenshaw's, only to find them engaged with Rebels coming across the Meadow Bridge. Stone pulled them out too and retreated east towards Shady Grove Church.[36]

Lieutenant Haywood of the 7th North Carolina had a starkly different view. He encountered about 200 Yankees, whom he attacked and drove off, capturing their camp and a flag at Atlee's. This was probably the camp of one of the 8th Illinois Cavalry detachments, as Branch says that Haywood's flag was a cavalry guidon.[37] Haywood pressed forward and engaged Stone at Widow Crenshaw's. Stone put up such a fight that Haywood called in another company as reinforcements, and had to begin replacing the other exhausted companies.[38] Robert Hoke's 33rd North Carolina now joined the fight at Branch's direction.[39] In the end, Haywood captured a full company of the 13th Pennsylvania Reserves.[40] At 12:00 p.m., McClellan wired that he had just heard that his pickets north of the Chickahominy had been driven in.[41]

Just South of Richardson's Crossroads,
a Mile South of Pole Green Church

With so much intelligence that the Valley Army was nearing Mechanicsville, McClellan sent troops to look for Jackson.[42] About noon, the cavalry of Brigadier Emory, the 17th New York Infantry, and four cannons arrived at Richardson's crossroads, and about noon were surprised to find the 18th Massachusetts Infantry marching towards them *from* Mechanicsville. The 18th had taken the wrong route. Hearing reports of Confederate cavalry threatening Old Church, 10 miles in his rear towards White House Landing, General Emory left four companies of the 18th Massachusetts and two guns of Benson's Battery M, 2d U.S. Artillery (6 Ordnance Rifles), and hurried away. Col. Barnes of the 18th brought up another two companies, but other than that he was utterly alone.[43]

Ewell's Division, on the Road
to Shady Grove Church

Ewell's skirmishers had two units of Valley Army cavalry in front of them,[44] and General Jackson himself accompanied Ewell's column.[45] Late in the morning, their guide, Lincoln Sydnor, missed the turnoff on the road that led to Totopotomoy Creek and Shady Grove Church. General Ewell threatened to string him up, but Jackson personally intervened and Mr. Sydnor lived to tell the tale.[46] About 11:00 a.m., the Yankees attacked; Jackson sent a note to Stuart that he was engaged with the enemy.[47] The Yankees had strewn the road with obstructions: "Logs were thrown into the road, and trees felled across it, their leaves perfectly fresh, and when the twigs were broken showing the fracture had just occurred. The flying axemen were not fifteen minutes ahead, and our march pushed them so that after a while the obstructions ceased."[48] The obstructions gave Capt. S.G. Pryor, 12th Georgia, Trimble's Brigade, time to write a letter to his wife from "Ashland this side 10 miles."[49]

With the Valley Army, on the Road
to Pole Green Church

After turning south at Lebanon Church, Stuart's cavalry met Union videttes at Taliaferro's Mill, about two miles east of the Valley Army. The Federals quickly retreated, then contested Stuart's advance to Overton's/Dr. Shelton's,[50] but then retreated further east, out of the way. Stuart sent the 1st Virginia Cavalry ahead to secure the bridge over Totopotomoy Creek, on the road to Pole Green Church, about two miles east of where Ewell's Division was nearing the creek, which crossed both roads. Stuart himself waited for the Valley Army, no doubt keeping a wary eye out.

Totopotomoy Creek, on the Road
to Pole Green Church

The intrepid Col. Farnsworth of the 8th Illinois Cavalry had not been idle. Shortly after 1:00, he sent a company up the Pole Green Church Road to look for the enemy.

About 3:00,[51] Farnsworth's men "tore up"[52] the bridge and then found Stuart's men bearing down on them, with Confederate infantry close behind. Brigadier Hood's Texans of Whiting's Division went forward as skirmishers, and Reilly's Rowan (NC) Battery (2 Parrotts, 2 captured Yankee boat howitzers, and 2 Confederate guns)[53] opened fire to drive off the Yankees, and to signal Powell Hill.[54] Hood's men were so close on Farnworth's cavalrymen that the latter left axes in the trees they were chopping down.[55] Facing most of the Valley Army, the Federals beat a hasty retreat.[56] Stuart's men repaired the bridge in half an hour and secured the area around Pole Green Church[57] while the Texans removed the tree obstructions south of the bridge.[58] Farnsworth moved further south, towards Richardson's Crossroads, where he had infantry support from the 18th Massachusetts.

At Union headquarters, General McClellan wrote a letter to his wife, in the middle of which he "received the positive information that Jackson is en-route to take us in rear."[59]

Ewell's Division, on the Road to Shady Grove Church

Two miles west, and closer to Mechanicsville, Ewell's men crossed Totopotomoy Creek at 3:00 p.m., only to finally bump into the Yankees: "Early in the afternoon the cavalry in front were seen halted. Instantly, you could hear all down the ranks, 'Look out boys, fight on hand! Cavalry videtting to the rear!' 'Bring forward the First Maryland,' was the order an [aide] brought from General Ewell. Going past the cavalry to the front we found the enemy's pickets, which companies G and E … immediately drove in—following them rapidly and driving in their supporting force, which skirmished obstinately. This began about 3.00, and we believe we were the first guns fired in the great Richmond battles."[60]

The skirmishing Yankees were more troopers of the 8th Illinois cavalry.[61] Ewell ordered the 1st Maryland to drive the enemy across Totopotomoy Creek. Soon the Marylanders and Jackson himself could see Branch's men to their right marching to Mechanicsville.[62] In their front, the 8th Illinois cavalry had concealed infantry support from the 2nd Pennsylvania Reserves.[63]

"'What's that firing, Colonel?' said General Jackson to Col. Johnson as the latter rode up to General Ewell to ask if he should drive them off. 'It's the enemy's skirmishers in a thicket.' 'Why don't you stop them?' 'Can't do it, sir, without charging them, or shelling the place.' 'Well sir, you must stop that firing; make them keep quiet!' 'Very well, sir,' said the colonel, and riding off he brought up two pieces of the Baltimore Artillery.[64] At the first two shells the Yankees fell back and we were not disturbed until late at night."[65]

The road to Shady Grove Church, and Mechanicsville beyond, was open.

At the Confederate End of the Meadow Bridge

General Order 75 specified that Powell Hill should cross Meadow Bridge when "the movements of [Branch and/or Jackson] were discovered."[66] In his report of March 5, 1863, Powell Hill claimed that he set his men in motion at 3:00 p.m. because he had "no intelligence" from Branch nor Jackson, and was unwilling to "hazard the failure of the whole plan by longer deferring it."[67] This seems rather improbable. The 7th North Carolina and

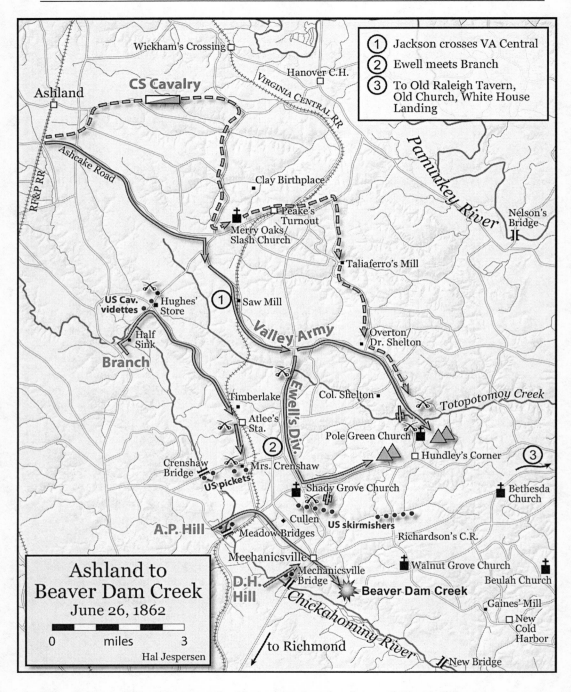

Ashland to Beaver Dam Creek
June 26, 1862

0   miles   3

Hal Jespersen

Map legend:
1. Jackson crosses VA Central
2. Ewell meets Branch
3. To Old Raleigh Tavern, Old Church, White House Landing

the 13th Pennsylvania Reserves had been in a short but heavy skirmish fight that morning at Atlee's about two miles away. About 2:00, they were going at it at Widow Crenshaw's, about a mile to Powell's direct front. About 3:00, the Valley Army's Baltimore Artillery started booming away, two miles in Powell Hill's direct front, at Shady Grove Church. Pvt. T.M. Bigbee, 5th Texas, Hood's Brigade, Whiting's Division was on the road to Pole

Green Church two miles east and heard the Baltimore Artillery: "Late in the evening of June 26 Jackson fired the signal gun that he was in position. Hill at once attacked...."[68]

Hearing Jackson's guns, Powell Hill launched his men across the Meadow Bridge at about 3:00 p.m.[69] Charles Fields' brigade led, and the 40th Virginia was his lead regiment. The 40th rushed across the bridge at the double-quick[70] and drove off Stone's pickets, who had been guarding the bridges and the Meadow Bridge Road,[71] and turned southeast on the Cullen Road.[72] Nearing Mechanicsville, the Yankees on the Beaver Dam Line opened up on him with infantry and artillery.[73]

Richardson's Crossroads

Col. Barnes and his four companies of the 18th Massachusetts watched a lot of movement, but nothing really happened.[74] In midafternoon, Union infantry under Brigadier Martindale showed up and deployed south of the crossroads.[75] At least Col. Barnes was not alone any more. They could hear the firing but nothing much happened to them, either.[76] At 3:15 p.m., McClellan wired to Brigadier Fitz John Porter, commanding the Yankees on the Beaver Dam Line at Mechanicsville, "From all you tell me it would seem best to hold your position at least until dark...."[77]

Due East of Atlee's Station, Between Widow Crenshaw's and Shady Grove Church

Ewell's Division of the Valley Army was marching south on the road to Shady Grove Church when it contacted Branch's brigade between Widow Crenshaw's and the church. Captain Campbell Brown beheld a magnificent sight: "[T]he appearance to our right, marching straight towards us of Branch's brigade, which was in column of regiments, moving across the open field with colors flying—and presenting as fine a sight as one ever see's [sic]. It was the first & only time I ever saw troops moving in such an order except on parade...."[78]

A member of the 37th Virginia also saw the end of Branch's attack; apparently Col. Stone was giving as good as he got: "Our column being at a halt, I rode a little way to the right and viewed from an elevation for a brief space of time a part of this battle, half a mile away. The Confederates by a brilliant charge swept the Federals from the field, but by counthercharge of fresh Federal troops the decimated Confederate ranks were in turn forced back over the same open field, which, however, was quickly recovered by fresh Confederates, leaving the dead and dying of both sides lying on this bloody field, promiscuously intermingled."[79]

Brigadier Branch conferred with General Ewell himself, and then went back to the action at Widow Crenshaw's, only to find, about 3:30 p.m., that the Yankees had withdrawn, and that Powell Hill's crossing at Meadow Bridge had put him out of the fight.[80]

On the Chickahominy River at Chickahominy Bluffs, Overlooking the Mechanicsville Bridge, About 4:00 P.M.

Word of the big operation had leaked at least through the Confederate Army. Late in the afternoon, a bevy of officers and influential civilians gathered at a bluff overlooking the Mechanicsville Bridge. "On this hill, in range of the enemy's guns, a group of distin-guished Confederates were assembled, composed of President Davis, Mr. Randolph (Sec-retary of War) Generals Lee, Longstreet, and D.H. Hill, waiting to hear General Jackson's guns on the north side of Mechanicsville…."[81]

Major Joseph Brent recorded the scene: "No one had any theory about the delay of Jackson, which was a cause of great anxiety…. Suddenly the lookers on … began looking with interest, and then Genl. Lee himself … joined them…. [He] continued his obser-vation for a few minutes, and then descended to the road. Advancing to Genl. Longstreet, he said, 'Those are [A.P.] Hill's men,' and then, in as quiet a tone as if he spoke of the weather, he said, 'General, you may now cross over.'"[82]

The "delay of Jackson" claim seems rather odd, because by the time Powell Hill crossed his bridges, Jackson had communicated with Branch, and Valley Army guns had opened fire at Shady Grove Church, and at Totopotomy Creek. Jackson himself was only two miles away, exactly where he was supposed to be, according to General Order 75 and the Merry Oaks Communiqué.

General Lee rode west to the Confederate earthworks between the Meadow Bridge Road and the Mechanicsville Road.[83]

McClellan's Headquarters, Trent House

Shortly after the firing commenced, General McClellan ordered his chief engineer, General John Barnard, to find a fallback position for the troops in the Beaver Dam Creek Line that they could hold as a bridgehead if the rest of the Army were to move north across the Chickahominy. Barnard opined that it would be impossible to hold all of the Federal bridges, but that the two best ones, named the Woodbury Bridge and the Grapevine Bridge, could be held, as they were only a few hundred yards apart. Barnard crossed the Chickahominy to take a look when a rider approached him with additional instructions from McClellan. The fallback line was to be in the area between Dr. Gaines' Mansion and the Grapevine Bridge. The rider was a young lieutenant named George Armstrong Custer.[84]

June 26, 1862, 2301 East Grace Street,
Church Hill, Richmond Virginia

Word of the impending battle had spread among the civilians in Richmond.[85] Char-lotte Cross Wigfall's father, Louis Wigfall, went to see General Longstreet, going from Richmond itself to the Confederate end of the Mechanicsville Bridge, a trip of a few miles, but which took him three to four hours.[86] Thirty-five-year-old Eliza Carrington was one of Richmond's bluebloods with a Bohemian streak, socializing with the likes of Edgar Allan Poe and Swedish singing star Jenny Lind.[87] She was making preparations for an outing that day. She had been invited to spend the day with John Minor Botts at his estate Half Sink, seven miles up the Brook Turnpike.[88] This gave her a sense of adventure, as the Unionist Botts had recently been arrested and jailed for suspected treason and was now under house arrest at his Henrico County farmhouse.[89] Carrington had a pass, and rather than take the shorter route up the Brook Turnpike, she and her companions made their way to Mechanicsville, and then down the Brook Turnpike. She would later recall: "The excitement on the Mechanicsville Turnpike was more thrilling than I could conceive. Men riding and leading horses at full speed; the rattling of their gear, their canteens and arms; the rush of the poor beasts into and out of the pond at which they were watered. The dust, the cannons on the crop roads and fields, the ambulances, and a long line of infantry awaiting orders…. No ball could be as exciting as our ride this evening…. I realized the bright rush of life, the hurry of death on the battlefield."[90]

Most of the civilians did not bother to travel all the way to Brigadier Branch's jumping-off point. "Hundreds of men, women and children were attracted to the heights around the city to behold the spectacle."[91] Both the Confederate officers and the civilians watched as Fields' Brigade moved slowly down the Cullen Road and into Mechanicsville.

4

They Were All Cut to Pieces

The Beaver Dam Creek Line

The Yankees were waiting for them. McCall's Pennsylvania Reserves called themselves a corps, but they were actually only a division of three brigades, under Brigadiers Reynolds, Seymour, and Meade. The latter's men were in reserve. The former two were lined up behind Beaver Dam Creek, about a mile east of the town of Mechanicsville.[1] Seymour was nearer to the river, with Reynolds to his right and north.[2]

Beaver Dam Creek cuts southerly through an east-west ridge, making "abrupt" banks almost a hundred feet high on both sides. Only one road crosses the creek, passing near Ellison's Mill (the Ellison's Mill Road), about ¾ mile from the river.[3]

For the soon-to-be-unfortunate Rebels, McCall liberally studded his lines with artillery, especially near the roads. Cooper's Battery B, Pennsylvania Light Artillery (six 10 lb. Parrott rifles[4]), and Kerns' Battery G, Pennsylvania Light Artillery (6 howitzers[5]), each had four of their six guns just north of the Mechanicsville Road, blocking the way to Gaines' Mill. Smead's Battery K, 5th U.S. Artillery (4 Napoleons[6]) had two of its 6 guns just south of that road. Kerns' other section (two guns) were covering the road from Mechanicsville to Ellison's Mill Road. South of them but at the northern tip of the swamp was Dehart's Battery C, 5th U.S. Artillery (six Napoleons). Smead's other four guns were at the southern tip of the swamp. Edwards' Combined Batteries L and M, 3rd U.S. Artillery (six ordnance rifles[7]) were further south of them, near the bluff of the river valley. Easton's Battery A, Pennsylvania Light Artillery (4 Napoleons) was in reserve. Thirty cannons would greet any Rebels they saw.[8]

Truman Seymour's Brigade held the Ellison's Mill crossing, the 12th Pennsylvania Reserves from the river to the road and the 10th Pennsylvania Reserves north of the road, behind the southern half of the swamp, and split by Smead's guns. The 9th Pennsylvania Reserves was initially in reserve. From the 10th's northern flank, Brigadier Reynolds' 8th Pennsylvania Reserves were behind the northern half of the swamp. Dehart's Battery came next, with Reynold's 5th Pennsylvania Reserves just south of the Mechanicsville Road. Reynolds' 1st and 2nd regiments covered the area from the road north. The 1st Pennsylvania Reserves and the 13th Pennsylvania Reserves were out picketing Mechanicsville and Meadow Bridge but would join the main line when driven in. The 4th Pennsylvania Reserves were behind that line, just in case.[9] Meade's other three regiments were in reserve, with Griffin's Brigade, of Morell's Division, tasked to help if needed.

Col. Landers' 1929 map of the Battle of Beaver Dam Creek (Library of Congress).

McCall had about 8,600 men, entrenched in an impregnable position, with 32 guns, roughly one cannon per 269 men.[10]

Lee had not anticipated that the Yankees would make a stand at Beaver Dam Creek.[11] They were supposed to realize their predicament and retreat. Lee was not sure in what direction they would go, but they should have at least *gone*. Instead, they had dug in and started shooting. By making a stand at Beaver Dam, McClellan had called Lee's bluff. General Lee crossed the river and stationed himself at Mechanicsville, a small hamlet, during the battle. Mechanicsville consisted of three stores and two shops.[12]

Between Mechanicsville and the Beaver Dam Creek Line

As Field's men left Mechanicsville on the Ellison's Mill Road, a "concentric"[13] fire of Union artillery smote their column, and forced them to deploy into line of battle to the northeast.[14] Pegram's Purcell Artillery (six Parrotts)[15] was put on the Mechanicsville Road, with two of Field's regiments on either side of it.[16] Poor Pegram was but a plaintive squeak against the bark of McCall's five batteries. Kerns' and Cooper's batteries (8 guns) at the Mechanicsville Road crossing, apparently had quite an effect, as Powell Hill's second brigade, J.R. Anderson's, was ordered to swing wide to the north and flank it while McIntosh's Pee Dee (South Carolina) Artillery (two Napoleons and two ordnance rifles) was put out to help poor Pegram and to keep Kerns and Cooper busy.[17] Archer's Brigade was ordered up on Field's left, but broke apart on the way, the 14th Tennessee getting lost.[18] Soon Braxton's Fredericksburg Artillery (two ordnance rifles and four smoothbores[19]) was sent up to help Macintosh. The next brigade, Dorsey Pender's, was ordered up to the right of Field but it lost the 16th North Carolina on the way.[20] Maxcy Gregg's Brigade would act as a reserve.

In the meantime, Johnson's Virginia Battery was sent to help Braxton.[21] Casting about for more men, Powell Hill grabbed Roswell Ripley's brigade, which was leading Harvey Hill's following division. As soon as it was across the Chickahominy, Powell Hill ordered it to attack the Ellison's Mill crossing, more or less with Pender.[22] In the space of two hours, Powell Hill had 12 guns and five brigades, about 10,000 men, headed at the Yankee line.

They never had a chance. The Union artillery smote pieces out of the Rebel lines as they advanced. As they moved closer, whole sections of battle lines fell. When the Union infantry opened up at about 200 yards, whole ranks of companies fell, but the regiments as a whole moved on to their doom; Brigadier Field described it as "the most destructive cannonading I have ever known."[23] His brigade, and Archer's, attacked along the Mechanicsville Road, making it to the valley of the creek before being stopped cold[24] by the 5th Pennsylvania Reserves. Field's men had the easier time of it. The Yankees across from Archer were marksmen, and claimed over 200 of his men.[25] Pender's brigade broke into pieces. The 16th North Carolina had already disappeared, losing 200 men in its effort.[26] The 22nd North Carolina somehow wound up behind Field's men. The 34th North Carolina broke off to the south and disappeared. The 38th North Carolina and the 2nd Arkansas Battalion made it into the creek, only to be slaughtered therein. Up until the time of his wounding, Col. William Hoke of the 38th says he lost 29 of his men. Lt. Col. Armfield, who took over, afterwards could find just 35 men of the 420 who started the charge, an effective casualty rate of 92 percent.[27] Just after this debacle, the 34th North Carolina arrived to suffer much the same fate, losing many of its officers.[28] Ripley's brigade broke in half; the two regiments (48th Georgia and 34th North Carolina) that actually arrived at this deathtrap position were the lucky ones. The other half attacked to the south at the swamp. The 44th Georgia to the north lost 321 of its 500 men, including most of its officers, while the 1st North Carolina lost 42 of its privates, and its entire command staff.[29] One company could only find 20 of sixty men afterwards.[30]

General Lee, his plan up the spout and his men being slaughtered, watched the debacle from Mechanicsville. Then President Davis and his enormous retinue showed up:

All over the plain, the spiteful shells were bursting in fury. Riders went down; horses were slain; guns were disabled. Many of the green troops were in a frenzy. Lee sat through it all as if he thought he was invulnerable. Nearby, though, was the President, with members of his Cabinet and a coterie of politicians. One explosion might kill all of them. They must go to a place of safety. Lee rode over to Davis. "Mr. President," he asked with a frigid salute, "who is all this army and what is it doing here?" Davis knew what Lee meant. He squirmed in his saddle. "It is not my army, General," he said. "It is certainly not my army, Mr. President, and this is no place for it." Davis was stunned. "Well, General, if I withdraw, perhaps they will follow me." He lifted his hat and rode down the hill. His companions, crestfallen, trooped after him. He disappeared, and Lee did not know till later that Davis had gone only far enough to get out of his sight. Then he halted quickly, but not before a soldier at his feet had been killed by an exploding shell.[31]

The Beaver Dam Creek Line

The Yankees did not make especial note of the wholesale destruction of these regiments. Capt. Cooper, Battery B, Pennsylvania Light Artillery noted that he had fired 800 to 900 rounds during the engagement from his six guns.[32] The 10th Pennsylvania Reserves reported that the rifle pits were "held."[33] The 12th Pennsylvania Reserves talked more about the action to their left (1st North Carolina and 44th Georgia) than their own. The 7th Pennsylvania Reserves, Edwards' Battery L/M, 3rd U.S. Artillery, and perhaps the 9th Massachusetts get the credit for annihilating the 1st North Carolina and 44th Georgia.[34]

The only place the Rebels made any progress was at the extreme northern end of the Union line. Just outside of Mechanicsville, J.R. Anderson's whole brigade had been ordered to swing wide to the north after Kerns' cannons. On the way, the brigade disappeared in the thick forest, so the 35th Georgia was sent to find the Yankee line. Most of J.R. Anderson's brigade hit the 1st and 2nd Pennsylvania Reserves, but the 35th Georgia, 14th Georgia, and 3rd Louisiana Battalion were able to make it across the creek.[35] With his line possibly flanked, McCall called up Griffin's brigade. The 9th Massachusetts broke off and went south to its date with Ripley. The 4th Michigan and 14th New York relieved the 2nd and 1st Pennsylvania Reserves, bottling up J.R. Anderson's toehold.

For James B. Dickerson of the 4th Michigan of Griffin's brigade, the battle was a trying one. Private Dickerson was frequently leaving the ranks. As the regiment went into battle, he slid his trousers down, tied them to his upper legs, and "kept up by hobbling along and suffering from diarrhea simultaneously."[36] Nightfall ended any aggressive maneuvering. Private Bores was particularly active in fighting the foe after dark, firing several times at the flashes of Rebel sharpshooters. He stopped when he realized that he had been shooting at fireflies, but claimed his effort as a great contribution to Union arms.[37]

In two short hours, the Confederates had lost almost 2,000 men, primarily in ten or so regiments. The pasting that the Mechanicsville regiments received would make them almost useless for the rest of the week. Half of Ripley's brigade had been annihilated. Pender, Field, and J.R. Anderson, half of the division, were still in shock. Only Archer's little band would recover quickly. The Yankees, on the other hand, lost fewer than 200 men.[38]

The Battle of Beaver Dam Creek was a debacle. As of 5:00 p.m., present in Mechanicsville were Generals Lee, Powell Hill, and Branch. Branch knew that the Valley Army was at Shady Grove Church from his conversation with Ewell about 3:00. This was only about a mile from Mechanicsville. Branch certainly reported personally to Powell Hill when the former arrived in Mechanicsville, as his brigade was available to support Powell Hill's attack.[39] In his report, Powell Hill specifically says that he did *not* order his brigadiers "storm" the Union works[40] until General Ripley arrived. Harvey Hill says that he was with Ripley's brigade (it was leading the divisions) and received "several" messages from Lee and one from Davis to hurry a brigade to Powell Hill's support.[41] It was Lee himself who ordered the storming of the Beaver Dam Creek Line, and is responsible for the "disastrous and bloody repulse."[42]

Powell Hill blamed Stonewall Jackson, who, according to Powell Hill, was supposed to attack the Yankee flank. The Federals' "position along Beaver Dam Creek was too strong to be carried by a direct attack, and expecting every moment to hear Jackson's guns on my left and in rear of the enemy, I forbore to order the storming of their lines."[43] He further complained, "It was never contemplated that my division alone should have sustained the shock of this battle, but such was the case, and the only assistance received was from Ripley." In other words, despite 20,000 men at his right hand, under the eye of the commanding general, Powell Hill expected Jackson, with 15,000 men at his left hand, to spontaneously come to his aid. In truth, if Lee had wanted Jackson to actually attack, all he had to do was tell him to do so. General Ewell and General Jackson were at Shady Grove Church, less than a mile away; it is a matter measured in hundreds of yards whether they were closer to Powell Hill than Harvey Hill and Ripley were. Moreover, the uncooperative Yankees had a reinforced brigade out there at Richardson's Crossroads to prevent Jackson from doing precisely what Powell Hill wanted him to do. The 2nd Pennsylvania Reserves were in place along the eastern branch of the creek, Farnsworth's Cavalry and the 18th Massachusetts were at Richardson's, and Martindale's whole brigade was due just south of them, in all about 4,000 men. The brigades of Griffin and Butterfield, and Sykes' whole Regular Division, were within supporting distance, with their own and excess artillery. If Powell Hill had gotten his way, Lee would have only 25,000 men attacking 20,000 Yankees, half of them in an impregnable position with artillery lined up almost wheel to wheel. This sort of attack was precisely what Operation Chickahominy was designed to avoid.

Evening of June 26, 1862, Half Sink Farm, Henrico County

Eliza Carrington arrived and found the traitor Botts and his family listening to the roar of artillery and the crash of musket fire. Her companion and "most intimate friend" was 44-year-old Elizabeth Van Lew, a very conflicted slaveowning abolitionist. "Crazy Bet," as Richmonders called her, was also a Yankee spy.[44]

After Dark, June 26, 1862

The Valley Army had arrived at Pole Green Church about 5:00 and bivouacked. All were two miles away from Powell Hill and the Beaver Dam Creek Line. At sundown, about 7:30 p.m., a force of Yankees approached Jackson's camp from the east, on the Old Church Road. Stuart's Horse Artillery opened fire.[45] It was all quiet after that.

Top: Van Lew House, Richmond, Virginia, ca. 1900 (Library of Congress). *Bottom:* Drawing of Pole Green Church, May 1862 (courtesy Historic Pole Green Church Foundation).

The 1st Maryland and 13th Virginia did not have a restful night. After dark, a body of Federals arrived to recover two abandoned artillery pieces, and did so. The Marylanders crept back into the area and slept on their arms.[46]

The Yankees' stand at Beaver Dam had thrown off the plan, and it was clearly time to update it. General Lee called a conference of his division commanders. Powell Hill "left Mechanicsville" at about 8:30.[47] Harvey Hill says that he "received an order" at 9:00 p.m. on the 26th to march through Mechanicsville and east on the road to Bethesda Church the next day.[48] Only General Lee could give orders to Harvey Hill. Lee's aide-de-camp Charles Marshall expressly says that Lee met with Longstreet and the two Hills until 11:00.[49] Jeb Stuart was also probably there. And so was General Jackson.

The Merry Oaks Communiqué told Jackson that the Valley Army could use the Mechanicsville–Bethesda Church Road to move east, or, alternatively, use the Walnut Grove Church–Bethesda Church Road to move east. The 9:00 order to Harvey Hill changed that by giving Hill the Mechanicsville–Bethesda Church Road, forcing Jackson to use the other one. It strains credulity to think that Jackson himself was not present for this change. As set forth above, just a few days earlier, Jackson had ridden fourteen hours to Richmond though tenuously secured country for a meeting with Lee and the other division commanders. Lee had been in communication with Jackson every day for the last four days. In his report, Brigadier Ewell points out that the march to Shady Grove Church and Pole Green Church were "under the immediate direction of the Major-General commanding."[50] This puts Jackson himself at Shady Grove Church late in the day on June 26, about two miles away from Lee, with Powell Hill's 10,000 men between his route and the Yankees. It would take Jackson less than an hour to get to Mechanicsville from Shady Grove Church. The Rev. Major Dabney, Jackson's chief of staff, saw Jackson near Pole Green Church with "the sun less than an hour high," about 7:30, about two and a half miles from Mechanicsville.[51]

The next credible sighting of Jackson himself is at about 9:00 a.m. the next day, when Jackson himself says that he was with the Valley Army when it crossed the eastern branch of Beaver Dam Creek near Richardson's Crossroads.[52] He was also seen just north of Walnut Grove Church around 10:00 a.m.[53] General Order 75 does not mention Walnut Grove Church at all. Lee's communication of June 25 mentions it, but only as a waypoint in the future; it does not order Jackson to move there from Pole Green Church. How did Jackson know to march south from Pole Green Church to Walnut Grove Church instead of east from Pole Green Church to Bethesda Church and Old Raleigh? How did Jackson know to meet Lee at Walnut Grove Church? How did Stuart know to ride east at dawn? Because they met with Lee at Mechanicsville. Finally, William Augustus McClendon, a private in the 15th Alabama, Trimble's Brigade, Ewell's Division wrote, "It is said that Jackson and Ewell rode into Richmond that night, a distance of 15 miles, and had a conference with President Davis and General Lee and formed their plans for the attack the next day."[54]

No minutes of this meeting, nor even any mention of it, exist, but it is not difficult to discern what happened at this meeting. The easier topic was how to get where they wanted to go. The Timberlake Map rather peters out east of Walnut Grove Church, Bethesda Church, and Old Raleigh. In fact, according to it, there is no way to get directly from Walnut Grove Church to Cold Harbor; the upper road east from Walnut Grove Church cuts south past Stark's and runs west of Gaines' Mill. This would put Jackson and Powell Hill on the same road west of Gaines' Mill. Undoubtedly a local guide spoke up, probably Seaton Tinsley, Fannie Gaines' husband and General Lee's personal guide.[55] The others, Captain C.C. Dabney and John Henry Timberlake, 4th Virginia Cavalry (with Jackson),[56] and Lt. Thomas Sydnor[57] (with Harvey Hill)[58] probably also chimed in.

The map was inaccurate; the road past Stark's did not lead to Gaines' Mill, but to Beulah Church, north of Cold Harbor. This information was dispositive. Harvey Hill would march past Pole Green Church to Bethesda Church on a wide end run, and then south to Beulah Church and Cold Harbor. Jackson would march on a shallower end run, from Walnut Grove Church to Beulah Church, and then to Cold Harbor. As part of the new situation, Lee gave Jackson operational control of Harvey Hill's division. Powell Hill would stick with the original plan, on the road from Mechanicsville to Walnut Grove Church to Gaines' Mill. Longstreet would use the River Road, close to the river. At dawn, Stuart would go east from Pole Green Church, making sure that the Yankees had not moved northeast towards Old Church, and clearing any of them from Harvey Hill's route. The infantry commanders would all meet at Walnut Grove Church the next morning, after they had taken the Beaver Dam Creek Line.

The more difficult topic was whether they should stay with the plan. Beaver Dam Creek had "miscarried"[59] and had been a "fiasco"[60] and the Yankees were still on the Beaver Dam Creek Line. Despite the battle, nothing had really changed. Jackson was where he was supposed to be, in a position to move either south or east. Powell Hill and Longstreet were where they were supposed to be. Harvey Hill would be on an end run, with Jackson on the inside track doing the same thing. Those Federals had to either stand or run. What if they stood?

Since the Yankees had fought Powell Hill to a standstill at the giant trench of Beaver Dam Creek, they might do the same at the next one, allowing the bulk of the corps to withdraw behind that.[61] The next logical place for the Yankees to fight was the Powhite Creek, which runs from Gaines' Mill past Dr. Gaines' Mansion to the Chickahominy, because from Mechanicsville east, five Union bridges spanned the Chickahominy. The one closest to Mechanicsville was the New Bridge. Both sides had pickets at the ends of it. But one rickety bridge is not enough over which to move a corps harried by the enemy. It also led into the Confederate lines, so the Yankees were not likely to use it to escape. A few miles on though, four more bridges, one with abutments, crossed the river. These were Woodbury's, Duane's, Grapevine/Sumner's Upper Bridge and one other, all relatively close to one another. There were more bridges further down, but they were pretty far away. Defending Powhite Creek would protect these bridges, and allow the Yankees to flee, or reinforce north of the Chickahominy. Powhite Creek was the logical choice for their next stand. From the Confederates' point of view, standing was not much of an option. The Reinforced Valley Army (the Valley Army plus Harvey Hill's Division) would be behind their right flank at Beulah Church. Powell Hill and Longstreet could push them onto the bayonets of the Reinforced Valley Army, or it could attack from that place and crush the Federals between the jaws of a gigantic vise.

If the Yankees ran, they had to go either east to White House Landing or south across the Chickahominy. If east, the Reinforced Valley Army could deal them a "side blow."[62] If south, they had to pass through the chokepoint of the bridges with Lee's whole army after them; that could easily turn into another debacle on the scale of Napoleon at Berezina or Leipzig. General Lee had all of the Yankees' options covered. But he was still unexpectedly stuck at the Beaver Dam Creek Line.

One of Longstreet's brigades, Wilcox's, had made it to Beaver Dam Creek itself and was holding there.[63] Powell Hill could pin them to the front, while Longstreet reinforced Wilcox and hit their southern flank, and Jackson moved south from Pole Green Church. If they made a stand at the Beaver Dam Creek Line the next morning, the Yankees would either be crushed from two sides, or forced out of the Beaver Dam Creek Line. Either way they jumped, Lee was ready for them.

The Mechanicsville conference ended about 11:00. Lee and his entourage rode back across the Chickahominy to spend the night at Ravenswood Farm, about a mile from the river.[64] Jackson and Stuart rode back to Pole Green Church, where Jackson spent the night.[65]

McClellan's Headquarters

General Barnard returned to the Trent House to make his report about dark, only to find that McClellan himself had repaired to General Porter's headquarters at the Beaver Dam Creek Line. At 10:00, McClellan requested Barnard's presence by telegram; Barnard showed up around midnight with his findings. McClellan stood to return to the Trent House, and Barnard stayed with Porter. Porter hemmed and hawed for about an hour about holding where he was and retreating in daylight, or decamping immediately to the new position. Barnard pointed out that if Porter waited until daylight, the troops in the Beaver Dam Creek Line would be harried by Confederates from behind and Jackson from the left as they fell back. At about 1:00 a.m., Porter issued the order for the bulk of his troops to fall back to the area that protected the bridges.[66] At 3:00 a.m., Porter received official orders from General McClellan to defend the area Barnard had reconnoitered, along Boatswain's Creek, *half a mile east* of Powhite Creek and Gaines' Mill.[67]

Almost everyone around Richmond knew that Stonewall Jackson was on the way, and would arrive from the north. Though Stuart's cavalry had largely screened the march, the affair at Totopotomoy Creek the day before had forced Jackson to deploy an infantry brigade, thus tipping his hand. During the night, Union pickets probed Jackson's huge camp at Pole Green Church.[68] Jackson had arrived, in full force, and for the Federals, it was time to quit Mechanicsville.

5

The Retreat to Gaines' Mill

Along the Beaver Dam Creek Line

Brigadier Martindale pulled out of his position near Richardson's shortly after 1:00 a.m.,[1] neglecting to tell the 18th Massachusetts, which was still supporting Farnsworth's cavalry.[2] Brigadier Griffin marched off about 2:00 a.m., as did Brigadier Meade.[3] Sykes' men started east at 2:30 a.m.[4] Butterfield's Brigade, of Morell's Division, sleeping near Sykes, also came back east, dropping off one regiment to remove the heavy guns at the Hogan House.[5] Brigadier Reynolds had sent one of his small regiments, the 5th Pennsylvania Reserves, east at midnight.[6] Brigadier Griffin's men followed after them,[7] along with Kingsbury's Battery D, 2nd U.S. Artillery.[8] About 4:00 a.m., Kerns' Battery G, Pennsylvania Artillery took off.[9] Tidball's Battery A, 2nd U.S. Artillery probably left about this time, ordered to cover the retreat from Gaines' Mill itself.[10] By 5:00, Brigadiers Reynolds and Seymour left with the bulk of their brigades.[11] At daybreak, all that was left of the impregnable Union infantry line were 6 companies of Stone's 13th Pennsylvania Reserves in pits near the Ellison's Mill Road, Berdan's U.S. Sharpshooters, and four companies of the 9th Pennsylvania Reserves.[12] The 12th Pennsylvania Reserves was still nearby but heading out. As for the artillery, only some of Cooper's Battery B, Pennsylvania Light Artillery were there to meet the Rebels.[13]

West of Beaver Dam Creek, Dawn, June 27

Cooper's guns bid the Confederates good morrow shortly before dawn, most of his fire falling on Marmaduke Johnson's Virginia battery way back in Mechanicsville itself.[14] General Lee himself was in Mechanicsville at that time.[15] Harvey Hill's Division had marched "at an early hour,"[16] but had to wait for the Federals in the Beaver Dam Creek Line. These were the right end of Stone's 13th Pennsylvania Reserves.[17] Hill sent two brigades, under Brigadiers Garland and George Anderson, on a flanking movement north up the road to Shady Grove Church, and then east and southeast. After an hour and a half of shelling and musketry,[18] about 8:00 a.m., the Confederates unleashed their legions against the terrible Union works. Powell Hill brought up his freshest brigade, that of Brigadier General Maxcy Gregg. It would attack along the Mechanicsville-Walnut Grove Church Road. Pender's battered men would attack south of the road center again. They took about an hour to get into position.[19] Further south, two of Longstreet's brigades, under Brigadiers Featherston and Pryor, had replaced Brigadiers Ripley[20] and Colquitt[21] (both of Harvey Hill's Division) during the night, and would storm the works nearer the river. Once Cooper's guns got going, Featherston, with Pryor in support, moved up to the creek and began firing at the four companies of the 9th Pennsylvania Reserves, which Featherston himself described as "greatly superior numbers."[22] Pender's men joined in, only to be stopped by the glutinous creek and precipitous banks.[23] Stopped cold and under fire, Pender sent for more artillery,[24] while Featherston sent for more infantry.[25]

General Porter's rear guards had read the situation perfectly, and abandoned the line as soon as the Rebels came forward. The four companies of the 9th Pennsylvania Reserves left Ellison's Mill with great enthusiasm, and were shelled for the first mile of their retreat.[26] This left the 12th Pennsylvania Reserves in the lurch. They lost 20 prisoners. One company was cut off near the mill and almost surrounded before squeaking away.[27] With Featherston and Pryor across the creek, the rest of the Union line collapsed.

The previous afternoon, one of Berdan's Sharpshooters, Private McCaul, had returned from sneaking a dead comrade back to Wisconsin for burial. He returned with a box of cigars and a bottle of whiskey for his comrades, which he shared out. He joined the Mechanicsville fight in shirtsleeves and civilian pants, carrying a double-barrel target rifle that weighed 19 pounds.[28] Private McCaul would need both barrels, as Companies C and G of the Berdan Sharpshooters were assigned duty as General McCall's rear guard, as were the survivors of Col. Stone's 13th Pennsylvania Reserves.[29] The rear guard fired most of their ammunition, and bugged out. One company of the 13th was sent out to destroy the bridge at Ellison's Mill.

Brigadier Pender launched his men up the hill, chasing out Private McCaul and his fellow U.S. Sharpshooters with great vigor.[30] Brigadier Gregg sent two companies up the hill, doing the same to the right end of Stone's 13th Pennsylvania Reserves, and capturing their flag.[31] According to the Yankees, General Reynolds showed up about 8:00 a.m. and ordered them quietly out of the line.[32] The Sharpshooters were only half a mile away when the Rebels poured into their just vacated rifle pits.[33]

With the impregnable line taken, Gregg's men pushed further forward at 7:35 a.m.,[34] entered a Union camp, and found "immense piles of flower [sic] and bacon burning."[35] They pushed on, "towards Walnut Grove Church."[36] Brigadier Featherston stopped in place and rebuilt the Ellison's Mill Bridge across Beaver Dam Creek,[37] which took an hour or two.[38]

Morell's Division, on the Retreat to Gaines' Mill

McCall's Division would be in reserve on the 27th, so Martindale's and Griffin's brigades of Morell's Division were ordered to their camps near the Curtis and Dr. Curtis houses and told to pack up[39] so that McCall's regiments could get past and to Gaines' Mill first. Morell's men reached camp about daybreak, a march rate of about 1 mile per hour.[40] Captain Sampson, 22nd Massachusetts, Martindale's Brigade, was out with pickets and somehow got the order to retreat behind Boatswain's Creek, to the east of Powhite Creek, instead of reporting at the Curtis Camp. Discovering the error, he hurried back west against the tide, but met the rest of the 22nd marching east. Initially ordered to come along, Sampson, by "vehement urging," was allowed to hurry to the camp to retrieve knapsacks and destroy anything left behind.[41]

Apparently some of Brigadier Griffin's supplies were without transport, so Morell fired them to deny them to the Rebels.[42] One of his men tells the story of some of those supplies. Several weeks before this, salt beef had been issued as rations,[43] but the men refused to eat it and piled hundreds of pounds of it up at the commissary tent in protest. William Harrer, a drummer with the 14th New York, Griffin's Brigade, took 25 pounds of the stuff down to Powhite Creek and boiled it for 24 hours, trying to get the salt out. He finally succeeded, but it "looked like old curled up shoe leather…." This morning, Harrer and his brother crossed Powhite Creek on a fallen tree near where he had boiled the beef for so long.[44]

The Gaines family was still looking after the deathly ill Dr. Curtis at his home between Walnut Grove Church and Gaines' Mill. Early in the morning, a Yankee officer arrived and informed them that they would need to vacate and head for White House Landing. The Union army was making a stand, and artillery was already in place around the house. This was probably Lt. Pennington, of Battery A, 2nd U.S. Artillery (6 ordnance rifles). With their quicker horse batteries,[45] Captains Tidball (Battery A, 2nd U.S. Artillery, 6 ordnance rifles) and Robertson (Battery B/C, 2nd U.S. Artillery, 6 ordnance rifles), had been ordered to fall back and harass the oncoming Rebels from long range. Tidball was in a position on the Walnut Grove Church–Gaines' Mill Road, about halfway between the Mechanicsville position and the mill itself, near Dr. Curtis' house. One of his sections, Pennington's, was detached, and probably near Walnut Grove Church, covering the eastward bend of Beaver Dam Creek and the road from Pole Green Church.[46] Robertson was in a peach orchard near the William Fleming Gaines House.

South towards the Chickahominy River, Brigadier Butterfield had been tasked with removing the heavy guns in emplacements near the Hogan House and Dr. Gaines' Mansion at 3:00 a.m.[47] The 44th New York was tasked with destroying the Federal bridges across the Chickahominy.[48] The 16th Michigan stood guard[49] as the crews of the monstrous weapons limbered up and trundled towards the Chickahominy.[50]

Sykes' Regulars camped at Camp Lovell, near the Hogan House.[51] They were up at first light and ordered to march across Boatswain's Creek.[52]

The Regulars had no transport, and also destroyed a huge quantity[53] of supplies: "On the site of the brigade commissary were boxes of hard bread, barrels of flour and pork, and a large quantity of miscellaneous stores piled in a huge heap…. A match was then put to the tents and thousands of dollars of property was burned. Barrels of whiskey broken over the piles made the whole a blazing mass."[54]

They also plundered the sutler's inventories:

> Knapsacks were then slung and we started off again with so much plunder that our battalion could have engaged in the sutling business. Every fourth or fifth man had a box of cigars under his arm and every man had a cigar in his mouth, puffing away like a steam engine. Officers' coats that had been selling at $18.00 were scarcely worth bringing away. Packages of soap, more than enough to keep the whole army in lather for a month, were crammed into pockets or anywhere that offered room. Razor strops were carefully stored away, even by men who never shaved. Pots of pomade and bottles of oil were carried off to the extent that if opportunity had been given, most men would have been as greasy faced as Aaron after the anointing.[55]

At least they had edibles, having been issued "beef with warm blood still in it" and "adamantine crackers," the ubiquitous Yankee hardtack, but no coffee.[56]

Warren's Zouave Brigade spent the night in a cornfield, moving out at 4:00 a.m.[57] One officer's mien was noted: "Captain Partridge appeared to be in an unusually serene

Siege guns like these were posted at the Gaines' Mansion (Library of Congress).

frame of mind…. He had given directions as to the disposition of his body in the event of his falling on the field, and remarked that he would not live to fight in many battles."[58]

Slowly, in dribs and drabs, Porter's Fifth Army Corps made their way across Powhite Creek, and then Boatswain's Creek, reaching there at about 8:00 a.m.

Several hours' march east, the Union men were concentrating behind Boatswain's Creek, but having some problems of their own. Passing three full divisions over the cart-width bridge at Gaines' Mill led to an immense traffic jam. Wagons, ambulances, and volunteer artillery crammed onto the approaches to the only bridge across Powhite Creek, delaying McCall's retreat for several hours.[59]

While the Valley Army marched south towards Richardson's, General Stuart's cavalry went east at dawn on the Shady Grove Church–Old Raleigh–Old Church Road. The "Old Raleigh" route had been mentioned in Lee's "Merry Oaks" Communiqué that Jackson received late on June 25: "Perhaps it would be better for one of your columns to take the road by Walnut Grove Church, and the other the road by Bethesda Church, or Old Raleigh, whichever you find most advantageous."[60] With the decision made to bring the Valley Army south to Col. Richardson's and Walnut Grove Church, the "Old Raleigh" route had to be cleared for Harvey Hill's use, and this was precisely what Stuart did. At Mrs. Gregory's, he turned southeast towards Bethesda Church. Union cavalry detachments, including some of Rush's Lancers, resisted his advance, but were driven off. Finding no sizeable Union force at Bethesda Church, Stuart detached Col. Martin's Jeff Davis Legion (Mississippi), the 4th Virginia Cavalry, plus one rifled cannon from the Stuart Horse Artillery, and sent them east towards Old Raleigh and beyond it, to Old Church.

Stuart and the balance of his command cleared the lonely and desolate road south from Old Raleigh to Cold Harbor.[61]

The Valley Army awoke early and was on the march from Pole Green Church at 4:00 a.m.[62] The men were asked to check their cartridge boxes for ammunition; in Winder's Division, each man only had between ten and twenty cartridges.[63] Ewell's Division was in the lead again.[64] The 13th Virginia and 1st Maryland were again out as skirmishers, with Brockenbrough's Baltimore Artillery in support.[65] Col. Isaac Seymour's Louisiana brigade was in the lead this time, and the 6th Louisiana soon relieved the Marylanders.[66]

Ewell's men crossed the road west to Shady Grove Church, then turned south toward Richardson's Crossroads. They soon crossed yet another branch of Beaver Dam Creek; Col. Richardson's house was just beyond it.[67] Jackson, as was his habit, was ranging ahead of his troops, usually riding 600 yards in front of the skirmishers.[68] In his report, he says that he "halted to dislodge a force of the enemy on our right [west] near the intersection of the road then occupied by us with the road leading from Mechanicsville to Bethesda Church." The Yankees saw Ewell's Division "moving down from my command." At the same time, Jackson and the Yankees saw Harvey Hill's command marching northwest on the Mechanicsville-Bethesda Church Road.[69] Ewell's division continued south, but the rest of the Valley Army stopped to let Hill's men go by.

Early the morning, the intrepid Col. Farnsworth had left Capt. Medill's company of the 8th Illinois cavalry north of Richardson's Crossroads with instructions to report Rebels coming from the direction of Pole Green Church. The rest of his men departed in the night with Brigadier Martindale. Captain Medill heard the early morning fracas towards Mechanicsville, as did the 18th Massachusetts. Medill had the 18th Massachusetts form line of battle with a section of Benson's Battery M, 2nd U.S. Artillery (2 ordnance rifles) facing north at Col. Richardson's.[70] With the whole Valley Army in his front, and Harvey Hill's host coming up his left rear, about 25,000 men, Barnes and Medill received orders to march their five companies to the rear, which was done, with much understatement, "in good order and without undue excitement."[71]

Harvey Hill's Division went through Richardson's Crossroads about 8:00 a.m. headed for Cold Harbor, about 8.5 miles away.

After clearing the Beaver Dam Creek Line, Powell Hill's men rested near the Puller House. Brigadier Gregg soon formed his brigade to resume the pursuit. The 12th South Carolina and the 1st South Carolina Volunteers[72] were beside each other in the first line, the 1st Volunteers on the right and the 12th on the left; each sent out skirmishers.[73] The

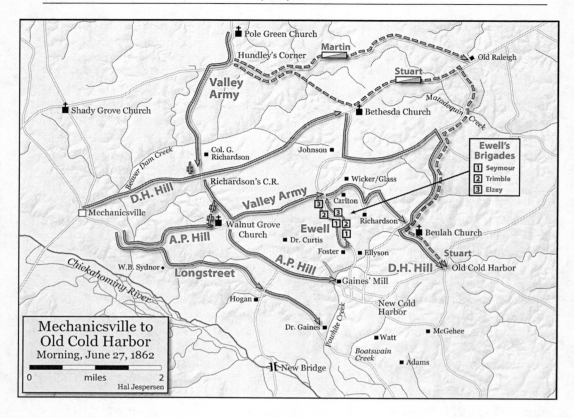

Mechanicsville to Old Cold Harbor
Morning, June 27, 1862
0   miles   2
Hal Jespersen

13th South Carolina and the 1st South Carolina Rifles were in a second line, with Cren-shaw's battery behind them.[74]

In this formation, Gregg's Brigade marched toward Walnut Grove Church. Passing through Union camps,[75] the brigade turned slightly north, and was hit by artillery fire.[76]

Shortly after passing Col. Richardson's, the 1st Maryland saw a heavy column of infan-try off to its right (west). From his position, Jackson could not discern whether they were the Yankees evacuating the Beaver Dam Creek Line or the Confederates who had driven them from it. At the same time, a cannoneer of Marmaduke Johnson's Virginia Battery, with Powell Hill, says the sight of glinting bayonets in the woods caused his battery to unlimber and prepare to fire. Jackson was quicker. He ordered the Baltimore Artillery to fire two shots in their direction. These two shots wounded two skirmishers of the 1st South Carolina Volunteers.[77] That regiment went into battle formation and advanced.[78]

Two officers rode out from Jackson's column: "A fearful tragedy was inevitable, but averted by the coolness and daring of Captain F.A. Bond and Lt. G.W. Booth ... these officers, at the imminent peril of their lives, boldly rode forth in the direction of the advancing lines, and followed by the watchful and anxious eyes were soon seen to enter their skirmish line and confer with the officer in command. They returned, and to the relief of all, reported the advancing troops to be friends who had taken a wrong road and were thus out of position. A moment more and the head of Jackson's column would have been engaged with [Powell Hill's]."[79] A member of Ewell's Division recalled, "[W]hen it became known that we were Jackson's troops from the Valley, [we] were greeted with shouts of applause. Every now and then a shout would be heard on front or rear and pass along the line in our direction. The men would immediately say that Jackson, or 'Old Jack' as they familiarly called him, was coming. In a few minutes, General Jackson and his staff would pass."[80]

Despite this inauspicious beginning, Brigadier Gregg pressed on and halted his men near the Walnut Grove Church at 9:10 a.m.[81] As General Jackson rode south towards the Walnut Grove Church, he met Walter Taylor, Lee's aide-de-camp, who directed the hero of the Valley to a meeting at the Church itself. When they arrived, Powell Hill was already present. According to a member of Jackson's staff, Harvey Hill was also present.[82] About 9:30, General Lee himself arrived.[83]

General Lee sat on a cedar stump, while Generals Jackson and Powell Hill conferred with him. Their respective staffs stood a distance away. John H. Daniel, editor of the *Richmond Enquirer*, was known as a fancy dresser and apparently outshone the generals in his haberdashery that day as a volunteer aide to Powell Hill.[84]

The purpose of this meeting was to update the situation. The Yankees had abandoned the Beaver Dam Creek Line, but no one knew quite where they were. Observers on the south side of the Chickahominy had not seen any 20,000 men cross, so the Yankees had to be on the north side of the river. Stuart's cavalry had not reported any large body of the enemy fleeing north, so they had to be to the east somewhere. Looking at the Timberlake Map, the next best place to defend was Powhite Creek, between Gaines' Mill and Dr. Gaines' Mansion.

While the generals planned, their staffs no doubt chatted. Stonewall Jackson's guide was Pvt. John Henry Timberlake, 4th Virginia Cavalry.[85] His ancestral home was just north of Atlee's Station, on the Virginia Central Railroad. General Lee still had with him Fannie Gaines' husband, Seaton Tinsley.[86] Thirty-seven years later, J.W. Mattison, of the First South Carolina Rifles, vividly remembered Walnut Grove Church and the first time he saw Stonewall Jackson.[87]

Lee apparently met with Powell Hill first, ordering him to hurry on to Gaines' Mill on the road south from Walnut Grove Church.[88] Lee then met with Jackson, and changed the plan. The short version of the General Order 75 plan was that Powell Hill and Longstreet would drive the Yankees towards White House Landing, and the Reinforced Valley Army would bushwhack them at Cold Harbor. Yet those Yankees had made a stand at Beaver Dam Creek, and were impudently not doing what Lee anticipated. This increased the chances that the Yankees would make a stand north of the Chickahominy, probably behind another creek. According to Charles Marshall, Lee opined that if McClellan saw the Valley Army threatening White House Landing, he might reinforce the Union troops north of the Chickahominy and go after Jackson.[89] In that case, Powell Hill and Longstreet could hit the Yankees' exposed left flank. Either way, the Valley Army still needed to be behind the creeks at Cold Harbor with Harvey Hill's Division. Lee ordered Jackson to take the road east from Walnut Grove Church.[90] The meeting ended about 10:00, after a sandwich lunch.[91] Harvey Hill's men had now passed, and the whole Valley Army moved south. As it arrived at the church, Jackson turned them left, to the east.[92] Ewell's Division was in the lead, and Jackson set a grueling pace.

Col. Martin was in command of the portion of Stuart's cavalry sent towards Old Church. Meeting Stuart (who had come from Bethesda Church) at Old Raleigh, he found Union cavalry videttes, more men from Rush's Lancers, about two miles west of Old Church, near Lenny's.[93] Pushing east, Col. Martin came upon a daunting sight: "I must confess I felt a little creeping of the flesh when I saw this splendid looking body of men, about 700 strong, drawn up in line of battle in a large field two or three hundred yards off, armed with long poles with glittering steel points…. The appearance they presented was certainly very fine, with a tall forest of lances held erect and at the end of each, just below the head, a red pennant fluttering in the breeze."[94] Heros von Borcke admired "their fresh, well-fitting [blue] uniforms turned up with yellow, a fine martial appearance."[95]

Von Borcke continued: "Down upon them we swept with a yell, at full speed. They lowered their lances to a level and started in fine style to meet us midway, but long before we reached them the gay lancers' hearts failed them and they turned to fly. For miles the exciting chase was kept up; the road was strewn with lances thrown away in their flight…."[96] Col. Martin attributes the collapse of Rush's men to the firing of the Blakeley gun.[97] He also noted the retreat of infantry, some 1000 to 1500 in his estimation.[98] These were the 17th New York and the 18th New York, which had arrived, no doubt, still "in good order and without undue excitement," from Richardson's Crossroads, somehow avoiding Stuart's cavalry and Harvey Hill's Division. Together with Gibson's Battery M/G 3rd U.S. Artillery and a section of Smead's Battery K, 5th U.S., they fled, or, according to Col. Lansing of the 17th New York, "made a rapid march, arriving at Tunstall's Station [i.e., McClellan's Army] in four hours."[99] Col. Martin returned to Old Raleigh and headed towards Old Cold Harbor to join Stuart.[100]

Longstreet's Division, Near the Chickahominy River

Once Brigadiers Wilcox, Featherston and Pryor had taken the Beaver Dam Creek Line, a single horseman rode east. Presently he saw a boy on the top floor of a barn looking at him, and beckoned to him with his hat. The boy came running. It was his little brother, Henry Clinton Sydnor. The elder took him to the general, where the "Little Rebel" told all he knew about the Yankees.[101]

General Longstreet ordered his command southeast down the Chickahominy. Brigadier Wilcox dropped off the 8th Alabama to repair the bridge at Ellison's Mill for artillery, sending the rest of his brigade towards the river and forming line of battle with three regiments, the fourth immediately behind. Brigadier Pryor was in a similar formation on Wilcox's left.[102] Soon they came to the W.B. Sydnor house,[103] where Henry's parents told them the Yankees had just left.[104] After passing through a deserted Union camp, Wilcox's men broke out into the open. To their left, they could see Ewell's Division of the Valley Army at Walnut Grove Church.[105]

Longstreet was operating his division in two halves, the leading half under the care of Brigadier Wilcox. Pulling Featherston back, Wilcox put his own brigade on line south of the River Road, with Pryor's in line just to the north, and moved east.[106] The other half, under Longstreet, followed the first half. The brigades of Wilcox and Pryor moved forward again through the woods south of the William Fleming Gaines house.[107]

Near Dr. Curtis' House and the Hogan House

After leaving Walnut Grove Church, General Lee rode to Brigadier Gregg and Col. Hamilton, 12th South Carolina, and gave additional instructions.[108] Soon artillery boomed towards the east. A Confederate battery south of the river fired a shot at Capt. Robertson's battery.[109] Robertson changed the front of his left guns, and started shelling the woods when a section of Tidball's battery opened fire at the Rebels on the road. After a few shots, both batteries decamped, Tidball pulling back down the road to Gaines' Mill, and Robertson going cross country to the Hogan House.[110]

Gregg's brigade now moved forward on the road to Gaines' Mill. Soon they came upon the camps of Morell's Division, near the Curtis and Dr. Curtis houses. While the burning camps were a sight, an even greater sight was the burning bridge train.[111] Col. Tilton of the 22nd Massachusetts had fired the lot before abandoning his camp.[112] Armies always have a need to cross rivers, and McClellan's was no different. To build a temporary bridge, boats, called pontoons, were floated in the stream and connected together, and then flooring was laid across them. Each pontoon was a sort of wagon in itself, and resembled a Jon boat, except that these were 31 feet long. The bridge train was usually 34 pontoons, 22 wagons full of flooring materials, four wagons of tools, and two rolling blacksmith forges, a total of 62 vehicles.[113] It is no wonder that this destruction made quite an impression.

Soon afterwards, Gregg received a communiqué from Longstreet asking the former to meet him at Hogan's House.[114]

After speaking with Brigadier Gregg, General Lee and his staff had ridden to Hogan's House and made it their headquarters. General Lee met here with General Longstreet,[115] who also met with his brigadiers, Wilcox, Featherston, and Pryor. The house and outbuildings were in bad shape, having been in the center of long-range artillery duels over the Chickahominy. In the house itself, a large bloodstain was found under a large cannonball hole in the wall.[116] General Lee was at the south entrance to the house, wearing a blue uniform. General Longstreet was sitting in a chair in the yard, his feet propped up on a tree, and devouring sandwiches. His gray uniform had faded to brown. Brigadier Gregg had arrived; his black hat was in deplorable shape and the starts at his throat "dingy and ragged." Brigadier Featherston stood out as one of the few older men without beard or moustache.[117]

A courier arrived, bearing word from General W.N. Pendleton, south of the river, that he could see the enemy in great force to the east, near Dr. Gaines' Mansion.[118] It appeared to Lee that the "great force" was just a large rear guard, and that the Yankees were withdrawing south across the Chickahominy. Lee sent a telegram across the river, ordering General Magruder to shell the woods.[119] That telegram also gave a situation report at the time: "General Longstreet's Brigade [Division] is on the road from Hogan's House to Dr. Gaines.' Genl. A.P. Hill is on the road from Walnut Grove Church to Cold Harbor via Gaines' Mill. Genl. Jackson's command support[ed] by D.H. Hill is on the road to Cold Harbor turning Powhite Creek. I think it probable that the enemy is in force behind Powhite Creek, crossing the Chickahominy on his line to Golding's by Fair Oaks Station along your front...."[120]

A flurry of orders went out. Powell Hill must vigorously pursue on the road to Gaines' Mill, putting out skirmishers to connect with Longstreet's skirmishers[121]; Longstreet's skirmishers and division must press forward toward Dr. Gaines' Mansion. An immediate attack could crush the rear guard, clog the bridges with panicked Yankees, and destroy a large part of the Union Army.

Near the Millpond of Gaines' Mill

Fannie Gaines Tinsley left Dr. Curtis' house wearing slippers and carrying a baby bag. Her jewelry box and trunk of wedding presents was left at Dr. Curtis.' Mrs. Gaines took a live chicken for Dr. Curtis to eat at some point. At the gate, Toler showed up with his vegetables; Dr. Gaines told him to go get the Gaines' carriage from the mansion and meet them at the mill. The Yankees wanted to take the carriage, but Toler refused because "Miss Fannie and Miss Jane [Mrs. Gaines] was walking." Dr. Gaines went to a Yankee officer and asked that he be allowed to collect his walking family in the carriage. The officer agreed, but only as far as the mill.

Dr. Gaines got out Dr. Curtis' buggy and hauled Curtis into it. Mrs. Gaines, Fannie Tinsley, Hattie the baby, and Mary, the nurse/cook, started walking towards Dr. Gaines' Mill, about a mile away.[122] The women were making their way through the woods towards the mill and came upon the camp of the 5th New York Zouaves. An old Irishman came out and said, "Messay, is you ronning?" Mother said, "Yes, and it's what you'll be doing pretty soon!"[123] The man was a member of Company B, 5th New York, which had been

The ruins of Gaines' Mill (Library of Congress).

Opposite: **A Union pontoon bridge unit (Library of Congress).**

left behind to fire the camp.[124] The party came to an open field; cannonballs were crashing, plowing up the ground, and going over their heads. They took shelter in a ravine; Mary went ahead with the baby. At the mouth of the ravine Fannie and Mrs. Gaines saw many Yankees looking down at them. Mrs. Gaines went all the way up the bank, but Fannie faltered halfway up. Mrs. Gaines threatened to leave her, then shamed her up the bank: "Don't you see all of these Yankees looking at you?" When Fannie reached the top, Mary and Baby Hattie had disappeared. They pressed on towards the mill.

As the two women came to the mill dam, fourteen Yankees were already there. An officer let the ladies pass, and even took Fannie's baby bag and helped her across the dam. He then asked Fannie the way to White House, saying, "I never expect to fight the rebels again, I had just as soon fight the devil as fight them." Fannie told him to follow the telegraph wires. Mary and Hattie were still nowhere to be found. Fannie and Mrs. Gaines found themselves at the intersection of two roads. One road went around a hill to Foster's; the other went up the hill to Magee's house.[125] "Mother told Fannie to go look to see if Mary and Hattie were at Foster's while she would go check Magee's." Mrs. Gaines saw the young people going into Magee's, and sat down to rest in a Yankee camp at top of the hill. Soon a soldier told Mrs. Gaines that a "good old man" lived at Magee's, and that she should go there. Mrs. Gaines told him that she would leave if she were in his way. Just then, Fannie arrived, and the pair went to Magee's. The Yankees fired the camp just as the women left.

Drs. Gaines and Curtis were both already at Magee's. When Fannie arrived, the Gaines carriage was bouncing off through a field with both doors open and so full that Yankees were spilling out, some even standing on the steps. Toler was walking; he had dismounted because the Yankees were going to take him to White House as a contraband. While they were at Magee's, a small piece of shell hit house. The Gaines, now augmented by other neighbors fleeing the battle, left to take shelter at Mr. Ellyson's, about a mile away to the northwest.[126]

6

Geography

The simplest reason why the Battle of Gaines' Mill has been misunderstood is that two years later, the Battle of Cold Harbor occurred at almost the same spot. Gaines' Mill involved about 42,000 Rebels headed southeast, and about 27,000 Yankees trying to stop them. The later Cold Harbor fight involved 108,000 Yankees heading southwest, and 59,000 Rebels trying to stop them. The Gaines' Mill fight took most of a day; Cold Harbor took almost two weeks, and by 1864, the soldiers had learned to dig. Both sides dug enormous trench lines that bisected the Gaines' Mill battlefield, and are still in existence in some places today. Even worse, the armies burned wood for heating and cooking, and built roads for supplies, so much so that they changed the natural lay of the land and the groundcover. In short, any map of the Gaines' Mill battlefield made after June 12, 1864, is inaccurate, unless based on an earlier map. And therein lies a tale.

The largest archive of Civil War materials is the *Official Record of the War of the Rebellion*, published from 1881 to 1901. In 1891, a book of the maps from the war was published as an *Atlas to Accompany the Official Records of the Union and Confederate Armies*.[1] Unfortunately, the Yankees did not have access to much of the Confederacy, and so their maps are very large-scale maps of states and regions thereof. When they had military operations in an area, their cartographers would make a smaller scale, more detailed map. The Confederates would do the same thing. Many of these maps wound up in the *OR Atlas*; however, the veterans started writing about the war in 1866.[2] Accordingly, they did not have much if any access to the military maps. In 1868, the Southern Historical Society was formed to preserve the Confederate records and history.[3] Soon the veterans were writing about their war experiences. By 1882, a magazine, *Southern Bivouac*, was also collecting and publishing memoirs. In 1883, *The Century Magazine* was also publishing war stories, which would ultimately become *Battles and Leaders of the Civil War*.[4] By 1889, the Confederate soldiers had coalesced into the United Confederate Veterans, who began their own magazine in 1893.[5]

The earliest postwar line map of the Battle of Gaines' Mill is found in Dabney's *Life and Campaigns of Lieutenant General Thomas J. Jackson*, dated 1865.[6] It is not to scale, General Lawton's brigade is mislabeled "Dawton," it mixes divisions and brigades, and it has a giant Confederate battery shooting at Powell Hill's Division. It has the Peter McGehee's house where James McGehee's house was, and leaves out the Adams House altogether. Its best feature is that it does not contain a road leading from New Cold Harbor directly to the Watt House.

In June of 1885, *The Century Magazine* published a new map, which has been repeatedly used to confuse since. On this map, there is only one McGehee house, but it is *east* of the Grapevine Road, and in the woods. The James McGehee house is *west* of the Grapevine Road, and in a clearing. The *Century* map has the Union cavalry charge late in the day hitting Longstreet's flank on the west side of Boatswains Creek; it actually happened nearer the Adams House. Worst of all, it has the road leading from New Cold Harbor directly to the Watt House. That road was built to supply that end of the Confederate lines during the battle of Cold Harbor in 1864.[7] In 1862, there was only a path to a spring across the creek, rather than a giant "superhighway" from New Cold Harbor to the Watt House and Union rear.[8] Additionally, the map does not show much of the timberlines.

In 1879, the United States Geological Survey was created to make topography maps of the United States. These were published by 1892. By 1929, the U.S. Army War College had Col. Howard Lee Landers put battle information onto topographical maps. Unfortunately, the topographical map in 1929 is not an accurate reflection of the battlefield in 1862; it still has the "Watt House Freeway," though the battle information is somewhat accurate.

The *OR Atlas* maps became available in 1891. Gaines' Mill and its environs appear on only a few of them. Plate 77 is an 1867 map of the greater Richmond area; it shows how the 1864 entrenchments went right through the Gaines' Mill battlefield.[9] A map of Mechanicsville and Gaines' Mill is found in the Southern Historical Society Papers, apparently drawn by someone in Pender's Brigade, Powell Hill's Division.[10] With a few exceptions, all of the *OR Atlas* maps are too large in scale, or focus on the 1864 battle. Every map since 1866 has been based on either the *Century* map the *OR* maps, or a topographical map, and accordingly, they are all wrong, to varying degrees. If only there were some 1862 maps of the area.

Enter the Confederate Engineering Department. Unfortunately the Timberlake Map does not lend any insight to the battlefield of Gaines' Mill. Gilmer Map 544, however, does. This is an official map, dated 1862, in 1/80,000 scale. Gilmer's name is on it and he became chief engineer in August of 1862. It mentions Merry Oaks, as well as New Cold Harbor and Old Cold Harbor, and shows where the Battle of Malvern Hill was fought, indicating that it was made official sometime after July 1, 1862. And as usual with anything pertaining to this battle, it is ripped in half right across the battlefield itself. Happily, Gilmer Map 548 is a rough draft of it, and it is not torn in half. Since Gilmer Map 548 is the closest in time, it is probably the most accurate.

In his June 26 reconnaissance, General Barnard crossed the Chickahominy at the Grapevine Bridge. From there, he took the road by McGehee's House. Indeed, there is a road from the Grapevine Bridge past McGehee's house. This is listed on various maps as Mrs. McGehee, or James McGehee. From there, the road goes directly to New-Coal Harbor, also known as New Cold Harbor. This is the first mention of this place in any of the records. From there, Barnard rode to Dr. Gaines' Mansion. Then he crossed Boatswain's Creek east on to the "spur on the right of Dr. GAINES." This would be where the Watt House is. He then went through the woods to New Coal Harbor. Indeed, the Gilmer map shows woods between the Watt House and New Cold Harbor. Barnard then went to Old Coal Harbor, and then down the road towards Dispatch Station, which is on the Richmond and York River Railroad just north of the Chickahominy. Another road leads from the Grapevine Bridge to Dispatch Station; Barnard found this and took it back to Barker's Mill, near the Grapevine Bridge.

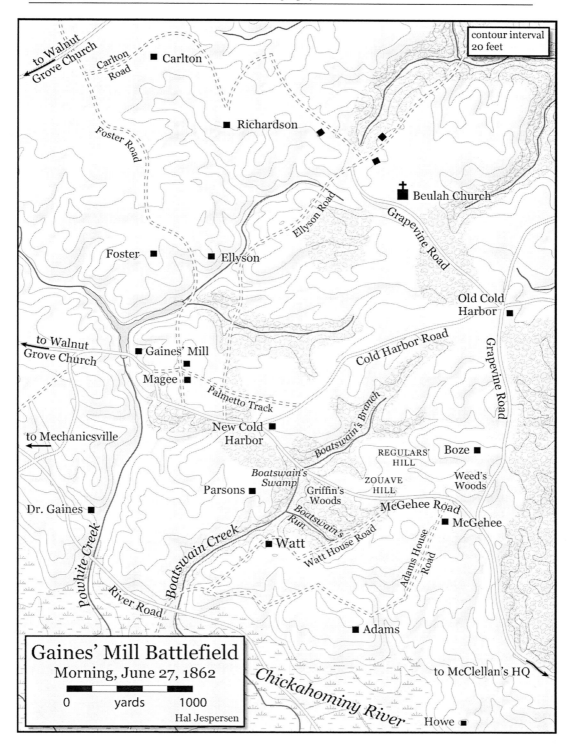

to Walnut Grove Church

Carlton Road

Carlton

Foster Road

Richardson

Ellyson Road

Beulah Church

Grapevine Road

Foster

Ellyson

Old Cold Harbor

Cold Harbor Road

Grapevine Road

to Walnut Grove Church

Gaines' Mill

Magee

Palmetto Track

New Cold Harbor

Boatswain's Branch

REGULARS' HILL

Boze

to Mechanicsville

Boatswain's Swamp

Griffin's Woods

ZOUAVE HILL

Weed's Woods

McGehee Road

Parsons

Boatswain's Run

McGehee

Dr. Gaines

Boatswain Creek

Watt House Road

Adams House Road

Powhite Creek

Watt

River Road

Adams

to McClellan's HQ

Gaines' Mill Battlefield

Morning, June 27, 1862

0   yards   1000

Hal Jespersen

Chickahominy River

Howe

Roads

It is difficult for a modern person to visualize what roads were like in the Civil War. Important roads were either planked with boards, or paved with stones. Unfortunately the area east of Mechanicsville and north of the Chickahominy River was not very important. Accordingly, "good" roads were two wagons wide, and dirt or mud, depending on the season, "Bad" roads were only one wagon wide. Where two roads intersect, a traveler essentially had three choices, as there were no road signs and few markers. Without a guide or directions, a traveler could easily get lost.

Roads were generally identified by a landmark at the other end. So, for example, if one is at Mechanicsville, the road east to Walnut Grove Church is called the Walnut Grove Church Road. If one is at Walnut Grove Church, the exact same road going west is called the Mechanicsville Road. At the same time, if one is in Mechanicsville, then the Walnut Grove Church Road is also the Bethesda Church Road, as that road leads past Walnut Grove Church to Bethesda Church; that road is also the road to Old Raleigh. In short, in the 1860s, the name of the road changed, depending on both the direction of travel and the destination.

Burnett's Tavern, Old Cold Harbor. Between the standing man and the house is a Civil War road (Library of Congress).

Since this battle developed from west to east, let us follow the roads in that direction to start. Four roads lead out of Mechanicsville.[11] One leads northwest; this is the road Branch followed to Mechanicsville (the Cullen Road). Another goes generally north to Shady Grove Church, where Ewell's Division of the Valley Army stopped on June 26. Another leads northeast past Richardson's Crossroads to Bethesda Church (the Mechanicsville–Bethesda Church Road).

The road that intersects this road from the north comes from Pole Green Church, where the Valley Army camped on the night of June 26. The 18th Massachusetts camped near at this intersection. This is the Pole Green–Richardson's Crossroads Road. From Richardson's Crossroads, a road leads east to Bethesda Church, and is the Richardson's Crossroads–Bethesda Church Road.[12] From Richardson's Crossroads, a road goes south to Walnut Grove Church. This is the Richardson's–Walnut Grove Road.

A road leads from Walnut Grove Church to Bethesda Church. About halfway down the Walnut Grove–Bethesda Road, a smaller road leads to the south, and immediately forks. One fork leads south past Foster's Quarters towards Gaines' Mill, called the Foster Road. The other fork leads to the Carlton house, and thence to Beulah Church, so it is called the Carlton Road. From Beulah Church, one road heads west past Ellyson's House to New Cold Harbor, which is the Ellyson Road. Another leads to Old Cold Harbor (the Beulah–Old Cold Harbor Road). At Old Cold Harbor, a road leads south to the Grapevine Bridge, so this is the Grapevine Road. A road also runs southwest, to New Cold Harbor. This is the Cold Harbor Road.

Also at New Cold Harbor, the Gaines' Mill–New Cold Harbor Road runs northwest to Gaines' Mill. From New Cold Harbor, the McGehee Road runs southeast, intersecting the Grapevine Road, which runs to the Grapevine Bridge. Just to make it all more confusing, a smaller road parallels the Gaines' Mill–New Cold Harbor Road, crossing the Foster Road and the Ellison Road. This is called the Palmetto Track, as Gregg's South Carolinians (Powell Hill's Division) used it, and we do not need another Gaines' Mill–New Old Harbor Road.

Back in Mechanicsville, a road leaves it and runs southeast to Ellison's Mill, and then northeast to Walnut Grove Church (the Mechanicsville–Walnut Grove Road). About halfway between the two, a road branches off southeast near Grubbs', past Sydnor's, to William Fleming Gaines' house (Dr. Gaines' son), past Hogan's (Selwyn) and to Dr. Gaines' Mansion (Powhite). This is the River Road.[13]

Buildings

Several important buildings exist on the battlefield itself. Since the Watt House is still extant, it is the most important. Hugh Watt built this house about 1836.[14] His widow, Sarah Bohannon Kidd Watt, was living in the house on June 27, 1862. This dwelling had several outbuildings and a spring.

General Morell used the Watt House as his headquarters, as it was directly behind the area entrusted to him. It is just east of Boatswain's Creek, and there is a path from it across that creek to the Parsons House (which also had a spring), which was vacant[15] at the time.[16] The house itself also had a pear orchard just east of it, at the top of a ravine which led down to the Chickahominy. This is Watt House Ravine. Boatswain's Creek and the Watt House Ravine form a circular plateau that juts out into the river valley; this is General Barnard's "spur." Another road branches east off of this, just at Boatswain's Run, and then about 100 yards later turns northeast to intersect the McGehee Road.[17]

Just to the east is another spur, formed by the Watt House Ravine and the Adams House Ravine. The Adams House sits on the circular plateau between them. The Adams House also had a spring and several outbuildings. From the Adams House, a road runs northeast to the McGehee House, and southeast to the Watt House Road. General Porter's headquarters was near the Adams House.[18]

The McGehee House is northeast of the Adams House. It was right behind the 1864 earthworks, and was probably destroyed at that time. It sits back from the McGehee Road. It is variously called James McGehee's or Mrs. McGehee's. This was probably the headquarters of General Sykes.

The house of Peter McGehee is northwest of it, deep in the woods. This is unfortunate, as this has confused many historians, who ignored the James McGehee House and placed the Federal line all the way into the woods at the Peter McGehee House, erasing the woods as they did so to force the map to make sense. This is in error; Barnard rode this area and specifically states where the right end of the union line was, and why:

> According to the force in which it was occupied, its left would rest on the first spur to the right (east) of Dr. GAINES' house, embracing the wood; or by contracting the front, rest on the spur where "WATTS'" house is, partially embracing the woods in front and running in front of Mr. GEE'S house. The right would extend past Mr. GEE'S house along the "Dispatch Station" road through the woods to the eminence near where a house is marked on the map, or *perhaps, still better, kept along the edge of the woods toward the Chickahominy.*
> …After reaching the ground, he [General Porter] decided to put his left on the spur of WATTS' House, and riding further along the position, he concluded he could not extend his right beyond the clearing and spur where MCGEE's house is.[19] [Capitals in original.] [Emphasis added.]

It is therefore clear that the right end of Porter's line was on clear ground along the woods that stretched to the Chickahominy. Looking to the Gilmer Map, the woods extend all the way down the Grapevine Road to the river; James McGehee's house is not in the woods, and is near a "spur." The "eminence" with the unnamed house on it is probably the house near Old Cold Harbor, to which the woods also extend.

Northeast of the McGehee House is the Boze House, also known as the Bowles House, or Mrs. Bates.[20] This is the unnamed house on the "eminence." It was between the trench lines in 1864, and was also probably destroyed then.

Going north on the Grapevine Road, we come to Old Cold Harbor. Here Mr. Burnett kept an inn. Legend has it that he served only cold food to those needing shelter ("harbor"), and thus the name Cold Harbor. This is dubious, as there was no tavern at New Cold Harbor at all, so what was new there? Also at Old Cold Harbor was Mrs. Stewart's House.[21]

West down the Cold Harbor Road, we pass the Garthright House, which is still extant but is not mentioned in any of the records. At New Cold Harbor we find two houses; one is the Stewart House, and the other is the Ingraham House, which was probably Lee's headquarters.

Northwest of New Cold Harbor, past houses belonging to the McGehees, is the actual mill belonging to Dr. Gaines. Following Powhite Creek South, we come to Dr. Gaines' Mansion. About halfway between the two was located Thaddeus Lowes' Balloon Corps camp.[22]

Creeks

Three creeks cut the battlefield from north to south. Elder Creek borders the battlefield east of the Grapevine Road, and is not on the map. It is militarily impassable, and protected the Union right. The westernmost is Powhite Creek, the location of Dr. Gaines' Mansion and his mill. It is in its own ravine, admirable shelter for troops.

In the center of these two is Boatswain's Creek. The "creek" part is the southern portion near the Watt House, which flows through a ravine with 20-foot-wide bottom and 50-foot banks rising at nearly a 45-degree angle on both sides. Moving north, it turns into Boatswain's Swamp just north of the Watt House, turning slightly northeast. Here the bottom is a hundred feet wide. The banks of the swamp are less steep, but where it crosses the McGehee Road the banks are 100 feet high. The watercourse turns slightly east and splits into several small creeks, which are Boatswain's Branch. This area is not as swampy, but still difficult. All three are filled with trees, dense undergrowth, and decomposing vegetation.

An 1865 image of unburied dead near Cold Harbor. The woods in the background give some idea of the dense foliage and underbrush in Boatswain's Branch (Library of Congress).

Just north of the Watt House, where Boatswain's Creek becomes Boatswain's Swamp, a run branches off to the east and then northeast to cross the McGehee Road. This is a critical landmark, and is called Boatswain's Run.

Timber

Any attempt to detail timberlines from 1862 will necessarily be imprecise. Starting with Gilmer Map 548, a large patch of woods can be found on the west side of Powhite Creek, just northeast of the Hogan House. Another belt of timber runs from New Cold Harbor to Boatswain's Run. Moving to the Cold Harbor Road, we find a large wood between the Carlton Road and Beulah Church, that extends down to within a half mile Old Cold Harbor itself. Moving west, another large forest starts about halfway down the Walnut Grove Church Road and extends east to the Carlton Road. Dr. Curtis' house is near this.

An important wood rose up between the intersection of the McGehee Road and the Grapevine Road. It was large, tall, and dense enough that it blocked the line of sight so that cannons could not shoot through it. These will be called Weed's Woods.

Moving back to the Cold Harbor Road, the Gilmer Map does not show any ground-cover around Boatswain's Creek, except at its intersection with the McGehee Road. On the other hand, the few drawings and many first-person accounts indicate that Boatswain's Creek, Swamp and Branch were heavily wooded.

The first-person accounts from the McGehee Road area also speak of woods. The *Battles and Leaders* map shows "Heavy Woods" about 300 yards wide on the Confederate side of Boatswain's Creek, Swamp and Branch.[23] A colorized version of that map shows that the woods around the southern portion of Boatswain's Creek were 75 yards wide. In front of the Watt House, there was an area of felled trees, extending for about 100 yards along the west bank of the gorge. On Boatswain's Branch, the woods increased from about 100 yards wide to 150 yards wide, and then petered out to "Slashings" near the Grapevine Road.

Hills

Between Powhite Creek and Boatswain's Creek, three small hills rise in the center of huge field between Dr. Gaines' Mansion and Boatswain's Creek. The one closest to the river is called Florida Hill, because the 2nd Florida occupied it for most of the day, as skirmishers. The one in the center is Virginia Hill, because Brigadier Pickett attacked here. The one closest to the Gaines' Mill Road is called Carolina Hill, because Pender's North Carolinians went into battle there.

On the west side of the creek, there is a hill just south of the intersection of Boatswain's Creek and Boatswain's Run. The northern part of this hill is a sheer drop of 30 feet or so. The southern part of this hill is a steep grade, but manageable. Since in later years the top of it would be a gravel pit, it is called Gravel Pit Hill. Following the McGehee Road southeast across Boatswain's Creek, Griffin's Hill is south of the McGehee Road and enclosed by Boatswain's Run. Here a brigade under Griffin's command controlled the creek crossing. It is wooded, and also called Griffin's Woods. Just north across the McGehee Road is Zouave Hill, where the 5th New York Zouaves started the battle. Going further east, past where Boatswain's Run cuts the McGehee Road, one finds Regulars' Hill, named by Timothy Reese in his book on the United States Regulars.[24] Behind Regulars' Hill is the McGehee House. Just to the west, along the McGehee Road, is another small hill, at the intersection of the Watt House and Adams House Roads and the McGehee Road. Here the McGehee Road cuts through the hill, and it therefore is "sunken." A fence ran from the McGehee Road roughly north-south into the woods, more or less dividing Zouave Hill from Regulars' Hill.[25]

7

Porter's Dispositions

Beginning at dawn, brigades, regiments, companies, and odd groups of stragglers began slowly arriving at the ground General Barnard had scouted. Required by McClellan to defend a specified position north of the river, General Porter disposed his troops to defend it for as long as possible. Based on his experience the day before, he knew that there were hordes of Confederates to the west, in army strength. He also knew that there was another host somewhere to northwest.[1] His southern flank was covered by the rest of McClellan's army, so that side was secure. His rear was covered by the impenetrable woods and swamps east of the Grapevine Road. Porter merely had to defend to the west and north.

The Confederates could move along several major roads into Porter's position. The ones to the west could come down the River Road, past Dr. Gaines' Mansion, or they could come down the Mechanicsville Road, which would take them to Gaines' Mill. Given the numbers which had appeared the day before, they would probably have to use both. Since this threat was concretely identified, Porter would post his main strength to the west, behind Boatswain's Creek.

There was concrete intelligence of another Rebel army to the north, but they had not really shown themselves. Two roads led from the north. One, the Foster Road, was rather small and led more or less to Gaines' Mill. The other, the Beulah Church/Grapevine Road, was better, and since it led to the river, it was a probable avenue of attack. Porter could cover the Foster Road with the same troops covering the road to Gaines' Mill. The Grapevine, however, would need its own division.

Porter had about 20,500 infantry in those three divisions, so he chose the shorter line that Barnard had scouted.[2] General Porter had another concern. His corps' firearms were a factor in determining how he posted his troops. By the summer of 1862, about half of his men were armed with modern rifled firearms, which fired a .58 inch diameter bullet with reasonable accuracy out to a range of over 300 yards. The other half were armed with older smoothbore firearms, which fired one .69 diameter ball and three .36 inch diameter balls, devastating at a range of 150 yards, but useless beyond. Accordingly, he was forced to use the regiments with rifles on more open ground, and the ones with smoothbores everywhere else. Sykes' Regular Division, all with rifles, came across the Gaines' Mill Bridge first, about 10:00 a.m.[3] Porter posted Sykes' division facing northwest.

General Porter's staff. Lt. Custer is reclining on the right with the dog (Library of Congress).

Sykes' Division

General Sykes had 4,500[4] men and two of the three possible attack routes in his front. He disposed his two most solid brigades to cover them. Lovell's brigade was made up of one small regiment, the 2nd United States, and three small battalions of fewer than 300 men each. Accordingly, this would be the reserve brigade. Sykes' whole front was a ridge, barely divided into two parts by the end of Boatswain's Run; to the west of the Run was Zouave Hill; to the east was Regulars' Hill. The McGehee road ran along the top of both, and in places made an admirable trench. However, if Sykes formed his troops in that road, the enemy could come to within about 100 yards before they could be seen due to the slope of the ridge face. Accordingly, Sykes decided to use the road as a covered position for his reserves. He put his infantry roughly halfway between the McGehee Road and the woods of Boatswain's Branch.[5] The open ground to their front was the text-book optimum killing zone for their Springfield rifles.

Sykes had two organic artillery batteries, both armed with rifled cannon. He could not put them at the McGehee Road-Grapevine Road intersection, because Weed's Woods were in the way of shooting at Old Cold Harbor. Accordingly, he placed Weed's Battery I,

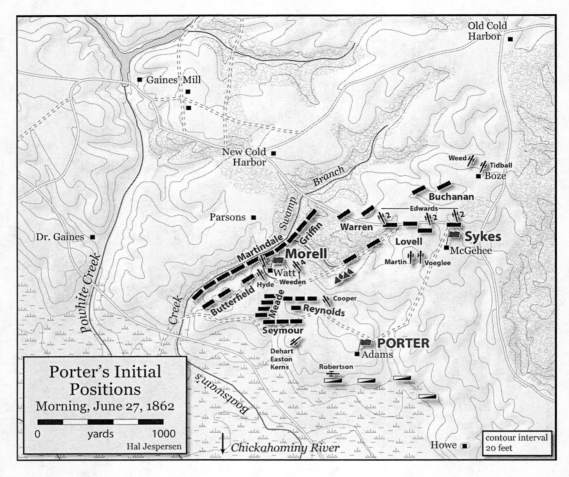

Porter's Initial
Positions
Morning, June 27, 1862

0   yards   1000
Hal Jespersen

contour interval
20 feet

5th U.S. Artillery (6 ordnance rifles) "on the knoll"[6] north of the Boze House.[7] This was not a perfect position, though; Weed could not support the infantry without turning his guns from northeast to west. Sykes' other battery was Edwards' L/M, 3rd United States Artillery (6 Parrotts). Since another division's guns (Martin's Battery C, Massachusetts Light Artillery; 6 Napoleons) secured Sykes' left, Sykes initially spread Edwards in two-gun sections along the McGehee Road and west of Weed's Woods.[8] With Martin able to hit New Cold Harbor, and Weed able to hit Old Cold Harbor, Edwards' guns could shell the Cold Harbor Road between those two points and the field in front. Shortly after noon, Tidball's Battery A, 2nd U.S. Artillery (6 ordnance rifles) reported to Sykes. Since his front was already well covered with guns, Sykes decided to super-anchor his right flank and sent Tidball to take position to the right of Weed and the 4th U.S.[9] This put the 4th U.S. between Weed and Tidball.[10] These twelve guns would control the Grapevine Road north to Old Cold Harbor.[11] With his artillery posted, Sykes had to defend the ground in between. Buchanan's Brigade would hold the east half of the front, and the east. Warren's Brigade would hold the west.[12]

    Brigadier Buchanan put two regiments in the open field, the 12th U.S. and the 14th U.S., each about 417 men. The 12th was directly in front of the McGehee House. The 14th U.S. was about 80 yards behind the 12th's right.[13] For the time being, the 3rd U.S. was put

Officers of the 14th U.S., Sykes' Division, May 1862 (Library of Congress).

in the McGehee Road to the left (west) of the knoll occupied by Hayden's section (2 guns) of Edwards' Battery L/M, 3rd U.S. (6 Napoleons).[14]

Warren's Brigade consisted of two regiments of Zouaves. These were troops fitted out in North African garb with red pants, blue jackets, and red caps. While called the "National Zouaves," the 10th New York had its bright uniforms in storage, and were wearing regular army blue.[15] The 10th had its left end in the woods where Boatswain's Swamp meets the McGehee Road, with the balance of the regiment in the open.[16] The 5th New York, however, was in full Zouave glory, in the open, on the brow of the hill, facing northwest, between the 10th New York and the 12th U.S.[17] In their red pantaloons, the 5th would be the most visible regiment on the field that day.

Sykes' final brigade was Major Lovell's, who was commanding because Col. Chapman was ill.[18] It was behind the gap between the Zouave right and the left of the 12th U.S. The 2nd U.S. was posted in the McGehee Road behind Edwards' battery as the core of the divisional reserve.[19] The 6th U.S. was behind the road, on the reverse slope, to its right.[20] The 10th and 17th U.S., each being small, were consolidated (10/17 U.S.)[21] in the road to the 2nd's left.[22] The 11th U.S. was detailed as protection for the artillery, and put in Boatswain's Run near the McGehee Road.[23]

Bouncing up from the across the river came Voeglee's Battery B, six huge 20-lb. Parrott rifles. Designated with some irony as Battery B, New York *Light* Artillery, Voeglee would apparently set up just behind the McGehee House, on the highest ground possible, and extend the artillery's reach beyond the Cold Harbor Road.[24] His line formed, facing northwest, the Regulars and Zouaves, 4,200 infantry with 18 guns, and waited for the enemy. Unknown to them, Engineer General Barnard's line had a major flaw.

Top: Stereo view of the 5th New York Zouaves in company formation (Library of Congress). *Bottom:* Gigantic 20-lb. Parrott rifles of Voeglee's Battery B, 1st New York Light Artillery. Note their size compared to the horses in the near background (Library of Congress).

McCall's Division

Once Brigadier Sykes had his orders, McCall's 8,600[25] Pennsylvania Reserves, half rifles and half smoothbores, began coming in. They had fought the day before and retreated all night, and needed a rest.[26] Porter needed to put McCall's Division where it would be out of the way and safe from artillery fire. He therefore ordered McCall to take up a position in the Watt House Ravine.[27] Meade's Brigade, wearing stylish white canvas leggings, was on the west side of the stream at the bottom, facing generally west.[28] The 7th Pennsylvania Reserves were on the left of the line, with the 3rd, 4th, and 11th to its right.[29] Reynolds' Brigade formed to the east, on the other side of the stream. From west to east were the 8th, 1st, and 5th Pennsylvania Reserves.[30] The 2nd Pennsylvania Reserves were in line behind them.[31] Truman Seymour's Third Brigade, the 9th, 10th, and 12th Pennsylvania Reserves, was formed behind the other two brigades.[32] Col. Seymour had been present at Fort Sumter when the Confederates fired on it to start the war.[33]

McCall did not put his artillery in the ravine, but in the flat land above. Cooper's Battery B, Pennsylvania Light Artillery (6 Napoleons) unlimbered almost due north of the infantry, on the Watt House Road. Easton's Battery A (6 Napoleons), and Kerns' Battery G, (6 Howitzers), both Pennsylvania Light Artillery, were on the bluff above the Watt House Ravine, facing towards the Chickahominy in case the Rebels tried an end run along the River. Joining them was Dehart's Battery C, 5th U.S. Artillery (6 Napoleons). Robertson's B\L, 2d U.S. Artillery (6 ordnance rifles) was south of the Adams House, at

Company F, 7th Pennsylvania Reserves, Meade's Brigade (Library of Congress).

The 44th New York, Butterfield's Brigade, Morell's Division, on dress parade, 1861 (Library of Congress).

an angle to the others, covering the river valley itself. Smead's Battery K, 5th U.S. Artillery (4 Napoleons), was between Cooper's Battery and the infantry.[34] Smead's guns had fired 350 rounds of ammunition at Beaver Dam Creek. He was ordered across the Chickahominy to replenish shortly before noon and did not return until nearly dark.[35]

Morell's Division

Morell's Division had been ordered to stop by their camps to give McCall's men a chance to pass them. Since the main Confederate threat was from the west, Porter personally posted Morell's Division, mostly smoothbores, along Boatswain's Creek and Swamp, with its right on the McGehee Road, and its left on the bluff where Boatswain's Creek meets the river valley.

From Boatswain's Run south to the bluff at the Chickahominy River Valley, Boatswain's Creek, almost knee deep, runs in what is best described as a gorge. Each bank is about 45 feet above the creek itself, and the two banks are at the same level. The banks rise at about a 40-degree angle. A person standing at the creek looking east or west cannot see anything but the appropriate edge of the bank, trees and sky. From the creek, one cannot see Carolina Hill, nor Florida Hill. One cannot even see the Watt House.

General Porter ill-advisedly put his main line down in the gorge, near the creek. This position would protect the men from artillery fire, conceal the line from the Rebels, and allow it to blast sky-lined Confederates if they stopped at the edge of the bank to fire. On the other hand, the main Union line was for the most part useless. Down in the gorge they could only fire at the edge of the bank, about 30 yards away and 15 yards up. That line would essentially have only one opportunity for effective fire, because the enemy could be, with gravity's help, past the edge of the bank in a couple of seconds. Moreover, smoke from their first firing would obscure the bank, and then lie in the gorge. Even if their first fire killed every man in the enemy's first rank,[36] most or all of the second rank could be down the bank with their bayonets before the Union line could reload. Because of the shortcomings, Porter posted other regiments on the eastern edge of the gorge.

Here they were on the same level as the western side of the gorge, and could see (and fire) out to Florida, Virginia, and North Carolina Hills, about 150 yards away, perfect range for their smoothbores.

General Morell commanded 7,400 men in three brigades under Brigadiers Butterfield, Martindale, and Griffin. Butterfield would anchor the division's left to defend against Rebels coming down the River Road or along the River Valley. The valley was not too much of a concern, as Irwin Sumner's Division was on the heights just across the Chickahominy with several batteries of siege artillery. The monstrous guns could lay waste to any column in the valley, and Sumner's infantry could also help out. Porter covered his side of the valley with a cavalry screen and excess artillery. Accordingly, Porter would put his leftmost regiment on the bluff at the end of the creek.

Butterfield's Brigade

The 44th New York of Butterfield's Brigade was to be this leftmost regiment.[37] It went into the gorge and took up a line directly behind the creek itself.[38] They started felling trees on the west side of the creek, dropping them with the branches toward the enemy to form an abatis. Some of the felled timber went to build a dam on the far left of their line, in case Rebels came north up the creek.[39] The 16th Michigan was not put in the gorge, but "up top," 150 yards behind the 44th New York.[40] To their right, Butterfield stationed the 83rd Pennsylvania[41] down in the gorge. Col. Campbell of the 83rd described the topography as "an intricate gorged rivulet, thickly overgrown with briar and brushwood."[42] In this position, they "could not fire a shot"; the rear regiments would have to shoot over the gorge.[43] The right (northern) half of the 83rd Pennsylvania was higher than the left, and could see over the edge of the west bank. Nevertheless, they too built a breastwork of "felled trees and rubbish,"[44] which they completed in half an hour.[45] The 12th New York was behind at the edge of the gorge, 25 feet above the Pennsylvanians. Butterfield had about a thousand men in each of his two lines. His regiments sent out skirmishers across the field in front towards Powhite Creek.[46]

By the time Brigadier Martindale arrived with his brigade, Generals Porter and Morell were nowhere to be found. Butterfield instructed Martindale where to put his men, and also to put the first line in the gorge. Martindale protested. Boatswain's Creek itself was easily jumped and its banks easily climbable. Martindale "insist[ed] that we were placing our men on the defensive in the last ditch."[47] Martindale wanted his front line on the *west* edge of the gorge, where they would be concealed and actually able to shoot at the enemy in the open towards Powhite Creek. Butterfield replied that Porter had required the first line in the gorge. Not satisfied, Brigadier Martindale sought out General Morell, who overruled his objections.[48] Martindale's men went into the gorge, in a worse arrangement than Butterfield's.

Martindale's Brigade

Martindale had six regiments, about 2,500 men. Four of his regiments went into the gorge. The 1st Michigan was on the right of Butterfield's 83rd Pennsylvania, and was Martindale's leftmost regiment. Next came the 25th New York and then the 13th New York.[49]

The men in the gorge immediately started to make breastworks on the east side of the creek and their own abatis on the west side of it.[50] Seventy-five yards behind, and 30 feet above, was the 22nd Massachusetts, on the flat land near the Watt House, and directly behind the 13th New York.[51] They felled "great pines" for a barricade,[52] 4 feet high.[53] Some distance to its right, up on top, was the 2nd Maine.[54] Martindale had about 2,000 men in the gorge, and only 1,000 behind them. Still anxious, Brigadier Martindale managed to obtain General Morell's permission to send two companies of the 1st Michigan and four companies of the 25th New York out as skirmishers.[55]

Griffin's Brigade

Morell's final brigade was that of Brigadier Charles Griffin. Boatswain's Creek turned into Boatswain's Swamp in his area, so his leftmost regiments went into the gorge. Accordingly, he put the 4th Michigan into line in the ravine,[56] prolonging Martindale's front line. Griffin also put the 14th New York along the creek, extending the line to Boatswain's Run.[57] The east side of the gorge here was much less steep than towards the Chickahominy, rising gently for about 200 feet.[58] That feature bisected the 14th New York's line, so two companies were put on Griffin's Hill.[59] The 4th Michigan and the bulk of the 14th New York were a battle group[60] under Col. McQuade of the latter. The other two 14th New York companies operated more with the 9th Massachusetts when it returned from skirmishing, and are included in that term. The 9th Massachusetts would go to their right, on Griffin's Hill, but had been detailed to skirmish at the Mill. The 62nd Pennsylvania was formed in a second line at the Run behind the regiments in the gorge.[61] Since one of Griffin's regiments was missing, Morell gave him a contingent of Berdan's United States Sharpshooters to cover his front as skirmishers.[62]

General Morell had four artillery batteries organic to his division, two from Massachusetts, one U.S., and one from Rhode Island. Since there were three routes through his front, he posted his guns to control them. Hyde's Battery E, Massachusetts Light Artillery (6 ordnance rifles) was posted several hundred yards south of the Watt House, behind Butterfield's brigade,[63] but with the woods in front they were effectively masked and of little long-range use. On the other end of his line, on Griffin's Hill, Morell posted Martin's Battery C, Massachusetts Light Artillery (6 Napoleons).[64] This location would prove to be the key to the battlefield. The final route was Mary Jane Haw's path to Parson's Spring, running through Martindale's front from the Parsons House to the Watt House. It was too narrow for a full battery, so Morell covered it with two guns of Weeden's Battery C, Rhode Island Light Artillery (6 ordnance rifles) under Lt. Bucklin.[65] The other four guns, under Lt. Waterman, were over behind Boatswain's Run supporting Griffin, but also masked by the woods.[66] With no room for him, Morell kept Kingsbury's Battery D, 5th U.S. Artillery (6 Parrotts) in reserve at the Watt House for the time being.

Although Morell's men were General Porter's most powerful division, the latter had managed to cut its fighting ability in half before the first shot was fired. Of Morell's 13 regiments, only 6 were on the flat land behind the gorge and able to fire at the Confederates coming from Florida, Virginia, and Carolina Hills. The other 7 were in the gorge and useless until the Rebels were coming down the chimney.

Other Fifth Corps Units

Attached to the Fifth Corps was a small cavalry detachment. Fewer than 700 men, it was nevertheless separated into two "brigades." The First Brigade, about 470 men under the command of General Phillip St. George Cocke, was made up of five troops[67] of the 5th United States Cavalry and six troops of the 6th Pennsylvania Cavalry, Mrs. Newton's despised Rush's Lancers. The rest constituted the Second Brigade, four troops of the 1st United States Cavalry and 39 men in the Provost Guard.[68] Porter put Cocke's horsemen down in the river valley, below the bluff, to intercept any Rebel attacks there.[69] The 4th Pennsylvania Cavalry was also on the field, but under Porter's personal direction,[70] and was sent to wait at Sumner's Upper/Grapevine Bridge.[71]

Just across the river valley at Golding's Farm were eight more 20-lb. Parrott rifles under Kniereim (Battery D) and Diederich's (Battery A) New York Light Artillery.[72] These guns could not only sweep the river valley, but shell almost all the way to New Cold Harbor.

General Porter established his headquarters near the Adams House.[73] General Morell had his at the Watt House,[74] and General Sykes had his behind the McGehee House.[75] Its troops posted by about 10:00 a.m.,[76] the Fifth Corps waited in the steamy heat. In a few hours, the temperature would be 100 degrees in the shade.[77]

8

If We Whip Them Before Richmond, We Shall Have Peace

Gregg's Brigade, Powell Hill's Division

As Gregg advanced east on the Gaines' Mill Road, his men saw the results of Porter's withdrawal. Camps were found abandoned, with equipment and stores burning. The Federals had destroyed as much as possible before they left, though some of the camps seemed intact.[1] West of the mill itself, the South Carolinians found large quantities of army supplies and sutler stores that had been destroyed or partially destroyed: "We found coffee, cheese, can goods, and a general assortment of eatables not entirely destroyed that we soon appropriated to our personal use. We had cheese on toast for dinner. The fire and hot sun had toasted them thoroughly. This was our first meal at Uncle Sam's expense, but not the last with some of us."[2]

Pender's Brigade, Powell Hill's Division

Pender's brigade was behind Gregg in the order of march, and had skirmishers out south of the road, connecting with Longstreet's skirmishers to the south.[3] They "passed through several camps from which the enemy had fled, with such precipitancy as to leave even their 'Love Letters,' and the signatures of their sweethearts behind them."[4]

On at the north side of the road in a field stood a large lonesome tree. John Whetmore Hinsdale, Pender's adjutant, noted that Powell Hill had stationed himself at this tree, and received a communiqué from Generals Jackson and Whiting, reporting that they were in the woods to the north, and driving the enemy before them.[5] This was probably more Whiting than Jackson. About 10:00, Jackson had left Walnut Grove Church with Ewell's Division.[6] Ewell's Division was at the time the best in the Valley Army, and arguably the whole Confederate Army, having fought and marched through the Valley Campaign. Whiting's men were fine troops, but new to the Valley Army and not used to Jackson's grueling pace. Pvt. Fletcher, 5th Texas, of Hood's Brigade, wrote, "My old friend A.N. Vaughn … suffered tortures on the march, as one of his heels had blistered so badly nearly all the thick skin under the heel had separated from the foot, but … he would not drop out of ranks. He would say, 'Bill … I have made up my mind to go into the next fight if I wear off to my knees.'"[7] Not quite yet tough as nails, Whiting's Division simply could not march as fast as Ewell's. Additionally, as a member of the 4th Alabama, Law's Brigade observed, "As on the day before, we met with obstructions of felled timber, which together with the enemy's sharpshooters very much retarded our progress."[8] Though Harvey Hill was out to the east, and Stuart's Cavalry further east, Whiting was deep in enemy territory, and ambush was a very real possibility. This made him keep close watch and move carefully.[9] The tree fellers and sharpshooters were probably from the 8th Illinois Cavalry, Capt. Medill's company, who were the ones who had obstructed near Totopotomoy Creek the day before and who had decamped from Richardson's Crossroads that very morning. By 11:30, Whiting's Division was just north of Hogan's House when Whiting sent word to Powell Hill at the lonesome tree.

Dr. Gaines' Mansion

Major Joseph L. Brent, an aide to General Magruder, who was holding McClellan at bay south of the river, crossed the Chickahominy and visited Dr. Gaines' Mansion. He found it deserted, except for two Yankee pickets, who were dead. One "presented a strange appearance with a large air bubble projecting from his nostrils."[10]

General Wilcox's forward half of Longstreet's division was moving down the River Road from Hogan's. Pryor's brigade, the advance guard, arrived at Powhite Creek first.[11] Pryor sent out "a few companies" including Co. D of the 14th Alabama[12] as skirmishers, who drove the Federals from Powhite Creek back halfway across the huge field between Powhite and Boatswain's Creeks.[13] With no real idea of what was behind the Union skirmish line, Brigadier Pryor decided to find out. Pryor brought up his brigade's battery, Maurin's Donaldsonville (Louisiana) Artillery, to shell Boatswain's Creek from near the Gaines Mansion.[14] Their shells fell on the 1st Michigan down in the gorge, and the 22nd Massachusetts, up top behind them. The former observed, "[T]he enemy commenced firing shot and shell, which fell and burst among and near the men, costing us a few lives."[15] The 22nd noted that the shelling "did very little injury,"[16] but it was apparently an intense barrage: "The enemy seemed determined to have this position, for they rained metal enough into this piece of woods to drive out any body of troops that were unprotected."[17] Over across the Chickahominy River, an enemy battery in the open was just what Col. Arndt, 1st Battalion, New York Light Artillery was waiting for. He had two batteries of 20-lb. Parrott guns, and now he had a juicy target. His monstrous weapons opened fire on the Louisianans, giving them "a great deal of annoyance."[18] During the artillery duel, General Wilcox arrived. He could see one line of Federals about halfway to Boatswain's Creek, and another along Boatswain's Creek.[19] He tried to get a better view. Just as he took position behind a tree, a cannon shot smashed into it. General Wilcox scrambled back down into the ravine.[20]

Under cover of this fire, Pryor sent his whole brigade, about 1400 men, over Florida Hill towards Boatswain's Creek. Pryor's men met a relatively thick skirmish line consisting of two companies of the 1st Michigan[21] and four companies of the 25th New York[22] (Martindale's brigade), and a like number from the 83rd Pennsylvania, 44th New York, and 16th Michigan, of Butterfield's brigade,[23] who fell back to Boatswain's Creek. As the Confederates got nearer, they were blasted by the skirmishers and the up-top regiments behind them.[24] This was the whole point of the exercise: to entice the main line to fire and reveal themselves. The 22nd Massachusetts gave them such a "reception that few lived to tell the tale,"[25] but M.B. Hurst, 14th Louisiana, observed that his regiment only received artillery fire, probably from across the Chickahominy, and fell back about 20 yards.[26] Brigadier Pryor determined that the enemy were "in great force." With no hope of replying to the Federal guns, the Donaldsonville Artillery was withdrawn.[27] Kniereim's and Diederich's fire would keep all of Longstreet's artillery off the field for the rest of the day.[28] One of Pryor's regiments stayed out as skirmishers, but fell back to Powhite Creek.[29] In the meantime, Brigadiers Wilcox and Featherston had brought up their men, who were immediately shelled, and were sheltered in the woods near the Gaines Mansion.[30] General Longstreet halted further attacks until Powell Hill's Division came up.[31]

Powhite Creek, Near Gaines' Mill

Four companies of the 1st U.S. Sharpshooters under Lt. Col. Ripley were posted along Powhite Creek south of Gaines' Mill. Late in the morning, General Griffin himself rode up and transmitted General Porter's "wish" that "reliable" men be sent out to ascertain the whereabouts of the enemy. Captain McLean, Company D, asked for a sergeant and 10 others to volunteer for "special work." Sgt. Hetherington was cautioned to be as quiet as possible and not to fire except to defend themselves. Hetherington and his men went north towards the millpond.[32] They crossed the western branch of Powhite Creek, and were probably the Yankees who were staring down at Fannie Gaines Tinsley and her mother.[33] They crept through the woods north of the millpond, and soon came upon Whiting's Division, marching east on the Walnut Grove–Bethesda Church Road.[34] A whole new Rebel division was news indeed! Hetherington hurried to get the news back to headquarters, but on his way he ran into Brigadier Gregg's skirmishers, who blocked the way back to Porter's position. Though one man was wounded and captured, and with some hairbreadth escapes, Hetherington's scouts made it back to their own men, and claimed to be the first ones to engage the Rebels at Gaines' Mill.[35]

Powell Hill's Division, Gregg's Brigade,
Just West of Gaines' Mill

As the South Carolinians approached Powhite Creek, they came under fire from Federal skirmishers posted along eastern bank.[36] A South Carolinian recalled, "As soon as we came in sight, being in their deserted camp, the enemy opened fire on us from the hill opposite. We returned the fire quickly taking shelter behind boxes, barrels or whatever lay about. But before I had reached a cluster of empty barrels, I felt a bullet strike my right foot. Looking down, I saw a dent in the edge of my shoe sole, near my big toe."[37] One of Barry Benson's comrades was hit. Benson dragged him into a tent, where the soldier told Benson to tell his sister, "Give her my love, and tell her I died for my country."[38]

These Federals were from the 9th Massachusetts, of Griffin's Brigade.[39] They had fallen back east with the general retreat, but were ordered back west to the mill.[40] Col. Cass was under the impression that two other regiments would be up to help, but for some reason, they never came.[41] When the men of the 9th Massachusetts arrived, they found Tidball's Battery A, 2nd U.S. Artillery (6 ordnance rifles), and Robertson's B/L, 2nd U.S. Artillery (6 ordnance rifles), on the eastern side contesting the crossing.[42] It had taken Tidball two hours to get into position because of the traffic jam at the bridge. Once across, he destroyed it and took up a position to shell the road to Gaines' Mill.[43] Robertson had been harassing the Rebels all morning from a position on Carolina Hill, but now hustled off the main line.[44]

Ordered to delay the Confederates as long as possible, Col. Cass of the 9th Massachusetts initially ordered two companies to line the eastern bank of Powhite Creek. The other eight were formed in the woods between New Cold Harbor and the McGehee Road Bridge across Boatswain's Creek.[45] Defending the bridge at the mill were some of Berdan's 1st United State Sharpshooters attached to General Morell's division.[46] More of Berdan's men were to the south of them.[47]

Stopped by the enemy fire, Gregg brought two regiments on line, ready to force a crossing of the creek. Col. Cass, on the other hand, reinforced his line with two more companies. Gregg countered by bringing up two sections of Andrews' 1st Maryland Battery to shell the woods,[48] and by sending his skirmishers charging down the hill at the double-quick,[49] across the creek, and up the opposite side.[50] The two regiments followed them down the hill, only to be stopped by Powhite Creek. With the 9th's men driven back from the top of the eastern bank, Gregg rebuilt the bridge for his artillery to use. While that was being done, the 12th South Carolina crossed over the milldam,[51] where Fannie and Mrs. Gaines had crossed. The repairs took some time.

The 1st South Carolina Volunteers "partook of liquor and provisions left by the enemy around the mill."[52] In the meantime, the First South Carolina Rifles had reached the mill without opposition.[53] As soon as the bridge was finished, Gregg sent his own artillery, Crenshaw's Battery, across Powhite

1ST REGIMENT

BERDAN'S U. S.

SHARPSHOOTERS !

Lieut. Winthrop, detailed from Washington to recruit for this Regiment will

"SHOOT IN"

all who may apply, this day, in the field in rear of residence of S. Arnold Esq.
Shooting to commence at 8 o'clock, A. M. and at 2 o'clock, P. M. Saturday, 26, Oct., 1861.

1861 Recruiting Poster for Berdan's 1st U.S. Sharpshooters (Library of Congress).

Creek and up the hill to support his infantry and skirmishers.[54] An officer of the 11th U.S. remarked, "Here some shells from the heavy guns of the enemy, reached us, and shrieking over our heads, exploded beyond. The first shell demoralized one of the officer's contrabands, that dropped the haversack and blanket he had, and rushed towards the enemy."[55]

The Irish 9th had withdrawn to the cover of the woods just east of the mill.[56] Cass, realizing that the enemy now had a couple of regiments across the creek, again reinforced his skirmishers, sending up another two companies, who formed in the woods just east of the Magee House.[57] Cass' skirmishers now covered the Gaines' Mill Road, the Palmetto Track, and the Foster Road. Berdan's Sharpshooters were covering Carolina Hill.

In their rush across the creek, the South Carolinians did not bother to search the mill itself. Later, 25 Yankees came out of it and were captured.[58]

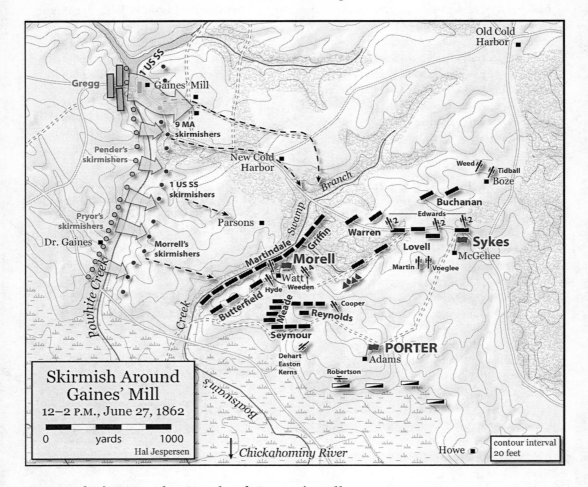

Skirmish Around
Gaines' Mill
12–2 P.M., June 27, 1862

0   yards   1000

Hal Jespersen

contour interval
20 feet

Pender's Brigade, South of Gaines' Mill

As soon as Gregg's brigade was across Powhite Creek, Pender's brigade crossed[59] and turned south, following the Gaines' Mill–New Cold Harbor Road. Pender was to drive the Yankees from the area to Gregg's right, along the road south and then east from Gaines' Mill to the Ingraham House. A miscommunication occurred; Col. Riddick and the 34th North Carolina promptly disappeared down the road. Pender's remaining regiments, the 16th, 22nd and 38th North Carolina, and the 2nd Arkansas Battalion, went south of the road, and soon ran into more of the U.S. Sharpshooters.[60] The Federals slowly withdrew,[61] but put up such a fight that Pender "found [his brigade] weak,"[62] and asked for support from Brigadier Archer's Tennessee brigade. In the meantime, Pender put the rest of Andrews' Battery out as bait to unmask any federal batteries that might be lurking behind the woods to the east. It didn't work.[63]

On the Palmetto Track, North of the Stewart House

The 9th Massachusetts skirmishers were not giving up without a fight. The 1st South Carolina Volunteers pushed them east towards the intersection of the Foster Road and the Cold Harbor Road, a place known locally as New Cold Harbor.[64] Gregg's reaction was to bring his whole force up, extending his line north, to his left.[65] The whole brigade then made what Powell Hill described as the "handsomest charge in line I have seen during the war."[66] General Gregg noted, "For a good part of the distance the line advanced at the double quick." The advance was also "steady and rapidly under the fire of the enemy's skirmishers."[67] Pvt. Mattison, 1st South Carolina Rifles, focused on one man's fate: "One Yankee was seen running across the old field in our front, some 200 yards distant, I suppose. Several shots were fired before he fell."[68] The line had moved about half a mile in the open when Union artillery opened fire.[69]

Captain John Edwards' Battery L/M, 3rd U.S. Artillery (6 Parrotts), had been split up and his guns placed in twos to support General Sykes' line on the high ground north of the McGehee Road. Hearing the skirmish fight, Edwards conducted Lt. Hayden's section (two guns operating together) forward towards Boatswain's Branch. They soon opened fire on Gregg's brigade, visible across the stream.[70] Hayden's firing had some effect on the 1st South Carolina Rifles, as Pvt. Mattison remarked that when it started, it was "uncomfortably near, and gave us what is called 'bomb ague.'"[71]

With artillery firing and a whole brigade of Rebels bearing down on them, the 9th Massachusetts realized that it was time to go. While the other companies took off, Major Hanley with two companies made a stand at the line of an abandoned sutler wagon laden with socks. Some of his men liberated new socks despite the danger. Hanley rallied his men, who fired one more shot, and the whole line ran for the main Union line.[72] Company I had had both of its senior officers killed in the skirmishing; it was now commanded by Lt. Boyd and was the rear guard of Hanley's detachment. A shell exploded near Boyd and broke his leg. Boyd called to his pard,[73] Sgt. John MacNamara, to help him off the field. MacNamara found two men to help, and put Boyd on William Winn's back. MacNamara and the other supported Winn under the shoulders, and all three made for the Union lines. Confederate fire hit Boyd and came out Winn's chest, and also wounded MacNamara in the calf. The sergeant ordered the other man to run, and was himself soon overrun by the Confederates. The latter tossed him a canteen of water and pressed on.[74]

The 1st South Carolina Volunteers witnessed a very similar scene:

> We shot down several of the enemy as they retreated across the open field, but one of them, after lying a moment, rose and attempted to follow his flying comrades. By this time the uninjured ones had passed out of sight, so this unfortunate was left to the fire of our whole line. The excitement became intense. A perfect shower of balls was hurled after him, striking up the dust before, behind and all around him. But still he staggered on, striving but the more vigorously as the danger increased. Cries of "Kill him!" "Shoot him!" "Down with the fellow!" and other of rougher cast, resounded from every side, but shoot as we would he succeeded in reaching a clump of pines, where we found him soon after, exhausted by fatigue and loss of blood.[75]

Gregg's brigade crossed the Cold Harbor Road still under artillery fire; Dr. Clinkscales, 1st South Carolina Rifles, was killed.[76] Underneath the artillery duel, the South Carolinians were moving into the woods north of Boatswain's Swamp.[77] Not yet challenged, they moved across Boatswain's Branch, sent out skirmishers,[78] and lay down in the woods.[79] Gregg asked for permission to attack with his brigade immediately, but

Powell Hill refused,[80] no doubt remembering what had happened when he attacked by brigades the day before at Beaver Dam Creek. Powell Hill would bring up his whole division, and deploy it to Gregg's right, extending the Confederate line towards the river. Hill also sent a request for a demonstration to Longstreet, whose men were arriving on Powhite Creek near Dr. Gaines' Mansion.[81]

Powell Hill's Division at Gaines' Mill

The rest of Powell Hill's Division was crossing the creek at Gaines' Mill and deploying for a fight. Branch's Brigade had been next in the order of march and was told to follow the Palmetto Track to the Foster Road, and then march south to New Cold Harbor. As they moved toward New Cold Harbor[82] the leading regiment, the 7th North Carolina, put out two companies as skirmishers, with the rest of the regiment in line of battle as support and the 28th North Carolina behind. The other three regiments were coming down the road, but stopped just short of New Cold Harbor. As soon as they passed into the woods southeast of New Cold Harbor, the 7th North Carolina skirmishers ran into more of the 9th Massachusetts.[83] The balance of the 7th and the 28th North Carolina immediately came up, causing Brigadier Griffin to have the 9th fall back.[84] The 9th withdrew faster than the 7th chased it, and took position on Griffin's Hill, just behind the creek.[85]

J.R. Anderson's[86] brigade was next. He was sent down the Gaines' Mill Road–New Cold Harbor itself, cautioned that the enemy was in force up ahead.[87] Anderson put out skirmishers and flankers, and found enemy skirmishers at the Ingraham House. Anderson drove these off and marched his brigade through the woods and out into the field between Powhite Creek and Boatswain's Creek.[88] Andrews' Maryland Battery went into firing position behind him, several hundred yards southwest of the Ingraham House.[89]

General Archer's Tennessee Brigade did not just support Pender's North Carolinians, but relieved them. Braxton's Fredericksburg Artillery was with Archer. Braxton's battery was odd, having 4 smoothbores and two "Burton and Archer" rifles.[90] These extremely rare guns were made by the Bellona Arsenal, the Confederacy's second largest armaments producer, in Chesterfield County, 14 miles west of Richmond, which had once been a silkworm farm.[91] Braxton went into battery on a small rise near Dr. Gaines' orchard on Powhite Creek.[92] Powell Hill filled the gap between J.R. Anderson's right and Archer's left with his remaining brigade, the small one of General Field's Virginians.[93] Pender moved north to support General Branch.[94]

Having received Powell Hill's request for a diversion, Longstreet, near the Gaines Mansion, ordered Wilcox to have Pryor send one regiment to drive the Union skirmishers in and back and to follow them to their supports.[95] Longstreet sent acknowledgment back to Powell Hill at about 2:30 p.m.[96]

Porter's Headquarters, Near the Adams House

Hetherington's Sharpshooter scouts uncovered the presence of an additional army marching east, in addition to those currently discovered to the west. Though not in a pickle yet, General Porter wisely sent to McClellan for reinforcements.[97] At 2:00, General McClellan contacted William B. Franklin's VI Corps and alerted Slocum's Division, about

8,000 men, for a move across the river.[98] Slocum's Division had the usual three brigades. First in the order of march was Newton's brigade of 2600 men. Brigadier Newton commanded three New York regiments (18th, 31st, and 32nd New York) and the 95th Pennsylvania. His brigade was more colorful than most. The Pennsylvanians were a quasi-Zouave regiment, but much less ostentatiously uniformed than the 5th New York.[99] The 32nd New York had several companies from California who had shown up the year before in New York Harbor and had tendered their services to that state.[100]

Slocum's second brigade consisted of the 1st, 2nd, 3rd, and 4th New Jersey regiments and until recently been commanded by Brigadier Phillip Kearny, who had visited Summer Hill Plantation. They were now under Brigadier Taylor. All four regiments were large, with over 600 men each. Six companies of the 2nd New Jersey were detached, and did not cross the river, so Taylor had about 2400 men.

Brigadier Bartlett's 2504 men brought up the rear. His was a conglomerate brigade of two New York regiments (the 16th and 27th), the 5th Maine, and the 96th Pennsylvania. The 16th New York was the envy of the army, as their colonel had just provided the whole regiment with cool straw hats.[101]

Slocum would bring his divisional artillery over with his brigades. Lt. Porter's Battery A, Massachusetts Light Artillery would accompany Bartlett's Brigade.[102] With the Jerseymen would go Hexamer's Hoboken Artillery, designated as Battery A, New Jersey Light Artillery[103] (4 Parrotts, 2 howitzers)[104] Newton would escort Upton's Battery D, 5th U.S. Artillery[105] (4 Parrotts, 2 howitzers)[106] Slocum began moving his lead brigade at 2:30, but the march took an hour and a half[107]; he would not arrive until about 4:00.

Powell Hill's Division

With the receipt of Longstreet's reply communiqué, Powell Hill was ready to unleash his whole division on the Yankees. Gregg's brigade would head south southeast to Zouave Hill and the 10th and 5th New York (Warren's Brigade) with Edwards' Battery L/M 3rd U.S. Artillery (6 Parrotts); Branch and Pender would head southeast to hit Griffin's Hill, where the 9th Massachusetts (Griffin's Brigade) waited. J.R. Anderson and Field would hit Boatswain's Swamp near Boatswain's Run, defended by the 14th New York and the 4th Michigan of Griffin's Brigade. Archer would attack the 13th New York and 2nd Maine of Martindale's Brigade and Bucklin's section of Weeden's Battery C, Rhode Island Light Artillery (2 ordnance rifles). Powell Hill's 9,500 men in 6 brigades with the support of 14 guns[108] would strike about 8,200 Yankees in four and half brigades also with 14 guns.

Fannie Gaines Tinsley and her entourage worked their way a mile north to Ellyson's, north of Gaines' Mill, between the Foster Road and the Ellyson Road. Since no one had eaten, Mrs. Gaines killed the chicken, cut it up, and put it in a pot to boil for soup. At about 3:00 p.m., just as it was coming to a boil, a cannonball smashed into the chimney, probably from one of Voeglee's 20-lb. Parrott guns. The soup was forgotten as the group fled out the door further north, even leaving their hats. Dr. Curtis could not go on, so Dr. Gaines hid with him behind big trees.[109]

9

I Confess I Did Not Know
What Hard Times Were
Until I Was Under Jackson

Harvey Hill had made good time marching east along the Mechanicsville–Bethesda Church Road. His column turned south at Bethesda Church, and then turned *north-east* near Johnson's.[1] From there, he marched about 1.25 miles, and then turned right (south-southeast) onto the road from Old Raleigh to Beulah Church, approaching the latter from the north, a march of about 1.5 miles. He could do this because at dawn General Stuart's cavalry had cleared the Federals from the area around of the Raleigh–Beulah Church–Old Cold Harbor Road.[2] (See Mechanicsville to Old Cold Harbor map, page 52.)

At the end of the conference at Walnut Grove Church, Jackson had instructed his guide to take him to "Cold Harbor." At Walnut Grove Church, General Jackson turned the head of his column, Ewell's Division,[3] to the left (east) on the Walnut Grove Church–Bethesda Church Road.[4]

Three roads intersect the Walnut Gove Church–Bethesda Church Road from the right (south) before one reaches the important one, the Carleton Road. All three lead to Dr. Curtis', west of Gaines' Mill. The Carleton Road leads directly south, but it forks and heads to Beulah Church and then to Old Cold Harbor.[5] John Henry Timberlake, Jackson's guide, led the column east, past the first three roads, and turned south on the Carleton Road. About an eighth[6] of a mile south of the intersection, the road forked. Timberlake led the column south. The Rev. Major Dabney later wrote:

> After marching for a mile and a half, the booming of artillery in [Jackson's] front caught his ear, and he demanded sharply of his guide near him: "Where is that firing?" The reply was, that it was in the direction of Gaines' Mill. "Does this road lead there?" he asked. The guide told him that it led by Gaines' Mill to New Cold Harbor. "But," exclaimed he, "I do not wish to go to Gaines' Mill. I wish to go to Cold Harbor, leaving that place to the right." "Then," said the guide, "the left hand road is the one that should have been taken, and had you let me know what you desired, I could have directed you aright at first."

The Gilmer Map shows that instead of heading east on the left fork (the Carleton Roaf to Beulah Church and Old Cold Harbor) Timberlake had taken the right (south) fork onto the Foster Road towards Gaines' Mill and New Cold Harbor.

Ewell's Division only had 4,000 infantry in it. Brigadier Seymour's Louisiana Brigade

(1,300 men) was in the lead, with Trimble (1,244 men), and then Elzey (1,293 men), excluding artillery. With ranks of men four abreast, it would take up about 1.5 miles of road.[7] The other Valley Army divisions were behind it facing east, on the Walnut Grove Church-Bethesda Church Road, in the following order: Whiting, Lawton, and Winder, together taking up 4.5 miles of road.[8] Dabney goes on to say that "nothing remained but to reverse the column, and return to the proper road."[9] Again, Dabney's words are misleading. "The column" did not mean the whole Valley Army; it was far too large to occupy the whole Foster Road. They just "reversed" Ewell's Division. In other words, everyone simply faced about, putting Elzey in the lead, Trimble in the middle, and Seymour at the end. Campbell Brown remembered this maneuver: "Our line of march was at right angles, or nearly so, to that of the evening before … for Jackson after riding with us for two hours directing the march, suddenly changed its direction so much that we came into the proper road with the rear of our line leading, if I am not mistaken. I was sent to recall some of the skirmishers, who had to hurry in order to catch up with the column. This second change was made by turning square to our [original] left…."[10]

Dabney reveals that reversing the column and turning onto the Carleton Road only took about an hour.[11] This makes sense: in reversing a column, all of the command staff has to shift from the front of their unit to the rear of it, and let the men know about the change.[12] The "booming" that Jackson heard was Tidball's and Robertson's batteries firing at Gregg's skirmishers from the bridge near Gaines' Mill. These two batteries were perhaps a mile south of Foster's, and the timberlines would have funneled the sound of the guns right up the Foster Road to Jackson's ears.[13] The Reverend Dabney was anxious over the lost hour, and brought the matter up with Jackson, who replied, "No, let us trust that the providence of our God will override it, that no mischief shall result."[14] Jackson's instinct was correct.

When he left Walnut Grove Church at 10:00, he had set a grueling pace to Old Cold Harbor, about three and a half miles away. Jackson's fastest long-distance march was 57 miles in 51 hours, a march speed of 1.1 miles per hour.[15] The secret of "Jackson's Foot Cavalry" was partially that they marched a tenth of a mile per hour faster, but more importantly they did so for a longer time, at one instance for 16 hours in one day. Their fastest short-range march was 2 miles per hour, going into battle at Front Royal.[16] On June 27, Ewell's Division was marching at a blistering pace. Campbell Brown, of Ewell's staff, says that his division was finally on the right road two hours after leaving Walnut Grove Church.[17] It is two miles to the Foster Road, and Ewell's whole division went a mile down it, reversed, and was ready to head to Old Cold Harbor, all in two hours. This means that by about 12:00, Ewell's Division had marched about three miles in two hours, a grueling march speed of 1.5 miles per hour, and was only a mile and a half from Old Cold Harbor.

They never made it. When the Valley Army's advanced party reached the Beulah Church Road, they found Harvey Hill's Division marching by. The Rev. Major Charles Dabney recollected, "Just as I was about to turn southward, at the crossing, Genl. D.H. Hill an old friend met me at the head of his column. He had known me only as a clergyman and Theological teacher and had not heard of my entering military service." He exclaimed, "Dr. Dabney is this you? What on earth are you doing here?" I replied, "Trying in my poor way, general to help defend our country." "You are in uniform," said he. "Yes, and in commission as chief of Jackson's staff." "There," said he, "halt your column. Don't you see your men and mine are almost mixed together? I am ordered by the commander in chief to take the advance." I halted our column until his division swept by, a magnificent body of soldiers.[18]

Old Cold Harbor was a little over half a mile away.[19]

Old Cold Harbor

The Cobb Legion,[20] Col. Martin commanding, was part of Stuart's cavalry force; it was ahead of Harvey Hill's column and arrived at Old Cold Harbor about 1:00.[21] Stuart himself was already there; Stuart reported that when he, Stuart, arrived, *General Jackson was already there*.[22] Stuart ordered Martin to guard the area to the east.[23]

By 2:00, Harvey Hill's Division, Harvey Hill himself, Stonewall Jackson, the Reverend Dabney, and Capt. Campbell Brown of Ewell's Division, and probably General Ewell, were all at Old Cold Harbor.[24] From Old Cold Harbor, the firing that could be heard was Gregg's Brigade at Gaines' Mill itself, which to Jackson's trained ear did not sound much like hordes of Yankees being driven into the arms of the Reinforced Valley Army. Stonewall Jackson sent Capt. James Keith Boswell to General Lee for orders.[25] Jackson and his entourage rode south on the Grapevine Road to assess the situation.[26] Jackson and his staff, along with Harvey Hill and his staff, rode south past Beulah Church and then even further, past Old Cold Harbor. Soon "several federal batteries were let loose upon the group of horsemen it was almost point blank range." Hill's front regiments "tumbled upon their breasts and there was nothing for us to do but gallop back."[27] These "batteries" were Capt. Stephen Weed's Battery I, 5th U.S., who thought he was shooting at some Confederate cavalry, not half of the Confederate high command.[28]

Dabney's horse was unbroken to gunfire and terrified; Dabney was near the rear of the pack. Capt. Sandie Pendleton turned and shouted that Jackson ordered, "Scatter, scatter right and left we make too much of a target there."[29] This is hardly the reaction of an exhausted, confused general. The Rev. Major Dabney found some lower ground with a spring, watered his skittish horse, and "ate a morsel of sandwich" before finding Jackson again.[30]

Jackson suggested that Harvey Hill bring up a battery to drive Weed's guns off, and stayed to watch.[31] Bondurant's Jeff Davis (Alabama) Artillery had only four guns that day, two ordnance rifles and two howitzers.[32] Bondurant's men whipped their horses into a gallop and came jingling up, talking position on the right (west) of the Grapevine Road near the Stewart House at Old Cold Harbor.[33]

Bondurant's opening shots were off the intended target, but hit the 4th U.S., Major Delozier Davidson commanding, just to the east of Weed's Battery I, 5th U.S. (6 ordnance rifles). "As soon as the enemy opened fire, Major D. Davidson … left the field, saying he was going for reinforcements…. He then almost immediately retired to the rear without informing anyone of his intentions, and has not been heard of since. He left his horse…." Major Collins took over the regiment.[34] Captain Weed and his gunners saw Bondurant open fire and returned fire at about 1,000 yards' distance.[35] Bondurant's men were also receiving small arms fire from the 4th U.S.'s skirmishers.[36] After half an hour, Tidball's Battery A, 2d U.S. Artillery arrived with six more ordnance rifles. The predicament of the Jeff Davis Artillery became extreme: "In fact the missiles of death were so thick it would seem no living thing could exist in its range. From this fire men and horses fell in rapid succession."[37] Even caissons (two limbers together) were hit,[38] and exploded with a blinding flash and thunderous roar. Tidball recounted, "It required only a few minutes to silence the enemy … and to cause him to change the position of his guns."[39] By this time, Bondurant's battery was almost out of ammunition,[40] and "badly crippled.[41] In addition to the caissons, it lost 18 men (out of about 100) and 28 horses (out of 32).[42] Bondurant pulled out three of his guns, but left one with orders to only fire on advancing infantry. That gun pulled out when the 4th U.S. skirmishers were almost on it.[43]

Bondurant's difficulties were well worth it. Though he had little effect on Weed and Tidball, the 18-gun artillery duel well to the east was heard by all of the Confederates to the south and west, even by the civilians in Richmond. In Longstreet's Division, a staff officer rode the line with the news, which was met with cheers,[44] "Stonewall was at them!"[45] Moreover, Boswell had reached General Lee when Weed and then Tidball opened up on Bondurant's Jeff Davis Artillery.[46]

As Harvey Hill's Division arrived, two brigades went forward to the Cold Harbor Road, Brigadier Garland on the east side of the Grapevine Road and G.B. Anderson on the west side of it. Rodes' Brigade had arrived at Old Cold Harbor; Harvey Hill wanted Rodes to support Garland for an anticipated attack straight down the Grapevine Road.[47] Garland demurred, as the federal guns (Weed, Tidball, Edwards, and perhaps Voeglee) would make mincemeat out of his right flank as it tried to negotiate the thickets east of the Grapevine Road.[48] Jackson himself nixed the plan,[49] and ordered Harvey Hill to pull Garland[50] and Rodes[51] back into the woods east of Old Cold Harbor itself.

To Stonewall Jackson, the Yankees were not getting pushed onto his bayonets, but Lee's orders were clear. "For a time, General Jackson held his troops back in the margin of the woods looking towards the highway…, in the hope that the enemy, retreating … would expose their flank to a crushing blow…."[52] In 1896, Dabney clarified that this wait was very short. He thought that Jackson "complied with General Lee's order to wait and hit the retiring McClellan a side blow in rather an impatient and brief fashion. The sound of the firing on our right taught him that McClellan was not retiring. When I overtook Jackson he had already completed his dispositions for putting D.H. Hill's division into action. He was also just completing similar arrangements for Ewell's Division."[53] For once, a Confederate commander had the nettlesome problem of having too many troops almost in the right place. Jackson had 25,000 men stacked up for a couple of miles[54] on two roads that led into one, and Yankees in his front. He did not need an order from Lee to know what to do. Hill's men would act as Jackson's reserve while he brought the Valley Army forward. Jackson himself then went to hurry Ewell's Division up.[55]

Jackson rode north past Beulah Church to Ewell's lead brigade, that of Brigadier Arnold Elzey, and ordered them to clear the woods to the west. "Jackson himself personally rode along with Genl. Ewell forming the troops, and told him that the woods ahead were full of the enemy."[56] A member of Carrington's Charlottesville Artillery (2 ordnance rifles, 2 howitzers, 2 smoothbores)[57] wrote that "in a few minutes a group of generals rode up alongside and had a very animated conversation."[58] Carrington's guns were attached to Elzey's brigade as its organic artillery, and normally would have been that brigade's trail unit. This places Jackson, Ewell and probably Elzey near the tail end of Brigadier Elzey's column, and near the head of Brigadier Seymour's column. It was shortly before 3:30 p.m.[59]

Campbell Brown thought something was odd, as Carrington's Battery was out in the open within musket range of the woods and had not yet been disturbed.[60] Jackson ordered a strong skirmish line into the wood, followed by Elzey's main body,[61] and then left, heading north up the Grapevine Road toward Beulah Church. Everyone held their breath as the skirmishers crossed the Grapevine Road, expecting the skirmishers to walk into a blistering volley from the hidden Yankees, but nothing happened. An officer came out of the woods to report no enemy had been found. General Ewell sent Brown after

Jackson for new orders.[62] Jackson found General Ewell first, and gave his orders. Ewell's brigades were already in line of battle and 200–300 yards away. Just as Ewell "dashed off to overtake his men," the Rev. Major Dabney rode up. Jackson turned his horse to Dabney, and

> quickly began with admirable clearness and precision … putting all his remaining brigades into action…. Jackson's words were about these: You know Major, these troops are now standing at ease along the line of march from Richardson's crossroads [H.C. Richardson's, on the Carleton Road]. Ride back rapidly along that line and tell the commanders to begin instantly an echelon movement, beginning from the left next to Ewell's right brigade; tell each brigade commander to follow as his guide the right regiment of his neighbor on his left and keep as nearly within supporting distance as possible. Thus, Whiting's left regiment will follow and support Ewell's extreme right under Brig. Genl. Trimble, while the rest of Whiting's regiments will keep alignment, as closely as possible, with their own left. So, Lawton's left regiment will follow and support Whiting's right, etc. But tell them that if this guidance fails at any point, form line of battle and move to the front, pressing to the sound of the heaviest firing and attack the enemy immediately wherever found. As to artillery, each commander must use his best discretion. If the ground will at all permit tell them to take their field batteries and use them. If not, post them in the rear.[63]

Forty-one years after the fact, Dabney was able to paraphrase this order clearly, yet some have condemned it as unintelligible.[64] Simply put, instead of all the units advancing south on one line, e.g.:

^Ewell^Whiting^Lawton^Winder^

which would require Ewell to wait while the others came up to his line, Jackson wanted them to move south in successive lines, supporting one another, viz:

^Ewell^

^Whiting^

^Lawton^

^Winder^

(Carets indicate direction.)

In this formation, Ewell could move immediately, with the others catching up. It was the fastest way to deploy 12,000 men in the same direction. Dabney's 1866 map roughly shows the positions and order of Whiting (Hood and Law), Lawton, and Winder (everyone else); Jackson essentially wanted them to head south en echelon, but, recognizing the difficulties of the terrain, if the formation failed, everyone was to find *some* Yankees and attack.

Unfortunately, the Rev. Major Dabney had diarrhea. This may explain why he had to catch up to General Jackson when the latter was with General Ewell. Recognizing this, Jackson stopped Dabney as he was about to gallop off, and sent Quartermaster Major Jno. Harman instead. Dabney could see that Harman did not understand what Jackson meant, and "put in a hot expostulation. No, Genl. Jackson, let me go; don't consider my health, this is no time for anyone to hold back, I am well enough to ride my horse, that is enough for you, let me due [*sic*] my own proper task. He listened but kindly replied; 'No you shall not go; I see you are not well and I will sfard [safeguard?] you this afternoon. I can't afford for you to have a regular breakdown now. I need you too much. I mean to spare you this evening. Maj. Harman can do it very well and he shall go.'"[65]

Dabney had a low opinion of Major Harman, calling him a "frushing [?] wagon master and horse dealer without education." As Harman rode off, Dabney was "in a state

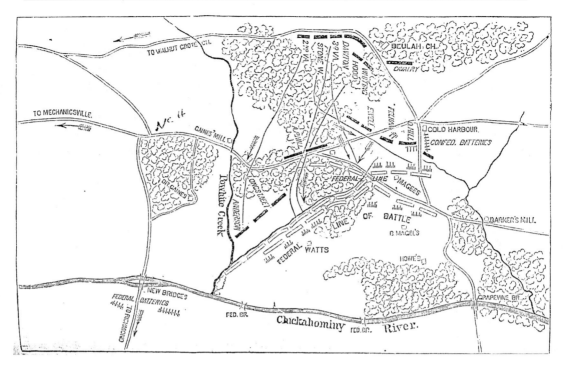

The Rev. Major Dabney's 1866 Map (author's collection)

of anxious misgiving." Jackson gave Dabney unspecified "lighter duty"[66] elsewhere. While Dabney was gone, Campbell Brown, Ewell's aide, found Jackson and reported no Yankees in the woods, and asked for instructions. The general told Brown that he, Jackson, had been misled about the location of the enemy, and Ewell should attack, inclining to the left, towards the firing.[67]

Having arranged the troops that were facing the enemy, Jackson set himself to the next task, getting the rest of Ewell's men moving. Jackson rode a short distance to Brigadier Seymour's Louisiana Brigade. Major Roberdeau Wheat had been in the throes of a death premonition all day, but lost it when he saw Jackson.[68] "Seeing him, Wheat spurred his horse out to greet his commander. 'General, we are about to go into a hot fight and it is likely that many of us may be killed … let us do the fighting. Just let me tell them that you promised not to expose yourself and they'll fight like—ah—Tigers.' Jackson took Wheats hand, shook it, and said 'Much obliged to you, Major, I will try not to go into danger unnecessarily. But, Major, you will be in greater danger than I, and I hope you will not get hurt. Each of us has his duty to perform, without regard to consequences; we must perform it and trust in Providence.'"[69] The Louisiana Brigade, now the "Louisiana Tigers," moved out. It was about 4:00 in the afternoon. Jackson then rode to meet with General Lee at New Cold Harbor.[70]

And here must die a myth. Since 1862, eminent historians have claimed that Jackson, exhausted, befuddled, dull, and lost in the wilderness, disappeared into oblivion on June 25 and rematerialized too late to help at Gaines' Mill on the 27th.[71] In fact, Jackson had communicated with Branch at 9:00 a.m. on the 26th; had communicated with him again around 3:00 p.m. near Shady Grove Church; was not ordered in by Lee on June 26;

had met with Lee that night at Mechanicsville; had met Lee about 10:00 the next morning at Walnut Grove Church; had communicated with Powell Hill at Lonesome Tree at about 11:30; and had sent Boswell to Lee from Old Cold Harbor about 1:00. Dabney specifically says that Bondurant's guns were silenced at 2:00 and had been firing for half an hour by that time.[72] This places Jackson's visit to Weed's guns sometime around 1:00. Col. Martin arrived at Old Cold Harbor at 1:00, finding Stuart, who found Jackson already there. Jackson and his staff arrived at Old Cold Harbor sometime between noon and 1:00. As for being lost, Jackson had not one, but two guides, the Reverend Dabney's brother and Timberlake, whose own kin had drawn the map in Jackson's pocket. Jackson himself, with Harvey Hill, and his division's vanguard, reached his exact assigned position at or before the time that Powell Hill reached Gaines' Mill,[73] and while General Lee was still at the Hogan House.[74] Let this evidence put a stake through the heart of this odious legend.

10

A Soldier Feels No Fear
While Fighting

Powell Hill ordered an attack shortly after 2:30.[1] This unfortunate statement in his report has led many to believe that he actually attacked at 2:30, or thereabouts.[2] It takes some time to get orders to commanders, and then to get 9,000 men out of road march formation and into attack position.[3] According to Brigadier Gregg, his whole brigade was across Powhite Creek at the Mill at 2:00. It reached Boatswain's Branch at 2:30, and sat idle until 4:00.[4] Two of his three regimental commanders agree.[5] Branch's Brigade reached Gaines' Mill itself between 3:00 and 4:00 p.m.,[6] and entered the fight about 4:00 p.m.[7] None of the other brigadiers mention the time they entered the fighting, but Brigadiers Pender, Field, J.R. Anderson and Archer were all behind Gregg and Branch in the order of march. Accordingly, after 4:00,[8] the brigades attacked one after the other,[9] each essentially cueing on the initial firing to their left. Powell Hill's attack lasted a little over an hour; there was a short lull about 5:30, after which reinforcements made a second attack.

The Battle of Gaines' Mill is singularly characterized by brigades and regiments fragmenting, then banding together in groups for more fighting. This work will refer to such *ad hoc* formations as Battle Groups, usually, but not always, named after the commanding officer.

The brigades of Gregg, Branch, J.R. Anderson, and Archer were in the first line. Pender's Brigade was following Branch, and Field's Brigade followed Anderson. The two brigades in support necessarily made contact with the Federals after the line in front of them. This creates an odd attack order, which was Gregg, Branch's 7th and 28th North Carolina, hereinafter Battle Group Lane, the balance of Branch's Brigade (33rd, 37th, 18th North Carolina), Anderson, Field and Archer, and finally Pender.

Gregg's South Carolina Brigade, Along Boatswain's Branch, Facing Zouave and Regulars' Hill

Before Powell Hill's attack order, Maxcy Gregg's South Carolina Brigade had cleared the area between New Cold Harbor and Boatswain's Branch, and had advanced deep into the woods, crossing Boatswain's Branch. There, he halted while Hill waited to hear from Longstreet. Crenshaw's (Virginia) battery was brought to a narrow opening in the woods[10] on the high ground behind Gregg, near the Stewart House, and opened fire on two Union

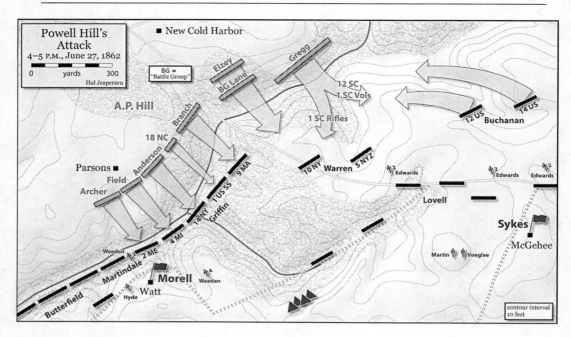

guns.[11] Lt. Pyne, 6th U.S. Infantry, watched: "From where I was standing, I saw the enemy coming out with his artillery onto an open space between the woods … and throw the first shell at the Zouaves and 10th NY who were in the field about 100 yards ahead of us."[12] Crenshaw had six guns, two howitzers, two Parrotts, and two smoothbores.[13] His target was the Union infantry,[14] but Hayden's section of Edwards Battery L/M, 3rd U.S., Artillery (6 Parrotts), spotted him. Warren had ordered Lt. Edwards out into the open to shell Gregg as the South Carolinians crossed the Cold Harbor Road, and he was still there. Edwards remembered that "a constant shower of shell and solid shot fell in and around the section."[15] Major Clitz' 12th U.S. went forward with these two guns as support, and lay down about 80 yards behind them.[16] Crenshaw claimed that after the infantry "scattered" he battled three Union batteries and must have kept up a lively fire,[17] as Brigadier Warren claimed that Crenshaw alone was "several batteries."[18]

While underneath this artillery duel, Brigadier Gregg rearranged the brigade. The First South Carolina Rifles were brought up to the first line, on the right of the 1st Volunteers. While at the 1st Volunteers, Brigadier Gregg told its 16-year-old color bearer, Jimmie Taylor, that he did not have to march that day. Taylor refused: "General you gave these colors to me. I shall bear them." Once Gregg was gone, Taylor pinned his name to the back of his jacket.[19] The 13th South Carolina was left in the second line.[20] The 12th South Carolina put out two companies as skirmishers in front of the first line.[21] A "pine thicket" (the point of woods on Zouave Hill) extended out into the open in front of the 1st Volunteers in the center, so it would still have its cover when the 12th South Carolina emerged from the woods, but it would also slow them down.

Gregg's Brigade was rather opposite the gap between Warren's New York Zouave Brigade and Buchanan's U.S. Regular Brigade. Warren sent one company of the 5th New York Zouaves out as skirmishers in the woods of Boatswain's Branch towards New Cold Harbor; Buchanan had one company of the 14th U.S. doing the same, but towards Old Cold Harbor.[22]

Sykes' Division, on Zouave and Regulars' Hills

The 5th New York Zouaves skirmishers were Company E, which advanced down to the edge of the woods with orders to pick off Crenshaw's gunners.[23] Company E was armed with the Sharps infantry rifle, a longer version of the carbine carried by the 8th Illinois Cavalry. Not only did it fire three times faster than the usual infantry weapon, it was deadly accurate at longer range. Crenshaw's men and horses started to drop,[24] but the Zouaves were suffering too. Sgt. Chambers' rifle was struck by a solid shot, smashed to pieces and sent him flying, knocking a lieutenant down, but with no further harm. One man's pet dog, who liked to chase solid shot, was wounded.[25] In the 14th U.S., Buchanan's Brigade, a shell hit at the feet of a color bearer near Jonathan Hager, knocking several men off their feet, but not exploding.[26] At the 2nd U.S., along the McGehee Road, Augustus Myers wormed his way into the ground so hard he broke the crystal and hands of his watch.[27]

The Zouave skirmishers prompted Brigadier Gregg to get moving. His two companies of skirmishers from the 12th South Carolina advanced, drove in the Zouave skirmishers, and hurried to Gregg's left to get out of the way.[28] There they attacked, or were attacked, by the 14th U.S. and driven back to the Branch.[29] While the Zouaves of Company E were in the woods, explosions killed some men in the main body of the regiment. Martin's Battery (or perhaps Voeglee's) had cut their fuses too short, and had rained metal on the Zouaves.[30] Warren had the 5th New York stack its wings in the sunken part of the McGehee Road.[31] The 10th New York had also suffered from the friendly fire, and was pulled back into the woods on Griffin's Hill, along the McGehee Road, and stacked its wings. This opened two corridors for the artillery behind them to fire through. Brigadier Warren wanted artillery support on his left, and so he ordered Lt. Edwards to send two guns, Kelly's section, 600 yards to the left, near the 10th New York.

To General Sykes, all indications were that the Rebels were coming, and in force. He sent to General Porter for support; Porter ordered General McCall to bring up the brigades of Meade and Seymour. Soon McCall's First Brigade, Reynolds,' left its covered position between the Adams and Watt Houses, and moved up near the McGehee House.[32]

Having fired for two hours, Crenshaw withdrew his battery 200 yards to the rear for a 45-minute rest, and drew more ammunition.[33] Thus, his firing stopped for most of Brigadier Gregg's attack.

Boatswain's Branch

About 4:00,[34] Brigadier Gregg personally gave the order to the South Carolina 12th, the 1st Volunteers and the First Rifles to advance. As the first line came out of the woods, Federal artillery opened fire from 350 yards away, killing and wounding 5 men of the 12th with its first volley.[35] The gallant 12th advanced about a hundred yards into the open, only to find that the 1st Volunteers were still thrashing though the pine thicket, as were the First Rifles. The 12th opened fire, hoping that the 1st Volunteers would untangle themselves, which they soon did, but the three regiments essentially attacked one after the other.[36] The First Rifles had been tasked with taking some Union cannons to the right, near the 10th New York in the woods, but attacked last.

Federal artillery pounded the South Carolinians.[37] Col. Hamilton, 1st Volunteers, observed, "In a short time I saw a brigade moving down on us."[38] Hamilton was unsure whether these were Yankees, thinking that perhaps the First Rifles had broken through and had come around to his front, so the two Confederate regiments foolishly stopped firing. The Federals didn't, firing a series of battalion volleys[39] that "seemed to sweep the earth."[40] Major Clitz of the 12th U.S. dropped off a company, changed front,[41] and double-quicked west towards the 12th South Carolina, as did the 14th U.S., coming in on Clitz' right. The 3rd U.S. was brought forward to the edge of the woods to assist the 12th U.S. skirmishers in covering the right and rear of these two regiments.[42] From this position, Major Rossell, 3rd U.S. could see the Rebel infantry and cavalry moving at Old Cold Harbor, and sent an officer to warn General Sykes.[43] When the 1st Volunteers came out of the woods, they met canister[44] fire from one of the batteries, and so did the 2nd U.S. in the McGehee Road. One private screamed as something hit him in the bottom. It was a piece of the packaging of a round.[45] The Fifth New York Zouaves opened on the 1st Volunteers from the front, and even the 10th New York was shooting at them from the right.[46]

The 12th South Carolina engaged for a short time and then retreated back into the woods of Boatswain's Branch, but to the left (east) of their original position.[47] The 1st Volunteers had charged out of their thicket, and suffered severely. Young Jimmie Taylor, carrying the blue Palmetto Regimental Colors, fell dead almost immediately. Private Pinckney took them up, only to be mortally wounded in a few seconds. Private Holmes reached for the flag, but was felled.[48] Corporal Hayne picked them up, stained with blood, until he fell. By now the regiment was falling back in some haste, leaving the flag. Color Corporal Crochett rushed out to fetch it, but he dropped with the flag. The "stalwart and lion-hearted" Dominick Spellman then picked it up and carried it back into the woods.[49] Col. Hamilton himself even carried the colors for a while.[50] The 1st Volunteers also fell back to Boatswain's Branch, also to the left of their original position. In the retreat, both regiments were disorganized; Jonathan Hager and the 14th U.S. "drove them twice out of the woods to the hill beyond where we could see them running for dear life."[51]

Warren's Brigade, on Zouave Hill

When Gregg's two regiments fell back, the 5th New York happened to be right in Crenshaw's sights, and he opened fire with a will.

Crenshaw's fire devastated the 5th New York. Dirt and sand from a shell blinded Cpl. Feeney, who headed for the rear, only to then be hit in the groin.[52] Stricken men bled to death in the hot sun. The regiment's band had piled their saxhorns and other instruments safely in the woods, only to see them blown to smithereens by a direct hit. Two of the five bandsmen took off for the rear.[53] Brigadier Warren pulled the Zouaves back up the hill into the sunken part of the McGehee Road, but the regiment was too large; it stacked its two wings behind each other and squeezed in.[54] This was not all that much better; though sheltered from Crenshaw's fire, Union artillery shooting over their heads now caused casualties. Cpl. Thomas "Pony" Southwick remembered that "every shot and shell fell with great accuracy almost in the midst of our crowded battalion."[55]

Martin's Battery C, Massachusetts Light Artillery (6 Napoleons) were about 200 yards behind them, and the Zouaves thought that it was the culprit.[56] However, Crenshaw was about a thousand yards away, and premature explosions of Martin's fire is improbable.

On the other hand, Voeglee's Battery B, New York Light Artillery, with their huge 20-lb. Parrotts (that "German Battery"), were further back; several other regiments complained about their fuze-setting[57] abilities, so it was more probably Voeglee. One shell crushed the skull of one of the three Gilligan brothers.[58] Lt. Thomas "The Fiend" Cartwright's arm was mangled in the sunken road. Col. Hiram Duryea, 5th New York, shifted his men left (west) to get out of the friendly fire, but this was into Boatswain's Run, causing some of the men to wait, standing in the water and muck.[59] The 10th New York pulled back into the cover of Griffin's Woods.

First South Carolina Rifles, at the Bottom of Zouave Hill

With Warren's Brigade driven back up the hill by Crenshaw's fire, Gregg's First South Carolina Rifles charged up Zouave Hill towards Griffin's Woods at the double-quick, wherein "were posted seven regiments of the enemy, including the Pennsylvania Reserves."[60] The Rifles split in half, the left wing absorbing the skirmishers, and heading towards the McGehee House, while the right wing moved towards the woods[61] and 10th New York, lying prone.[62] The 10th rose up; it and the First Rifles fired at each other virtually at the same time, 35 yards apart,[63] but the Rifles charged, and drove the New Yorkers back.[64] Col. Marshall reported "some of the men having it hand to hand, clubbing their rifles, then dispatching four or five with the bayonet; many taking deadly aim through the forks of trees."[65] As the 10th New York fell back, the First Rifles continued to head south, penetrating the woods so far the that 10th was driven back to the camp, where the 62nd Pennsylvania and Battle Group Skillen were waiting. Battle Group Skillen could see the 5th New York through the woods. They and the 10th New York counterattacked: "At the same time, we charged through the woods, and drove the rebels through the woods, beyond the road."[66] At times it was hand to hand.[67] J.W. Mattison, of the First Rifles, was severely wounded deep in Griffin's Woods. As the First Rifles retreated, the Federals came in and Mattison was left behind the Union line. He chatted with the Yankees, until one demanded his cartridge box at bayonet point. He would have a front-row seat for more fighting on Griffin's Hill.[68]

5th New York Zouaves, on Zouave Hill

Seeing the left wing of the Rifles out in the open, Col. Duryea shouted, "Now men, the time has come; up and do your duty!" Company I, which also had Sharps infantry rifles, scrambled out as skirmishers and opened a devastating volley fire on the left wing of the First Rifles, now only about a hundred yards away. While the Zouaves were unstacking, Company I was hammering with the South Carolinians. Since the Rebels had to stop to shoot, the skirmishers would fire a company volley from their breechloaders, then fall to the ground to avoid the return fire. The Confederates would advance, and the skirmishers would rise up and nail them again. Company I withdrew when the First Rifles came close to charging distance.[69] Captain Partridge of Company I was shot through the heart just as the skirmishers were ordered to retreat, but his killer was paid back with eight bullets in return. When the front was clear, the order rang out, "Advance the Colors, advance the Colors!" The Zouaves charged bayonets[70] and went screaming down the hill.[71]

Lt. Higgins of the First Rifles saw the Zouaves maneuvering and gathered about 30 men, who "poured into the ranks of the Zouaves such a deadly fire as to bring their left to a standstill."[72] The Zouaves saw it differently: "Some of them stood until the Fifth was within thirty yards of them, firing steadily, and with good aim. They were nearly all shot down...."[73] At the same time, the 10th New York had gained the upper hand and was firing at the First Rifles' right wing from Griffin's woods.[74]

Failing to see the 1st Volunteers or the 12th South Carolina, Col. Marshall claimed that he ordered a retreat, but the Zouaves saw them waver, break, and flee for the woods.[75] Col. Marshall led the remnant of the First Rifles to the right, down the McGehee Road to Boatswain's Branch, and reformed his men.[76] A good portion of the 12th South Carolina and 1st Volunteers returned to the woods and kept fighting.[77]

11

Then We Got Down
to Our Knitting

Boatswain's Branch, at the Foot of Zouave Hill

When Branch's North Carolina brigade arrived at New Cold Harbor, it was initially ordered to spread itself from Brigadier Gregg's right to Brigadier J.R. Anderson's left, but immediately ran into the Federals.[1] Brigadier Branch received an order from Powell Hill to send two regiments, the 7th North Carolina and the 28th North Carolina, about 930 men, to the left (north) of the McGehee Road, towards Brigadier Gregg, and to keep his other three regiments in reserve.[2] Branch's lead regiment, the 7th Carolina, went forward into Boatswain's Branch, floundering across a lake, and up the opposite side.[3] The two companies in front as skirmishers immediately ran into their counterparts[4] from the 5th New York Zouaves, who were skirmishing for all of Warren's Brigade. Col. Campbell ordered his own skirmishers out of the way and advanced his regiment to a rail fence.[5] Col. Warren, whose 5th New York was under attack by Gregg's Brigade, moved the 10th New York down into the woods along Boatswain's Branch. Col. Bendix, 10th New York, split his regiment in half, fighting two sets of Rebels with each half, known as a "wing." "The National Zouaves immediately delivered a galling fire upon the Rebels advancing across the field, and at the same time engaged those who were coming through the heavy timber."[6] The left wing in the woods with the 7th North Carolina had it the worst. "The contest in these woods was fierce for a time…. It was the first battle for us…. The color company fired with its front rank kneeling … the fire of the Rebels being simultaneous with our own…."[7] It was soon hand to hand; Private William Williams was run through by a Confederate bayonet.[8] "A forward rush of the Tenth almost cleared the enemy from our own portion of the woods, and now the brigade reformed…."[9]

The Rebels had indeed mostly left the woods. Col. Campbell's seven companies fell back, but his three companies of skirmishers crashed into Col. Lane's 28th North Carolina, claiming that Campbell had ordered a general retreat.[10] Thinking that it applied to his regiment also, Lane's 28th North Carolina marched out of the woods, only to run into Brigadier Branch, who ordered them right back in.[11]

Griffin's Brigade, in Griffin's Woods

After the skirmish fight, the 9th Massachusetts of Griffin's Brigade had rallied, less casualties and stragglers, just behind Boatswain's Branch, in the woods in the corner of the McGehee Road and Boatswain's Branch. The 14th New York was to the 9th's left, and the 4th Michigan to the 14th's left.[12] The 4th Michigan and 8 companies of the of the 14th New York (under Col. McQuade) were along Boatswain's Swamp[13]; two companies of the 14th, under Lt. Col. Skillen, were also on the swamp, but on the north side of Boatswain's Run.[14] The run was wooded, and separated the 4th Michigan and the 14th New York from Griffin's Woods. Augmenting Skillen's men were four companies of Berdan's Sharpshooters, with Sharps infantry rifles.[15] The two companies of the 14th New York and the U.S. Sharpshooters form Battle Group Skillen. The 9th Massachusetts was on Battle Group Skillen's right, and Martin's Battery was to its right and rear, on the Watt House Road, 140 yards from the woods.[16] Griffin's Brigade had about 2,500 infantry, but about 700 of them were south of Boatswain's Run; Griffin's Woods contained about 1,800 infantry.

Branch's Brigade North of the McGehee Road

After meeting Brigadier Branch, Col. Lane marched the 28th North Carolina back down the McGehee Road and was about to wheel them into line facing the 10th New York. Branch personally then hurried to bring up his remaining three regiments to send them down the McGehee Road and turn south into Griffin's Woods. The 37th North Carolina was in the lead,[17] with the 33rd and 18th behind them, in all, about 1,000 men. As the 37th North Carolina reached the east side of the branch and turned south, the 9th Massachusetts opened fire. Col. Lee's 37th broke northwest under this fire, taking the right wing of Col. Lane's 28th North Carolina with it.[18] Lane's left wing men joined Col. Campbell's seven companies and held the ground at the foot of Zouave Hill.[19]

Ewell's Division, Valley Army

Ewell's Division had been ordered forward because Branch was "hard pressed."[20] Brigadier Arnold Elzey's Brigade was first in the line of march and had outdistanced Ewell's other two brigades, those of Trimble and Seymour. General Ewell sent Elzey's men in north of the McGehee Road.[21] "Here we formed in the edge of the woods, behind an old rail-fence, with our right on the road…. Our position was an excellent one, and we held it with but little fighting. In the meantime, our troops, both to the left and right, were more heavily engaged,"[22] recalled French Harding of the 31st Virginia. When the balance of Elzey's men arrived, the 13th Virginia and the 7th North Carolina,[23] Branch's Brigade, were pulled out and went to the Parsons House with Trimble and Seymour, leaving only the 31st Virginia, 44th Virginia, and 58th Virginia near Zouave Hill.[24] These three regiments, about 500 men, fought with Col. Lane's 28th North Carolina, Branch's Brigade, constituting Battle Group Lane.

South of the McGehee Road, in Griffin's Woods, the 33rd North Carolina came up, deployed in line of battle and moved forward. Col. Lee rallied the 37th in Boatswain's Branch and went right back in again. The regiment stopped, and opened fire[25] right into the backs of the 33rd. "When discovering all was not right, we fell back a few yards, reloaded, rallied and fired again.... When becoming better satisfied that all was not right, we fell back about 200 yards to a branch, reloaded and rallied a second time, when a majority fired a third time.... Major [Col.] Cowan of the 33rd North Carolina Regiment came down with outstretched arms, screaming 'Cease firing, cease firing, gentlemen, cease firing,' for we were killing our own men."[26] Col. Lee of the 37th stomped about, "looking more like a maniac or a mad man at the time, than the Honorable Colonel of the Regiment." While the 37th was sorting itself out, the 33rd charged. The 9th Massachusetts fired one volley and broke.[27] The rallied 37th came up[28] and joined the 33rd. Brigadier Branch's last regiment, the ill-fated 18th North Carolina,[29] could not find a passable portion of Boatswain's Branch, and so it headed so far south that it only knew that the balance of the brigade was on its left.[30]

The 9th Massachusetts not only broke, but streamed to the rear in confusion, leaving a gaping hole in the federal line. The left flank of Martin's Battery C, Massachusetts Light Artillery (6 Napoleons) was utterly unprotected from the North Carolinians. Theoretically, if the Confederates drove hard, they could take Martin's Battery from the west and split the Union line at its center, but with only two regiments against all of the supporting Yankees, this was unlikely. Much simpler and more likely was that the North Carolinians would change front south, flank Battle Group Skillen and the 14th New York, and open up a brigade-sized hole in the Union center, through which more Rebels could pour. Lt. Col. Ripley of the U.S. Sharpshooters (Battle Group Skillen) now held Brigadier Griffin's right flank. To save his men, Ripley pulled his own right flank back, lining it up on Martin's Battery in the distance and effectively changing front from west to the northwest.[31] Griffin's Brigade had just been driven off their most advantageous position, the 100-foot-high eastern bank of Boatswain's Branch. Griffin's Woods became no man's land.

The 9th Massachusetts' collapse probably disordered the 62nd Pennsylvania, Griffin's reserve regiment,[32] elevating a crisis to near disaster. Now Griffin's reserve regiment, which was in reserve for precisely such an emergency, was useless. If Branch's men pressed forward, the two regiments, about 600 men, could easily come within sight of the McGehee House and all Griffin could do was have the 4 companies of Battle Group Skillen shoot at them as they passed by.[33] Charles Griffin was an artillery battery commander who had received command of his brigade just 24 hours earlier; he had been a general for about two weeks.[34] Now half of his brigade was in chaos and it had opened a huge hole in the center of the Union line. Griffin sent for help.

2nd Pennsylvania Reserves, South of Griffin's Woods

Brigadier Reynolds responded to Griffin's urgent call. Major E.M. Woodward, who would win the Medal of Honor for capturing over 300 men of the 19th Georgia (Archer's Brigade, Powell Hill's Division) and its battle flag at Fredericksburg in December of 1862, witnessed what happened. "[O]n the double quick they moved to the edge of a heavy swampy woods.... General Reynolds soon rode up and ordered our regiment to advance into the woods, clear it out, and take position on the extreme edge.[35] Col. McCandless not entirely liking the order, asked the General's permission to move in at right angles to the position assigned to us.... The General was silent for a moment, his face bearing an expression of great perplexity and dissatisfaction, when he replied 'Colonel, General Porter is fighting the battle on certain parallels, and his orders will have to be obeyed.'"[36]

The 321 men of the 2nd were to the left and rear of Easton's Battery A, Pennsylvania Light Artillery (4 Napoleons), which was firing northwest, parallel to the 2nd's line; the regiment was posted between Easton's guns and the Watt House. The Rebels were on their left flank, and the 2nd was facing north towards the 5th New York on Zouave Hill. Woodward noted that the regiment was "in a better position to attack our own troops than to inflict damage on the enemy."[37]

Branch's Brigade

The 2nd Pennsylvania Reserves witnessed their own demise: "Steadily the solid columns of the foe were advancing on our left, their leading lines dressed in our uniform, showing no flag, and treacherously crying out they were our friends and not to fire on them.[38] But we were not deceived, and poured into them a left oblique fire with good effect. But onward they pressed until almost upon us when they poured into us a deafening roar of musketry, above which the artillery fire at the time could scarcely be distinguished."[39] The 33rd and 37th North Carolina were within point-blank range for their smoothbore muskets. These fired ammunition known as "buck and ball," three small lead balls and one large one. These muskets were useless beyond 150 yards, but devastating within voice range. Each North Carolina volley sent 2,400 projectiles downrange into McCandless' men. Just then, fire from the 9th Massachusetts and the 62nd Pennsylvania[40] slammed into the 2nd from the rear. It was too much. "Overpowered, flanked, and with the enemy in our rear, with scattered remnants of other regiments in the excitement of the moment firing into us, we broke and were scattered through the woods, fighting the best we could from behind trees, until finally we were headlong out, with our muskets thoroughly heated, and our ammunition almost out."[41] The 2nd rallied 300 yards to the rear near Easton's Battery.[42] It had stopped Branch's Brigade and had allowed Griffin time to rebuild his line. The 9th Massachusetts and 62nd Pennsylvania drove the North Carolinians back "a half a mile."[43]

18th North Carolina and 14th New York,
Near Boatswain's Run

Not much had happened on the front of the 14th New York, so Col. McQuade put out skirmishers and allowed the men to break formation and rest. Lt. Col. Skillen sat on a fallen hemlock tree and chatted with Captain Harrer. Suddenly, the 18th North Carolina appeared from out of nowhere. Utterly surprised, Skillen stood up on the tree and ordered his men to fall in and commence firing. It was too late. The first volley mortally wounded Skillen and Captain Harrer, though the men made it into formation and began firing.[44]

Col. McQuade was just as surprised, and his 8 companies were near panic. McQuade snatched the colors from the color bearer, held them aloft, and shouted, "Rally on the colors, men, I'll stand by you to the last!" His men rallied, and opened fire.[45] The 18th North Carolina's attack was murderous. "All I could hear was 'Oh! Oh! Oh! Oh!' When the brave men were hit by the merciless lead which brought them down." The 14th was losing a man per minute,[46] but it counterattacked, driving the 18th back.[47] The U.S. Sharpshooters, experts at skirmishing and scouting, joined in, noting with curiosity that "the affair lost its character as a picket fight and partook of the nature of line of battle fighting."[48]

Branch's Brigade

The North Carolinians slowly retreated, and the Northerners pressed forward, the lines about 150 yards apart, to a very slight ridge that ran roughly north and south through the center of Griffin's Woods. Branch's Brigade had shot its bolt, losing about 20 percent of its men. The 33rd North Carolina suffered only 30 casualties or so[49];

The uniform coat that Lt. Col Skillen wore at Gaines' Mill. Note the damage to the elbow (courtesy Shiloh Relics, Savannah, Tennessee).

the 18th North Carolina lost 68 in this one battle, out of about 389 engaged, or about 17 percent, and felt blessed at that amount.[50] The 37th North Carolina was still organized and ready for another go, but by the end of the day, would lose about 23 percent of its men.[51]

The attack had alarmed the Federals. Half of a fresh brigade had broken, as had the regiment sent to the rescue. With the rest of Sykes' and Morell's lines holding their own, Griffin's Hill was the weak point. A regiment that broke once was more likely to break again. Brigadier Seymour's 9th and 10th Pennsylvania Reserves were called out of reserve to reinforce Griffin's Woods. It was a prudent move, as Dorsey Pender's Brigade of North Carolinians was reinforcing Brigadier Branch.

12

Column After Column
Melts Away Like Smoke

Between Powhite and Boatswain's Creeks

While the other brigades of Powell Hill's Division were throwing themselves at the Regulars and Griffin's Woods, J.R. Anderson's Georgians, Field's Virginians, and Archer's Tennessee Brigade attacked near the Parsons House. General Longstreet technically honored his word to Powell Hill about a diversion, by sending one regiment of Pryor's Brigade.[1]

J.R. Anderson's brigade consisted of the 14th, 35th, 45th and 49th Georgia, and the 3rd Louisiana Battalion, about 2500 men. Field's Brigade consisted of the 40th, 47th, 55th, 60th Virginia, and the 22nd Virginia Battalion, but only had about 1,000 men. The 40th Virginia was under the command of Col. J.W. Brockenbrough, whose sister, Judith Brockenbrough, had received the lurid letters about Rush's Lancers and other Yankee depredations. Brigadier James A. Archer was an unlikely candidate for command of a Tennessee brigade. A Virginian, his appointment to the 55th Virginia (now in Field's brigade next door) had miscarried, but in May of 1862, Brigadier Hatton of the Tennessee Brigade was killed at Seven Pines/Fair Oaks, and Archer was raised to command it.[2] His brigade, about 1100 men, consisted of three Tennessee Regiments (1st, 7th, and 14th), the 19th Georgia, and the 5th Alabama Battalion.[3] Brigadier Pryor moved his whole brigade up, but actually sent only the 14th Louisiana.[4]

Anderson, Archer, and Pryor formed the first line, with Field behind Anderson. J.R. Anderson probably formed his men in two lines. The 45th Georgia was on the left flank, the 35th Georgia on the right flank,[5] with the 14th Georgia in the center. The 49th and 3rd Louisiana Battalion were in a second line. Behind them, Field's men formed in two lines, the 47th Virginia and the 40th Virginia in the first, the 55th Virginia and 22nd Virginia Battalion in the second, with the 60th Virginia behind as a reserve.[6]

For once that day, a Confederate attack had artillery support. The battered remnant of Pegram's Purcell Artillery (four Napoleons), attached to Pender's Brigade, went into battery in a garden at New Cold Harbor[7] and opened fire. Braxton's Fredericksburg Artillery was near Dr. Gaines' Mansion "on a little rise." "Right back of our position was an old ditch which had washed out a channel 3 or 4 feet deep and whose banks were overgrown with sassafras bushes."[8] Captain M'Comb, 14th Tennessee, recalled Braxton's fire on the enemy to his front.[9] Andrews' First Maryland Artillery was "on the banks of a stream, playing over the heads of our infantry as they advanced to the assault." "During this time, our guns were playing on the enemy's batteries and supports of reserve infantry."[10]

The Tennesseans formed their line in an apple orchard[11] on the east side of Powhite Creek[12] near Braxton's guns.[13] For this attack, Archer kept the 19th Georgia in reserve, and put the rest of the brigade in one line. Apparently the 5th Alabama Battalion was in the center of the brigade[14] with the 7th on its left and the 1st and 14th on its right (south).[15]

Martindale's Brigade, Along Boatswain's Creek

Anderson, Field, and Archer, about 4,500 men, were attacking what was probably the most heavily defended portion of the Union line. It was held by the southern half of Griffin's Brigade, the 14th New York and the 4th Michigan, and the northern half of Martindale's Brigade, the 2nd Maine and 13th New York, with the 22nd Massachusetts in support, about 2,500 men. Only the 13th New York was in the ravine bottom; the rest were "up top," shooting across the ravine. The 22nd Massachusetts probably had longer-range Enfield rifles. Both the 4th Michigan and the 2nd Maine, about 1000 men, were armed with smoothbore muskets that fired "buck and ball," and tripled a unit's short-range firepower. The brutal arithmetic of smoothbore combat dictates that each time they fired, 4,000 projectiles went downrange. If just 1 percent hit, then 40 targets were rendered *hors de combat* with each volley. Firing every two minutes, assuming ammunition held out, 1,000 men firing buck and ball could expect 1200 hits over one hour's time.

All of the Federals except the 14th New York had breastworks. The 4th Michigan "built up breastworks of logs rails & bales of hay[,] Cos A & F had a first rate one of bales of hay … our breastworks did good service."[16] The 22nd Massachusetts "strengthened our position by felling great pines and constructing with them and smaller trees a barricade."[17] Capt. Sampson of the same regiment noted that the barricade was augmented with fence rails.[18] The 13th New York's barricade "protected the men very much."[19] Behind the barricades and the infantry was artillery support from two guns, Lt. Bucklin's Section of Weeden's Battery C, Rhode Island Light Artillery (6 ordnance rifles), firing through that gap in the woods that Brigadier Martindale found that morning. It was arguably Beaver Dam Creek all over again, but without as much artillery.

Anderson's and Field's Brigades

Anderson's line charged through the woods at the double-quick.[20] The Georgians met a blast of fire 100 yards from the Union line that stopped them cold, and they opened fire.[21] Field's front line opened fire, as did his second, seemingly elevated above his first by the slope of the hill. They were not as elevated as they thought, as either the 55th or the 22nd Battalion killed or wounded some in the 47th; the front line had to lie down to load.[22] The 14th Georgia was apparently directly in front of Bucklin's guns, as its "advance was stopped by a rain of cannon shot."[23] Bucklin's first shot was aimed at a Confederate flag; the second shot dropped it. "Our artillery mowed them down like grass and slaughter heaped on high its weltering ranks."[24] Captain Weeden, the battery commander, was less sanguinary in his description, saying that Bucklin's fire of shrapnel and shell[25] were "bursting in the enemy's line as they appeared on the crest beyond the ravine." It was too much: "[I]n a moment or two, unable to stand the deadly fire to which it was subjected, [the 14th] gave way and fell back, breaking through the supporting column of Field, throwing his line into temporary disorder."[26] The Georgians broke, which disordered Field's Brigade, and they fell back, too.[27]

Anderson's men retreated right over Field's Brigade back to the safety of Virginia Hill. "Just at this critical moment… [My] attention was attracted to a general officer, of commanding figure, who was moving along the broken line endeavoring to rally his men and exhorting them to stand firm. Seizing the colors of one of the regiments, he planted them near the crest of the hill, and by entreaty and example soon gathered around it the more intrepid of his command."[28] General Anderson led his men forward twice more, only to be driven back twice more.[29] The 35th Georgia stayed put, but finding that the rest of its brigade and Archer had fallen back, it, too fell back behind Virginia Hill.[30]

Archer's Brigade

From Powhite Creek, Archer started moving his men slowly forward to Virginia Hill, where Field joined him. Then he gave the command "Right Shoulder Shift, Charge!"[31] toward the Union line, 600 yards away behind the Parsons House. The Tennesseans raised the Rebel yell and "charged the enemy in his stronghold."[32] When Field's men reached the Parsons House, their lines disintegrated, but they reformed on the other side of it[33]; they now lagged behind Archer's Brigade, advancing on its right.[34] "The artillery and musketry opened on us from every quarter as soon as we came into range. The roar was deafening and furious; men fell on all sides, but the line pressed forward." Sgt. Wrenn of the 5th Alabama Battalion was shot in the chest. As he told a comrade to keep advancing, a ball entered his brain and killed him.[35]

When the Tennesseans were 150 yards from the Federals, they opened fire[36] in response to "a fire that nothing could live under."[37] Since Archer's men were closer, the Federals concentrated their fire on them.[38] Presently, Brigadier Archer's men began to waver, so Archer himself rode out in front and yelled to his men, "Follow me!" Inspired, the men broke into a charge headed for the ravine.[39] Inside the Union abatis, twenty steps from the ravine,[40] they found that the banks of Boatswain's Branch here are very steep, making about a 40-foot cliff, rather than a hill, on either side. If they went down into the gorge and had to fall back, they would be slaughtered as they tried to climb back out. Archer's men stopped on the west side of the ravine in place and attempted to trade firepower through the woods with Martindale's more numerous men.

Color Bearer Ledbetter, 5th Alabama Battalion, was wounded in the hip, dropped the battalion's colors, and tried to limp back to safety. Then another ball hit his wrist and tore off his thumb. As he looked back to see if the Yankees were coming to get him, he was hit a third time, nicking his chin. Unfortunately, he was going the wrong way, and fell into the ravine. Another soldier helped him out, and he crawled back 600 yards to Powhite Creek.[41] The color bearer of the 1st Tennessee was not so lucky; the 13th New York captured that regiment's flag and took prisoners from every regiment in Archer's brigade.[42] Brigadier Archer says his men fell back of their own accord, but had they not done so he would have so ordered.[43] Unsupported and heavily outnumbered, Archer fell back behind Virginia Hill, more or less in the open, lay down, reorganized, and waited. In the meantime, Field's men had gone to ground and were holding the line when Brigadier Field ordered them to retreat. This was "not very well executed,"[44] according to Brigadier Field. In fact, his brigade broke and streamed to the rear.

14th Louisiana, Pryor's Brigade

As the 14th Louisiana crested the hill between Powhite and Boatswain's Creeks, it "drew upon itself a heavy fire of musketry."[45] It also prompted fire from those heavy Union batteries across the river.[46] The whole exercise revealed what Pryor already knew: "I found him [the enemy] to be in very great force."[47] To Butterfield's Brigade, along Boatswain's Creek, it looked like a full-scale assault in concert with the Rebels hitting Martindale and Griffin to the north.[48] Butterfield called up one gun of Hyde's Battery E, Massachusetts Light Artillery (6 ordnance rifles) and it began shelling Pryor's men.[49] The 44th New York and the 83rd Pennsylvania opened fire at about 200 yards, staggering Pryor's men, and driving them back.[50]

The Yankees did not think much of this particular attack. Divisional commander General Morell said merely that it was "repulsed." Brigadier Griffin and his regiments hardly even noticed it. Brigadier Martindale remarked that the Rebels returned his first fire at long range, tried to hold the hilltop, then fell back, out of reach.[51] From the reserve position of the 22nd Massachusetts, above and behind Martindale's other regiments, the Confederates "broke and ran back to the cover of the woods,"[52] and "but few lived to tell the tale."[53] Brigadier Martindale had at least some anxiety about this attack, as he sent to Brigadier Butterfield for help. The 12th New York and 16th Michigan arrived from Butterfield's brigade, alas, too late to assist.[54]

Each of J.R. Anderson's Georgia regiments lost about 25 percent. Field's front line regiments (40th and 47th Virginia) both lost over 25 percent; the 60th Virginia lost 14 percent; and the 55th Virginia lost only 5 percent. It would rally and join in a later attack.[55] Archer's brigade had taken a beating. The Tennesseans lost the bulk of their 320 (29 percent) casualties in this attack.

Confederate Headquarters, New Cold Harbor

Powell Hill's Division had shot its bolt, but had set the stage for final victory. As they hunkered down behind any available cover, the men of Jackson's Valley Army would take over the effort and with it most of the glory. To stop Powell Hill, Griffin and Martindale's men had fired off a good portion of their ammunition. This created two problems. First, Martindale's men were approaching the point where they would have to be replaced for want of bullets. Second, their muskets were becoming fouled from the powder residue and took longer to load. From this point on, Brigadier Martindale's firepower would decrease as his men ran out of ammunition or took more time to fire what they had. Rather than bringing ammunition up, the practice at this time was to replace whole regiments as they ran out. This is not as bizarre as it may sound. Ammunition was supplied in 1000-round boxes, each weighing about 100 pounds; to resupply 400 men with only 40 cartridges each would take 16 boxes of explosives, which if ignited by any of the hot metal flying through the air would be devastating. Adding to the problem is that many regiments had two companies with rifles and 8 companies with smoothbores, both of various calibers. Replacing the whole unit was easier, but it created confusion and removed a large part of the available firepower until the two formations could switch positions. As the afternoon wore on, this procedure would result in disaster.

13

A Dense Woods
and an Ugly Marsh

Seymour's Louisiana Brigade, Ewell's Division, Near Beulah Church

After giving his orders to Quartermaster Major Harman, and speaking to Major Wheat, Jackson rode to New Cold Harbor to meet with Lee, probably down the Ellyson Road. In the interim, Col. Walter Taylor, of Lee's staff, had ridden up to Ewell with orders from General Lee to attack.[1] Clearly, Lee knew where to send an aide to give orders to the Valley Army.

Fourth Alabama Regiment, Law's Brigade, Whiting's Division, on the Carleton Road

About 2:00, Whiting's Division had been resting in the road for over an hour. While lying in the road, "a splendidly equipped ambulance drawn by a find pair of bays came driving slowly through the regiment in the direction we were marching." Recognizing the Confederate flag, the [Irish Yankee] driver inopportunely inquired, "Who be you?" He was instantly mobbed by the men looking for eatables. Sergeant Parker shared with Pvt. R.T. Coles a "cap full of nice, ripe, red currants … and no two soldiers ever enjoyed a more refreshing repast." The driver had been out in the country foraging for the headquarters mess.[2]

Elsewhere on the Carleton Road

Fannie Gaines Tinsley, Mrs. Gaines, the baby, and the nurse separated from the group, and fled slowly north from Ellyson's into the woods. While the far woods were being shelled "all the time," they came upon a lone Confederate at a spring, and the astonished soldier asked, "Where did you come from?" The women told him that had been behind McClellan's lines for six weeks. The soldier replied that he was one of Stonewall Jackson's men, who were all at the top of the hill. Fannie recollected, "When we got up there, we found ourselves in the midst of the whole army." An officer rode up, and, finding three women and a baby in the middle of the army, also inquired as to where they had come from. The ladies recounted the six weeks again. The officer advised them to move on, or the men would smother them with questions. A servant came up to take the nurse through the lines, and he did. An officer escorted the two women and the baby up the Carleton Road, away from the fighting.[3]

With the Valley Army, on the Carleton Road

After running his errand, the Rev. Major Dabney was still anxious about Harman in the first place, and not hearing any 12,000 men entering the battle, realized that he could not quickly find Jackson and bring the absence to his attention. He took it upon himself to see what had happened: "But no matter, I did not take a commission to get favor or promotion, but to do some good for my bleeding country … this battle will not be lost for red tape's sake, if I am cashiered tomorrow morning…." Dabney rode back up the Carleton Road.

Sure enough, the rest of the Valley Army was resting in place. When he found Whiting, Dabney inquired if Harman had come. Whiting, who also had a dim view of Harman, replied in a surly tone, "That man Harman has been here, with a farrago of which I could understand nothing." Dabney asked, "[D]id he tell you that it was the general's wish you engage the enemy immediately?" "No," replied Whiting, "just the opposite, that I was to await further instructions, and you see I am waiting." Dabney gave him Jackson's now stale orders, and rode off before Whiting could "cavil." Dabney found that the other commanders had gotten the same botched order, and got them moving.

Whiting's Division, on the Carleton Road

According to Dabney, sorting out the Harman mess had taken two hours.[4] General Whiting says he got the word at 3:00.[5] Brigadier Hood says that he *arrived* at the battlefield between 4:00 and 5:00 p.m.[6] Brigadier Evander Law says that his men arrived "by 5 o'clock."[7] Whiting's Division consisted of two brigades. Brigadier John Bell Hood commanded the Texas Brigade, the 1st, 4th, 5th Texas, the 18th Georgia and the Hampton Legion[8] Infantry, about 2,100 men. Whiting's other brigade was under Evander Law, who commanded the 2nd and 11th Mississippi regiments, the 4th Alabama, and the 6th North Carolina, about 1,900 men. The Rev. Major Dabney must have imparted some sense of urgency to Whiting, as the 6th North Carolina dropped its knapsacks[9] and his brigades double-quicked[10] towards the firing.[11]

Nevertheless, progress was slow though "underbrush, swamps, quagmires, etc."[12] They marched through fields, crossing creeks, climbing hills, and "finally wad[ing] a swamp about 100 yards wide and waist deep in mud and water.[13] The "waist deep lagoon"[14] must have been a new experience, as three members of the 4th Texas, and one of the Hampton Legion, specifically mention the depth.[15] This was probably the Gaines' Mill millpond. Law's 4th Alabama passed through "General Porter's" camp, "with everything intact, tents, officers' tables and other camp furniture standing as if it was their intention to return after a temporary absence."[16] Pvt. Hankins, 2nd Mississippi, remembered that they were out of water and none was available.[17] Before going through the swamp, Capt. Robbins delivered a prayer to the kneeling 4th Alabama, as was their custom.[18]

As they neared the fighting, they came under federal artillery fire. "The grape and canister were coming thick and fast, and it seemed as though those screaming, shrieking shells bursting around us would never stop. We ran down a hill, then waded a sluggish stream that was waist deep to me, and I held up my cartridge box in order to keep my ammunition dry. Beyond the stream we climbed its back, then crossed an old field, and were halted behind a skirt of woods."[19] "Louder and fiercer it grew until it really seemed as if heaven and earth were coming together," although it caused no casualties in the 18th Georgia.[20] The Texans were not so fortunate. In the 4th Texas, "a fellow's head was smashed" and his brains scattered on his comrades near him. In the 5th Texas, two men in front of Pvt. Fletcher were slowing things down by "dodging and stooping" at every crash. Fletcher spoke harshly to them and finally told them to straighten up, that Yankee shells that would miss in front would take off their heads when stooping. Seconds later just that happened.[21] In the 11th Mississippi, shot and shell were passing through the ranks. When they stopped to catch their breath, some lay flat, some squatted. Pvt. Chambers was squatting 10 feet from a Texan, when a cannonball hit the Texan's head and took it off; the head hit another man, covering the man, his gun, and his blanket with gore.[22]

Trimble's Brigade, Ewell's Division, Passing Through New Cold Harbor

As the 15th Alabama of Trimble's Brigade passed, Private McClendon saw Generals Lee and Jackson meeting at a nearby house.[23] McClendon remembered the event because it was the first time he had ever seen General Lee. The meeting was again the cause of jubilation. "The two soldiers shook hands in the midst of tumultuous cheering from the troops...."[24]

The conversation between General Lee and the Hero of the Valley is lost to history, and as such has created more myths. One myth is that at this meeting Lee asked Jackson if the latter's men could stand the vicious fighting that was being heard. Jackson is alleged to have replied, "They can stand anything; they can stand that." This exchange was first recorded by Judith McGuire at 10:00 p.m. on the night of June 27, 1862, having been reported to her by General Thomas Jefferson Chambers, a Texas land speculator and ne'er-do-well who was then an aide to John Bell Hood, of Whiting's Division. According to Chambers, Jackson's alleged reply was, "General, I know our boys, they will never give back," meaning that they would not allow the Yankees to drive them back.

By 1867, John Esten Cooke, J.E.B. Stuart's ordnance officer, and by then a writer of turgid "Lost Cause" prose and treacly Southern romances, reworked this episode into "They can stand that," even though he was not present at the conversation.[25] Unfortunately, in his 1867 book, Cooke added to this anecdote by claiming that when Jackson rode up, Lee said "'I am very glad to see you, I had hoped you had been with us before.' Jackson made a twitching movement of his head, and replied in a few words, rather jerked from the lips than deliberately uttered."[26] The source of this addition is a mystery. If this additional conversation ever happened, Jackson probably replied that he had been a bit busy arranging Harvey Hill's 10,000 men and getting his own 12,000 reinforcements up, jerking his head in those two directions. Nevertheless, this is the probable source of the "Jackson was late" myth.

At their meeting, Jackson certainly informed Lee that he had ordered the whole Valley Army at the Federals, and his reasons why. Lee probably concurred; if Powell Hill needed help so quickly, it was abundantly clear that the Yankees were not going to fold up easily for a "side blow." One of the two decided that Harvey Hill could be thrown in, too. The Beaver Dam Creek fiasco[27] and Powell Hill's attack were difficult bloody lessons, but had taught a valuable lesson. Attacks by brigades, and even combinations of brigades, had not worked. This time combinations of *divisions* would attack.

As Lee noted in his report, "The principal part of the Federal Army was now north of the Chickahominy."[28] He was not far wrong. A lot of ink has been spilled about McClellan's 100,000-man army. However, in 1870, Surgeon General of the Army Joseph K. Barnes commissioned a medical history of the war, as an aid to future army medical management. Part of this study was determining the disease rate of the troops, which was broken down by campaign. For each campaign, each illness was classified, such as epidemic catarrh and orchitis,[29] the number of cases of all diseases counted, and compared to army strength by month, all based on the official military records. For the month of June 1862, McClellan's Army had a strength of about 76,000 men, 15,000 of whom were ill. If the 15,000 were unfit for duty, McClellan only had about 61,000 effectives total.[30] Even without this data, Lee realized that about a third of the Federal army was north of the Chickahominy. This was the decisive battle. If Porter could be crushed today, the war could be over, just as Cornwallis' surrender in 1781 had effectively ended that war.[31] Longstreet and Harvey Hill were at hand. The Valley Army was close at hand. Get them all moving. Send every fresh man and gun forward; attack the enemy wherever found, break his lines, and cut off the Yankees at the Grapevine Bridge before nightfall.[32]

After the 4:00 meeting, an august personage arrived at Lee's headquarters. Austin Dobbins, of the 16th Mississippi, Trimble's Brigade, saw General Lee meeting with President Jefferson Davis. When Davis saw that the 16th was from his home state, he shouted, "Hurrah for Ole Missisip!"[33] But something was amiss. Trimble's men, including Private McClendon, were the trail brigade of Ewell's Division, but the rest of the Valley Army had not shown up yet.

Near Gaines' Mill

Whiting's men debouched from the woods under artillery fire about halfway between Gaines' Mill and the Ingraham House at New Cold Harbor. There, Brigadier Law himself noticed a battery "at the edge of the field, badly cut to pieces and silent." Indeed, there was no Confederate artillery then in action on that part of the field.[34] This was Crenshaw's battery, which had been withdrawn from New Cold Harbor.[35] General Whiting himself was deluged with supplicants from diverse commands begging for assistance.[36] Whiting ignored them, and headed toward New Cold Harbor. There he saw Brigadier Trimble, and asked him where his troops should go. Trimble "strongly advised" Whiting to go in half a mile to the right (south); disorganized troops were "confusing" the McGehee Road area.[37]

About 4:30, General Whiting and Brigadier Hood met General Lee.[38] Private Hamby, 4th Texas, recalled:

> [A] conference was held between Gens. Lee, Whiting and Hood, which ended by Lee and Whiting riding rapidly away. In a short while Gen Lee returned and ... inquired of General Hood, who was only a short distance from us.... He at once saluted Gen. Lee, who said that the efforts to break the enemy's line in front of us had been unsuccessful and that it was of the utmost importance to do so. Gen. Hood replied "We will do it." As Gen. Lee turned his horse to ride away, he lifted his hat and said "May God be with you."[39]

Hood's version was similar; he "arrived about 4:30 p. m. at the Telegraph road ... here I found General Lee seated upon his horse. He rode forward to me and extending his usual greeting announced to me that our troops had been fighting gallantly, but had not succeeded in dislodging the enemy; he added: 'This must be done. Can you break his line?' I replied that I would try."[40]

Pvt. Crozier observed some discussion of taking an annoying set of Union guns: "All at once I saw General Hood ride at a gallop from a group of officers out into an opening on our right.... [Hood said to Lee] I can take that battery with my old regiment."[41] General Jackson arrived, and Judge Stevens floridly described the meeting between Generals Jackson, Whiting, and Hood.

> The immortal Stonewall, mounted upon his trusty sorrel, shoots by like a flying meteor, his countenance emitting a blaze of glory. He seems a very war god transformed as by magic from a tired awkward looking cavalryman of the ranks, to a very personification of a man born to command; to lead men over every obstacle and drive before him every opposition. The flashing eye, the erect form, the firmly set mouth and the determined expression which lit up his countenance can only be imagined, never described by mortal pen. The impulse of his men is to cheer him. A gentle wave of his hand and we forebear. "Genl. Hood, wheel your men into line and prepare for action."[42]

Capt. Owens, 4th Texas, inspired his men by reciting from Sir Walter Scott's poem, *Marmion*.[43]

Lawton's Brigade, on the Walnut Grove–Bethesda Church Road

The Rev. Major Dabney was not the only one anxious about the Valley Army. After putting his division in, Ewell had ridden back to New Cold Harbor to lead in reinforcements, and sent Campbell Brown[44] to find Lawton; Brown found Brigadier Lawton.[45] A member of the 31st Georgia recalled, "The day was clear and warm, and our officers kept us on the move at 'quick time' until afternoon, when a staff officer, who had ridden forward returned and informed our general that the engagement had been in progress all the morning; that General Lee so far had made no impression on the enemy's works and had gotten the worst of the day's fighting, and to bring his men to the front at 'double quick' as we were needed there."[46] Lawton pushed his men forward at a trot.[47]

Lawton's command had started north from Georgia in early June with about 6,000 men,[48] but now were down to about 3,500.[49] By June 12 they were in Lynchburg, Virginia, where Private William Wilkinson was happy the find that the brigade was joining Stonewall Jackson: "[H]e is fighting nearly every day and never gets whipped.... He marches his men nearly all the time and when he gets into a fight he knows how to manage them."[50] On June 17, Lawton had met General Jackson, and noted, "I have six Georgia regiments and a Virginia battery, the largest brigade in the field anywhere in the

Confederate States. I have seen a good deal of 'Stonewall' Jackson and my impressions of him do not differ from what I expected—great energy and will without much system—capable of any amount of endurance, he is rather indifferent to the comfort of his troops, they are broken down very fast—he is silent and mysterious."[51] When Lawton's men arrived at Staunton, "there was a great pile of new Springfield muskets that had been left on the numerous battlefields by the federals and picked up by our men, and we were told to exchange our old guns for these.[52] Lawton's Brigade was larger than Ewell's three brigades, and only a little smaller than Whiting's Division of two brigades. On the march east, they "were packed in box cars like sardines...."[53] On the march to Ashland, the officers were pushing them to the limit and keeping every man in ranks, except those who went for water.[54]

Lawton says he received orders to cut cross-country at 5:00.[55] Col. Griffin, 26th Georgia, says he started at 4:30.[56] Capt. Battey, 38th Georgia,[57] says he started running at "about 5 o'clock." Col. Douglass of the 13th Georgia[58] says he arrived at the fighting at 5:00, as does Berry of the 60th Georgia.[59] While his stragglers caught up and caught their breath[60] near New Cold Harbor, one asked an old gentleman who looked like a preacher (probably Mr. Magee), "Old man, how far is it to hell?" The man responded, "My dear sir, I am afraid you will find out pretty soon."[61] Brigadier Lawton himself and Campbell Brown, Ewell's aide, went to New Cold Harbor for orders.[62]

It was the first time Campbell Brown had ever seen General Lee. He was sitting on his magnificent gray horse, Traveller, at New Cold Harbor. He ordered Brigadier Lawton to stay in reserve for the time being.[63] Campbell Brown went down the McGehee Road to find General Ewell.

Lawton's Brigade

Brigadier Lawton's double-quick dash cross-country had exhausted the men, so he stopped them for a rest while he went for orders. A member of the 38th Georgia recalled, "We halted and stacked arms and enjoyed a short rest in a pine thicket just out of range of the shot and shell. We saw Lee and Jackson on a little knoll with their field glasses scanning the front and the field generally. With them was General [J.R.] Jones ... also General Lawton.... They seemed to be consulting and seemed anxious and uneasy. Suddenly they seemed to have come to some decision, for they separated, and Captain Lawton ... called for the 31st and 38th Georgia regiments ... we marched some distance through a thicket."[64] The 31st and 38th Georgia, under *Captain* Edward Payson Lawton (the general's adjutant and brother) now became Battle Group Georgia; they moved down the McGehee Road from New Cold Harbor toward the fighting.

Brigadier Lawton, with the other four regiments (Lawton's Brigade) went in another direction. "Having no knowledge of the local geography, and failing to find any staff officer who could direct me at what point I should enter the fight, two regiments standing in an open field were pointed out to me as having just retired from the woods, whence the enemy had driven them. I at once moved by the flank through the interval between these regiments, promptly formed line of battle, and accepted for my brigade the position which they had abandoned."[65]

Winder's Division, on the Carleton Road

Carvel Hall, another of Ewell's aides, found Winder and ordered him to leave the road. Capt. McHenry Howard, on Winder's staff, thought it odd that one of Ewell's aides would be giving orders to Winder, as only Jackson and Lee were above Winder in the chain of command.[66] Hall went to the rest of the Winder's Brigades and ordered them south, too.[67] Brigadier Winder says he received the order between 4 and 5 p.m.[68] Winder's Division fragmented, too. Winder and the Stonewall Brigade waited for Lawton's men to pass,[69] and then headed due south. When they reached the Ellyson Road, they turned southeast, winding up at New Cold Harbor,[70] but were sent to Old Cold Harbor. Fulkerson's and Cunningham's Brigades just followed Lawton, but were blocked by the troops in front, and were the last to arrive on the battlefield.[71] Fulkerson's and Cunningham's Brigades followed General Whiting towards General Longstreet's men, but in doing so Fulkerson lost the 1st Virginia Battalion, which joined the Stonewall Brigade.[72]

Harvey Hill's Division, Near Old Cold Harbor

Harvey Hill's division was brought out of its position east of the Beulah Church Road to Boatswain's Branch to extend the line from Gregg's Brigade east.[73] Once again, Boatswain's Branch had its effect. "In advancing we had a dense swamp to cross, with tangled undergrowth … [which] produced much confusion and a lapping of brigades and the separation of regiments from their proper places."[74] The left of the division was most affected, as they came in more or less on top of the remnants of Gregg's Brigade. Brigadier Ripley, "while searching for position,"[75] on the far left of the division, lost the pitiful remnant of the 44th Georgia,[76] who had been slaughtered at Beaver Dam Creek the day before. Ripley found "some portion" of other Confederate troops, and the 48th Georgia was squeezed out of line, and ultimately sent to assist R.H. Anderson, way over in Longstreet's area.[77] These other Confederate troops were the relatively intact 14th South Carolina,[78] the remnants of the 13th South Carolina,[79] and the remnants of the 12th South Carolina.[80] Since these acted in concert with Col. McGowan's 14th South Carolina, this group will be known as Battle Group McGowan. Battle Group Lane was to the right of Battle Group McGowan, along Boatswain Branch with its right on the McGehee Road.

Colquitt's Brigade, on Ripley's left (east), also disintegrated. The 23rd Georgia, 28th Georgia, and 13th Alabama never made it out of Boatswain's Branch.[81] Brigadier Rodes had similar problems. "[U]pon emerging from the swamp and striking the field beyond, three of my regiments 5th, 12th, and 26th were found on the left [east] and behind [G.B.] Anderson's brigade, which was in front of us." The 3rd and 6th Alabama were on G.B. Anderson's right.[82] Further on, the 3rd Alabama stacked up behind yet another regiment[83] where they did not fire a shot, but heroically "remained firm as a rock amid surging billows."[84] The 6th Alabama fared better; it passed the 3rd and went on alone.[85] G.B. Anderson's Brigade, leading the division, made it more or less intact through Boatswain's Branch, as did Garland's North Carolinians.[86]

Longstreet's Division, Near Dr. Gaines' Mansion

General Longstreet's Division had arrived on the field shortly after noon, and he had decided that the Federal position was at best impregnable, and at worst a death trap.[87] When Powell Hill asked for help, Longstreet sent out only one regiment from his whole division, which he claimed was acting as a reserve.[88]

Longstreet's 9,500-man division had been divided in two.[89] The larger portion, Battle Group Pickett, was led by Brigadier Pickett, who would achieve fame in Pennsylvania a year hence. This group also contained Richard H. Anderson's South Carolina Brigade and Kemper's Virginia Brigade. It is named for Pickett because his men led the attack, and Richard H. Anderson's brigade was split up. This portion contained about 4,964 men.

Brigadier Wilcox commanded the other half of the division, a three-brigade battle group consisting of his own (Alabama), Featherston's Mississippi, and Pryor's multistate. This part of the division, about 4,537 men, had arrived first, and were near Dr. Gaines' Mansion while Powell Hill's men were crossing at Dr. Gaines' Mill, to the north.[90] Pryor's brigade had been first in the line of march,[91] and so had deployed to cover the arrival of the rest of the Division. It had battled Butterfield's skirmishers all afternoon,[92] and had pushed them back across Powhite Creek and over Florida Hill.[93] Brigadiers Wilcox and Featherston, in that order, began arriving late in the afternoon and were safely ensconced in the gorge of Powhite Creek.

With General Longstreet at the Gaines' Mansion

At 5:00 or so, Longstreet received Capt. Mason,[94] who bore a message from General Lee imploring Longstreet to get moving, "or the day was lost."[95] Longstreet passed the word to Battle Groups Wilcox and Pickett to make an attack. Battle Group Pickett was to send two regiments to drive in the Federal skirmishers[96]; Battle Group Wilcox was to send one. The former's contribution to the action consisted of the 8th and 18th Virginia regiments in skirmish order, who did little or nothing but provoke a violent response from across the creek.[97] The 2nd Florida (Pryor's Brigade), on the other hand, stormed over Florida Hill, and "drew upon itself a heavy fire of musketry." This time, their attack was so furious that Brigadier Butterfield used all four of his regiments,[98] aided by the heavy guns across the river.[99] Finally wrecked after several hours of skirmishing and the attack across the open field, the 2nd Florida fell back into Powhite Creek.[100] It had lost almost a quarter of its men.[101] When the battered Floridians returned, they found the rest of the battle group preparing for the big assault. Since the attack with Archer earlier in the afternoon was the "diversion," Longstreet called this second one a "feint," as he had just received Lee's order to attack.[102]

In response to Longstreet's order, Brigadier Wilcox formed his men behind Florida Hill. Wilcox's Alabama Brigade, 1,850 men, was closest to the Chickahominy in two lines, facing east, the 10th on the left and the 11th on the right. In the second line, the 8th was behind the 10th, and the 9th behind the 11th. To the Alabamians' left, Pryor formed his 1,400 men in one line,[103] with 14th Louisiana near Wilcox, then the 14th Alabama and 3rd Virginia, with Coppens' Zouaves on the end.[104] Behind and between the two front brigades, Brigadier Featherston's 917 men were formed in one line.

Brigadier Pickett's Battle Group consisted of three brigades. His own was made up of Virginians, and held the 8th, 18th, 19th, 28th and 56th Virginia regiments, about 2,400 men. Several hundred yards behind Pickett's Brigade was Kemper's Brigade, more Virginians in the 1st, 7th, 11th, 17th and 24th regiments, about 1,469 men. Between these two lines was the South Carolina Brigade, which had suddenly come down with "bomb ague." C.B. Fleet, of the Braxton's Fredericksburg Artillery recounted:

> [R.H. Anderson's] brigade disappeared in this ditch for protection, the only men visible being the General and his staff officers who were all mounted and had to stand it. One man of his staff attracted my attention by his apparent fright. He was white as a sheet and was the most frightened looking man I ever saw. Finally, after the arrival of other reinforcements, orders were given to form line of battle for a charge. Gen Anderson called out "Fall in my brave boys!" Not a man stirred. Again he called out "South Carolina to the rescue! Fall in, men!" Still no men appeared. The General, very mad and excited pulled out his pistol and yelled "Get out of this ditch or I'll shoot every last man of you!" and called on his staff to bring the men out. They came out then, joined in the line of battle and went forward and did splendid work.[105]

The 2nd South Carolina Rifles, the 6th South Carolina, and 4th South Carolina Battalion, 545 men, formed line of battle between Pickett and Kemper. The other half, 550 men in the 5th South Carolina and the Palmetto Sharpshooters (under Col. Jenkins), was banished to the river valley to protect the whole division's flank (Battle Group Jenkins).[106] By the time the 2nd Florida limped back to Powhite Creek, Battle Group Wilcox was ready to go,[107] but Battle Group Pickett was not. The former would go when they heard firing to the north.[108]

Just at this point, about 6:15 p.m., General Whiting met Longstreet and asked where to be put in.[109] Whiting formed his division on Battle Group Pickett's left while Longstreet rode to Battle Group Pickett.[110]

South of the Chickahominy River, Confederate General John Magruder was watching the battle. From his vantage point, he could see Federals in some threatening position, and sent his aide, Major Haskell, to tell General Lee about it. After a harrowing escape from the Yankee videttes, Haskell rode to New Cold Harbor, delivered his message, and went to join his old friend General Longstreet.[111]

Over on Boatswain's Creek, Butterfield was in good shape. His men had toyed with Pryor all day long, and were ready for another attack. Behind him, Hyde's Battery E, Massachusetts Light Artillery (6 ordnance rifles) was supporting him, facing west, and he also had gotten infantry reinforcement in the form of the 7th Pennsylvania Reserves, who were in a third line in the woods. Since the heaviest attacks, so far, were to the north, on Martindale's front, Brigadier Butterfield let the 7th go. It filed north, forming a line south of Bucklin's two guns, facing west.[112]

While Whiting, Longstreet, and Harvey Hill were bringing their men up, the reinforcements for Powell Hill attacked. Gregg's Brigade attacked at Zouave Hill, Pender's Brigade of Powell Hill's Division attacked Griffin's Woods, and Ewell's Division attacked past the Parsons House. It was about 5:30.

14

Fixed Bayonets in the Hands
of Resolute Men

The Union Lines

After battling the First South Carolina Rifles, the 10th New York had exhausted its ammunition, and was relieved by the 6th U.S.[1] These regulars went into the north end of Griffin's Woods facing generally west, with other Union troops to its left, and more to their right front. Those on the right promptly fired into Capt. Hendrickson's three left companies, causing the other Northern troops on the left of the 6th U.S. to break, which in turn caused the 6th U.S. to break. While the exact positioning is difficult to discern, the 14th New York and 9th Massachusetts were also involved in this fiasco.[2] The 6th U.S. was rallied and returned to its position.[3] With the 6th U.S. holding their left flank, the 5th New York Zouaves and Brigadier Buchanan's 12th U.S. and 14th U.S. had shifted back northeast.[4] While Sykes' right had generally been quiet, except for the artillery shooting at Old Cold Harbor, his left and center had been assailed for two hours[5]; they would soon be utterly exhausted and out of ammunition. Anticipating this, McCall's Division of Pennsylvania Reserves was at hand.[6] Reynolds' Brigade, about 3,000 men, was sheltering just behind the McGehee Road. McCall's other two brigades, under Meade and Seymour, were behind them,[7] near the McGehee house. Meade and Seymour would support Brigadier Griffin's men, who were in about the same condition as Sykes'.

Slocum's troops, another whole division, was further behind the McGehee House. Bartlett's Brigade was positioned to support Sykes' front, and the other two brigades could support Morell's front, Newton to support Griffin, and Taylor's New Jersey Brigade to support Martindale. Not much had happened in front of Butterfield so far, but Porter was out of troops; Butterfield would have to make do.

Boatswain's Branch, at the Bottom of Zouave Hill

The 13th South Carolina had been in support of the original brigade line. While crossing Boatswain's Branch, it had become somewhat disorganized, but moved up to the woods on the other side eventually, and relatively intact.[8] Gregg ordered it to stay put right there, so it could blast any Yankees pursuing the 12th and 1st Volunteers.[9] Unfortunately, those two never showed up, so the 13th stayed put. Just at that moment, the 14th

South Carolina arrived to the 13th's right.[10] It had been detailed to outpost duty, but had joined the brigade by a forced march.[11]

After annihilating the First South Carolina Rifles, the 5th New York had charged down the hill on the survivors' heels.[12] Battle Group Lane and the remnants of Gregg's Brigade stopped the Zouave drive.[13] "[T]he New York Zouaves dressed out in their red breeches, long red caps, charged down on them and drove them … back to the woods."[14] "About 5:00 p.m., our turn came, and we were furiously attacked. The first Federals that reached our side … were dressed partly in red. They came no farther," said French Harding of the 31st Virginia. "We maintained our position with but little loss, throughout the battle." Harding had fired his 40 rounds of ammunition when he heard Private "David Shelton inhale the smoke laden air so loudly that I turned to see what was the matter. He had been shot through the fleshy part of his left hand between his thumb and forefinger."[15] Both sides were now trading fire at close range in the edge of the woods when the 14th South Carolina arrived and drove the Zouaves back.

It was the Zouaves' turn to suffer. For a time they held their own; 8 companies of the Zouaves were using Johnston & Dow waterproof and combustible cartridges,[16] which about doubled their firepower; the two Sharps infantry rifle companies, E and I, had triple firepower. It was not enough. The storm of lead coming from the woods took its toll; the Zouaves fell back and left a thick line of dead and wounded. They fell back again, and then again, but the Zouaves were not about to give up. Color Sgt. John Berrian shouldered his blue New York State regimental color, stomped forward about 30 yards, planted his flag in the ground, and "looked defiantly around him." Color Sgt. Allison soon joined him with the national colors. Aghast, Col. Duryea and the officers screamed at them to come back to the line; the Rebels were so close that a sortie might capture he flags, but the pair ignored them. Inspired, the 5th New York gave a "yell never heard off the battlefield, so demoniac and horrid that men in peaceful times cannot imitate it," and charged forward, driving the Rebels further back into the woods.[17]

The Confederates rallied, and charged right back, driving the Zouaves back. John Urban, of the 1st Pennsylvania Reserves, observed, "[W]e could distinctly see the desperate nature of the fighting. Neither side appeared to think of loading their muskets, but depended entirely on the bayonet."[18] Col. Duryea, 5th New York, concurred: "Our line was several times forced to yield … but as often advanced and regained the ground at the point of the bayonet."[19] Seeing the melee, General Sykes sent in his immediate reserve, ordering Brigadier Lovell to send the 2nd U.S. and the battalion of the combined 10th and 17th U.S. (10/17th U.S.), about 500 men, to Warren's aid.[20] On the way, reserve regiments shouted, "Go in, Second Infantry, and give them hell!"[21] The 2nd and the 10/17th fixed bayonets, went down Zouave Hill, and waded into battle on the 5th New York's right. "Our colors were planted on the very brow of the rise and we dressed [aligned] on them as we did when on parade."

This spectacle drew the attention of the Confederates, 200 yards away. Augustus Myers recalled, "As soon as I began to fire at the enemy, I was inspired by very different feelings from what I had experienced while lying inactively in the road, being shelled by the enemy and unable to reply.… I now had a strong desire to inflict all the damage I could on the enemy. I was cool and collected and took deliberate aim with every shot…." Bullets began to buzz around the Federals' ears, and Myers heard an odd noise. "Presently my comrade … pitched forward on his face to the ground, exclaiming with a groan, 'I've got it!'" The odd noise was a ball smashing the comrade's thigh bone.[22] The

2nd U.S. was moved back a few paces and ordered to kneel or lie down. Myers fired prone, "until I saw a man a few files from me receive a horrible wound which opened his face from forehead to chin."[23]

The men of the 2nd had been firing at their own volition, but were soon ordered to fire by command, and by company. Such group firing concentrates the regiment's firepower, usually in response to an oncoming foe. In this instance, "the Rebels retired into the woods and for a little while their firing ceased; then it commenced again in a more feeble way."[24] A member of the Pennsylvania Reserves narrated the scene to his men before they went in: "At that moment, the Second Regulars turned fiercely upon the almost exultant rebels, and made a desperate charge. Thereupon the captain exclaimed 'They're charging! They're charging!' Presently the rebels broke and fled to the wood; and the captain grew enthusiastic, and eagerly exclaimed: 'They're skedaddling! They're skedaddling! ... GIVE 'EM –LL!'"[25] These Confederates were probably the remnants of the 1st South Carolina Volunteers, the 12th South Carolina, and the 13th South Carolina.

Myers continues, "The day was intensely hot, my clothing was saturated with perspiration, the barrel of my gun was so heated by the fierce rays of the sun and the firing that it seemed to burn my hands and I was almost afraid to reload it without giving it time to cool off."[26] As the Zouaves and Regulars fought, the steel barrels retained more heat than they radiated, and rifles became hotter and harder to handle. The steel can become so hot it alone will ignite the gunpowder, usually taking off a finger or two of the loader. Moreover, the black powder used as a propellant fouled the inside of the barrel slightly with every shot; after about 35 shots, loading slows considerably as the inside diameter of the barrel occludes. Ramming the ball down is the most time-consuming step of loading, taking approximately 10 seconds with a clean rifle. The dirtier the barrel, the harder and slower the ramming.[27] With staggering losses, running low on ammunition, and their rifles barely operable,[28] Reynolds' Brigade came down the hill to relieve Brigadier Warren's men. The 5th New York had impressed the Regulars. "The Zouaves, on our left front, behaved splendidly. There was no flinching, no dropping to the rear. They stood like heroes to their work, under a murderous fire."[29] The 5th New York paid dearly for these accolades. Of about 450 men, it lost 140 of them here, around 31 percent.[30]

Reynolds had three regiments, the 1st, 8th, and the combined 5th and 13th Pennsylvania Reserves,[31] about 2,500 men.[32] Zouave Colby, whose smashed knee made his tuberculosis moot, waved his tasseled fez[33] and cheered as the Pennsylvanians arrived.[34] The 5th New York was in bad shape. "The regiment was completely disorganized, and left the field in squads. Its ... commander [Col. Duryea] stayed for some time with our regiment.... When the two Colonels met, Col. Roberts [1st Pennsylvania Reserves] remarked, 'Well Colonel, they have used you up pretty badly'; to which Duryea replied, 'Well, yes, but by the Eternal'—pointing with his sword to the heaps of rebel dead—'I think we have paid them back in their own coin!'"[35]

Reynolds' men advanced into a gruesome spectacle. "The ground was so thickly covered with dead and wounded that it was with the utmost difficulty we could advance without treading on them. To accomplish this the regiment[s] were compelled to break ranks and get over the ground as best they could...." "Some of the dead had their heads broken in by blows from the butts of rifles, and others lay dead with bayonets thrust

Opposite: **Kingsbury's Battery D, 5th U.S. Artillery in June of 1863 (Library of Congress).**

through them, the weapon having been left sticking in their bodies…. [A]ltogether, it was the most sickening sight I had ever witnessed."[36] A member of the 8th Pennsylvania Reserves also remembered their advance: "We marched to the right of the Second Regulars, and lay down under the hill. We saw many horrid sights while lying there. Men staggering from the field with mangled hand or arm, or limping off—a leg covered with blood—an officer now and then—were being carried off, covered with blood, groaning in agony."[37]

Regulars' Hill, East of Reynolds' Brigade and Just West of Weed and Tidball's Batteries

Earlier in the day, when the 1st South Carolina Rifles attacked the Zouaves, Brigadier Buchanan slid the 12th U.S. and 14th U.S. to the west, and had the 3rd U.S. come forward to the woods to cover where they had been. Shortly after the 3rd arrived, Major Rossel saw signs of a major attack, and sent Capt. Walker to warn General Sykes.[38] About the same time, Captain Lay, commanding the skirmish company of the 12th U.S., lost his nerve and disappeared. His men, leaderless before the impending attack, also decamped, all the way to Brigadier Buchanan.[39] This left the front of the 12th U.S. without any warning line should massed Confederates appear out of the choking underbrush.

About this time, Kingsbury's Battery D, Fifth U.S. Artillery (6 Parrotts) reported to General Sykes with only four of his guns.[40] Lt. Edwards' six Parrott rifles were still dispersed in three two-gun sections across the front. Hayden's section thereof was between Weed's Woods and the McGehee Road–Grapevine Road intersection, so Kingsbury joined him, going into firing position on his right (east) near the intersection of the McGehee Road and Grapevine Road. This created an apparent "battery," of Parrotts, two of Hayden's guns and four of Kingsbury's.

Kingsbury's arrival did not go unnoticed by the Confederate cavalry. J.E.B. Stuart offered to send in the Stuart Horse Artillery until Jackson's own artillery could come up, and Jackson agreed.[41] "The only artillery being under my command being Pelham's Stuart Horse Artillery, the 12 pounder Blakeley and Napoleon were ordered forward to meet this bold effort to damage our left flank. The Blakeley was disabled at the first shot."[42] This left only one Napoleon to duel with Kingsbury's 4 Parrotts, and, only 1,000 yards away, Weed and Tidball's 12 ordnance rifles. Captain Pelham yelled, "Blakely gun crew, drag your gun out of range! Men of the Napoleon Detachment, follow me to a new position!" At the new position, Pelham said, "Men, we Alabamians are all that stand between the advancing Yankee batteries and General Jackson's troops. We must rout them so that the Valley infantry can push ahead and join in the main attack." With the gunners singing "La Marseillaise," Pelham opened fire[43] at extreme range, but the federal gunners soon shifted their attention. The attacks on the Zouaves and 2nd U.S. prompted Kingsbury to swing his fire to cover them, and to bring up his other two guns, making it an eight-gun battery.[44]

Ominously, about this time, Sgt. Major Evans, 12th U.S., reported "whispers that the left of the corps had fallen back."[45]

Boatswain's Branch, Near Old Cold Harbor

Major Rossel, 3rd U.S., was right. The major attack he feared was Harvey Hill's Division struggling through Boatswain's Branch. Brigadier George Anderson's North Carolina brigade was in the lead.[46] The 4th and 30th North Carolina were probably in the first line, with the 2nd and 14th in a second line. The brigades to their right (Rodes, Colquitt and Ripley) hit the worst part of the morass, well churned up by Gregg's Brigade, and disintegrated. The 2nd North Carolina was near them and was disorganized by friendly fire.[47] The 4th, 14th, and 30th North Carolinas, about 1000 men,[48] retained their cohesion and made it through. Brigadier Rodes made it across Boatswain's Branch with one regiment, the 6th Alabama, and attacked more or less with G.B. Anderson.[49]

As the four regiments moved forward, the 14th North Carolina "suddenly … encountered a line of battle concealed in the underwood. Our line halted and poured a volley into their ranks. Volley after volley followed as we advanced. Soon the enemy gave way."[50] A member of the 30th North Carolina remembered, "Here was our first fire in regular line of battle, and it was a heavy one too."[51] Their target in the woods was the 3rd U.S.

Just then, over to Anderson's right (west), the 6th Alabama, 4th North Carolina, and 30th North Carolina found the 12th U.S. Sgt. Major Evans, 12th U.S., recounted: "[T]he enemy is pushing up a column concealed by the woods directly in our front. Not only do they try to hurl us back frontally, but attempt to turn both our flanks and cut us off."[52] "The ringing of the smooth bore balls and buckshot as they whistled past made a deadly music."[53] "Now the Zouaves are falling back and all our men of the 12th and 14th were lying down. Suddenly a yell as from a thousand Indians breaks from the woods, and shots strike thick and fast from another direction.… Our battery on the road to our rear opens with case and canister so close that we cannot move until they cease firing."[54] These guns were the Hayden/Kingsbury eight-gun battery.[55] "[Canister's] peculiar cracking sound is sharply menacing, and in this instance was so close that some of our men were wounded by our own fire."[56] Because of the acute danger of fratricide, measured in inches, firing canister over the heads of prone infantry is about as dangerous a practice as one could find on a battlefield at the time. Things were getting desperate.

The 14th U.S. was between the 12th and the 3rd when the latter suddenly retreated. "We would have maintained our position … but the 3rd [Infantry] … on the death of Major Rossell fell back without giving us notice when the rebels then directed their fire upon the 14th."[57] With its right (east) flank[58] wide open, the 14th had to retreat or be slaughtered.[59] "The 14th U.S. rises, pours in a volley, and falls back in good order.…" The 12th kept up its fire, covering the 14th. The 14th was halfway to the McGehee Road when they stopped and fired another volley.[60] The 12th rose up; "Ready! Aim low! Fire! Every piece is discharged in a withering volley."[61] The 12th made it halfway to the McGehee Road when it was volleyed by Confederates and broke: "Step now men, if you ever stepped!"[62] one officer cried. Major Clitz went down with a wound to the leg.[63] The Regulars fell back in different degrees of disorganization all the way to the McGehee House.[64]

Weed and Tidball's 12 guns, with the 4th U.S. between them, were still at the tip of Boatswain's Branch. When the Regulars pulled out, the two batteries also had to fall back or face capture. Both were almost out of ammunition, and headed towards the Chickahominy, out of the fight.[65] The Grapevine Road was now open, at least to the McGehee Road; the Hayden/Kingsbury battery was behind Weed's Woods and could not fire effectively to the north. At the same time, the right (east) flank of Sykes' infantry, Reynolds'

Brigade, was in the air.[66] At the worst possible time for the Union effort, General Harvey Hill, West Point Class of 1842, Mexican War hero, and headmaster of the North Carolina Military Institute,[67] rode forward to further direct the assault.[68]

With General Sykes, on Regulars' Hill

Sykes' front line regiments had been fighting since early afternoon and heavily engaged for over an hour. Sykes' men were low on ammunition, especially the 5th New York and the 10th New York. All had started with 60 rounds; the 5th was almost out.[69] All of the Regulars were exhausted. Of Sykes' men, the 12th and 14th U.S. had started with about 500 men each, and each had almost 45 percent casualties. The 10th New York had about 31 percent casualties, while the 5th New York had 36 percent.

Gregg's Brigade fared even worse. The 13th South Carolina lost 12 percent. The 1st Volunteers lost 29 percent, the 12th lost 34 percent, and the 14th lost 45 percent. The First South Carolina Rifles, who made it all the way, lost a staggering 59 percent. Sykes' Division was about twice the size of Gregg's Brigade at the start. Gregg's Brigade had lost 40 percent of its men cutting Sykes' Division down by a quarter.

With Brigadier Buchanan's 3rd, 14th and 12th U.S. falling back, Sykes' right was collapsing. Reynold's Brigade, to their left, was in danger of being flanked, or, worse, completely cut off. General Sykes called on his last reserves, Bartlett's Brigade of Slocum's Division, sheltering behind the McGehee House. The brigade artillery, Porter's Battery A, First Massachusetts Light Artillery (6 Napoleons), could not find a firing position, and had been sent to the rear.[70]

With his whole northern front collapsing, General Porter sent an urgent message to McClellan for additional reinforcements. General McClellan tasked Sumner's 2nd Corps with this duty; General Sumner ordered General Richardson of his First Division to send two more brigades. Thomas Meagher's Second Brigade and William B. French's Third Brigade began moving at 5:00.[71] Brigadier French was in charge,[72] but since Captain George Armstrong Custer had already been across the river, he guided the movement.[73] French's men were near Fair Oaks Station, about 4 miles away.[74] He could not possibly arrive until about 8:30.

South of the Cold Harbor Road

After his first attack, Brigadier G.B. Anderson had gone back into the woods only to find Brigadier Garland's men moving up.[75] General Harvey Hill himself then arrived to find Brigadiers Anderson and Garland planning an attack southwest on the now exposed flank of the Pennsylvania Reserves' line. Anderson pointed out that a Federal battery slightly to the southeast would enfilade such an attack, but Garland was willing to risk it, and then, so was Anderson.[76] The guns to the left were Hayden/Kingsbury's eight-gun battery, near and south of Weed's Woods firing northwest in support of Reynolds' Brigade. General Hill ordered three of Elzey's small regiments (the 25th Virginia, 52nd Virginia, and 12th Georgia, about 500 men,[77] hereinafter Battle Group Virginia) out of battery protection[78] to go down the Grapevine Road and attack the guns from the eastern side.[79] Garland's Brigade would attack due south at the guns.[80] Garland's leftmost (east) regiment was the 200 men of the 5th North Carolina,[81] with the 800-man 20th North Carolina to its right (west), with parts of the 1st North Carolina and 3rd North Carolina (190 men; Ripley's Brigade) and the 5th Alabama (300 men, Rodes' Brigade) to their right. George Anderson's Brigade was to Garland's right, and Rodes' Alabamians to his right. Colquitt and Ripley's brigades were stacked up behind Battle Group McGowan,[82] on Rodes' right. Battle Group Lane was to McGowan's right.[83]

Old Cold Harbor

General Jackson returned to Old Cold Harbor after his meeting with Generals Lee, Whiting and Hood. Henry Kyd Douglas was already there, and recalled: "[S]omeone handed him a lemon—a fruit of which he was specially fond. Immediately a small piece was bitten out of it and slowly and unsparingly he began to extract its flavor and its juice. From that moment until darkness ended the battle, that lemon scarcely left his lips except to be used as a baton to emphasize and order ... he never for an instant lost his interest in that lemon and even spoke of its excellence."[84] Another man wrote, "[Stonewall Jackson] sat quietly on his sorrel sucking a lemon and watching through his glasses the progress of the fight. Presently a staff officer of Gen. Ewell galloped up and exclaimed, 'Gen., Ewell says, sir, that it is almost impossible for him to advance further unless that battery ... is silenced.' 'Go tell Major [Andrews] to bring sixteen pieces of artillery to bear on that battery and silence it immediately' was the prompt reply."[85]

With Weed and Tidball gone, Stonewall Jackson ordered Valley Army artillery forward. Sixteen guns of Ewell's Division, deployed near Old Cold Harbor, allowing Pelham's sole gun to pull out. Their rifled guns could hit Griffin's Woods, while the others could hit the McGehee Road–Grapevine Road intersection. These were Brockenbrough's Baltimore Artillery (1 ordnance rifle, 1 Blakeley, 1 Parrott, 1 howitzer),[86] Carrington's Charlottesville Artillery (2 ordnance rifles, 2 howitzers, 2 smoothbores),[87] and Courtney's Henrico Artillery (1 rifle, 5 smoothbores[88]).[89] The aim of Kingsbury's Battery near the McGehee Road-Grapevine Road intersection worsened significantly once these batteries opened up.[90] Jackson also ordered up some of Harvey Hill's guns. Bondurant's (Alabama) Artillery had done its part, but Fry's Orange (Virginia) Artillery (1 ordnance rifle, 1 howitzer, 3 smoothbores)[91] and Rhett's (South Carolina) Artillery (1 Napoleon, 1 howitzer, 2 smoothbores), with Clark's Battery, were brought up; Jackson would soon have a grand battery of about 30 guns.[92]

Though not all of the same division, four brigades, 7,200 men,[93] more or less, constituted the Confederate lines, between New Cold Harbor and Old Cold Harbor. They would make a single attack on Sykes' shaky line all the way from Boatswain's Branch to the McGehee Road.

Behind the McGehee House

George Townshend, correspondent for the *London Times*, could not stay away:

[A]t three o'clock I called for my horse ... that I might witness the battle. It was with difficulty that I could make my way along the narrow corduroy [road], for hundreds of wounded were limping from the field to the safe side, and ammunition wagons were passing the other way.... Before I reached the north side an immense throng of panic stricken people came surging down the slippery bridge. A few carried muskets, but I saw several wantonly throw their pieces into the flood, and as the mass were unarmed, I inferred that they had made similar dispositions. Fear, anguish, cowardice, despair, disgust were the predominant expressions of the upturned faces. The gaunt trees, towering from the current, cast a solemn shadow upon the moving throng, as the evening dimness was falling around them, it almost seemed that they were engulfed in some cataract.

A fugitive tried to take Townshend's horse, but Townshend kicked him in the chin.

The thick column parted left and right, and though a howl of hate pursued me, I kept straight to the bank, cleared the swamp, and took the [River] road toward the nearest eminence. At every step I met wounded persons. A horseman rode past me, leaning over his pommel, with blood streaming from his mouth and hanging in great gouts from his saturated beard. The day had been intensely hot and black boys were besetting the wounded with buckets of cool lemonade. It was a common occurrence for the couples that carried the wounded on stretchers to stop on the way, purchase a glass of the beverage, and drink it. Sometimes the blankets on the stretchers were closely folded, and then I knew that the man within was dead. In one place I met five drunken men escorting a wounded sergeant; the latter had been shot in the jaw, and when he attempted to speak, the blood choked his articulation. I came to an officer of rank … four men held him to his [saddle], and a fifth led the animal.[94]

15

There Is Hot Work on That Hill Yonder

Pender's Brigade, Attacking Griffin's Woods

Earlier in the afternoon, Dorsey Pender's Brigade (16th, 22nd, 34th, and 38th North Carolina) had crossed Powhite Creek at Gaines' Mill, and had been sent on a wide sweep south in an effort to surround the Union skirmishers fighting Brigadier Gregg. Somehow the 34th North Carolina disappeared, causing Brigadier Pender to ask for support. Archer's Brigade relieved him, and Pender marched back to New Cold Harbor, where he found the errant 34th, and was ordered to support Brigadier Branch. Pender's Brigade hurried down the McGehee Road to Griffin's Woods.[1]

On the way, the 16th North Carolina witnessed a bizarre episode. A terrified woman came out of nowhere and ran screaming down the road, "bare headed with her hair down and flying back."[2] Pender formed his brigade in two lines with the 38th and the 22nd Virginia Battalion in the second line.[3] Once across Boatswain's Branch, Pender found the 18th North Carolina, Branch's Brigade, added it to his line,[4] and soon found the Yankees.

After Branch's attack, the 9th Massachusetts and the 62nd Pennsylvania remained in the woods. Pender's men "drove the enemy slowly," but the 9th Massachusetts broke again.[5] This forced the 62nd Pennsylvania and Battle Group Skillen to fall back or be flanked. The 62nd fell back faster than Pender's men could follow it; Pender's two right regiments, the 16th and 22nd North Carolina, outdistanced his left ones, heading southeast, and made it all the way through Griffin's Woods into the Union camps along Boatswain's Run.[6]

Union Brigadier Truman Seymour had worked the guns that defended Fort Sumter a year earlier, and had been an infantry general for about two months.[7] One of his three regiments had already been sent to support Kingsbury's Battery D, 5th U.S. Artillery (6 Parrotts) on the Grapevine Road. He led his remaining regiments to reinforce Griffin's beleaguered men. His remaining two regiments, the 9th and 10th Pennsylvania Reserves, were armed primarily with smoothbores. Both regiments moved up to Boatswain's Run, behind Griffin's men, facing northwest. The 10th was now Griffin's Reserve.

Pender's men forced the 9th Massachusetts and 62nd Pennsylvania out of the woods, and drove southeast, breaking the Union line at the camps on the outskirts of Griffins Woods. There, the 16th and 22nd were viciously counterattacked on their right flank by three Yankee regiments. Pender sent for support, but his men were too hard pressed.[8]

The 62nd Pennsylvania's slow withdrawal allowed the routed 9th Massachusetts to reorganize. When the 62nd returned to the line, its color bearer planted the flag and the 62nd formed line around it. The 9th Massachusetts and the 9th Pennsylvania Reserves joined it, and at "Charge bayonet,"[9] the three regiments charged onto Pender's flank. Lt. Hinsdale of Pender's Brigade was certain all was lost.[10] The 16th and 22nd fell back, causing Pender's left regiments to follow suit.[11] Pender's men fell back fighting "diagonally"[12] to the northeast, with the three Union regiments on their heels.

Pender's men fell back across the clearing in Griffin's Woods, but one regiment made a rear-guard stand in the clearing. The 62nd Pennsylvania stopped in the clearing, where "It was now 'give and take' in the open without cover," recalled Charles Henry Veil, an aide to General Seymour.[13] He and the general had just spoken to Col. Samuel Black, 62nd Pennsylvania, when Veil saw "a minnie [sic] ball strike him between the eyes, killing him instantly.[14] The 9th Pennsylvania Reserves kept going, only to run into the 37th North Carolina, which had returned to the fight.[15] The 9th was staggered by a "tremendous fire from a fresh body of the enemy," and broke. Its panicked retreat disordered the 62nd and the 9th yet again, all of whom fled back east.

The 6th U.S., Lovell's Brigade, Sykes' Division, witnessed the chaos. It had just arrived at the northern edge of Griffin's Woods when "the two or three companies comprising my left flank received a heavy volley of musketry from a body of our own troops stationed diagonally to the right had front of my line. This unexpected event and the falling back at the same time of a body of volunteers on its left caused a momentary confusion in the ranks."[16] Col. Jackson of the 9th Pennsylvania Reserves described the rout with florid Victorian doublespeak: "In falling back across the open field, which was done under a galling fire, there was much disorder and a complete mingling of the several regiments, in consequence of which, and the wild ineffectual firing arising therefrom, an effort was made to rally the different regiments, but without success."[17] Such verbiage was necessary, as the 9th only had about 6 percent casualties.

Once again, half of Griffin's Brigade had broken, and the hole in the Corps' center yawned open. Brigadier Pender took advantage of it. Now reinforced, his men advanced into the breach.[18]

The only regiment at hand that could stop Pender was the 10th Pennsylvania Reserves, near Boatswain's Run, under the enterprising Col. James T. Kirk. "When the command was given to charge bayonets, they sprang to their feet and made for the enemy." The 10th crossed Boatswain's Run in its trek, "and charged into the woods, only to be met by a Confederate volley, which did not even stagger the regiment," but hit Private Andrew Roy just above the groin and killed a close comrade. The Rebels broke, pursued by the 10th Reserves, but counterattacked and drove them back. Private Roy lay between the lines watching the fighting,[19] which Roy described as "a terrific fire" and Col. Kirk described as "severe and desperate."[20] Confederate bullets kicked up dirt around him, spattering his clothes. Roy watched the 10th make another counterattack before he was carried away on a stretcher.[21]

Crenshaw's Richmond Artillery, Near New Cold Harbor

Crenshaw's Battery had been firing all day, and the stress began to tell on its guns. The incessant firing had broken the axles of two guns, probably the antiquated 6-lb.

smoothbore guns. The other two bronze guns were so hot that embers extinguished with the sponge between every shot instantly reignited, threatening to burn through the thick wool powder bags and fire the round while the gunners were still pushing it down the barrel. With only his two Parrotts in firing condition, three caissons damaged, and almost out of ammunition,[22] Powell Hill ordered Crenshaw out. The battery lost so many horses that officers' mounts were pressed into service to move the guns, and even then two of the guns had to be withdrawn by hand. Capt. Marmaduke Johnson's Richmond Artillery (2 howitzers, 2 smoothbores)[23] replaced Crenshaw[24] during Pender's attacks. With only four guns, Johnson had a wider field of fire through the narrow opening in the woods than Crenshaw.

The 9th Massachusetts had lost 39 percent casualties, and the 62nd Pennsylvania 28 percent. The 9th Pennsylvania Reserves, which broke almost as soon as it was engaged, only lost 10 percent. The 10th lost 17 percent. Pender's Brigade lost about 30 percent.

General Porter had had it with Griffin's Woods. The enemy had almost broken through it twice, and the men were exhausted and low on ammunition. He'd replace what was left of Griffin's four regiments, now down to about 1,700 men, with eight regiments, two whole brigades, those of John Newton and George Taylor, of Slocum's Division, some 5,400 men.[25]

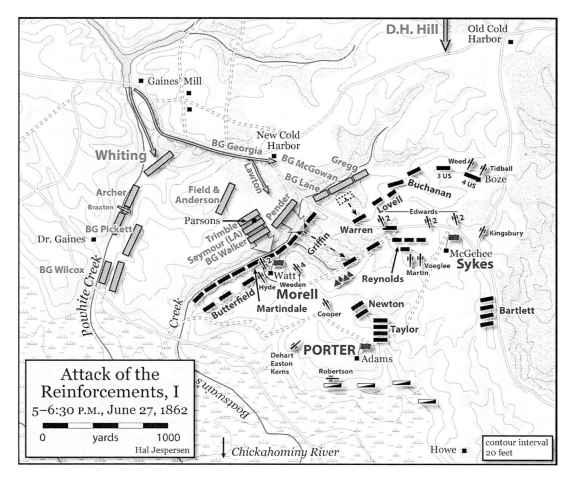

Near the Parsons House

Brigadier Arnold Elzey had left three small regiments (Battle Group Virginia) as battery supports at Old Cold Harbor several hours earlier, leaving him with only four small regiments. His brigade now consisted of the 13th, 31st, 44th and 58th Virginia, about 600 men.[26] General Ewell sent these into Boatswain's Branch with the 31st's right resting on the McGehee Road. When the balance of his division showed up, all of Elzey's regiments were in the line except the 13th Virginia, so Ewell detached it and took it with him. The 7th North Carolina of Branch's Brigade, was also unoccupied, so he took them along, too,[27] creating Battle Group Walker. Col. Walker, 13th Virginia, had the unique distinction of having been dismissed from the Virginia Military Institute in 1852 for insubordination; he had challenged Professor Jackson (now "Stonewall") to a duel.[28] As the 13th left New Cold Harbor, a shell (probably from Martin's Battery, Massachusetts Light Artillery (6 Napoleons) almost wiped out the color guard.[29] The survivor, young Sergeant George Cheshire, took them up (the 13th was only carrying a blue Virginia flag),[30] saying "They are mine now!"[31] Walker's men then moved south in column "in the direction of heavy musketry."[32] General Ewell ordered Battle Group Walker into battle at a knoll near the Parsons House.[33]

In moving, the 7th North Carolina disappeared; Walker's men went in alone, under artillery fire from Bucklin's guns. Capt. Samuel Buck, 13th Virginia, observed, "After struggling under some heavy underbrush and over a marsh we moved by the left flank, formed ourselves immediately in front of the Yankees' breastworks where our own troops were in deadly conflict; on we went, until within a very short distance not over 100 yards, when we received a terrible volley from behind the works which killed and wounded a great many of the regiment. I had a hole shot in the knee of my pants. Five of the company fell dead within a few feet of me."[34] Another member of the 13th recalled, "[I]nstantly we were engaged in a deadly contest at close range, sometimes almost together and at no time more than 50 yards apart. The smoke became so dense that the men could only locate the enemy by the flash of their guns…. The volleys of musketry were so loud we could not distinguish the report of the cannon. But we could see the effect of the shot and shell as they cut down the trees around us."[35]

With General Ewell at New Cold Harbor

Having told Elzey's Brigade and Battle Group Walker where to go, General Ewell and his staff rode to New Cold Harbor to bring up the rest of the Division. Ewell halted the Louisiana Brigade waited for Brigadier Trimble.[36] After Trimble had passed New Cold Harbor, General Lee and President Davis, Confederates burst out of the woods away from the fighting. Brigadier Trimble noticed that some of these troops were partially organized.[37] The organized and the disorganized broke through Trimble's column, separating part of the 15th Alabama[38] and the 21st Georgia from the rest of the 15th Alabama, the 16th Mississippi, and 21st North Carolina, all of whom promptly disappeared. Col. Cantey and two companies of the 15th Alabama wound up in with the Louisiana Brigade and are included with them.[39] Some delay was caused by the officers of the 21st Georgia pointing out that their Colonel, John Thomas Mercer,[40] was in his cups and had already passed out in a pine thicket. Brigadier Trimble ordered Mercer's arrest and put Lt. Col.

Hooper in charge of the 21st Georgia.[41] General Ewell and Brigadier Trimble both were with the unlost portions of the 15th (now under Lt. Col. Trentlen) and the 21st Georgia. Pvt. McClendon, 15th Alabama, stepped into a muddy spot and sank almost up to his knee. When he pulled his foot out of the muck, he left his shoe but went on, half barefoot. General Trimble happened to be present, and ordered McClendon to dig his shoe out.[42] Ewell himself took command of Trimble's men, and sent Trimble himself to find his errant regiments.[43]

General Ewell formed the Louisiana Brigade (about 1,300 men) with Brigadier Trimble's two regiments (about 600 men) behind them as support.[44] Before it went in, an officer, either Col. Harry Hays of the 7th Louisiana or Col. Seymour,[45] commanding the brigade, rode across the 9th Louisiana's front and "shouted in clear and piercing tones: 'Louisianans, the famous Pennsylvania Bucktails are behind breastworks at the top of yonder hill!... Remember Butler and New Orleans; remember your sweethearts, your wives, your mothers! Will you go to the rise of that ridge? Will you go?'" The brigade gave the rebel yell,[46] and moved forward.

Battle Group Walker

The combined firepower of three Union regiments chewed up Walker's men, but they held their ground in the "hottest and most prolonged infantry fight I ever saw," as Col. Walker, 13th Virginia put it. "[A]s I passed along the line I saw the brave little color-bearer standing bolt upright in an exposed position, holding the colors aloft, unmindful of the Minie balls that were whistling thick around." Col. Walker motioned for him to get behind a tree, but the man did not do so. "Before I reached him the colors went down, and the color bearer pitched forward ... saturating the bunting with his life's blood. I beckoned one of his comrades to me, and we lifted his body and picked up the flag, wet and dripping with his blood.... The bunting was riddled, and the staff in three places nearly severed in twain, so that it was too weak to be borne by the regiment."[47] Walker's attack made quite an impression. The 3rd[48] and 4th[49] Pennsylvania Reserves, Meade's Brigade, arrived, with the 3rd joining the 4th Michigan's line in the firefight,[50] the 4th remaining in support.

The 13th "was barely able to hold its ground" when Major Wheat, free of his death premonition, nonchalantly asked Col. Walker how his regiment was getting along. Walker related his desperation. Wheat asked, "Why don't you charge them?" "Not strong enough," replied Walker. The 13th and its 300 men were facing three big Union regiments. Wheat calmly retorted, "My brigade is coming up, and I intend to charge them."[51]

Major Wheat led the charge, still on horseback. "When [his] men came up, he rode in front of his men, sword in hand, and waving it over his head commanded 'Charge!'"[52] And charge they did, struggling through the muddy bottom of Boatswain's Swamp,[53] and up the other side. The 6th Louisiana saw Yankees at the top of the hill and opened fire, only to be slaughtered while floundering through the water and the felled trees. Col. Seymour was shot off his horse and died immediately, lying in the muck at the bottom of the ravine.[54] The 9th Louisiana made it up the side of the ravine, crested a small rise in the woods, and were hit by a perfect hailstorm of bullets."[55] The 9th balked, searching for unseen Yankees, and opened an uncertain fire.[56] The 6th made it 30 more yards, and then broke.[57] Wheat, who was so proud of his wharf rats, walked his horse through the underbrush 10 yards ahead of the 9th's line and fell from his horse[58] 40 yards from the Union works, shot through the eye and brain.[59] One man reported 8 men fell within ten yards of him. The loss of the charismatic Wheat took the fight out of the 9th, as did the "murderous" fire.[60] The 6th and 9th broke,[61] carrying the 7th and 8th with them, "driven from the field."[62]

Trimble's Brigade, Ewell's Division

Ewell flung Trimble's two following regiments into the fray to save his line. These two regiments now join Battle Group Walker. The 15th Alabama[63] and 21st Georgia, about 600 men, had supported the Louisiana brigade. As they went forward, the Parsons House split the 15th Alabama, part of which had to maneuver around it.

Private McClendon could see Zouaves.[64] McClendon fired a shot at them, and turned to see one of his friends shot in the stomach trying to plug the spurting hole with a canteen cork. The 15th dressed its main line on a rise in the woods. Their skirmishers were "fighting a regular line of battle" just over the rise. The 15th was still under artillery fire, and the musketry volleys "were as a regular roll. You could not distinguish one gun from another." McClendon heard "heavy volleys" of musketry to his left. As the 15th went over the rise, they opened fire. They could hear the Yankees cheering, and could see their own men falling, but could not see the enemy in the smoke. The fire was so intense that the 15th took a knee and kept firing. The noise was so loud that McClendon could not hear his musket fire; he felt it do so from the recoil only. He fired so much that the weapon became too hot to handle, so he picked up another. Just at that moment, a man in the rear rank fired his musket too close to McClendon's head[65]; he drew back to hit the offender with his musket butt, but the man apologized, and they both kept firing. McClendon carried grains of powder in his neck for the next 44 years. Soon the 15th ran low on ammunition. Men were sent to the rear for more; in the meantime McClendon and his mates gleaned cartridges from the fallen, but this too ran out.[66] General Ewell rode up, and ordered the prone men to fix bayonets and hold. Ammunition soon arrived, and the 15th kept firing.[67] The 21st Georgia met remnants of the Louisiana Brigade while going in. One said, "Boys, you are mighty good but that's Hell in there."[68] The Georgians went forward into a "very warm reception, both of musketry and shell."[69] Cresting the rise in the woods, the 21st was soon fully engaged.

The cheering of the Yankees was the ill omen of more of them. More cheering heralded the arrival of the 11th Pennsylvania Reserves, also of Meade's Brigade, and the 4th New Jersey of Taylor's Brigade.[70] Battle Group Walker was "nearly whipped twice and it was with only the greatest exertion they could be rallied and induced to hold the position." It was General Ewell himself who did a lot of the rallying. "General Ewell gave us and the Alabama regiment his presence and attention and by his cool courage and brave example did everything to encourage the men until reinforcements arrived."[71] Lt. Col. Hooper of the 21st Georgia, his arm shattered, turned command over to Capt. Nisbett, who ordered a retreat behind the rise on the west side of Boatswain's Swamp and kept fighting.[72]

General Ewell knew that he had nothing left to stop a concerted Union push at his lines, but did not know that the Federals had no intention of doing so. He therefore rode his horse along the line, ordering phantom troops into line.[73] Col. Trentlen of the 15th

Alabama followed suit, as did Private Frank Champion, 15th Alabama.[74] Miraculously, none were hit. Behind Ewell's line, Campbell Brown was on his way back to General Ewell when he was stopped by terrified men pouring out of the woods from the south. "These I knew to be Louisianans and to leave a gap in the line. Col. Cantey of the 15th Alabama with two of his companies also came out—but they as well as Col. Stafford's 9th La. And parts of the 8th La. and 7th La. were in some sort of order & soon came under the control of their officers. I concluded that my first duty was to rally these men and as Seymour had been killed to get some one to take command of the Brigade. This took ¾ hour of hard work." Brown put Col. Stafford in charge; General Ewell thought that the rallied brigade was "somewhat nervous" and sent them to the rear "to let them be quite [*sic*] til needed."[75]

Martindale's Brigade

Brigadier Martindale had beaten off everything the Rebels could throw at him. The 4th Michigan and the two companies of the 14th New York had shot their bolt and they were pulled back to the support line. The 11th Pennsylvania Reserves and the 4th New Jersey moved up into their place. As Martindale surveyed his position, things were not looking good, though. "The right of our line, where Sykes' Division was posted, had at this time receded…. Already [Morell's] right had shown signs of suffering, and part of Griffin's regiments had retired, having been relieved." Focusing on his own front, Martindale realized that his own situation was to become much worse: "Looking through the partial clearing in front of my two pieces of artillery, I saw the enemy approaching in dense columns."[76] Whiting's whole division was coming his way.

16

The Bullets Whistled
Through the Leaves Like Fun

South of the McGehee Road, after watching Col. Black, 62nd Pennsylvania, fall from his horse dead, Brigadier Seymour (with the 9th Pennsylvania) gave Charles Henry Veil a message to carry. "As I turned my back on the firing, I got scared for the first time, as I recollect. I was trying to get up the hill as fast as I could with my horse, when all at once a lot of the enemy's guns opened from a new direction—on our right—and about the first round knocked off both my horse's forelegs and threw me over his head, but in the direction I wanted to go, so I kept going…. Confederate General Thomas "Stonewall" Jackson arrived from the Shenandoah Valley and was making his attack on our right flank."[1] Veil was somewhat correct; Jackson's 16 guns had opened up, Harvey Hill's men were about to come up Zouave and Regulars' Hills, and Brigadier Lawton's 2000 Georgians were on their way to Griffin's Woods, as was Newton's Brigade of New Yorkers.

Lawton had been ordered to support Ewell and headed his column towards the Parsons House. Entering Griffin's Woods, he met General Ewell himself, who was heading to New Cold Harbor for help. After the war, General Ewell told the Rev. Major Dabney "that he was whipped and his line disintegrating when he saw Lawton come up."[2] Brigadier Lawton reported, "As [Ewell] saw this long line advancing under fire, [he] waved his sword and cried out 'Hurrah for Georgia!'"[3] Ewell's men were holding the line on Boatswain's Creek just south of Griffin's Woods; Whiting's whole division was behind them, and Ewell knew it, so he suggested Lawton attack east, into Griffin's Woods.

Once again, Boatswain's Branch disorganized troops moving through it. "The extreme density of the wood and the sloppy, miry soil … made it evident that the different regiments of the brigade would soon be separated from each other. I therefore sent different members of my staff to the right and left of the line to press it forward and remained myself as near the center as possible."[4] This was prudent. The 13th Georgia led the order of march and went towards the Parsons House and the position of Ewell's men,[5] with five companies of the 26th Georgia.[6] These are designated Battle Group Douglass. The 60th, the 61st Georgia, and four companies of the 26th, all armed with rifles,[7] stayed with General Lawton.[8]

Slocum's Division

Newton's Brigade was led to the right of Griffin's Brigade[9] into Griffin's Woods by at least two of Porter's aides de camp, and promptly split up.[10] Brigadier Newton took charge of the 95th Pennsylvania, "Gosline's Zouaves,"[11] and 31st New York, the "Montezuma Regiment"[12] (Battle Group Newton), while Col. Matheson, of the 32nd New York "First California Volunteers,"[13] took command of the 32nd and 18th New York (Battle Group Matheson).[14] Newton stacked his regiments; the 95th was in the first line and the 31st in his second.[15] Matheson's regiments were initially side by side, with the 18th on the right.[16] Each man carried 60 rounds of ammunition.[17]

Battle Group Matheson

The 18th New York advanced first with "hearty good will" despite the spent balls whizzing by. As they approached Boatswain's Run, the goodwill diminished. "We could see heaps of killed and wounded before us, but we had no time to look at them." Ghastly casualties from the 5th New York Zouaves and the Regulars diverted their attention. Battle Group Matheson arrived just in time; the left half of the 26th Georgia's attack broke the 9th Massachusetts yet again, which disordered the 18th.[18] The 62nd Pennsylvania was also involved,[19] as was Battle Group Skillen. Private Harrer, 14th New York, recorded that the Confederates "opened a tremendous fire on our troops, drove us out from the shelter of the woods and forced us upon an open space…. In this movement I witnessed a scene of confusion among our troops which, I am glad to be able to say, in 19 battles afterward I never witnessed."[20]

Battle Group Newton

The 95th Pennsylvania, Gosline's Zouaves, entered Griffin's woods after Griffin's men had skedaddled; the 31st New York stopped at Boatswain's Run and lay down.[21] Gosline's Zouaves soon came upon Pender's remnants and a firefight erupted. General Newton ordered the 95th back to the 31st's line. Both regiments then charged together, cheering, and "driving the enemy before them."[22] Those enemy were Pender's men, and they did not get driven far; half of the 26th Georgia had just arrived, and the 61st was on the way. Private Nichols could see his comrades 200 yards away, and the Yankees 300 yards away.[23]

Battle Group Matheson

"About this time," the right wing of the 18th New York "received a terrific fire of grape and canister, the men lying down and taking the fire with great coolness."[24] Since the nearest Confederate guns were far out of canister range, this fire could only have come from Union guns, probably Hexamer's Battery A, New Jersey Light Artillery (2 howitzers, 4 Parrotts).[25] Col. McGinnis moved to his left, behind the 32nd New York.

Griffin's Woods

The 60th Georgia came up on the left of the 61st. Lawton now had 1,400 fresh men with rifles plus the remnants of Branch's and Pender's brigades facing Newton's 2,600 men. "The battle raged without intermission,"[26] reported Major McGinnis of the 18th. Both Newton and Matheson began over watching their regiments[27]; that is, one fights while the other rests in a second line. This cut their firepower in half, but the return musketry was so fierce that Private Sheldon, 18th New York, remarked, "We had to hug the ground as we advanced."[28] "We walk up to the scene of slaughter with a determined, steady tramp and serious pace, knowing there is no backing out,"[29] observed Pvt. Hawley of the same regiment. Private Weymer went down with a wound that would turn gangrenous; Sgt. Huntington had his shoulder hurt when a wounded comrade's rifle flew up and hit it.[30] Major McGinnis' horse was shot in the hindquarter.[31] Artillery explosions brought bittersweet news; the 18th's right wing buckled, but they were from Hexamer's Battery A, New Jersey Light Artillery (2 howitzers, 4 Parrotts)[32]; the New Jersey Brigade had arrived. Col. Matheson ordered a cease-fire in his Battle Group, as the woods were so full of smoke that the enemy could not be seen, and the New Jersey Brigade was rumored to be in their front.[33] Matheson had his men fall back 100 yards until the mess could be sorted out.

Suddenly, an officer materialized out of the smoke carrying a furled flag, exhorting the men to hold fire. As he rode to within 50 yards of the 18th's Company F, arguments arose. Some claimed to recognize him as a member of the 18th's staff, others were convinced that he was a Rebel. Sgt. Bantham aimed at him and ordered him to "come down" off the horse. Color Corporal Kearns did not hesitate, and shot the officer off his horse. His foot caught in the stirrup and the horse dragged him back to his own lines.[34] This did not end the indecision. Major McGinnis rode out and recognized a Confederate flag at 150 yards, approaching at the double-quick; he rode back to his men, while the Confederates opened fire.[35]

Elzey's Brigade, Battle Group Lane

"We thought he was dead when we reached him, and so left him," remembered Captain Harding of the 31st Virginia.[36] Brigadier Arnold Elzey had been shot through the head and face.[37] He was taken to New Cold Harbor and survived.[38] Unseen in the woods, his tiny regiments, and Battle Group Lane, had attacked almost due south, across the Boatswain's Branch-McGehee Road intersection, on Battle Group Matheson's right, which was the end of General Morell's whole line. His men gave the 18th New York "the most terrific storm of bullets we received at all, and many a brave man fell."[39] Cpl. Kearns, who had shot Brigadier Elzey, was hit four times while carrying the 18th colors, but survived. Private Shaw, officially 42 years old, but really over 50, ignored the graze to his head and "blazed away at the enemy."[40]

Col. Matheson's muskets were becoming too hot to load[41]; they were also running out of ammunition. "I don't think a man left the field with half a dozen in his box," Sgt. Alexander remembered.[42] Matheson sent Lt. Col. Pinto for reinforcements, but he returned alone. Matheson himself left, and found the 31st New York in Boatswain's Run.[43] Matheson ordered them to charge to his support. Advancing at the double-quick, the

The 95th Pennsylvania poses proudly with their Union repeating gun on the right (Library of Congress).

31st cheered as they went in and opened fire,[44] but Col. Platt of the 31st fell from a ball to the head. This disorganized the 31st, who promptly fired into the backs of the 18th. A major from the 32nd prevented a second volley.[45]

Col. Matheson's appropriation of the 32nd New York left the 95th alone and unsupported once again. Col. Gosline was mortally wounded, and Lt. Col. Town took over.

Col. Lane's 28th North Carolina swung around Elzey's right and crashed into Battle Group Matheson's right. "At this time the enemy appeared on my right flank," reported Col. Matheson, "which compelled me to change my original purpose. I instantly led the 31st forward to meet them, when we soon engaged with them…."[46] "[T]he enemy had turned our right flank, and was pouring a terrible fire upon us," wrote Major McGinnis of the 18th.[47] It was too much; Matheson ordered the 31st New York to retreat, and it broke. Just at this moment, the 95th Pennsylvania also broke.[48] With the Rebels only 30 yards away, the 18th and 32nd also broke. "It was every man for himself until he got out of reach of that murderous fire," recalled Private George Green.[49] Sgt. Bantham, who had hesitated to shoot Brigadier Elzey, recalled, "We were pretty much scattered, no order appearing to be possible, although each company kept together pretty well considering the manner in which we were pressed at last."[50] Private Pollard lost his way and wound up walking into the 13th North Carolina, Garland's Brigade, thinking it was the 18th New York. The Carolinians cheered him.[51]

Newton's Brigade suffered about 14 percent casualties in Griffin's Woods. The 32nd New York had the least, 7 percent, while 18th and 31st both had about 15 percent. Gosline's Zouaves suffered the most at 17 percent.

Edwards' Battery, 3d U.S. Artillery

Capt. Edwards' guns (6 Parrotts) were still split up into three gun sections along the McGehee Road. Lt. Hayden's was in front of the McGehee House, half a mile away; Lt. Brownson's was a quarter mile away; and Kelly's Section was near Griffin's Woods, between the other two. "[A]s our troops [Newton's Brigade] were breaking and running to the rear, I directed Lieutenant Kelly to limber up and retire." Capt. Edwards then rode to his center section.

Taylor's New Jersey Brigade

The center of General Porter's line in Griffin's Woods had collapsed yet again. General Porter himself took charge, ordered Taylor to send the 1st and 3rd New Jersey into Griffin's Woods, and then fired the men up. "Boys, Jersey is a small state but she is a big one! Three cheers for New Jersey. Go in!"[52] These two regiments entered Griffin's Woods, their line essentially connecting the two ends of Boatswain's Run.[53]

Taylor's men had two secret weapons. One had been used with great effect just that

The Duc de Paris receiving orders from General Porter, by Alfred Waud (Library of Congress).

afternoon. The whole brigade was armed with Johnson & Dow Waterproof and Combustible Cartridges, the same ones that had so helped Sykes' men. A New Jersey soldier described how advantageous they were: "[A]fter the pieces had become warm, it was only necessary to insert the cartridge [into the muzzle], give it a slight shock [tamp the butt on the ground], and it was home, thus greatly facilitating the rapidity of loading."[54]

The second secret weapon was somewhat more complicated. Attached to the 3rd New Jersey[55] were at least two[56] Union Repeating Guns. These were specimens of a primitive machine gun that Wilson Ager had invented in 1861 and advertised as "An Army in Six Square Feet."[57] When Abraham Lincoln saw a demonstration, the president remarked that the ammunition hopper resembled that of a coffee mill, and so the contraption earned the nickname of the "Coffee Mill gun."

Lincoln persuaded the War Department to purchase 60 of these by December of 1861.[58] While limited by technology, the gun was also on the cutting edge of it. It had a shield to protect the operator, and the barrel was designed to be replaced quickly in the field. It used a thick steel (not iron) casing for the powder, ball and cap, and had a turbine-forced air system to cool the barrel, all operated by a hand crank. All of this made it capable of 120 shots per minute using standard Johnston & Dow Waterproof and Combustible Cartridges. After the Battle of First Manassas, the 28th Pennsylvanian was stationed along the Potomac River. Henry Hayward, 28th Pennsylvania, described the Coffee Mill gun in a letter to his sister: "we have got 2 Union Guns that were presinted to the 28th. they are fired by turning a crank. the faster you turn it the more Rebels it will kill. it will throw a ball 4 miles. I cannot describe it but when the men saw it first they thought it was a sausage machine."[59] Slocum's Division, Bartlett's Brigade, also had at least three Coffee mill guns.[60] Col. Cake's 96th Pennsylvania was so proud of its gun that it had an image made with it.[61] Lt. Edward Burd Grubb (3rd New Jersey[62]) recalled, "Lying between the Fourth and Third [New Jersey], was a battery of seven machine guns, called the Union Coffee Mill Guns."[63] Sgt. James Dalzell, 3rd New Jersey, commanded the detachment.[64] The Repeating Gun Detachment was deployed somewhere along Boatswain's Run.

1st and 3rd New Jersey Regiments

The Rebels were even up in the trees. One New Jersey officer picked up an unused musket and shot a Georgian out of a tree a mere 20 yards away, and added two more to his score within minutes.[65] They were also on the ground; the two New Jersey regiments "exposed themselves to the leaden hail of an often unseen foe."[66]

4th and 2nd New Jersey Regiments

With his center somewhat stabilized, Porter sent one of his French volunteer aides, the Prince de Joinville, to Hexamer's Battery A, 1st New Jersey Artillery (4 Parrotts, 2 howitzers); Joinville personally relocated them 200 yards from Griffin's Woods, almost due south of the sunken part of the McGehee Road. Hexamer opened fire at Marmaduke Johnson's guns near New Cold Harbor, his smoke obscuring his guns and horses from Lawton's men in Griffin's Woods, who ceased fire.[67]

Morell's line between the Watt House and Boatswain's Run was hard pressed, so Porter sent another one of his aides, the Duc de Chartres, another French volunteer to Porter's staff, to the 4th New Jersey; the Duc babbled out instructions that it was General *McClellan's* order that Col. Simpson should move the 4th as the Duc instructed. Col. Simpson properly referred the Duc to Brigadier Taylor, much to the latter's surprise: "Who the devil is this, and what is he talking about?"[68] One of Taylor's aides translated. Taylor ordered Simpson to put the 4th New Jersey behind the regiment in its rear. Once the 4th had assumed the new position, the Duc ordered it into the woods, Brigadier Taylor concurring.

Simpson marched his men towards the Watt House, and went into line of battle 50 yards behind the 3rd Pennsylvania Reserves.[69] That regiment had been in the line as a reinforcement to the 4th Michigan when General Ewell's Division attacked. By now it was low on ammunition and the "muskets of the Third were now becoming so heated and choked with powder as to render many of them unserviceable and their fire perceptibly diminished."[70] The 4th New Jersey replaced them, with the 11th Pennsylvania Reserves in close support.[71] The 3rd Pennsylvania Reserves met General Meade on the way out, who praised their "cool valor," and ordered them to support Weeden's Battery C, Rhode Island Artillery (6 ordnance rifles). Weeden had 2 guns at the Watt House firing through Martindale's hole in the woods, and 4 guns north of it behind Battle Group Skillen/Battle Group Newton in Griffin's Woods.[72] The 3rd supported these 4 guns.

The 2nd New Jersey, all 261 men of it, were also sent to support the 4th Michigan of Martindale's Brigade.[73] Col. Tucker of the 2nd noticed, "Things are rather hot in there, and I rather think some of us will never come out."[74]

Battle Group Georgia

"Suddenly came … that command which … causes a soldier's heart to creep up in his mouth and his courage to ooze out at his finger tips … *load.*"[75] The 31st and 38th Georgia moved down the McGhee Road and took some time to cross Boatswain's Branch and deploy almost 1300 men. "After having loaded, our field officers informed us that [we] had been selected to charge two batteries of artillery and a body of infantry in our front…."[76] Battle Group Georgia was to be the right end of Harvey Hill's attack. The two batteries were Martin's Battery C, Massachusetts Light Artillery (6 Napoleons) and Edwards' L/M, 3d U.S. Artillery (6 Parrotts). The infantry was what was left of General Sykes' Division and Reynolds' Brigade.

17

We Had Been Pretty Well
Pounded Out That Afternoon

Zouave and Regulars' Hill, Along the McGehee Road

Bendix's 10th New York had left the fighting on Zouave Hill first, out of ammunition, and went into battery support for Voeglee's battery of 20-lb. Parrotts. The 5th New York Zouaves were the next to leave, but their march up the hill would not be easy. The several hundred men dressed in bright red pantaloons in the open on a hill had been seen by the sharp-eyed Confederate artillerists at Old Cold Harbor, who shifted their fire onto the McGehee Road.

While its regiment had been fighting on Zouave Hill, the 5th New York's "surgeon's party" had posted itself along the McGehee Road, probably in the sunken part, but when Jackson's 16 guns opened up from Old Cold Harbor, it forced them to move behind the McGehee House, which was little better. After they had raised their red hospital flag, "while I was assisting the surgeon to amputate an arm, a shell struck close beside us, and killed and wounded a number who were standing by…. To hear the trail of shot around us you would have thought that scarcely a bird could escape…. The cry 'There come some more Zouaves' was so often repeated while we were at work, that I knew the poor fellows were being terribly cut up. Soon the hospital presented such a sight that would sicken the strongest heart…. One poor fellow with a mortal wound grasped my hand and said with a smile, 'S—, I'm dying, but tis a good cause.'"[1]

Private Veil, 9th Pennsylvania Reserves, lost his horse and took a tumble at the first shots; the bulk of the barrage exploded all over Regulars' Hill. Col. Duryea of the 5th New York Zouaves knew that only discipline would keep his battered regiment from panicking at this new onslaught. He held them in place in the midst of the barrage, forcing them to dress their lines as if on parade, count off, and then march in proper military fashion up the hill through the barrage.[2] Crossing over the McGehee Road, the 5th met the 10th behind Voeglee's Battery of 20-lb. Parrotts[3] south of the McGehee House and east of the Adams House. Here both regiments "rested after their long fight."[4] Their idylls soon became less than restful. "The spent balls flying around them thickly, many of the men received stinging blows from them."[5]

Harvey Hill's attack had coalesced into three components. From east to west were Garland's Brigade with the 20th North Carolina near Old Cold Harbor, then Harvey Hill's other brigades and regiments (G.B. Anderson and Rodes) in the center, then Battle

Group McGowan, near New Cold Harbor. Hill's three components attacked at more or less the same time; but the units to the left of Garland were delayed by Reynolds' Brigade. Hill would unknowingly have a fourth component which would make all of the difference.

The artillery barrage continued while the Regulars fell back up Regulars' Hill behind Reynolds' Brigade. Captain O'Connell, commanding the 14th U.S., found that "their artillery had a true range of the battalion,"[6] at Weed's Woods. Sgt. Evans of the 12th U.S. wrote, "Directly in front of me six men fall in quick succession, so rapidly that I have to pause an instant to avoid trampling on them."[7] In the 3rd U.S., companies were led by sergeants instead of officers.[8] The Confederate artillery fire hurt Lovell's men, too. Capt. Dodd and a private of the 10/17 U.S. were also killed by artillery fire near the road.[9] Capt. Brindley, 2nd U.S., was killed retreating up the hill; the fire was so hot that the 6th U.S. broke, rallied on its colors, "now nearly shot to pieces," reformed, and "retired in good, or rather not bad, order."[10] The 12th U.S. attempted to form a line of battle behind Weed's Woods, and was joined there by the 14th U.S.[11]

While Garland's brigade and the 20th North Carolina went for Hayden's and Kingsbury's guns, Brigadier Rodes, Brigadier Anderson, and Battle Group McGowan attacked Reynolds' Brigade. The latter's three big regiments, about 800 men each, had more than replaced the 5th New York Zouaves, the 2nd U.S., and the 6th U.S. A small battalion (150 men) of the 13th Pennsylvania Reserves, and Companies C and G of the 1st U.S. Sharpshooters,[12] were sent forward some distance from the 8th Reserves' right flank, guarding the interval between the 8th's right and the 12th U.S.[13] A Sharpshooter noted, "One unfortunate field officer of a Zouave regiment was led off the field crying aloud at the loss of his nose, presenting a sight not easily forgotten."[14] The 8th Pennsylvania Reserves were to the left of the 13th, and the 1st Pennsylvania Reserves to its left, as they advanced into the carnage left over from the Zouaves' fight with Gregg's South Carolinians.

Battle Group McGowan

Battle Group McGowan was still in the woods when Reynolds' Pennsylvania Reserves came down on them. A member of the 14th South Carolina recalled, "Friday [June 27] was the most dreadful musketry that I ever heard in my life. The 14th Regt. held position where three Regiments had been compelled to leave but we never gave an inch for the Blue Jackets, but drove them step by step from the field…. I could stand in one place and count thirty Yankees within 20 yards. I think we killed three to one."[15]

Rodes' Brigade

In going through Boatswain's Branch, Rodes' Brigade had come up on George Anderson's men and split in twain. As Brigadier Rodes tried to sort the mess out, the 5th, 12th, and 26th Alabama formed line of battle and went forward without him. The 12th was behind the other two, and it watched the "front lines engag[e]"[16] the Yankees. The 5th and 26th "soon came upon the enemy in force. Continuing to move forward, the 5th + 26th Rgts. Ala. engaged and drove back four regiments of the enemy."[17]

Reynolds' Brigade, Pennsylvania Reserves

The 1st Pennsylvania Reserves had just arrived when it heard a yell "which was enough to make us believed that all of the demons of the lower regions had broken loose."[18] Col. Roberts of the 1st had them hold fire until the Confederates had cleared the woods. As soon as they did, the whole 1st Pennsylvania Reserves, about 800 men, fired at once, driving the rebels back. The unharmed 1st was ready for another go. The Rebels came out of the woods again, and the 1st blasted them again. The Pennsylvanians were congratulating themselves on such easy work when yet another attack, fresh troops and more of them, "determined to drive us from our position at any cost," came out of the woods. This time, the regimental fire only staggered the Rebels, who returned fire with their own regimental volley and charged. Each side stood at "close quarters" firing as fast as they could. Soon they were low on ammunition, and then out.[19] The 8th Pennsylvania Reserves lost at least four officers and dozens of men just getting to the right of the 1st Pennsylvania Reserves; their bayonet charge[20] forced the Rebels back into the woods, but exposed them to Confederate artillery fire and musketry from the woods.

The 8th was about 25 yards from the Confederate line, and firing as fast as it could, about two shots per minute; their 50 rounds of ammunition would last only 25 minutes at this rate, assuming their rifles did not clog up sooner. Private Darby recalled, "My musket had become foul and I dropped to the ground on one knee and was ramming away at the cartridge with both hands to get the load down when I felt something spattering over my face and left side, and on turning around I discovered that my comrade, George Proud's head had been dashed to pieces and his brains and fragments of his skull had been scattered over me."[21]

A Confederate sharpshooter had climbed about 15 feet up a tree, and took a shot at Col. Hayes of the 8th. He missed, but hit a private in Company C. Col. Hayes snatched a rifle from the ground and aimed at the sharpshooter. "Don't shoot! Don't shoot! I'm coming down!" cried the terrified man. Col. Hayes "pulled the trigger, and down came Mr. Reb."

The firing was horrendous. Nothing could be seen in the dense white cloud of powder smoke except the other side's gun flashes. The two lines were so close that Rebel balls would fling men into the air as they were hit. Men would "stagger, reel, and fall to the earth gasping for breath, the hot blood gushing from his wound." In almost no time, the 8th was out of ammunition; it faced about and hurried off with the 1st Pennsylvania Reserves, who were also out of ammunition.[22] The 5th Pennsylvania Reserves took their place; now it was just the 5th and the small battalion of the 13th holding back the Rebels.

Between Zouave and Regulars' Hills

Just as the 5th Pennsylvania Reserves were going in, the Regulars to their right collapsed, and Brigadier G.B. Anderson's attack pressed forward. Anderson's brigade was asymmetrical, with two regiments of about 400 men each, the 14th and 30th Carolina, and with two that totaled about 250 men, the 2nd and 4th North Carolina. The larger two were probably in the first line, which was slightly larger than the 5th Pennsylvania Reserves. The little 13th fired a volley from their Sharps infantry rifles, which

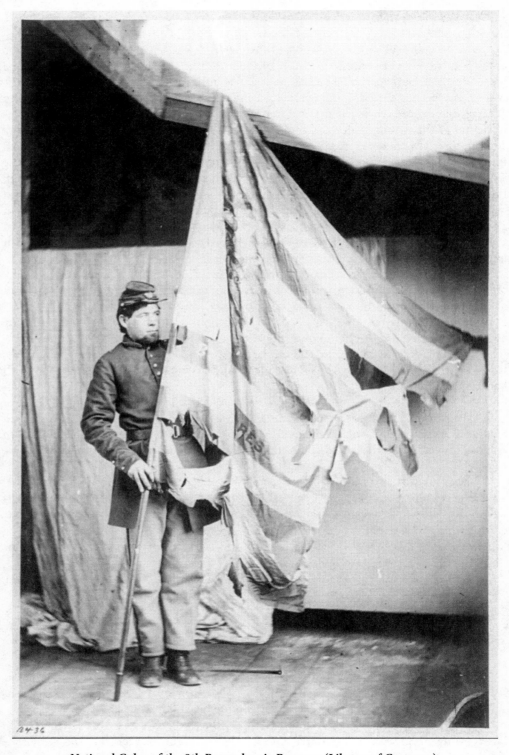

National Color of the 8th Pennsylvania Reserves (Library of Congress).

staggered the Rebels, and then the 5th charged down on them and fired at 150 yards, forcing Anderson's men back into the woods.

By now the 1st and 8th Pennsylvania Reserves were long gone, and Confederate artillery had opened on the 5th. A shell hit an "orderly, cut him in two in the middle; the upper part went up among the tree tops while the other stood on the feet part quivering, as it was done so quick."[23] A member of the 14th North Carolina remarked, "The musketry was furious."[24] Quartermaster Captain Blount took up the 30th North Carolina's colors and galloped forward, only to be shot dead.[25] The 30th and the 14th North Carolina surged forward with a yell.[26] The 5th Pennsylvania Reserves appeared to the 14th South Carolina to be making a flanking movement on their left, so it, too, attacked them.[27] Attacked on both flanks and by Rodes in front, the 5th Pennsylvania Reserves broke.[28] It was a hair's-breadth escape; had they remained five minutes more they would have all been captured.[29] The 1st and 5th had fired much, but suffered little; they each had but about 5 percent casualties. The 8th fared three times worse, with about 18 percent casualties. The little 13th lost 17 percent. The Confederates suffered more, about 37 percent in Anderson's two lead regiments. Of Rodes' men, the 5th Alabama lost about 21 percent, while the 26th lost 10 percent and the 12th 5 percent.

Garland's Brigade, Attacking Regulars' Hill

Garland's Brigade opened fire on the retreating Regulars, but their task was to silence the Hayden/Kingsbury Battery so that the troops to their left could move forward. After advancing into the open, Garland[30] ordered them to charge the battery, 400 yards away.[31] Though Hayden and Kingsbury were the target, Lt. Brownson's section was 500 yards west, just south of the McGehee Road, so Garland's men charged into the fire of *ten* Parrott rifles. After 200 yards, Brigadier Rodes, on the other side of George Anderson's Brigade, saw "the whole line having a moment before paused and hesitated, nearly if not the whole left of the division … broke and retreated in apparent confusion."[32]

Kingsbury's Battery, Near the McGehee Road–Grapevine Road Intersection

Battle Group Virginia threatened Kingsbury's Battery D, 5th U.S. Artillery (6 Parrotts) so badly[33] that he shifted his fire to throw to canister to its front,[34] keeping Kingsbury from helping Hayden. Musketry from the 5th North Carolina and Battle Group Virginia put the 12th Pennsylvania Reserves "under a galling cross fire"[35] by an "overwhelming force,"[36] causing them to precipitately retreat out of the fight. This forced Kingsbury to retire his six guns about 80 yards to the rear, east of the McGehee House and directly in front of the 16th New York.[37] Lts. Brownson and Hayden and their four Parrott guns were all alone.

Garland's Brigade

The confused retreat was not as bad as it appeared to Brigadier Rodes. Major Toon of the 20th North Carolina observed that the regiment "advanced about half way, under

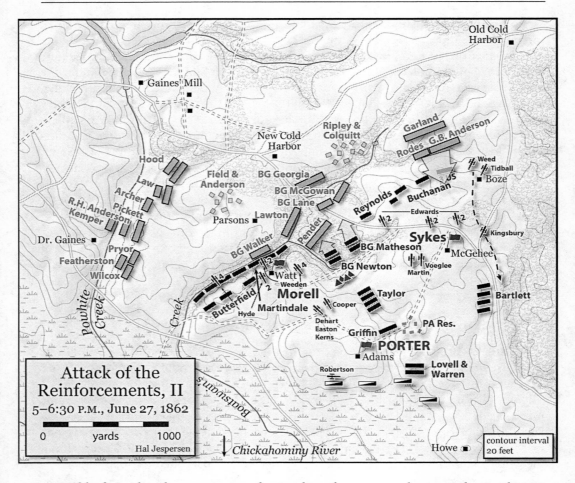

Attack of the Reinforcements, II
5–6:30 P.M., June 27, 1862

0   yards   1000

Hal Jespersen

contour interval
20 feet

Chickahominy River

a terrible fire, when by some misunderstanding the command retreated to within 20 yards of the woods. Here they were halted and the order to charge and take the battery was repeated and understood. The regiment immediately faced about, advanced rapidly amidst a storm of grape, canister and musketry, and charged the battery with a yell."[38] The regiments angled left. The 12th North Carolina recalled the "storms of shot and shell and the ground strewn with the dead and dying."[39] The 23rd North Carolina was in "full view of a battery on our left, which opened on us, as we went forward.... The men became excited and began to fire, but Col. Christie [ordered them] to stop the firing until they got closer. So [they charged] up the hill to the enemy's position."[40] Col. Iverson, 20th North Carolina, fell wounded early in the charge, and Lt. Col. Faison took over.[41]

Near the McGehee Road, the hastily retreating 14th U.S. turned and fired a volley, but the Rebels came on.[42] Brownson and Hayden began firing double canister,[43] and the Rebels came on still. With only two men left, Hayden fired one last round[44] and fell with a musket ball in the leg.[45] Horses fell; the gunners tried to cut the dead and dying ones out of the harnesses, but it was taking too much time; the Rebels were almost upon them. The cannoneers fled.[46] Jubilant, the 20th's color bearer clambered onto one gun and defiantly waved the battle flag.[47] The rest of the North Carolinians poured past the guns toward the McGehee Road and Lt. Brownson's guns.[48]

At that moment, Capt. Edwards arrived at Brownson's guns, to the left and rear of Hayden's. Half of Brownson's horses were already down, and Brownson was pulling out. "[Brownson] was in great danger of losing his section, as the rebels had gained the road in front. The two lead horses of one piece had been killed and the two surviving horses were shot as the piece was being limbered. This gun[49] was drawn to the rear by 2 horses." These guns safe, Capt. Edwards then galloped east to find Hayden's men and guns, but only found the wounded Lt. Hayden. Lt. Edwards lost in total 10 men, two guns, and 25 horses.[50]

16th New York, Bartlett's Brigade, Slocum's Division

Brigadier Bartlett's lead regiment was the Col. Howland's 16th New York, wearing Mrs. Howland's cool straw hats. The 16th, east of and behind the McGehee house, changed front and moved forward through Kingsbury's guns, silencing them.[51] Col. Howland admonished the regiment that he would not fire until point-blank range,[52] and with three cheers, "long and loud," charged at a run towards the lost guns,[53] ruining the attempt of the combined remnants the 12th and 14th U.S. to form a new defensive line.[54] One man, Solomon Burr, ran ahead of the line, calmly aimed, and fired. His shot struck home, killing Lt. Col. Faison of the 20th North Carolina, but a close-range Tarheel ball killed Burr, went through him, and seriously wounded another man.[55] Forty-two-year-old Pvt. Eliakim Sprague was shot, and died in the arms of Pvt. Persho Sprague, his son. Joseph Perry was hit in the thigh, lost an eye, and then used two muskets as crutches to walk two miles to a hospital. Only one man in the entire color guard was not hit.[56] Col. Howland was hit in the thigh but refused to go to the rear.[57]

20th North Carolina, at Lt. Hayden's Section, Edward's Battery

In the face of this charge,[58] the remnants of the 20th North Carolina, unsupported, fell back to the woods under Major Toon.[59] Sgt. Faison Hicks was with the 20th North Carolina and witnessed the charge:

> [T]he guns were located on the left, as we faced them, and in front of the house. My position in line was at the intersection of the [McGehee Road and Adams House Road]. I saw our troops turn the guns, and then gave my attention to my front, and fired several shots about the house. The captured guns not firing, I looked in that direction and saw that they were abandoned, and, knowing there had been no forward movement, on the part of our boys, I looked and saw our whole line had fallen back, and, the smoke having risen in my front and right, saw the enemy charge in a run towards the battery. They commanded me to halt, and as I could not fly, I ran back and joined our lines at the charging point, at which position the regiment continued to fire. I remember seeing a great many straw hats on the field....[60]

The 16th New York passed through the guns but was stopped after about a hundred yards, and promptly broke.[61] Lt. Hager, 14th U.S., wrote in a letter, "They received about one volley from the enemy and then retired in great disorder."[62] A member of the 27th New York left his description of the battlefield, which was printed in the *Richmond Daily Whig* on July 8, 1862. "As we steadily advanced, a portion of a regiment, the [16th] New

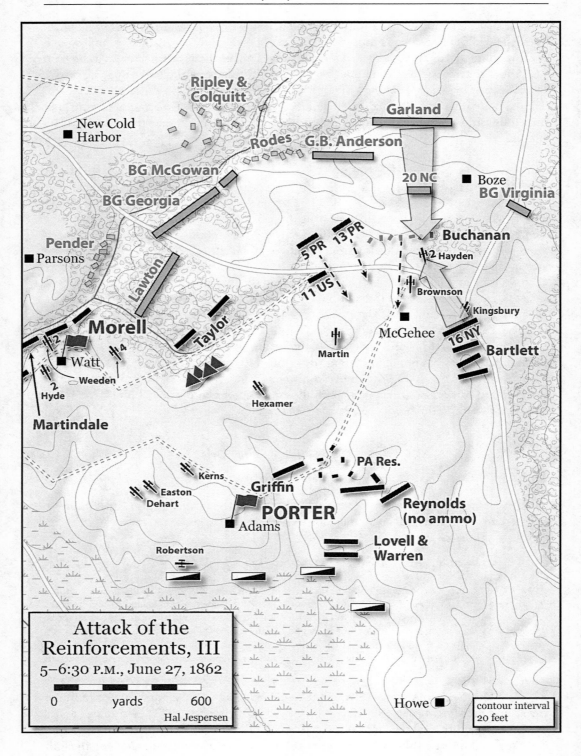

Ripley &
Colquitt

New Cold
Harbor

Rodes

Garland

G.B. Anderson

BG McGowan

20 NC

Boze

BG Georgia

BG Virginia

Pender
Parsons

Lawton

5 PR   13 PR

Buchanan

2 Hayden

11 US

Brownson

Morell

Taylor

Martin

McGehee

Kingsbury

Watt

2
Hyde

Weeden

16 NY

Bartlett

Martindale

Hexamer

Kerns

PA Res.

Easton
Dehart

Griffin

PORTER

Adams

Reynolds
(no ammo)

Robertson

Lovell &
Warren

Howe

Attack of the Reinforcements, III
5–6:30 P.M., June 27, 1862

0   yards   600

Hal Jespersen

contour interval
20 feet

York, I think, came rushing, driven back, and threatening to break our ranks and cause great disorder."[63] According to a member of the 96th Pennsylvania, "In a few minutes, what was left of the [16th New York] regiment, came tumbling down the side of our shelter, all broken up…. They were cut to pieces."[64] The fight for Hayden's guns was costly. In this one charge, the 16th New York lost 201 out of 485 men, more than 41 percent.[65] The 20th North Carolina lost 272 out of about 800 men,[66] a rate of 34 percent. Its flag had 27 bullet holes in it, but it held the guns for ten vital minutes.[67]

Battle Group Georgia

Col. Evans, 31st Georgia, was nervous. After a grueling cross-country run, his 1,300 green and untried troops were moving down the McGehee Road from New Cold Harbor through a debris field of broken units into dense woods that had totally disorganized veteran regiments. Pvt. Bradwell describes his experience:

> Col. Evans and the other field officers, mounted, ordered us to move forward; and as we did so he drilled us as if we were only on parade until we reached the margin of the creek, which we found to be a tangled mass of briers and undergrowth. Here he stopped us a moment to catch our breath and told us to lie down. He took a small Bible out of his breast pocket after he dismounted and read while we rested. As we fell down a shell from the battery on the other side of the creek came cutting the air just above our heads and plunged into the marshy place back of us, lifting a great quantity of mud and weeds many feet high and spattering us with it. This shell just missed our company, and I saw its effect and felt that the gunners would make short work of us…

After their rest, Battle Group Georgia moved forward across Boatswain's Branch, more or less in the footsteps of Gregg's Brigade. "We were soon through the thicket, and as we plunged into the muddy water, full of dead men and horses, many of our men fell prostrate in it and began to drink. When we got across, our clothes and shoes were dripping mud and water. Just ahead of us was a long line of South Carolinians, lying flat on their faces, holding the position until we should come. When they saw us they called: 'Come on boys, walk right over us.' This we did, as the ground was so covered with their bodies and there was nowhere else to step."[68]

Battle Group McGowan, at the Foot of Zouave Hill

After Reynolds' Brigade fell back, a "North Carolina regiment came up on our right and a Georgia regiment on our left," said Col. McGowan of the 14th South Carolina.[69] The North Carolina "regiment" was G.B. Anderson's men.[70] The Georgia "regiment" was Battle Group Georgia, who had burst out of the woods at the foot of Zouave Hill. With this reinforcement, Battle Group McGowan and Rodes' Brigade charged out of the woods.[71] G.B. Anderson's Brigade joined the line, and the huge attack swept up Zouave Hill and Regulars' Hill, during the precise ten minutes that Garland's men had taken Hayden's guns.[72]

Sykes' Front

The situation on Sykes' front was that of impending disaster. Thousands of Confederates were coming up Zouave and Regulars' Hills, and the Yankees had very little to stop them. Brigadier Bartlett was frantically trying to bring up the balance of his brigade. Sykes' regiments, including the Pennsylvania Reserves that had relieved them, were generally in a status of low usefulness, either from lack of ammunition, disorganization, casualties, or exhaustion. The more useful remnants were trying to form a line facing northwest from McGehee's on the right to Hexamer's Battery A, New Jersey Light Artillery (4 Parrotts, 2 howitzers), and then to the right end of the line of artillery that General McCall was creating about 300 yards in front to the Adams House. Warren's Brigade and other relieved regiments were grouped together a few hundred yards behind them, due south of the McGehee House and due east of the Adams House. The less useful ones were already headed towards the river. Sykes' front had collapsed; the northern end of General Morell's Division was utterly flanked by the rough equivalent of a whole Confederate division. We must now leave Sykes' front for a moment and move our focus to General Morell's front.

18

To the Wall of Death

Despite Ewell's Division of the Valley Army fighting furiously and to the death right in front of them, it was General Jackson's appearance at New Cold Harbor that fired up the hearts of Longstreet's men. A member of the 7th Virginia, Kemper's Brigade, recalled, "Not too long after the artillery had picked up its fire, word came down the line, 'Stonewall Jackson has arrived!' As word of Jackson's arrival spread through the ranks, great yells went up all along the Confederate line, and infantrymen, inspired by the knowledge that the recent victor of the Valley Campaign was on the field, rushed forward everywhere with renewed vim and vigor."[1]

General Longstreet had just arrived at Battle Group Pickett when General Whiting arrived and asked General Longstreet where to be put in.[2] Whiting's arrival gave Longstreet a fired-up reinforced division of almost 18,000 men,[3] substantially larger than the number that he would have in an assault in Pennsylvania one year hence. These men were approximately 57 regiments in 10 brigades; both regiments and brigades fractured into distinct parts, some of which then recombined in a different structure, thus requiring more Battle Groups. From north to south, these are Battle Group Douglass (13th Georgia and half of the 26th Georgia), Battle Group Trimble (21st NC and 16th Miss., 7th NC), Battle Group Texas (Hampton Legion Infantry and 5th Texas, part of 18th Georgia), Battle Group Hood (4th Texas, most of the 18th Georgia, 1st Texas, and Law's Brigade), Archer's Brigade, Battle Group Pickett (Pickett's Brigade and R.H. Anderson's Brigade) and Battle Group Wilcox (Pryor's, Wilcox's and Featherston's Brigades), all with essentially no artillery. Opposing them were 8,754 men of Martindale's Brigade and Butterfield's Brigade, with the 12 guns of Weeden's Battery C, Rhode Island Artillery (6 ordnance rifles) and Hyde's Battery E, Massachusetts Light Artillery (6 ordnance rifles), reinforced with all of Meade's Brigade of Pennsylvania Reserves, about half of the New Jersey Brigade, and 20 guns (12 Napoleons and 8 howitzers) from McCall's Division[4] under Captains Easton, Kerns, and Dehart. All of these Yankees had the tremendous advantage of rudimentary fortifications impressive enough for Chaplain Davis, 4th Texas, to label the Yankees' position as "the wall of death."[5]

Previous authors have written of this attack by following various units from start to finish, and then moving to another unit. Longstreet's attack developed generally from the west, and occurred in several phases. This work will follow all of Longstreet's units through each phase to the next, as the men experienced it themselves.

Morell's Division

On the Federal side of the creek, General Morell's line near the Watt House had been reinforced. The 4th Michigan (Griffin's Brigade) had been relieved by the 3rd Pennsylvania Reserves, which had then been relieved by the 4th New Jersey and 11th Pennsylvania Reserves.[6] The 4th Michigan was now up top behind the 2nd Maine and between the Watt House and Weeden's guns.[7] The 3rd Pennsylvania Reserves were also out of ammunition and behind[8] the 11th Pennsylvania Reserves and Weeden's Battery C, Rhode Island Light Artillery (6 ordnance rifles). Brigadier Meade congratulated them on their "bravery and daring courage."[9] The 4th Pennsylvania Reserves were behind the 2nd Maine,[10] as was the battalion of the 2nd New Jersey.[11] The 2nd Maine, 13th New York, 25th New York, and 1st Michigan were down in the ravine and claimed to be low on ammunition.[12] The 22nd Massachusetts was behind them, and alongside it was the 7th Pennsylvania Reserves, supporting 1st Michigan.[13] Brigadier Butterfield's men were still in their original positions south of Martindale's Brigade; the 44th New York and the 83rd Pennsylvania were down in the ravine, with the 83rd's right flank touching the left flank of the 1st Michigan. The 12th New York was up top behind the 83rd, and the 16th Michigan was up top behind the 44th, but further back than the 12th, behind the crest of the hill south of the Watt House.[14] Hyde's Battery E, Massachusetts Light Artillery (6 ordnance rifles) was about 100 yards south of the Watt House. One, then two sections, were detached to its left and sent up to the edge of the woods along Boatswain's Creek.[15] At this point, the only cause for anxiety was that there were no further reserves. Every regiment was either on the front line, supporting it, or out of ammunition.

Ewell's Division, on Boatswain's Creek

General Ewell did not have much of a division left. Most of Elzey's Brigade was at the McGehee Road; the Louisianans had been banished as "nervous"; the 21st Georgia, 15th Alabama, and 13th Virginia had been holding the line. The 21st Georgia continued to hold the line. The 15th Alabama had run out of ammunition. General Ewell rode up, found this out, and told them to fix bayonets and hold until the Texans arrived. An ammunition detail arrived just after General Ewell left. Private McClendon "looked down hill to rear and there comes the [5th] Texas half bent as if looking for a turkey. We greeted them with a cheer which they responded. They marched up to our position and halted, rectified their line, fired one volley down the slant through the bushes at the Yankees."[16]

Samuel Buck of the 13th Virginia recalled a brush with death: "One of the enemy came from behind the works in my immediate front while I was capping my gun, got within a few yards of me when he fell, having been shot at my request by a man at my side who turned out to be a South Carolinian. This was very close fighting. I fired 38 rounds and my gun barrel was so hot from rapid firing I could scarcely hold it in my hands."[17] Another member of the 13th Virginia, Boney Loy, had his Mississippi rifle become so fouled that he could not remove the rammer. A bullet then struck him in the thigh. This "roused his anger" and he shot at the Yankees, bullet, ramrod, and all. Another ball passed through his knapsack and lodged in his clothing, doing no harm. A third one passed through his lungs.[18] "The 5th Texas and a portion of the Hampton Legion first came to my assistance,"[19] and Ewell ordered the 13th Virginia to the rear. Two-thirds of the 13th had been killed or wounded.[20]

While his men were holding the line, General Ewell himself had not been idle. The reinforcements he had sought out arrived, right after Battle Group Texas. Brigadier Trimble showed up with his two lost regiments, as did most of Col. Campbell's 7th North Carolina of Battle Group Walker. With Battle Group Douglass from Brigadier Lawton, General Ewell had conjured almost a whole brigade.

Battle Group Douglass

The 13th Georgia, Col. Douglass, was in reserve because it had no bayonets.[21] The 13th was west of the Parsons House when Campbell Brown of Ewell's staff guided it into battle.[22] On the way, it picked up the 26th Georgia's five right companies. The woods were eerily silent, except for artillery fire muffled by the woods and felled timber.[23] Private Murray, 26th Georgia, recalled, "We went on in through a very thick, boggy branch where we found a great many dead and wounded Yankees. Some of these were lying in the water. I was so thirsty from fever and a long march and run to the battle till my tongue was swollen. I stopped, dipped up and drank water which I knew had Yankees blood in it. I am sure it was the best water to me that I ever drank. I have often thought that it saved my life."[24]

Battle Group Trimble

Col. Campbell's 7th North Carolina had moved right from the McGehee Road and followed one of General Ewell's staff officers to the Parsons House. Brigadier Trimble had found his two lost regiments, the 16th Mississippi and the 21st North Carolina, and led them to the Parsons House, where they joined the 7th North Carolina, thus creating Battle Group Trimble.[25] One of General Lee's staff officers rode up in haste and shouted, "General Lee says the enemy have been driven in on both flanks, but still holds his position in that woods. He directs you to drive them from it."[26] Trimble had learned a lesson from what had happened to his first two regiments. A Mississippian recalled that Trimble told them, "Don't depend on shooting; give them the cold steel!"[27] As Trimble's two regiments advanced to the ravine, an all too familiar episode recurred. A colonel met them and exclaimed, "You can't drive the enemy…. Four attempts have been made by 4 different regiments and each has failed." Gen. Trimble replied, "We can and we will drive them! Forward, boys, and give them the bayonet!"[28]

With Gen. Longstreet, Along Powhite Creek

General Longstreet was with Battle Group Pickett when General Whiting arrived. Longstreet rode out to meet him, indicated the best location for Whiting's men, and rode back to Battle Group Pickett with instructions.[29] Longstreet now changed Battle Group Pickett's orders from a diversion to a full assault. The same orders were sent to Battle Group Wilcox; it would attack when it heard Whiting and Pickett firing to the north,[30] but this would miscarry. While Battle Group Pickett was sorting itself out, Whiting's Division was arriving on the field.

Whiting formed his division in the woods, just south of the Gaines' Mill and west of New Cold Harbor[31] about 6:30. Each man had 80 cartridges.[32] His left brigade, Hood, was near the Parsons House. His right brigade, Law's, would hit the Federals just south of it.[33] The whole division would swing like a gate to the left, into and through the Wall of Death. Hood's regiments went in different directions, and did diverse things, all under the moniker of "Hood's Brigade," which has led to much confusion.

Hood's Brigade also initially formed in two lines,[34] facing south, with the Hampton Legion Infantry on the extreme left.[35] It would be the gate's hinge. The 5th Texas was on its right, and the 1st Texas on its right.[36] The 4th Texas and the 18th Georgia were initially in a second line with the 4th Texas on the left, the 18th Georgia on the right. Brigadier Law's men deployed to the right of Hood; the right end of the 4th Alabama, being the latch of the gate, was also in two lines. Before they were committed, the 4th Texas moved to the right of the 18th Georgia,[37] so it was actually behind the 1st Texas. The whole division would swing like a gate to the left and smash into the Wall of Death.

Once the attack started, the Hampton Legion[38] quickly came up on the left of Ewell's men and joined Battle Group Trimble. The 5th Texas quickly came up on General Ewell's right. To its right was the 1st Texas.[39] Law's Brigade was on its right, but stopped; most of Brigadier Hood's second line angled right and passed over it, so the 4th Texas was in front and its right became the latch of the gate. Law's Brigade started moving again once the 4th Texas passed over them, so it was slightly behind the 4th. Most of the 18th Georgia went with the 4th Texas. Since Hood himself was with this portion, it will be called Battle Group Hood. Two companies of the 18th Georgia[40] stayed with the 5th Texas. These make up Battle Group Texas, and went in near Boatswain's Run, to the left (north) of the 1st Texas.

Attack on Whiting's Division's Attack on the Yankee Line

(North)	Y
	A
Battle Group Texas>	N
1st Texas>	K
Battle Group Hood>	S

Battle Group Texas

At General Whiting's command, Battle Group Texas stepped off in the advance. They encountered Federal artillery fire when they reached the open ground.[41] As they approached Carolina Hill, they found a "thin line of Confederate soldiers."[42] These were the remnants of J.R. Anderson's Georgians. As they neared Boatswain's Creek at its intersection with Boatswain's Run, Battle Group Texas was "meeting great bodies of stragling [sic] men with wounded coming out of the fight sometime breaking our ranks so bad that it kept up a confusion."[43] "En route, we passed troops in a disordered condition, coming out, who said 'Don't go in there you will be killed.'"[44] A more lettered member of the 5th Texas wrote, "They [were] ordered to retire…. As they pass us to the rear, the effect upon our men is most trying to their nerves; they are literally cut to pieces … having left prostrate forms of more than half of their number at the breastworks they failed to carry."[45] Battle Group Texas "reached the line of battle in good order and found a portion of General Ewell's forces maintaining the ground against heavy odds."[46] These were what was left of the 13th Virginia (Elzey's Brigade), which had indeed lost half of its number, and Brigadier Trimble's 15th Alabama and 21st Georgia. Soon Battle Group Texas was "fronting that terrible place ... where the straglers [*sic*] said we could not take."[47]

"I opened fire with my regiment, and after firing some 30 minutes it was evident that the fire of the enemy was greatly reduced, and that the time for charging them was near,"[48] reported Col. Robertson. Suddenly, a staff officer rode up and "exclaimed, 'Stand boys, don't run for God's sake don't run, but die here!'" Lt. Col. Upton was standing nearby, dressed as usual in his wool battle shirt, black hat, two six-shooters at the hips with a huge sword, and a long-handled frying pan for "himself and the mess."[49] He jumped up with the fury of a madman and exclaimed, "Who in the hell are you talking to sir? These are my men, these are Texans—they don't know how to run and you leave here or I'll blow hell into you."[50]

Over across the River, General John Magruder was watching the battle. From his vantage point, he could see Federals in some threatening position, and sent his aide, Major Haskell, to tell General Lee about it. After a harrowing escape from the Yankee videttes, Haskell rode to New Cold Harbor delivered his message, and went to join his old friend General Longstreet.[51]

1st Texas

Pvt. Glover, 1st Texas, recalled that his regiment was ordered to "drive the enemy out of their breastworks which were formidable as any I ever saw."[52] As the 1st Texas advanced, it passed over one of Field's Virginia regiments "lying in a field."[53] It came up to the most formidable part of Boatswain's Creek. The western lip of the creek falls off here in a vertical cliff, perhaps 30 feet high, which stopped the 1st Texas' advance cold.

Battle Group Hood, Law's Brigade

"General Whiting ... formed the Mississippians in his brigade into a hollow square, and in that position we could hear him plainly... 'When the charge is ordered, there will be no order for retreat. I will lead you, and I believe you will carry the works,'"[54] recalled one private. General Whiting also visited the 6th North Carolina: "The gallant Whiting, riding a long in front of the line, raised his hat in acknowledgement of the salute, and called out, saying, 'Boys, you can take it!'"[55] General Whiting then rode along Law's whole line on a "spirited dapple gray,"[56] and ordered the men to load their weapons.[57] As they came out of the woods, the men studied the Yankee position, which was, in one man's words, "a perfect Gibraltar."[58] "[T]he Federal line was shrouded in smoke, and seemed fairly to vomit forth a leaden and iron hail."[59] Approaching Virginia Hill, "General Field's Virginia Brigade was found lying down in the field ... while the shrapnel and bullets poured into them thick as hail. They would neither advance nor fall back; they were perfectly exhausted and out of ammunition."[60] Lt. Col. McLemore, 4th Alabama, turned around and walked backwards, called cadence, "Guide center, keep the step-one, two, three, four, one, two, three, four," and continued calling out the step until we had passed over the Virginians, and then he gave the order to charge."[61] Passing over the crest, Pvt. Chambers "saw [Whiting] wave his hat and call 'Mississippians, Charge!' … with a roar, and as of one man we gave the Rebel Yell."[62] Chaplain Davis of the 4th Texas considered this "the most galling fire I ever witnessed."[63] Pvt. Samuel Hankins[64] said, "We had gone about 20 yards when Joe said to me, 'Let's drop our tin cups; they are just so much in the way.' Just then Bang! and Joe Compton fell on his face. I heard him groan, and I saw a stream of blood about the size of my finger shoot up through his thick black hair."[65] Just before cresting Virginia Hill, Chaplain Davis noted, "The storm of iron and lead was too severe; they [Law's Brigade] wavered for a moment, and fell upon the ground."[66] This stop opened a gap in the line; Brigadier Hood "commanded in his clear ringing voice, 'Forward!'"[67] and took the 4th Texas and 8 companies of the 18th Georgia (Battle Group Hood) over Law's prostrate men. Law's men laid down for just enough time for Battle Group Hood to pass over them.[68]

Battle Group Hood, 4th Texas/18th Georgia

Not all of Field's Virginians were skulking. One man jumped up, told his men that they were a disgrace, cast away his sword, took up a musket, and joined the 4th Texas. He was killed within a few steps.[69] Lt. Col. Warwick, 4th Texas, took up their colors and advanced, sword in one hand flag in the other.[70] Just as Battle Group Hood passed over Law's prostrate men and the crest of Virginia Hill, Col. Marshall, 4th Texas, shouted, "Close up that gap!"—and then, with blood streaming down his face, he fell forward on his horse's neck, and then to the ground.[71] The gap closed up, but another one was made.[72] The artillery fire was such that to Pvt. Crozier it "seemed as though those screaming, shrieking shells would never stop." The air was stifling with the smell of gunpowder, and though the sun was shining brightly, the day was nearly dark as night. A riderless horse bolted through the lines with its lower jaw shot off.[73] "Volleys of musketry, and showers of grape, canister and shell ploughed through us, but were only answered by a stern 'Close up—close up to the colors!'"[74] "Onward they rushed over the dead and dying … without a pause, until within about 100 yards of the breast-works." Here the Rhode Island guns switched to canister and their infantry had the range.[75] The "fire of the enemy was falling on us like drops of rain from a passing cloud," and closer to the Federal line they became "teeming showers."[76] Brigadier Hood wheeled his horse,[77] and: "At this critical juncture, the voice of General Hood was heard above the din of battle, 'Forward, Forward, charge right down on them and drive them out with the bayonet!' Fixing bayonets as they moved, they made one grand rush…."[78] Now the short-range Yankee muskets, obscured by the trees,[79] opened up. Half of the 4th Texas' right wing fell at their first fire.[80]

Law's men were right behind Battle Group Hood, and thus became part of it. "Men fell like leaves in an autumn wind, the Federal artillery tore gaps in the ranks at every step, the ground in rear of the advancing column was strewn thickly with the dead and wounded…."[81] That artillery was Bucklin's section of Weeden's Battery C, Rhode Island Artillery (2 ordnance rifles) at the Watt House. Lt. Col. McLemore, 4th Alabama, fell wounded.[82] The smoke had settled down heavily, and one standing erect could scarcely see ten feet in his front.[83] So many fell in Pvt. Hankins' company of the 2nd Mississippi that it was commanded by the 2nd sergeant.[84] "[N]ot a gun was fired in reply; there was no confusion, and not a step faltered as the two gray lines swept silently and swiftly on; the pace became more rapid every moment when the men were within 30 yards of the ravine, and could see the desperate nature of the work at hand. A wild yell answered the roar of Federal musketry, and they rushed for the works."[85] In Law's Brigade and Battle Group Hood, "In the very few moments it took them to pass over the slope and down the hill to the ravine, a thousand men were killed or wounded."[86]

Archer's Brigade

After his going at the Union lines with Powell Hill's attack, Brigadier Archer withdrew back to Powhite Creek, and sent his aide, Capt. George Lemmon, to headquarters for further orders. Capt. Lemmon never found Powell Hill, but did espy Whiting's Division coming at a run, and returned to Brigadier Archer with that information. Brigadier Archer decided to "move forward to the attack of the same position and [enter] it in the front line of attack."[87] His men formed up as Battle Group Pickett deployed to their right. John Hurst wrote, "[W]e were ordered on again, and but for my old friend and messmate, Ralph Cardin, I am afraid and declined to go. He said, 'Let's go, if it kills us all.'"[88]

Brigadier Archer advanced, with his brigade in two lines, slightly behind Battle Group Pickett but ahead of those on his left, Battle Group Hood. Having been brutally mauled the first time, Archer added his sole fresh regiment, the 19th Georgia, to the attack, and changed his tactics. Major M'Comb, 14th Tennessee, related, "General Archer ordered me to make a beeline for a [ravine] that was in our front…. As we passed General Field's brigade this time they moved with us…. One of General [Powell] Hill's aides, Capt. Frank Hill, came along our line very rapidly and said General Whiting was supporting us and General Jackson was to the left of us. This encouraged the boys very much…."[89] "As we passed General Field's brigade this time they moved with us."[90]

Col. Christian, 55th Virginia, had rallied some of Field's men, including the 47th Virginia,[91] and went back to the crest of Virginia Hill, where they kept up a fire on the Yankees. As they joined Archer's line, Color Sgt. Fauntleroy and the 55th's flag fell, and their line faltered. Private Nicholson snatched up the 55th's battle flag until he fell. Lt. Sydnor of the 40th Virginia took up the 55th's colors.[92] Another member of the brigade wrote, "The advance … was slow but steady, moving forward by rushes about 30 yards and then lying down until the supports came up, and then advancing again, until when about 30 paces from the ditch, Gen. Archer said 'Do not let the supports lie down.' As they came up he ordered: 'Forward everybody! We are going through!'"[93]

Brigadier Archer and his men arrived before Battle Group Hood. "Gen. Hood's line incorporated itself into our line…. When the first line [Hood] got within a few paces of us, the fire was so destructive they halted and only with difficulty could be moved up to join in with our line. We were greatly endangered by their firing in our rear."[94] Battle Group Hood was taking fire from the Union regiments up top, primarily the 22nd Massachusetts, not the ones down in the ravine. "But here there was defect in the enemy's position. They could not depress their guns to get our range, and from the infantry line they could not see us. Very little damage was done our ranks while passing though the abatis."[95] Brigadier Archer had crossed 600 yards of open ground between two huge Battle Groups and had reached the Union line first, but apparently neither Generals Powell Hill,

Longstreet, Whiting, Hood, nor Law ever mention it.[96] Archer's firing was heard half a mile away, by Battle Group Wilcox.

While the attack was going in, Major Haskell met General Whiting, who asked him to rally some skulkers and to reinforce the right of the division.[97]

Battle Group Pickett

Pickett's Brigade scuttlebutt had it that when General Lee had asked Longstreet for a brigade to assault the Union line, Longstreet demurred, saying, "I have a brigade, Pickett's, that will carry it, but it has been in the thickest of all the fights and has lost heavily. I don't like to send it in." Lee replied, "This is no time for sentiment. I must carry the place."[98] This is dubious, as General Lee was at New Cold Harbor and had been sending him messages from there. However, General Longstreet did meet with Brigadier R.H. Anderson. "My part of this work has not yet been accomplished and I have nobody to do it with but you." R.H. Anderson replied, "Well, General, what is it you want done?" Longstreet answered, "The enemy must come off that hill before night." R.H. Anderson "cheerfully" responded, "If any brigade in the army can do it, mine can."[99]

When Brigadier Pickett received Longstreet's attack order, his men were separated. Pickett himself, the 8th Virginia, and the 18th Virginia were advanced as skirmishers on the right, with the rest of the brigade under the cover of the northern crest of Florida Hill. The 19th Virginia had sent out skirmishers in its own front while the 28th and 56th waited back in Powhite Creek. Pickett had left Major Walter Harrison to watch over this part of the brigade while he, Pickett, was over with the 8th and 18th. Harrison was not to move until Pickett returned. Suddenly, Major Moxley Sorrell, an aide to Longstreet, rode up and ordered Harrison to forward the partial brigade. Vexed, Harrison rode to Longstreet, who was closer than Pickett, with the dilemma. Longstreet sent word to Pickett that the brigade would move instantly and the 8th and 18th were to form on its right as it passed by.

It took some time for Major Harrison to form his part of the brigade. The 56th Virginia was on the left, the 28th next on the right, and then the 19th.[100] When Maj. Harrison's part moved forward, it picked up the 18th and the 8th. R.H. Anderson's brigade was behind them[101] as they marched towards Florida Hill,[102] but there they stopped.[103] Kemper's men were put in the woods along Powhite Creek, and being the only Confederate reserves, they stayed put.[104]

Battle Group Pickett moved towards the enemy.[105] "The sun shone brightly and the atmosphere was clear, and every move that Lee's troops made could be plainly seen by the enemy,"[106] observed Lt. Cooper of the 8th Virginia. Major Harrison, an aide to Brigadier Pickett, recollected, "The fire from the enemy's batteries and small arms was terrific, but the brave old brigade pushed on. The officers were being fast thinned out. It was almost impossible to see or hear anything distinctly, such was the continual rush of shot and shell."[107] Lt. Wood of the 19th Virginia observed, "The smoke from their guns settled in the bottom between us, and not only concealed the enemy but shut out from their view their surroundings."[108] In other words, the Yankees' own smoke was blinding them, so they could not see to shoot effectively. "As soon as this advancing brigade reached the summit of the hill it was met by a storm of shot and shell I never saw exceeded except in the famous charge of Pickett's men at Gettysburg." About 75 yards from the

Yankees,[109] "Brigadier Pickett was within 10 paces of me when he was shot from his horse. When he fell, Pickett exclaimed, quite astonished, 'Somebody hit me!'" Pickett had taken a single Minie ball to the shoulder.[110]

Command devolved onto Col. Eppa Hunton, 8th Virginia,[111] but Hunton did not know it.[112] "Pickett ... being hid by the smoke of battle, approached to within 40 yards of their first line of intrenchment, where, in the intense heat and the dense smoke, they involuntarily threw themselves flat on the ground and commenced firing. The roar of musketry was so terrific that it was impossible to hear anything else."[113] Pvt. George Harris of the 19th Virginia was seen to go forward from the front line, take "deliberate aim, fire and fall back [into the line] to reload."[114] Col. Withers was mesmerized as the volume of fire caused bark from a walnut tree to fly off like sawdust.[115] Col. Hunton, 8th Virginia, rode up and asked Withers what they should do. "Push forward!" Withers screamed. "No troops can live long under a fire line this!"[116]

The right wing of the 56th Virginia was already wavering.[117] "There was some confusion—owing to the crossing of the fallen timber and other obstructions—and I suspect the brigade would have given way had not the Texans now charged with loud cries, inspiriting our men, and creating a generous rivalry to first carry the works."[118] "We had fired perhaps two volleys, when Col. Slaughter, with Corporal Gill, the color bearer, rushed ahead, shouting to us, "Charge them!"[119] Col. Withers, 18th Virginia, was mounted, and alongside his color guard. All eight men fell in the next 30 yards, as did Col. Withers, 40 yards from the Union line. Another ball hit him as he was carried away. Capt. Wise took over the 18th, only to have a leg shot off by a solid shot.[120] "The 'rebel yell' resounded over the din of battle."[121]

In his travels, Major Haskell came across the wounded General Pickett.[122] After crossing the open and arriving near the federal position, Haskell's stragglers flopped to the ground, joining those who were lying down.[123] Chagrined, Haskell tried to get them moving, finally snatching a flag from a recumbent color bearer. The bearer tried to get it back, and agreed to charge if the colonel would. Haskell rode over to the colonel, also lying down, and began poking him in the back with the butt of the flagstaff! Enraged, the colonel jumped up, but when ordered to charge, he took off in the other direction. Haskell followed and clonked him on the head with his sword, but the colonel kept going and fell.[124] Haskell's horse was then hit and bolted—straight into the Union lines.[125]

The sleeve removed from Brigadier Pickett's uniform coat when he was wounded at Gaines' Mill. Note the damage near the shoulder (courtesy Ian Hoffman and the National Civil War Museum, Harrisburg, Pennsylvania).

Pvt. Shotwell, 8th Virginia, declared that Pickett's men had absorbed the Yankees' attention, and their fire, while the Texans rushed them,[126] but Archer's Brigade, not Battle Group Hood, was to Pickett's left. Nevertheless, to Brigadier Pickett and his men must go the laurels of striking the enemy's works first, as Archer clearly states that Battle Group Pickett was ahead of him and that he was ahead of Battle Group Hood.

Battle Group Wilcox

Battle Group Wilcox was the extreme right of the whole Confederate line, and separated from Battle Group Pickett by some distance.[127] Wilcox's own brigade was nearest the river; Pryor's Brigade, less the 2nd Florida, was to its left, with Featherston's Brigade behind the center.[128] Wilcox's 10th and 11th Alabama regiments were in his first line, with the 11th on the right, and the 8th and 9th were in his second line, with the 9th on the right.[129] "At length the furious Rebel Yell was heard away to our left of our three brigades…. Word came down the line that Stonewall Jackson had just arrived from the Valley. Our men could be restrained no longer. With a wild unearthly yell the whole lone sprang forward…."[130]

Hearing Brigadier Archer's firing to the left, not Whiting's nor Pickett's, Brigadier Pryor jumped the gun,[131] advancing all alone in the open towards Boatswain's Creek. "Ascending the hill in front of this position, my men were staggered by a terrific volley at the same time that they suffered severely from the battery across the Chickahominy. I was compelled to retire them to cover in a ravine to their rear."[132]

Brigadier Wilcox jumped the gun, too. Neither Whiting's Division, nor Battle Group Pickett, had yet finished deploying for their attack[133] when Wilcox, Pryor, and Featherston crested Florida Hill. As soon as they did, Knieriem and Diederich's batteries began pounding all three from across the river with siege artillery, creating casualties and confusion.[134]

Pryor considered that "Wilcox had come to my assistance."[135] According to a member of the 14th Alabama, "A few hasty orders were given to the men when the command was given to go forward, and in an advance of a hundred yards we were in full view of the enemy's musketry. They opened a fire on us with terrible effect…."[136] Lt. Miller, 14th Louisiana, remembered, "The brigade followed Pryor across a wide field, first walking, then breaking into a run down a gentle slope towards Boatswain's Swamp…. When the Yankee muskets opened fire, the bullets tore ragged holes through the Louisiana line."[137] Miller had one ball pass through his sword scabbard and kill a man running next to him. "The bullets came so thick I felt a desire to see how many I could catch with my open hand stretched out."[138] "[O]ur columns advanced to within 50 yards of their nearest breastwork; we halted for a moment, and a few rounds from our boys [14th Alabama] dislodged them."[139] The 14th Louisiana "pushed on under the order to charge until the enemy was reached and driven from his entrenchments, losing in the charge over 100 men."[140] The 3rd Virginia fared little better. "We charged them … through a wheat field. We got in about 75 yards of them when they opened fire on us. I was wounded on the first fire in both legs…."[141] "In these assaults I sustained a very great loss—as much from the enemy's artillery as from his infantry fire…. A single shell killed and disabled 11 of my men," reported Pryor. In fact, his men were "almost annihilated."[142] "At last, with a terrific yell our brave men rushed down the hill, leaped the ditch, and drove the enemy from his position at the point of the bayonet."[143]

In Wilcox's Brigade, Col. Woodward, 10th Alabama, and Lt. Col. Hale both fell in the Yankees' first fire, as did most of the other 41 officer casualties in the brigade. The 8th and 9th Alabama were in the second line of Wilcox's Brigade and saw what happened ahead of them. "When [Wilcox's] first regiment got to the top of the hill it halted, the next one came up and halted on the same line so with the four regiments on our left."[144] Another private recorded, "[T]he order was given 'Forward, Guide Center, March! Charge bayonets!… [W]hen we came into view on the top of the ridge we met such a perfect storm of lead right in our faces that the whole brigade literally *staggered* backward several paces as though pushed by a tornado…. [T]hen the cry of Major Sorrel, 'Forward Alabamians! Forward!' and the cry was taken up by the officers of the different regiments and we swept forward with wild cheers over the crest and down the slope, and though at every step some brave one fell, we did not falter." Clayborne Thrasher was cut almost

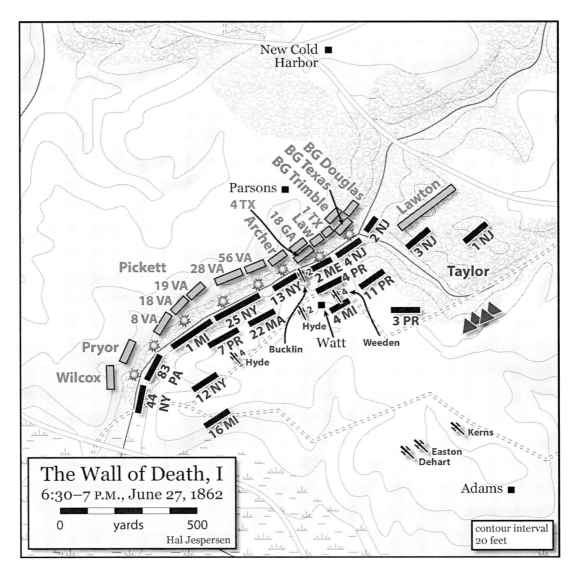

The Wall of Death, I

6:30–7 P.M., June 27, 1862

0 yards 500

Hal Jespersen

contour interval 20 feet

entirely in two by a cannon ball that struck him above his side; his head and feet fell together.[145] Pvt. Williams recalled, "When we came up, in place of halting on this line we raised the yell and double-quicked down the hill to the woods. It is a mystery to me how any of us escaped on crossing that ridge."[146] When the Alabamians' rear line overtook the first, Featherston's Brigade came up in the rear of Pryor's Brigade.[147] By this time, Battle Group Pickett was on the move to Pryor's right. Brigadier Wilcox noted, "Our men press[ed] on with unabashed fury."[148]

When ordering Featherston's Brigade to form behind Wilcox and Pryor, Brigadier Wilcox recognized the color bearer of the 19th Mississippi, Pvt. Jim Moser. Wilcox said to him, "'Jim, do you see the crest of the hill beyond this open field? When the command to charge is given, carry that flag to the top of that hill.' The command 'Forward, Double Quick, March!' was given. The colors obeyed, but the men hesitated. They were urged to follow the flag and the lines began to move, but wavered some. The flag had 'gotten away' from them when someone called, 'Jim, bring the colors back to this line.' To this Jim replied, 'Bring the line up to the colors! The colors are going where commanded!'" "Like lightning from Jove," Featherston's line moved up. Brave Private Moser later died wrapped in his colors.[149]

Brigadier Featherston would go on to report, "During this advance they were exposed to a raking fire from the enemy's artillery in front, as well as his long range rifles. The advance was rapidly made with unbroken lines…. The woods were reached with considerable loss in our ranks."[150]

19

At the Wall of Death

Battle Group Douglass

Just as the fresh troops arrived, 13th Georgia, in the front line, was staggered by a volley from the Federals only 40 yards away. Col. Douglass had his men lie down and prepare for a charge. Douglass sent his color bearer across the creek, with orders to plant the flag on the opposite bank. He did so, and gave the order to charge, but the regiment stayed put and opened fire.[1] Then someone claimed that they were firing on friends. Part of the regiment stopped firing, and part did not, so the regiment disintegrated.[2] While the officers were trying to reform it, the 26th Georgia came up beside them. "We were ordered to the right ... [we] went a short distance and advanced over the dead and wounded, friends and foes," remarked Private Murray.[3]

Just as they were negotiating Boatswain's Creek, the battalion of the 2nd New Jersey advanced to the brink of the hill and gave them a short-range volley.[4] The 26th and the 13th returned fire, and soon the Yankees fell back.[5] The 2nd New Jersey, having lost 21 percent of its men already, received fire from its left, realized it was flanked, and took off for the rear. It would lose another 40 men missing, bringing its casualty rate up to 37 percent.[6]

Battle Group Trimble

Battle Group Trimble was behind the left of the 5th Texas, and consisted of remnants of the 13th Virginia, 15th Alabama, 21st Georgia, and part of the 7th North Carolina, as well as all of the 21st North Carolina, 16th Mississippi, and Hampton Legion (South Carolina) Infantry. Here the Wall of Death consisted of felled trees, and then three lines of infantry, one lying, one kneeling, and one standing.[7] When the 7th North Carolina had "mov[ed] about a quarter of a mile, they were ordered to advance across a swamp and over an abatis of felled trees up a hill upon an intrenched position of the enemy."[8] With Battle Group Douglass on its left, Battle Group Trimble charged, "receiving heavy volleys from the opposite heights ... down the hill and over trees felled in the swampy ground to impede our progress all the time under torrents of musketry fire and bravely and rapidly ascended the hill, cheered on by the continuous shouting of the command 'Charge, men! Charge!'"[9] Even General Ewell joined in, shouting, "Now charge them, boys!"[10] "It would have required older and braver troops and engaged in a better cause to have stood firm against an onset so rapid, so resolute, so defiant."[11] As the Yankees fled, Trimble's men mercilessly shot them down.[12]

Battle Group Texas

"Col. Robertson [5th Texas] ordered 'Fix bayonet! Charge! Give them the bayonet my brave boys!' The old Indian war hoop, now called the rebel yell, was raised and but a few bounds over the dead was made, and we were standing at the brink of [the] creek and spring, pouring lead into the federals as rapidly as we could load our guns. We with the flag landed at the spring where the gulch [Boatswain's Run] began, and the best place to cross the creek. I without delay soon crossed and raised my gun to shoot the first federal I saw rise from his works, he ran looking back at me and someone shot him down."[13] The 5th Texas "charged with a yell that could be heard 5 miles off." "We charged them downhill we went into the branch up to our knees." Private Jackson outdid Private McClendon of the 15th Alabama; he lost both shoes.[14] Now underneath the smoke, the Texans could see the enemy.[15] Their fire had been so effective that the Yankees would not raise their heads above their works.[16] It was clear to Cpl. Brantley that the Yankees knew it was "death to stay and steel was the next thing."[17] The 5th Texas "climbed one … obstruction, with comrades falling like autumn leaves. And with bayonet shoved them from their works—and in less than 20 minutes had conquered their works."[18] Sgt. Onderdonk, then acting color bearer, was killed.[19] "Onderdonk, the color bearer crossed right behind me…. Soon as Onderdonk hit the ground he was shot down and the flag came down at my left. I caught it and looked back at him. He says, "Take it, I am shot.' I then dropped my gun, drew my sword bayonet raised the flag above my head with a yell, and moved with all speed for the heights," remembered Cpl. Brantley.[20] The 5th Texas had Enfield fusils, a shorter version of the more common Enfield rifle. Its lack of length was made up for by attaching a wicked-looking sword bayonet.

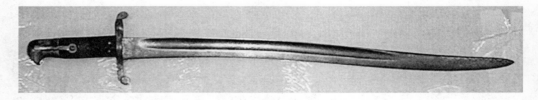

An example of Cpl. Brantley's sword bayonet (author's collection).

1st Texas

The 5th and 1st Texas were at a point on Boatswain's Creek where the west bank is higher than the east, and falls in a vertical 30-foot cliff. They were shooting down at the "Federal works beneath us," through "smoke so dense that we could not see them…."[21] "Our forces … aimed only by the flash of enemy guns & by guess."[22]

The 11th Pennsylvania Reserves (Seymour's Brigade) had just relieved the 4th New Jersey (Taylor's Brigade) after their fight with Ewell's Division. When put into the line, both General McCall and Brigadier Martindale told the Pennsylvanians that it was the weakest part of the line, and that it had to be held "at all hazards." "They did not see us ... and we let them come up to the edge of the ravine, when we poured a volley into them that sent them back reeling."[23] The 4th New Jersey, low on ammunition, retired to a second line.[24] "[W]hen line after line of the enemy's fresh troops bore down upon them in deadly conflict, they met such volleys from the men of the 11th as sent them staggering back; volleys that seemed like a continuous stream of fire."[25] It stopped the 1st Texas in its tracks.

Battle Group Hood

"Raising the Rebel Yell, we dashed across the creek which we found to have steep banks ... with sides cut to form a ditch."[26] Hood's right flank slipped and skidded down the slope of the ravine only to tumble onto Archer's Brigade.[27] "The onset was so furious and determined that seized with panic, the first line of Federals, taking time to fire only a few scattering shots, took to precipitate flight." The terror may have been caused in part by Capt. "Howdy" Martin, who led his company with a formidable Colt Dragoon six-shooter in each hand.[28] "Their panic communicated itself to the troops in the two lines behind them, and they too fled, pell mell, and probably with a prayer that the devil might save the hindmost, up and over the ridge in their rear."[29] "And in the next minute our battle flag was planted upon the captured breast work. The cowardly foe, frightened at the rapid approach of pointed steel, rose from behind their defenses, and started up the hill at speed. One volley was poured into their backs, and it seemed as if every ball found a victim, so great was the slaughter. Their works were ours, and as our flag moved from the first to the second tier of defenses, a shout arose from the shattered remnant of that regiment, and which will be long remembered by those who heard it; a shout which announced that the wall of death was broken...."[30] Pvt. Hunter was more succinct: "The regiment that was in my front gave back as soon as we pressed them."[31] "There a brave [Federal officer], on horseback, with his hat on his sword, [who] tried to rally them but they scarcely had time...."[32] Atop the breastwork, Lt. Col. Warwick waved his confiscated Virginia battle flag and shouted "Come on!" The 4th Texas had already lost 200 men.[33]

Law's Brigade crossed the creek where the 4th Texas had driven the Yankees back.[34] A member of the 11th Mississippi recalled, "At the foot of this hill we found solid log breastworks with sharpened sticks and a deep ditch. I personally was fortunate in being able to jump the ditch where the majority of the men had to jump into the ditch and get out as best they could...."[35] "Pvt. Jim Harrison fell into the Union ditch, shot one Yankee, and had another 23 men surrender to him. He took the officer's sword and pistol, and led them to the rear."[36]

The 2nd Maine (Martindale's Brigade) was defending this portion of Boatswain's Creek. Their left was on the grassy way to Parson's Spring; the 4th Pennsylvania Reserves,[37] with little ammunition, was behind them. Col. Roberts, 2nd Maine, reported, "At this juncture I requested one of the Pennsylvania regiments stationed directly in my rear, to relieve me, and I gave to my command the order to fix bayonets, when, to my surprise, the Pennsylvania regiment, rising up to relieve me as I supposed, went to the right about and retreated from the field in confusion. At this time the right and left flanks of our entire army corps having been broken, I followed suit with my own command."[38] The 2nd Maine lost 26 percent of its men, with more missing than wounded.

Col. Magilton, 4th Pennsylvania Reserves, reported, "[W]e were [there] but a few moments when our center gave way and we were cut off, and made our escape only be crossing the Chickahominy...."[39] The 4th had already been engaged once during the day, but lost only 10 percent casualties, as many missing as wounded.

Archer's Brigade

The short rushes of Archer's Brigade brought them to the ravine first. Capt. George Lemmon wrote, "There was a heavy line behind Archer and three or more on his right...."[40] Battle Group Hood was behind him, and Battle Groups Pickett and Wilcox were to the right. "We soon struck a branch where the enemy had felled all the trees and cut the branches, and it took some time to get through this abatis. And before we got through, General Hood's Texas Brigade caught up to us.[41] After passing through to the foot of the cliff we found an open level place of about 30 feet, which gave us a chance to reform our line, and we waited until the Texas boys could get through and re-form."[42] Brigadier Archer went into the ravine, followed a few moments later by Capt. Lemmon, who also fell into the ditch and had trouble getting out.[43] In the meantime, "General Archer and General Hood were old friends ... and it took very little time for them to decide what to do. They ordered the charge, and the boys raised the Rebel Yell."[44] Sam Taylor, 18 years old and carrying the 14th Tennessee's colors, was the first man to cross the enemy's breastworks.[45] As Captain Lemmon moved up the slope on the Union side of the ravine, he literally ran into another officer, Brigadier Hood himself. The two shook hands and moved forward, but Capt. Lemmon sprained his ankle at the third breast-work.[46] In the proud words of one Tennessean, "Gen Hood's line incorporated itself into our line and all went on together in the final storming of the enemy's position."[47] Archer's Brigade now becomes a part of Battle Group Hood.

The 13th New York (Martindale's Brigade) had its right end on the grassy way to Parson's Spring, and had thrown up works. "Our men stood their ground manfully, hold-ing the enemy in check until all their ammunition was expended, when we fell back to the second line of defense. The enemy, seeing us fall back, pressed us hard. Here our loss was severe."[48] The 13th put up more of a fight; it had 4 killed, 47 wounded, and only 29 missing, 39 percent of the regiment.[49]

Battle Group Pickett

Eppa Hunton's 8th Virginia, on Pickett's right, launched itself into the smoke-filled ravine,[50] with regiments to his left following suit. A member of the 8th Virginia remem-bered, "The charge was made, and our regiment with the 18th Virginia, moved straight across the stream...."[51] Lt. Wood, of the 19th Virginia, tried to jump across, but fell into the creek and was unable to extricate himself.[52] Pickett's men went "over the breastworks, and up thru a skirt of woods to an opening,"[53] but had lost heavily. Pvt. Irby, 18th Virginia, noted, "When at last the survivors reached the dich at the foot of the hill, they were sadly decimated, but on and up they went, till from its summit the stars and bars waved in tri-umph in sight of the scattered and flying foe."[54] The Virginians were "dashing across the gulley and the creek, up the slope driving the Yankees so rapidly from the first and second line of works that they could not reform in the third...."[55]

Major Haskell's horse was shot dead leaping over the Union breastworks and had the impudence to fall on top of Major Haskell and his flag.

> A captain, I think of a New York Regiment, ran up to me and grabbing the flagstaff called out to me, you damned little rebel, surrender. I held on and jerked him to me, striking him at the same time with my sword…. He at once jumped back and fired at me with his pistol, cursing me all the time and tugging at the flagstaff. I kept jerking it back and striking at him with my sword, while at the same time struggling to get from under my dead horse…. One ball from the pistol struck at the star of my collar and burned my neck like fire, while another struck my little finger, breaking it and smashing a … ring that I wore. Another just grazed my leg, but that one felt like a double heated, hot-iron and made me struggle so that I found myself free from my horse and on my feet. Our troops by this time were pouring in and the Yankees running, my opponent among them. I cut him down with both hands, expecting to split him, but my sword bounced off, knocking him to his knees. He rose and turned, facing me with his pistol in hand. I never doubted that he was about to shoot again and ran him through. He lived only a few minutes after, trying to say something.[56]

Pickett's left, the 56th Virginia, was attacking the 25th New York.

> [T]he 25th reserved fire until the enemy were halfway down the hill, and then opened fire on them. The enemy once wavered for a moment, and would have gone back, but for the impulsion of the mass behind. Major Gilbert stood just in rear of the colors shooting the rebels as they advanced with his pistol. Captain Bates was wounded here…. The break in the first line commenced to the left of our regiment, and ran like a wave through the whole line. I did not see Major Gilbert after he left the barricade … but I learned … that he fell, while going back up the hill to the second line. Capt. Ferguson … was mortally wounded.[57]

The 25th did not put up as much of a fight as did the 13th New York; it only lost 13 percent, with wounded and missing about the same.

Pickett's center and right, the 19th, 18th and 8th Virginia, hit the 1st Michigan, which was to the left of the 25th New York. Col. Roberts, 1st Michigan, is the only regimental commander to tell the unvarnished truth. The enemy "moved steadily on with a fire that cut down nearly ¼ of my command until up and onto us … the line broke and the men commenced a retreat. The men were borne back by sheer force of numbers."[58] Lt. Christiancy survived; his daughter married Brigadier Pickett's son.[59] The 1st Michigan officially lost 18 percent, more wounded than missing.

Battle Group Wilcox

"Jumping and clawing their way across the gorge, the Louisianans [Pryor's Brigade] had to reform their line on the other side … and charged once again."[60] "[T]hen some of the more active cleared at a bound; others jumped and scrambled up the opposite side."[61] "[We] drove the first line back pell mell upon the second and charging upon the heights upon this, it too broke and fled in confusion…."[62] "A feeble advance seemed to carry consternation to every mother's son of them and the whole three lines broke in flight up the hill."[63] Another participant mused, "How we ever got through that tangled mass of timber so rapidly has ever been a mystery to me, but we did it."[64] Pvt. Hurst noted, "They attempted to retreat in order, but we pressed them too closely. General Pryor was everywhere the firing was the hottest.[65] An Alabamian wrote, "By the time we had gotten across the front line, … frightened by our screams which sounded like 40,000 wildcats, had reached their second line and thrown them into confusion, and they, panic stricken, left their works and crowded to the top of the hill, thus preventing their artillery from firing into us…. [E]very man though only of saving himself. They threw down their arms and ran in one grand mass, out of the woods and down the valley beyond…."[66]

Pryor's Brigade hit the 1st Michigan and 83rd Pennsylvania. Lt. Col. Campbell of the latter reported that just before the Confederates attacked:

> Brigadier General Butterfield amidst a galling fire from his lines of support in the rear and that of the enemy in front, came coolly down the knoll, and, sword in hand, sized our colors, waving them repeatedly aloft. His presence at once stimulated with new vigor our now thinned ranks, when the general loudly shouted out, "Your ammunition is never expended, while you have your bayonets, my boys, and use them to the sockets!" The battle at this juncture raged furiously. The fire was tremendous. The trees were lopped and branches and leaves fell as thick as snowflakes, whilst the balls few like a hail-storm, the solid shot, grape canister and shrapnel unintermittingly scattering destruction in all directions.[67]

Brigadier Butterfield's actions would win him the Medal of Honor.[68]

Capt. Judson, 83rd Pennsylvania, wrote:

> Suddenly, as if from a thousand engines of death, there burst both from front and rear line, and from the batteries above, a living sheet of fire, and an overwhelming tempest of iron and lead. Under the shock of this tempest, the solid columns of the enemy quivered like a reed shaken in the wind. Huge gaps were made in their ranks…. Their color bearer fell at the first volley, but soon another daring fellow seized the flag and raring it triumphantly above the smoke of battle, fell pierced by a score of bullets. Again and again it was caught up … until five successive color bearers were shot down beneath it.[69]
>
> The enemy, failing to force our front and turn our left flank, now directed his efforts against our right…[70]
>
> Martindale's [brigade] … being overpowered by numbers … left our right exposed. The 83rd had noticed that something was amiss, which was an enfilading fire from the … artillery. Which began to pour upon us, from the direction of our own troops. One shot came hissing and whirling into our midst…. A hundred more, less fatal followed, making the woods hideous with the roar of constant explosions.[71]

The ordnance that McCall's Gunline was throwing at the Confederates to the 83rd's right was landing squarely on them.

Wilcox's Brigade

"The … ravine took us completely by surprise…."[72] "Just as we reached it we poured a volley into the front line of the Yankees,"[73] recalled Pvt. Barrett of the 9th Alabama. "When we got to the edge of the timber we … encountered the first line of the enemy's infantry, who were very much excited over our sudden appearance so close to them…."[74] Wilcox's men crossed "in spite of brush, briars and ditches."[75] Wilcox's Brigade met the 83rd Pennsylvania and 44th New York. Col. Rice reported, "On the left he was constantly repulsed … when an entire brigade of his forces charged upon our lines, [and] broke through the left of our forces on the right."[76] Pvt. Warner recollected, "[T]hen the enemy appeared on the crest of the hill in front of us, but they soon retreated before the sharp volley which we gave them. After a little they rallied … then the firing on the right became heavier, and the regt. on the right of us had retreated."[77]

20

Beyond the Wall of Death

Battle Group Douglass

The 2nd New Jersey soon fell back, with Battle Group Douglass on its heels.[1] Color Sergeant James Marshall tore the Union flag from the staff and wrapped it around his body, took up a musket, and fired as he retreated. Captains Bishop and Tay, and Lt. Buckley, tried to save Marshall and his colors, but in vain.[2]

Battle Group Texas

Cpl. Brantley, his flag, and his terrible sword bayonet reached the same camps that Pender's Brigade had entered. "At the top of this hill was a few tents, and I stopped near one of them, and there stood three officers and two privates talking earnestly.... When I ran up and yelled, one of them with an oath said there is a rebel now and raised his gun to shoot and as he did I threw the flag in their faces. He fired but did not hit. After that they all broke and ran down the hill."[3] Brantley had made it through Griffin's woods, but he was all alone. "I then looked for my regiment and saw the right wing many moving up to the spring to cross the gulch and the left wing going around the head of the spring, the Federals were still in their works. This crossing delayed the regiment but they were fighting desperately."[4] The delay was not long. "The Federals fled before us & fell in piles as they ran.... If ever I was bloodthirsty it was then."[5] He continues, "In following them, we passed through their encampments, and continued moving until we reached the top of the next hill, and there lost sight of them."[6]

Battle Group Hood

Pvt. Coles remembered, "Then on up the steep ascent over the second line at the crest of the hill, exposed to a deadly fire they pressed on until they had driven the enemy from his stronghold."[7] The 4th Texas had annihilated[8] the fleeing Federals in its front, and came out of the woods just north of the Watt House itself.[9] Cheers from the right signaled that the Confederates had broken through there.[10] As they reached the Watt House Road, the panting men of Battle Group Texas stopped for breath. Pvt. Polley, 4th Texas, saw thousands of Federals fleeing to his left,[11] where Battle Groups Douglas, Trimble and Texas were. To the right, even more Yankees were fleeing.[12]

"Just across the road from us was an acre lot inclosed by a rail fence. In its center stood a log stable, and from behind this an armed Yankee peeked out. Stringfield ... saw him and mounting the fence in hot haste, ran toward the stable.... Lt. Hughes, ...who never really takes the name of the Lord in vain, but comes perilously near it sometimes, sang out 'Go it Stringfield, go it! Kill him dod damn him, kill him!' But just as he reached the stable Stringfield was confronted by the muzzle of a loaded gun, and had it not been for Wolfe ... who instantly ... killed the Yankee, would have been killed."[13] Once the Federals had all fled, Battle Group Hood[14] could see McCall's Gunline open fire on them from 400 yards away to the east.[15]

Like Hood's men, let us take a breather and recount the artillery supporting Morell's Division at this point. Lt. Bucklin had two Rhode Island ordnance rifles in front of the Watt House, firing through the opening in the woods to Parson's Spring. The other 4 Rhode Island guns were about 200 yards north of the Watt House, and slightly east. Lt. Hyde had two Massachusetts ordnance rifles on the Watt House Road south of the house, and four more were further south up at the edge of the woods. Between the Adams House and the Watt House was McCall's Gunline, facing west. These were, from north to south:

Kerns' Battery G, Pennsylvania Light Artillery (6 howitzers)

Easton's Battery A, Pennsylvania Light Artillery (4 Napoleons)

DeHart's Battery C, 5th U.S. Artillery (6 Napoleons)

Cooper's Battery B, Pennsylvania Light Artillery (Library of Congress).

According to the Confederate accounts, the only two Union batteries on the entire field that day were Easton's and the Hoboken Battery, i.e., Hexamer's. Adding to that myth, Easton's guns were not only not in a position chosen by General McClellan himself, but also not directed in their fire by General McClellan in person.[16] Cooper's four Napoleons had already retired, and Hexamer's New Jersey Battery was technically behind Sykes' front, so there was a total of 28 guns immediately behind Morell's front. All of McCall's guns were bronze; all of the guns near the Watt House were black wrought-iron ordnance rifles.

Archer's Brigade

Archer's Tennesseans were just south of the Watt House, in front of Lt. Bucklin's two Rhode Island ordnance rifles.[17] Confederate fire had reduced his crews to three men out of six on each of the two guns,[18] and then the panicked men of the 13th New York had masked his fire. "When the Rebels raised that unearthly yell it made them tremble in their boots and they thought it was time to leave, and they did leave promptly...."[19] More probably the yell stampeded the few remaining horses, forcing Bucklin to abandon his iron guns.[20] "Our color bearer in the charge planted his colors on the cannon. His name was Taylor. He was presented a nice saber for his bravery, but declined to accept it."[21] Lt. Sydnor, 40th Virginia, with the 55th Virginia's flag, also mounted a gun.[22]

Battle Group Pickett

Since Pickett's right-hand regiment, the 8th Virginia, had entered the ravine first, his left-hand regiments were some distance behind, blocked by the fleeing 25th New York and 7th Pennsylvania Reserves.[23] The 8th and 18th Virginia penetrated though a gap in the line between the northern end of Butterfield's Brigade and the southern end of the 7th Pennsylvania Reserves, which had been up top behind the 25th New York. The 19th, 28th and 56th Virginia were slowed by the fleeing Yankees, so Pickett's line was wheeling to its left. Fearing that the brigade's breakthrough would be pinched off from the sides, Col. Strange, 19th Virginia, ordered his regiment and the 28th Virginia to halt in the woods.[24] The 56th, 8th, and 18th Virginia never received Col. Strange's order to stop. They continued charging on the heels of the fleeing 1st Michigan and 7th Pennsylvania Reserves[25] towards the Watt House Road and Hyde's Battery E, Massachusetts Light Artillery (6 Ordnance Rifles). Hyde's own two-gun section was about 125 yards south of the Watt House, and 100 yards from the woods.[26] One, and then three more, guns were sent up to the very edge of the woods, to bolster the Wall of Death about a hundred yards south of there, and between the woods and the Watt House Road.[27]

Behind the 13th and 25th New York

Brigadier Martindale reported, "Presently I saw one of Butterfield's regiments coming in order out of the woods. Their movement grew quicker. The right, too, was receding. At once the whole line gave way and retired in disorder."[28] In fact, this was his own 1st

Michigan, which disordered the right wing of the 12th New York (Butterfield's Brigade), hurrying up to seal the breach. Col. Richardson reported, "Our men were beginning to fire at the right oblique, when the right of my regiment was broken by the 1st Michigan Volunteers falling back through it."

22nd Massachusetts

Major Tilton, 22nd Massachusetts, reported, "They made a final and desperate effort to break through our lines, and they were successful, but not until our weary men were trampled upon by the hordes of Jackson's Army. The noise of the musketry was not rattling, as ordinarily, but one intense metallic din."[29] Pvt. Parker recalled, "The 22nd was taken by surprise when the 13th New York came streaming over the breastwork with the cry 'Get up boys and give them some!' The order came, 'Commence firing, shoot low!' And the response was a volley followed by firing as fast as the men could load. This galling fire delivered in the center of the rebel line staggered it, and they came on in the shape of a V, with the opening toward us. The enemy's left soon struck the opening made by the First Michigan when it was driven back, and we were flanked and enfiladed."[30]

Maj. Tilton continues, "The brave 13th and 25th NY, which had so long defended our front were soon compelled to retreat with the rest, falling back to our breastworks. Before many of the troops had fallen back to our breastworks I shouted for the men to rise and fire by file. At this juncture I was shot though the right shoulder, went to the rear, and was ordered to the hospital by Surgeon Prince." Major Tilton was captured at the Adams House hospital, and "was told by several prisoners in Richmond that Captain Sampson was the first man to run away."[31]

Capt. Sampson had a different view:

> [A]t an early period of this last attack Major Tilton was wounded and left for the hospital. Soon regiments posted on the right and left of the 22nd, who had no barricades, had to fall back, closely followed by an ambitious and exulting enemy. [W]e awaited them in confidence, and delivered a crushing artillery and musketry fire. The rebels were only 50 feet in the direction we were aiming, when Nowell was struck in the face. The concussion sounded like a blow given by an open hand. I turned to the left saying that Nowell was killed, and saw that the line was broken beyond our regiment. I ran the gauntlet with the fleetness of a deer....[32]

He adds: "In the open field Col. Gove endeavored to reform the line to rally the men."[33]

Pvt. Parker says, "Col. Gove was killed in the first rush of rebels from the woods. When the color bearer was shot, the enemy was right upon him. Cpl. Crone of the color guard fired point blank at the squad of rebels and picked up the colors. A rebel soldier seized them at the same moment, but Crone tore them from his grasp, and bore them safely to the [rear]. Cpl. Crone received a ball in the right elbow, which shattered the bone, and he afterwards suffered amputation. But he saved the colors, and his gallantry was highly commended."[34] "At this time the regiment was left without a field or staff officer. Upward of ½ of the line officers were killed or wounded. Over one half of the rank and file fell...."[35] The 22nd Massachusetts mustered only 300 men that night,[36] an instant casualty rate of 76 percent, with about as many missing as wounded.

7th Pennsylvania Reserves

The 7th Pennsylvania Reserves "was then ordered to move to the center of the line of Butterfield's Brigade, where it united with the 1st [Michigan] in resisting an attack on Butterfield's artillery.[37] Sgt. Alexander wrote, "[W]e were ordered up, so we double quicked to where we were wanted ... and on the edge of a deep ravine with rebels on the other side. We poured volley after volley into them ... until we had a ravine piled full of dead rebels." The enemy was in a patch of woods just forward of where the 7th finally halted. The order came to fire: "[W]e do so and instantly take cover wherever found."[38] Alexander dropped down behind one end of a line of fence rails that were only in front of the Reserves' left wing; the right wing was behind their knapsacks. "The enemy is slamming lead into our line thick and fast. We can hear their balls strike the rail pile. [Rolling onto his back to reload, Alexander] could see them cutting the sand continuously a few feet to the rear, two or three striking simultaneously."[39]

Sgt. Alexander continues, "[R]esting the Harpers ferry musket on the rail pile, I aim at where I thought the enemy might be." [I] did not see one of the enemy [because they were] concealed by very heavy undergrowth in the woods in front of our part of the line.... [T]he balls were still cutting the sand and whacking the rail pile, but it seems I must have always stuck my head up [to fire] when the balls were absent."[40] The 7th's right wing, with no fence rails, withdrew first.

Sgt. Heffelfinger takes up the tale: "I looked to my right, and our men falling back in disorder; looking to the left, I saw that there, too, our men were giving way. The retreat was not ordered.... one would call it none other than a perfect rout."[41] As he ran up the hill, "between the guns and the enemy there were hundreds of our men. [T]he murderous showers of grape and canister mowed down friend and foe alike."[42] These were 4 ordnance rifles of Hyde's Battery E, Massachusetts Light Artillery, who were also in the path of the Confederate juggernaut. Heffelfinger snatched up the regimental colors and was shot through the thigh. The ball shattered "a large dirk knife."[43] The 7th lost 50 percent, with more missing than wounded.[44]

Hyde's Section of Hyde's Battery E, Massachusetts Light Artillery

When the fleeing infantry passed, Lt. Hyde had Rebels on his left and front.[45] The Rebels, "filled with whiskey and gunpowder, the drunken devils,"[46] were only 35 yards away when all three guns fired a round of double canister,[47] but a rebel volley scythed through the battery and all four horses at one gun dropped, blocking it. Lt. Hyde fired one round of double canister, and ordered the other gun out, when his gun was overwhelmed.[48] Corporal Macomber ordered, "By Hand to the Rear!" The men strained at the carriages to get the 2000-pound gun moving, but soon too many fell to additional rebel gunfire, and they left the gun to save the men, taking the rammers with them.[49] The rebels planted their flag on one of these guns.[50]

Despite his order, all of the officers in Col. Strange's 19th Virginia had fallen, and some of the men did not get the word. Pvt. George Harris and one other man joined the 56th Virginia and pressed forward; Harris assumed command and led them at the guns, with hat in hand shouting to the men to come on. Pvt. Harris was the first man to put his hands upon the guns, and turn them on the enemy.[51] W.F. Clarke continues, "We moved after … the enemy—a great mass of humanity just ahead—with some artillery on a ridge just beyond this retreating enemy. We were so close upon them that their artillery could not harm us on account of their own men. They had time to fire only once after their men passed their artillery when the 56th Virginia and 18th Virginia of Pickett's Brigade captured the cannon and placed the flag of the 56th Virginia Regiment upon it."[52]

Phillips' and Scott's Sections, Hyde's Battery E, Massachusetts Light Artillery

Lt. Scott begins the story of the other two sections of Battery E. "Going into battery … in rear of the line of battle, we could not see the movement of troops on our right nor the brigades on our left front, as Butterfield and Martindale were beyond the wood. The sun poured down on us and while here the U.S. Mails were distributed, and many read letters from home and friends for the last time."[53] "We could hear the quick popping of a rapid firing gun."[54] Three guns were ordered up to the woods, two of Phillips' Section but only one of Scott's Section.[55] "We limbered up the left section and away we went to the woods, followed by the center section, Lt. Phillips, who took position on our right. These … guns were not idle. Through the woods we could see only parts of the rebel lines." Pvt. Chase recorded in his diary that they fired shrapnel with a one-second fuze.[56] Cpl. Spear recalled that Phillips only fired two rounds of double canister.[57] "But this time the thundering volleys of musketry told us that the hottest work of the day was before us…. But it was of no use; advancing at trail arms in one unbroken mass, they rushed thru the woods closing their ranks as fast as our fire mowed them down."[58]

Lt. Scott now takes up the narrative:

If we did not cut them down we did the small trees in our front, as they fell as if cut with a scythe…. [B]ut human endurance could not withstand the more than a double force pitted against us. The left of Martindale's brigade [1st Michigan] had been turned and the rebels were flanking us. We kept up our fire with the gun unaware of what had happened. Enveloped in smoke we could not tell want was going on far from us. At this point the infantry of our brigade came struggling up between our guns. Anxious to know how he fight was going on I said to a soldier, "What's the trouble below?" "Trouble enough," he said, "the rebels are crossing the ditch on our right." These were the 7th Pennsylvania Reserves, who claimed to be retreating because Scott's guns were hitting them.[59]

And then: "Looking to our left, we saw an officer mounted on a stone heap waving a flag. He cried out 'For god's sake men stand by your colors!'"[60]

Lt. Phillips continues:

The woods were full of smoke, and the bullets buzzed round our head like a swarm of angry bumble bees; still our artillery thundered away. My horse had a bullet in his flank and one sergeant's horse lay dead on the ground. As yet no men were hit, but louder and louder roared the musketry, and thicker and thicker buzzed the bullets, and suddenly, out poured our infantry in disorder, frightened and reckless….[61]

[T]hey made an attempt to rally, rushing out right in front of the muzzles of our guns, which were not 10 feet from the trees, but broke and retreated…. Still, as long as there was any hope I blazed away till all our men had retreated beyond me. Then I limbered up…. As far as I could see the hill was covered with our men, running in groups of two or three or alone, each one looking out for himself while 200 yards in front stretched a long line of rebel infantry, which had formed between us and the woods, their red flags flying, and their muskets sending the bullets flying around our heads after all the infantry had left. I unlimbered and fired one round of canister at a regiment with a red flag within less than 300 yards. We could see the gaps made by each discharge instantly filled up by fresh troops, and still on they came. Reluctantly we limbered up and commenced our retreat.[62]

The Confederates were 30 yards away.[63]

Lt. Scott now takes up the tale: "We received orders to retire in haste, which we did. Limbering up our guns with Phillips leading, we moved quickly down the slope to where we had left the Right [Hyde's] section of the battery. To my surprise, Lt. Philips as he came up [to Hyde's] section continued on at a trot. He had taken in the situation. As my section came on I saw something was wrong with the guns, but I passed quickly by.... I turned about to look ... up [the hill], passing the guns already captured...."[64]

Lt. Phillips recalled:

> So far both of my guns were safe.... [A] fence stopped us a little, and while passing through the gap we experienced the hottest fire of all. The rebels by this time lined the top of the hill, and poured a murderous fire into our retreating soldiers. As Blake's piece went thru the gap, down went one horse with a bullet in his jaw, throwing his rider, but the other horses pulled him thru and saved the gun. As Page's piece passed through down went four horses a one volley, and I told the men to leave the piece. I had hardly gone a hundred yards when my horse fell, shot through the leg, and as I tumbled I saw the rebel flag planted on [Page's] gun![65]

Lt. Phillips lamented the poor short-range performance of ordnance rifles: "Had we had a battery of [Napoleon] 12 pdrs. a regiment of dead men would have covered the field

Confederates capturing Lt. Hyde's guns, by Alfred Waud (Library of Congress).

before they would have got our guns, but our little pieces do not throw canister much larger than mustard box [about the size of two shoeboxes], and were never meant for that kind of work."[66] Lt. Scott was more sanguine: "It was a miracle or interposition of Providence that any of us escaped."[67]

J. Cooper, 8th Virginia, tells the Confederate side: "One battery of four guns, about 100 yards in their rear, out in a field, gave Pickett a parting salute of shot and shell ... and then fled with the others. [These] guns were parked [where] the left of the brigade had not yet reached. The 8th Regiment was ... on the extreme right of the Watt House, in pursuit of the fugitives, and as soon as they got within range ... the enemy opened fire with grape and canister.... Their terrible fire was of short duration, for as soon as the left of the brigade got close enough those guns were silenced and the fire in Pickett's front ceased...."[68] The 8th and 18th Virginia captured two Massachusetts ordnance rifles.[69]

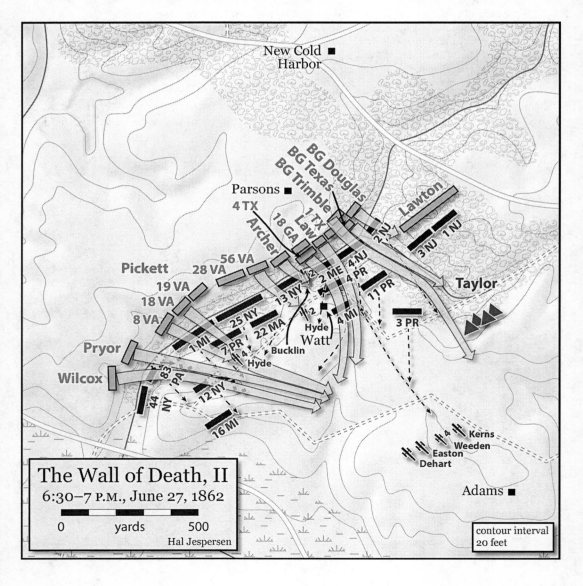

The Wall of Death, II
6:30–7 P.M., June 27, 1862

0   yards   500

Hal Jespersen

contour interval
20 feet

Battle Group Wilcox

Wilcox's Alabamians "made most of those three lines of Federals prisoners."[70] Some joined Pickett's men in taking the four Massachusetts guns. Pvt. Williams, 9th Alabama, thought, "It would have been better to stop in the woods, ... but we followed them into the field, and as soon as they uncovered their battery it was opened on us at short range, and—my God!—grape, canister, shrapnel and solid shot all seemed to literally pour on us. At this critical moment some of our troops assaulted and silenced this battery."[71] An Alabamian in another regiment remembered, "As we advanced into the open ground ... artillery confronted us.... In quick time we killed the horses and captured the guns and most of the men."[72] Even some of Featherston's men were in on it: "Hard pressed, they were compelled to abandon their artillery, four pieces of which were passed over by my brigade and a number of prisoners taken by them, and finally to flee in wild confusion."[73] The remnants of Pryor's men joined the remnants of Wilcox's men who were going forward with Battle Group Pickett.

To the south, Brigadier Butterfield was still trying to seal off the breach. "Gen Butterfield seeing our right broken ... also fell back and formed a new front on his original right flank."[74] If the Rebels reached the river bottom, they would cut the only two bridges that the Fifth Corps could use to escape. The 16th Michigan "was ordered to move by the right flank to support the right of the brigade, which was severely pressed and exposed to the flank movement of the enemy, who had now broken though the line to the right of our brigade and were driving the regiments on the right in disorder before them."[75]

21

Respite from the Wall of Death

Battle Group Texas

Capt. Weeden's 4 Rhode Island ordnance rifles were midway between the Watt House and Boatswain's Run, in front of 3rd Pennsylvania Reserves. The 3rd could clearly see the collapse of the line to their left. When the 3d Reserves lost its "cool valor" and broke, Weeden's battery opened fire, but after a few rounds they retired 100 yards "in haste" to rear, in the temporary safety of McCall's Gunline.[1] This was prudent, as Battle Group Texas was behind their right flank, and Battle Group Hood was flanking their left.

1st Texas

The slugfest with the 11th Pennsylvania Reserves continued, with the northerners getting the worst of it. Aaron Kepler was shot in the thigh and kept alive with a tourniquet. He and other wounded sought shelter, but finally "gathered dead bodies, and piled them around us in heaps, which gave us a slight protection."[2]

Battle Group Hood

As Battle Group Hood moved past the Watt House Road to the east, McCall's Gunline opened fire with "shot, shell and canister," but the range makes the latter unlikely.[3] McCall's Gunline was to the east, and Robertson's Battery B/L 2nd U.S. Artillery (6 ordnance rifles), was shelling them from behind the Adams House, to the southeast. Val Giles, 4th Texas, had come to from being knocked out and saw "hundreds of men passed me yelling, shouting, and swearing." Someone was dragging him behind an apple tree. "Limbs and leaves were falling all over me, cut from the tree by the lead and iron hail."[4] A solder in the 4th Texas recollected, "I could plainly see the gunners at work; down they would drive the horrid grape[shot]—a long, blazing flame issued from the piece, and then crashing through the fence and barn, shattering rails and weather-board, came the terrible missiles with merciless fury."[5]

Brigadier Hood had made it 200 yards beyond the Watt House into the pear orchard at the head of the Watt House Ravine, "a deep hollow down the middle of which ran a steep banked tortuous gully, almost impassable except at a few places."[6] That ravine ran at almost right angles to McCall's Gunline, about 300 yards away, to Hood's left front.[7] Brigadier Hood, leaning on a tree with his sword uplifted, sent word back to the rear for every man to join him.[8] The 4th Texas had lost all of its field officers by this point; Captain Davis was in command.[9] He led his men into the ravine, where they were protected from the shellfire.[10]

Brigadier Law himself, the 4th Alabama, and the 11th Mississippi[11] arrived, with the 18th Georgia right behind.[12] Brigadier Hood looked down the ravine and saw the Yankees trying to rally to the southeast. This was a portion of Brigadier Butterfield's Brigade, who were forming for a counterattack on Hood's flank from the river bottom at the end of the Watt House Ravine.[13] With his men still organizing and almost defenseless, Brigadier Hood left Brigadier Law in charge and went back to Boatswain's Creek to look for help.[14] Hood found Major Haskell, who had vanquished the New York officer in a sword fight, and was reforming his stragglers. "While I was doing this, General Hood came from my left. He spoke to me, offering to help me as I was very bloody. He … suggested that I join his men to his right."[15] Haskell's stragglers included part of the 6th North Carolina.[16] Hood also found R.H. Anderson, and asked him to advance, angling towards the Chickahominy to stop Butterfield's counterattack.

Battle Group Pickett

In the ravine, on the left of Battle Group Hood, the 8th Virginia[17] took a breather as men from Pryor's Brigade[18] and Wilcox's Brigade arrived.[19] "We of the stragglers brigade, as Col. Strange is pleased to designate us, had advanced over the undulating plateau until we came to a deep ravine at the base of the last and highest hill, which was crowned with the enemy's heaviest artillery. Those to the left would go around the head of the ravine, but we on the right had to cross over by the slow and tedious process of crawling down one side and crawling up the other. We had just gotten over in a very straggling condition."[20]

R.H. Anderson's brigade had followed Pickett's. "Anderson pressed up the steep ascent across the ravine and met with little resistance, although under a constant fire, while the battle was raging with more vigor to our left, where Hood's and Pickett's brigades were engaging the Federals."[21] Anderson's men focused towards the Chickahominy, where the remnants of Butterfield's Brigade were trying to rally.[22]

22

Return of the Wall of Death

Battle Group Trimble, Battle Group Texas

The left wing of the 15th Alabama expected a hand-to-hand fight, but "when we reached their line numbers of them lay dead or too badly wounded to be moved. This was the result of … engagement with 'buck and ball' when well directed."[1] One Yankee fired at them from behind a tree and took off at a run. McClendon and Calvin Kirkland fired at the same time. "We passed close by him and paused long enough to see several bullet holes in the back of his blouse."[2] Further on, McClendon noticed that Calvin had stopped and was looking at the ground. A terrified Yankee had crawled under some tree roots, but his feet were exposed. The two men sent him to the rear.[3] The smoke was so dense that the sun had turned "gloomily red."[4] McClendon and Kirkland were in the left wing of the 15th Alabama; the right wing was on the far side of the 5th Texas, and with it were the 7th North Carolina and remnants of the 21st Georgia (Battle Group Campbell).[5]

The 5th Texas came under fire from the New Jersey Union Repeating Gun Battery, near the camps that Pender had reached earlier in the afternoon. "I discovered a battery to my left, which was hidden from our view…. I ordered my men to fire on those around the battery as they ran, which volley cleared the battery…."[6] To the Texans' right, Battle Group Campbell could see McCall's Gunline in front of them firing towards the Watt House, and decided to charge.

Kerns' Battery G, Pennsylvania Light Artillery (6 howitzers) was on the northern end of McCall's Gunline.[7] Lt. Col. Haywood, 7th North Carolina recounted the charge:

> The colors, when the advance began, were in the hands of Cpl. Henry T. Fight…. He was instantly shot down, when they were again seized by Cpl. James A. Harris, of Company I; he was also shot down, when Col. Campbell himself seized the colors and advancing some 20 paces in front of his regiment, ordered them not to fire but to follow him. Within 20 paces of the enemy's line he was shot down, when Lt. Haywood again seized the flag, the staff of which had been shot in two, and advanced to the front of the regiment. He also immediately lost his life, where upon the flag of the regiment was carried out of the action by Corporal Peavey, of Company C.

The 7th's battle flag, about four feet square, had 32 holes in it.[8] The 7th had come within a stone's throw of Kerns' guns.[9]

The 21st Georgia also felt the sting of canister. Capt. Nisbett recalled, "The battery continued to fire until we got well up to them. A shell bursting just as it passed me, the concussion blew me up in the air six or eight feet. I turned a complete somersault but lit on my all fours as the men passed me towards the battery. As I sped through the air I thought my legs had been cut off by the shell and that the upper part of my body was flying through space. I instinctively felt for my limbs and found they were all right before I came to the ground…. We were so close to the cannon that grains of unburnt powder had stung my face and that, with the dense smoke, nearly blinded me."[10]

From Kerns' point of view, "The enemy made determined efforts to drive the battery from the hill. A heavy column was formed and charged … coming within 50 yards of the guns. Captain Kerns was wounded in the left leg, but standing by his guns continued to cheer his men. Grape and canister, double shotted, were poured into the advancing column, tearing men to pieces, and sending the masses reeling down the hill."[11] Six days later, Lt. Amsden reported, "The charge is said … to have been led by General Stonewall Jackson in person, carrying the colors."[12] "When within 20 paces of the battery, at a single round the whole front rank was carried away, the General and his flag were buried in the heap of slain, yet still rushed the infuriated enemy to the muzzles of the guns."[13] Easton's Battery A also opened up, noting that the Confederates were "*literally* mowed down in heaps."[14] Weeden's Battery C, Rhode Island Light Artillery (down to 4 ordnance rifles) helped with "some 40 rounds."[15] Chaplain Davis, over near the Watt House, watched as Battle Group Campbell, under the fire of at least 14 guns, "became powerless, and could do little else but seek protection under the crest of the hill from the guns above."[16]

Cavalry Brigade, Near the Adams House

U.S. Cavalry Brigadier Phillip St. George Cooke's aide, Capt. Wesley Merritt, returned from General Porter's headquarters near the Adams House with some alarming news: "Hasty preparations were made for the retreat of the headquarters, and everything was in the most wretched confusion." Even worse, when Merritt "reported to the headquarters … during his attendance there heard read a dispatch from General McClellan. It closed with his directions to drive the rebels off the field, and to take from them their artillery."[17]

1st Texas

The slugfest filled the woods and the ravine with even more smoke. Soon the Texans' fire slowed. "Firing almost ceased. An order was passed down the line to cease firing, that we were Shooting our own men. Our boys lay quiet for a few minutes, when Some keen eyed fellow discovered and Said they are Yankees Shure I can see the Blue uniform and the U.S. Buckles on their Shoulder Straps. Then the order to charge was given. You ought to have seen those Texans go forward over gullies, ditches. Through and over a dense mas of fallen timer, Onward Now into the Enemies works."[18] Some of the Texans passed by the left of the 11th Pennsylvania Reserves and the 4th New Jersey and out into the open near the Watt House.[19]

Battle Groups Hood, Pickett and Wilcox

The color bearer of the 18th Georgia planted his flag in the bottom of the Watt House Ravine, where the milling men rallied, quickly forming lines of battle for the attack on

McCall's guns. The officers conferred and organized the effort. The resulting line was based on the 18th Georgia. The remnants of Law's men supported its right end, and the remnants of the 4th Texas supported the left.[20] Further down the ravine, but unseen by Battle Group Hood, the survivors of Battle Groups Pickett and Wilcox (now Battle Group Pickett/Wilcox) rallied around the 8th Virginia. "[W]e confronted a battalion of artillery. Its fire was very destructive, and my regiment, being somewhat in advance, was halted a moment till the other regiments of the brigade came up."[21] These other troops were also from Pryor's and Wilcox's brigades.

Brigadier Hood, who had returned, called the men to attention. Just at that moment, Major Warwick interrupted, crying, "Wait a second, General, let me lead the charge!" and sprang in front of the regiment. "As the command 'Charge!' fell from Hood's lips, the line surged forward out of the ravine,[22] into the very jaws of Death itself."[23] Major Warwick, with his confiscated Virginia flag, was killed within 12 paces.[24] To Hood's right, the Pickett/Wilcox Group also charged,[25] independent of Battle Group Hood.[26]

Nothing happened to either for the first 70 yards,[27] but back by the Adams House the movement had been spotted.[28] "Smoke [was] now in thick curtains, rolling about like some half solid substance; the dust was suffocating. Suddenly word is passed down the line 'Cavalry!'"[29] McCall's guns opened again, but only from two pieces.[30]

The Charge of the Fifth Regulars at Gaines's Mill, 27th of June 1862, W.T. Trego, 1893 (courtesy U.S. Cavalry Museum, Ft. Riley, Kansas).

Behind the Adams House

Cavalry Brigadier Cocke had watched Morell's line crumble further, and led the 220 men of the 5th U.S. Cavalry forward past the Adams House, with the 125 men of the 1st U.S. Cavalry in a second line behind them.[31] "[I]t was the supreme moment for cavalry, the opportunity that comes so seldom on the modern field of war, the test of discipline, hardihood and nerve."[32] A few of Rush's Lancers joined the charge.[33] "Texans ... came running with wild yells, and they were a hundred yards from the guns. It was then the cavalry commander ordered Capt. Charles J. Whiting, with his regiment to charge...."[34] Cooke ordered the charge to give McCall's Gunline time to limber up and skedaddle.[35] "As soon as the battery on our right ceased firing Captain Whiting ... gave the order to charge."[36] The 5th walked for 20 paces (5 m.p.h.), then went to a trot for 60 paces (10 m.p.h.), then to a canter for 80 paces (15 m.p.h.), and then to a full gallop[37] (25 m.p.h.).[38] "The left squadron had but one officer present ... and when he fell it broke and threw the rest of the line into disorder."[39] "The regiment charged ... into a most galling fire until 6 officers out of the 7 had been stuck down."[40] "The column ... wheeled [away] to the right...."[41]

Battle Groups Hood and Pickett/Wilcox

The right of the Confederates saw them first. Pvt. Hogan, member of the 11th Alabama, Wilcox's Brigade, wrote, "But a new danger confronted us. Across the open field a brigade of cavalry dashed into view and halted. [Brigadier] Wilcox ... instantly rallied his Alabamians [and] formed them in squares."[42] A "square" is a difficult formation wherein a line of battle forms a hollow square with its bayonets outward.

Pvt. Hamby of the 4th Texas felt them first. "In a short while we felt the ground begin to tremble like an earthquake and heard a noise like rumbling thunder. To hear the trumpets sounding the charge, to see the squadrons coming at us at full speed, and to see their sabers glistening ... was a spectacle grand beyond description, and imparted a feeling of awe in even the bravest hearts ."[43] "[A] squadron of about 600 cavalry ... charged down on the right." Though alerted, Battle Group Hood did not have time to form square, but coordinated its fire with the Pickett/Wilcox formation. "When they were within about 40 yards of us, we poured a volley into them and prepared to receive them on our bayonets."[44] "[T]here came out from that ragged line a continuous sheet of flame."[45] "[D]own come horses and riders with sabers swung over their heads, charging like an avalanche...."[46] Pvt. Patrick Penn jammed his bayonet into a passing horseman, and the rider made off still impaled with the weapon. Another man skewered a rider and flipped him over his own head. The volley "broke their front, brought down their leader, [and] ... changed their direction...." Union Captain Whiting and all of his officers but one fell. "Horses and riders fell in heaps upon the ground, and the groans of the wounded and the shrieks of the dying could be heard above the roar of battle."[47] "[S]cores of their saddles were emptied and many a cripled steed left hobling across the field...."[48] "[Others were] frantic from bayonet cuts and Minnie balls.[49] "Horses without riders, or sometimes with a wounded or dead master dangling from the stirrups, plunged wildly and fearfully over the plain, trampling over dead and dying...."[50] "Cpt. Chambliss and four or five of his men and their horses were all shot down in a space of only a few yards..., Chambliss

Infantry formed in a square. Note the charged bayonets on the left side of the image (Library of Congress).

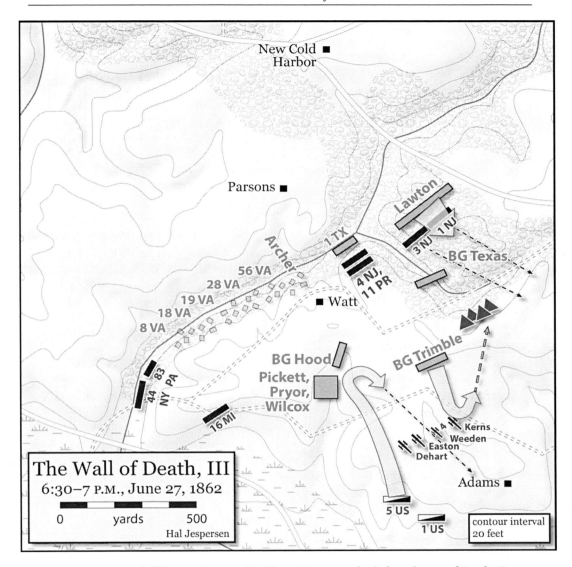

The Wall of Death, III
6:30–7 P.M., June 27, 1862

0   yards   500

Hal Jespersen

contour interval
20 feet

having three wounds."[51] Capt. George Todd, 1st Texas, to the left and rear of Battle Group
Hood was an eyewitness to the "charge and slaughter" of the cavalry.[52] "[S]uch destruction
I never want to see again," lamented Pvt. Hogan. "We were told that that brigade was so
nearly annihilated that it never attempted to rally."[53]

During the charge, the officers of McCall's batteries had called up their limbers to
snatch their guns away, but they were too slow. "Checked and broken … the mounted
fugitives came pouring through the battery, carrying with them to the rear all the available
teams and limbers."[54]

One of Rush's Lancers observed, "Wounded and demoralized artillerymen, mounted
on their battery horses, with cut traces, were flying in a disorganized and incongruous
mass from the dreadful carnival of death."[55] "The infantry cavalry and cannoneers, with
5 guns, mixed and moving at their utmost speed, gave to the mind the idea of GRAND
CONFUSION!"[56]

Battle Group Trimble

In the dense smoke and confusion, Battle Group Trimble charged again. A member of the 21st North Carolina remarked, "[I]n a field hard by where the enemy had a battery of six guns, [Fulton] led a dashing and magnificent charge, captured the entire battery and took a number of prisoners."[57] Thomas Verdery, 21st Georgia, wrote in a letter, "At last, the 5th Texas Regiment came up and, after firing about 5 minutes, that regiment with ours and the 15th Alabama, that is what was left of them, charged the enemy. We took one battery of six guns."[58] Another Georgian wrote, "I cannot see how I escaped getting hurt for there was five wounded and two killed in the crowd I was in. All I can see it was the will of the Lord to spare my lie a little longer."[59] Brigadier Trimble reported, "Parts of 3 companies of the 15th Alabama and fragments of 21st Georgia were the first at the guns, followed by the 5th Texas and the 18th Georgia."[60]

Battle Group Trimble attacked Kerns' Battery G, Pennsylvania Light Artillery (6 howitzers).[61] "While the battery was being limbered the enemy were within less than 20 yards of the pieces." "Guns Nos. 1 and 4 were left on the field, owing to lack of horses to bring them off."[62] Kerns put up a fight, firing 75 canister rounds alone. He lost 7 men killed, 11 wounded, and 10 horses.[63]

Battle Group Hood

"Just as this charge was made the left wing had come up within range of the guns, when one of them fired into Co. K, killing 2 men, wounding 6 others. Whole line halted to deliver their fires, which they did so effectually that for a moment the firing of the battery ceased and the infantry began to fall back. Col. Solon Ruff, 18th Georgia, … hat in hand, waved the boys onward…."[64] "Cavalrymen, artillery limbers and caissons … all rushed away in one wild sea of confusion, running for dear life."

Battle Group Hood was attacking Easton's Battery A, Pennsylvania Light Artillery, and its four Napoleons. "[W]e opened on them with double shotted canister…." Captain Easton was in the thick of it cheering on his men. "The enemy shall never have this battery but over my dead body." The Confederates obliged. "[O]ne cannoneer was shot at piece ramming down shot, another while adjusting a friction primer."[65] "Aye, the rammers as they were withdrawn from the pieces after putting home the last charge, actually touched the breasts of the rebels—their ranks were so near."[66] Major Haskell was with Battle Group Hood, still with his confiscated flag. "When I got to within a few feet of their guns, I marked a gunner fixing his lanyard into the friction primer. I made a run to cut him down before he could fire, but he was too quick. When I was not over ten feet from the muzzle the gun went off. The shot struck my right arm, crushing it and tearing it off at the shoulder. When it hit me, it seemed to knock me up in the air and spin me around two or three times … and then dashed me down with a force that knocked all the breath out of me. When I came to, I found my arm wrapped around my sword blade in a most remarkable manner."[67] The 4th Texas was nearby. "The battery in … our front [was] mowing down the 4th Texas like grain before the scythe. Take that battery boys! Like a flash of lightning the Texans move forward upon the seven gun battery; the gunners double shot it with schrapnell and sweep our ranks at close range … as the dying gunner fires his last gun into our ranks [he] is shot down at his gun. The horses are all killed or badly wounded."[68] Cpl. Foster, who carried the 18th Georgia's flag, mounted a gun and waved it.[69] Easton's battery lost all 4 of its guns.[70]

One private in the 4th Texas observed, "One battery with four guns got away."[71] This was Weeden's Battery C, Rhode Island Light Artillery (down to 4 ordnance rifles). Capt. Weeden reported, "We saw the enemy turning the left of the batteries. The smoke had filled the whole field to the woods ... the batteries were limbering to the rear in good order ... when the cavalry, repulsed, retired in disorder through and in front of the batteries. The caissons were exchanging limbers with the pieces.... Men were ridden down and the horses stampeded by the rush of the cavalry. The whole line of artillery was thrown into confusion ... and different batteries were mingled in disorder."[72]

Battle Group Pickett/Wilcox

Pvt. James recalled that after repelling the cavalry, the 8th Virginia "rushed up the hill and captured the guns that had not been carried off under cover of the cavalry charge."[73] The intrepid Pvt. George Harris, 19th Virginia, also of Pickett's Brigade, was in that charge, too.[74] The 14th Alabama, Pryor's Brigade, "quickly decided to take that battery—Alabamians, Virginians and Louisianans." Many of the Louisianans who were not so fleet as the Alabamians and Virginians, threw down their guns and empty cartridge boxes, and rushed forward with their bayonets in hand. Sgt. Henderson, 14th Louisiana, Pryor's Brigade, "while bearing gallantly the colors of the regiment, fell within 10 paces of the last battery, pierced by nine grapeshot. The entire color guard fell at the same time."[75] Swarming on, the rest of the 14th and Coppens' Zouaves attacked the gunners with bayonets and bare hands.[76] "We ran over their artillery, killing the gunners at their guns, and as this confused mass ... fled ... we kept close on them and shot them down by the hundreds and thousands. We were so close that pistol did as good as guns."[77] Corporal James Giles, 14th Louisiana, planted his flag on the guns.[78] Pickett's men insisted that Hood assisted *them.* "Just as the left of Pickett's brigade had captured those ... guns, Hood's troops entered the field, marching in column. [Lt. Cooper] saw and asked an officer what command it was, and was told by him that it was Hood's. Should that officer be living and see this, he would corroborate this; so would Gen. Pryor."[79]

Pickett and Wilcox had attacked Dehart's Battery C, 5th U.S. Artillery (6 Napoleons). "Canister and spherical case were used, with a great preponderance of the former." The Confederates succeeded in "flanking the battery, capturing several pieces, and driving the remainder from the field.... [T]he day might not have been lost to us had not our own cavalry ... rushed in disgraceful flight pell mell through our intervals while we were changing front.... [T]he three pieces and caissons that remained ... retreated."[80]

It is impossible to determine which regiment took whose guns, because the Federals don't know how many they lost, and the Confederates don't know how many they captured. In his report of March 7, 1863, Inspector of Artillery Brigadier William Barry reported that Weeden lost four ordnance rifles,[81] but Weeden's Report says he lost three, two of Bucklin's section and one mired.[82] Brigadier Barry says that DeHart lost 2 Napoleons, but DeHart himself says he lost three.[83] All agree that Easton lost 4 Napoleons and that Kerns lost 2 howitzers. Various Confederates claimed the capture of 26 guns at this location alone. Battle Group Hood claims 5 guns, and Battle Group Trimble claims 6, for a rather incredible beginning total of 11 guns, before adding any claims of Pickett's men. At its height, just before the cavalry charge, the Gunline contained Dehart (6 Napoleons), Easton (4 Napoleons), Kerns (6 howitzers), and Weeden (4 ordnance rifles), a total of 20 guns. Dehart lost three, Easton four, Kerns 2, and Weeden 1, for a total of 10.

Even more ludicrous are the claims of the cavalrymen. "It was a hard duty given this half of the 5th Cavalry," but it is easy for Cavalry Brigadier Cocke's pen to blame on it: Cocke even asserted that somehow the charge enabled "the batteries to get off" without mentioning that three of those battery commanders loudly blamed the cavalry's retreat for the loss of almost half of the 22 guns.[84] General Porter didn't fall for Cocke's attempt to blame Chambliss:

> [T]o my great surprise, the artillery on the left were thrown into confusion by a charge of cavalry coming from the front. The explanation of this is that although the cavalry had been directed early

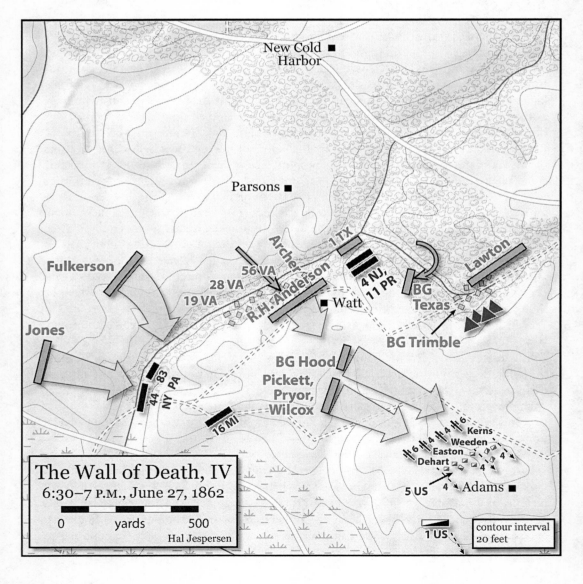

The Wall of Death, IV
6:30–7 P.M., June 27, 1862

0   yards   500

Hal Jespersen

contour interval 20 feet

in the day to keep below the hill [in the river bottom] and under no circumstances to appear on the crest, but to operate, if a favorable opportunity offered, against the flank of the enemy in the bottom-land, Brig. Gen. P. St. George Cooke, doubtless misinformed, ordered it, as I have since learned, to charge between our infantry and artillery upon the enemy on our left flank, who had not yet emerged from the woods. This charge, executed in the face of a withering fire of infantry and in the midst of heavy cannonading, resulted, of course, in their being thrown into confusion, and the bewildered horses, regardless of the efforts of the riders, wheeled about, and dashing through the batteries, convinced the gunners that they were charged by the enemy. To this alone is to be attributed our failure to hold the battlefield and to bring off all our guns and wounded.[85]

In September of 1862 Cocke was assigned to court-martial duty. After the war he was involved in an Indian massacre.[86] Nevertheless, upon his death, Merritt, who reported the chaos at Porter's headquarters to him, would claim that Cocke's charge was the sole reason Porter's entire Corps was not utterly destroyed.[87]

Behind the Adams House

The 14th New York had been relieved and was somewhere between the Adams House and the McGehee House. Pvt. Harrer watched as "from the point where the break occurred in the infantry line came a stream of flying fugitives, a mass of discouraged soldiers, some of them throwing away guns and everything that could hinder them from getting down the hill and over the creek. Everything now indicated a terrible disaster to our arms. In looking at the mass of running men, all rushing for the rear, I thought to myself: Now look out for another Bull Run…. On I went with the flying men…. I believe tears were in my eyes."[88]

When the Union lines broke, Col. Berdan was coming out of Griffin's Woods, and "saw not less than 12,000 of our men and officers, each apparently making quick time for the bridge."[89] Newspaperman George Townshend wrote:

> I have seen nothing that conveys an adequate idea of the number of cowards and idlers that … stroll off. In this instance, I met squads, companies, almost regiments of them. Some came boldly along the road; others skulked in the woods, and made long detours to escape detection; a few were composedly playing cards, or heating their coffee, or discussing the order and consequences of the fight. Their appreciation of duty and honor seemed to have been forgotten; neither hate, ambition, nor patriotism could force them back; but when the columns of mounted provosts charged upon them, they sullenly resumed their muskets and returned to the field.

Townshend rode up to the plateau to experience his personal Henry Fleming moment, and then joined Robertson's Battery B/L, 2nd U.S. Artillery.[90]

Robertson was in the path of the oncoming juggernaut. "The enemy advancing to within range, as soon as the [Union] infantry passed I commenced firing canister … a battery posted near me on the brow of the hill was forced to retire, leaving two of its guns on the field [Dehart or Kerns]. It was now getting to be dusk, and the enemy were appearing on the hill to my right, and seeing no support I limbered up to retire, when I was met by a squadron or more of Rush's Lancers, the officer of which informed me that he would protect my right."[91] According to the Lancers, it was a bit more dangerous. "Captain [Robertson] is moving off his guns to save them from capture. At this moment, an aid from General Cooke's staff, Lt. Wesley Merritt, dashed up … and asked him to give them another shot to check their advance, if possible. 'Who will support me, Lieu-

Robertson's Battery B/L, 2nd U.S. Artillery, May 1862 (Library of Congress).

tenant?' asked the gallant captain. 'The Lancers, sir,' was the reply."[92] The Lancers moved to Robertson's right, "lances poised, awaiting the 'charge,' if necessary." Robertson fired the rest of his ammunition, when a "perfect storm of bullets warn[ed the Lancers] to retire." Rush's men realized that they had become an anachronism. "[Our] weapon being unfitted for any service but the charge, we were held only to resist attack from the enemy and though severely exposed, had not the satisfaction of returning his fire."[93]

23

Conquest of the Wall of Death

Battle Group Trimble

Battle Group Trimble stopped at McCall's Gunline, where Battle Group Texas passed them going east.[1] The 21st Georgia was put in charge of 6 guns,[2] which they loaded and aimed to their rear, as a regiment was coming out of the woods. "We could not decide whether the regiment we saw coming up behind were friends or foes. I ordered Joe Glover, our color bearer, to step forward and unfurl his flag, which he did, and was shot through the calf of the leg by someone in that regiment. It was all I could do to keep our men from opening on them with small arms and artillery. However, we waved a handkerchief, and they did the same, and on finding out that they were surrounded they surrendered."[3] Afterwards, the Georgians enjoyed the spoils. "We had captured the camp of the Pennsylvania 'Bucktails,' intact, so we had plenty of rations, including gen-u-ine unadulterated coffee. There was a yellow vegetable in 50 pound caddies [which] the men would not eat. I knew it was pressed carrots and had some of it put in my beef soup. The men finding that I had not died from its effects … jumped on it."[4]

The 21st North Carolina had but 18 percent casualties, while the 16th Mississippi had 33 percent, indicating that the latter was in on the late day failed attack on the guns. The 7th North Carolina lost 46 percent. The 21st Georgia lost 32 percent, while the 15th Alabama, which had battered at the Wall of Death all day, lost 66 percent.

Battle Group Texas

The 5th Texas came up to the captured batteries and took a rest, still under fire from the Federals. Col. Robertson took a ball to the shoulder, and the colorful Lt. Col. Upton took over. Lt. Crute was lying down when he exclaimed, "Boys, they have put a hole through my coat." When he stood up, he keeled over with a groan, hit in the heart. His company was taken over by a sergeant.[5]

Col. Robertson reported:

My men, seeing the enemy flying across the field in the direction of … the Chickahominy continued to charge over the hill.… [N]ight was fast closing on us.… I thought it proper to recall my men.… On my march back I discovered a fire was being made upon my men from the camp though which we had just charged.…[6]

We then moved to the left and had not gone more than a few hundred yards, when we were fired into from the rear. This was so unexpected that it astonished us very much indeed. We immediately about faced and then saw about 50 yards before us a full regiment of federal infantry. We were just about to fire a volley into them, when they have made marked signs of surrender by throwing down their guns and waving their hats and handkerchiefs; still there were a few who seemed so nervous that they still held their guns, though they gave the same signs as their comrades....[7]

Pvt. Nabors continues, "[W]e came face to face with the [4th] New Jersey Infantry, with colors flying. Capt. Rogers ordered [a field officer] to surrender. He said he would to an officer of equal rank. Capt. Rogers drew his revolver and ordered him to surrender at once, which he did giving up his sword and pistols, also ordering his men to ground [their] arms.[8] The colonel of the regiment (it was the 4th New Jersey) rode up to us, and surrendered his sword to [Major Upton]. (That made it all right)."[9] Col. Simpson and Lt. Col. Upton had been schoolmates.[10]

From the Union point of view, Col. Simpson realized he had Rebels on his right and rear. He sent 2nd Lt. Josiah Shaw to determine the friendliness of these formations. Lt. Shaw returned with his clothes severely holed and no doubt highly agitated. Simpson attempted to escape, but ran into more rebels. The 4th was surrounded. "Simpson, who had told his men the day before 'We should go to Richmond tomorrow' had reason to rue his words."[11] Colonel Gallagher of the 11th Pennsylvania Reserves found himself in the same predicament. "Fighting and retreating until it reached the open field, it there found itself completely surrounded, with ranks sadly thinned and broken, ammunition nearly gone, and all chance of escape cut off."[12]

Somewhere in the mass of fleeing men in the river bottom, Brigadier Taylor inquired of Lt. Grubb, "Where is the 4th?" The junior officer answered, "Gone to Richmond, sir." Brigadier Taylor's eyes flashed in anger, "Young man, this is no place for levity!" Lt. Grubb replied, "They are captured, every man of them." Taylor wrung his hands and lamented, "My God, my God!"[13] The 4th New Jersey lost 45 killed, 103 wounded, and 437 missing. The 11th Pennsylvania reserves had 50 killed and 634 wounded or captured.

Still carrying his long-handled frying pan, Major Upton began collecting the swords of the officers. Upton put the frying pan in crook of arm while taking up officers' swords. "Finally, Upton's arms were so full of cutlery that he was forced to temporarily discard his precious skillet."[14] Within two months, Upton would be killed taking the flag of the 5th New York Zouaves at 2nd Manassas.[15] "After this, close to the left, another regiment was taken trying to get out. The regiments captured ... were the 2nd [Maine], 4th New Jersey, and 11th Pennsylvania. The number of flags [captured] I do not remember but it seems to me there were more than two."[16] The 5th Texas lost 14 percent of its men.

1st Texas

The 1st Texas now came up, passed through the captured batteries, and pursued the Federals all the way to the Adams House, where R.H. Anderson's Brigade had formed a line on their right.[17] The 1st Texas' losses were 18 percent.

Battle Group Hood

Brigadier Hood witnessed a remarkable sight. 'Just after my troops had broken the adversary's line, [Major Haskell] reported to me for duty, sword in hand, notwithstanding that one of his arms had been by a shot completely severed from his body. I naturally instructed him to go in search of a surgeon."[18]

After taking the guns, Battle Group Hood, what was left of it, kept going, too. "Still the work was not finished; the enemy had rallied behind some houses in front and in the garden, and kept up a sharp fire. We drove ahead, forced them to leave the houses, whipped them out of the garden and put them to utter rout." Hood's men had captured the Adams House. "Our own Regiment, now a mere handful, and led by Capt. Townsend, still rushed on towards the river, until ordered back for fear of being surrounded. It was by this time getting dark."[19] At the edge of the bluff, the 4th Texas had only 72 men out of 546, an instant casualty rate of 87 percent. Private Hunter's company lost 33 out of 52 men (63 percent).[20] Enough stragglers would return to the regiment to drop its casualty rate to 55 percent.[21] The 18th Georgia also went on, 400 yards past the captured guns, and was also ordered to fall back. It had lost 34 percent of its strength.

Law's Brigade also stopped. William Duncan, 11th Mississippi, had been killed; he was wrapped for burial in a cape his mother sent him, onto which he himself had sewn the buttons.[22] The 4th Alabama captured a whole company of the 6th U.S.[23] Alphonso Ames, 6th North Carolina, went to Parson's Spring and found a wounded Texan. "I asked him if his wounds were fatal and he replied, 'I don't think so. A ball has passed through my hips and cut the cords of my testicles.'"[24] President Jefferson Davis himself visited the brigade the next night.[25] The 6th North Carolina lost only 10 percent. The 2nd Mississippi lost 20 percent, the 4th Alabama 26 percent, and the 11th Mississippi a whopping 45 percent. Pvt. Hankins' company of the 11th Mississippi had but 16 of 76 men, an instant casualty rate of 79 percent.[26]

Archer's brigade was disorganized after taking Bucklin's guns. It wound up with about 100 men at the end of the day, an instant casualty rate of 91 percent.[27] All field officers of 19th Georgia, 1st, and 7th Tennessee had fallen, as well as 2 captains in the 5th Alabama Battalion.[28] Stragglers would lower the brigade casualty rate to about 25 percent. Capt. Lemmon reflected, "the federal troops were posted in the bottom [of the ravine], and the smoke of their own guns hung in their faces and obscured the charging brigade, so that they mostly overshot them, or the place could not have been taken."[29] Bucklin's two fine ordnance rifles were given to Captain Braxton, Fredericksburg Artillery.[30]

Fulkerson's Brigade, Valley Army, had followed Whiting and wound up with Longstreet's Division, where it was formed in line of battle and sent forward, following Wilcox's brigade. The 37th Virginia was on the right, the 10th in center, 23rd on the left. "The brigade moved forward rapidly with a shout, crossing the field and up to the enemy's works on the hill, which we found deserted, except by dead and wounded. We continued to advance until we came up to [Battle Group Hood] which being at a halt, the ... brigade was now also halted, and Col. Fulkerson went forward to ascertain the position of the enemy, when we received heavy fire from the right, and the gallant Fulkerson fell mortally wounded. The fire was returned by another brigade on our right...."[31] Command devolved onto Col. Warren, 10th Virginia, who relieved Battle Group Hood.[32] Lt. Wood, 37th Virginia, was present when the brigade lost its only man killed. Near the captured artillery, "My attention was attracted to the colonel. He had been struck and was slowly turning and sinking. I quickly put my arm about him and assisted him to the ground. I saw he was seriously hurt and had him borne from the field."[33] Col. Fulkerson had been backlit by setting sun.

Battle Group Pickett

Battle Groups Pickett and Wilcox also stopped at the guns. The irrepressible George Harris, 19th Virginia, "ordered the greater portion of the 2nd Federal Regiment [2nd U.S.] to surrender, but they fired into our men, when he ordered our men to return fire, whereupon they surrendered."[34] The 2nd did have 19 men missing. Pickett's men turned over 1,400 prisoners to the 7th Virginia, of Kemper's Brigade.[35] Pvt. J.K. Simmons was rumored to have captured a brigadier general, 2 colonels, and a Yankee flag.[36] Pickett's brigade's casualties mirror how they attacked, with the right forward of the left. The left regiment, the 56th Virginia, had but 13 percent casualties; the 28th 15 percent, and the 19th 16 percent, which did not include George Harris. The two right regiments, the 18th and 8th Virginia, who broke through the Wall of Death and captured two different sets of guns, had 27 percent and 24 percent casualties, respectively.

R.H. Anderson's Brigade, Battle Group Pickett

Following Pickett, R.H. Anderson had moved straight forward across Boatswain's Creek with the 6th, 2nd Rifles, and 4th South Carolina Battalion. Near the Adams House,[37] the remnants of the 12th New York and 16th Michigan made a stand.[38] Peter McDavid's bayonet was hit by a grapeshot and bent double. "After taking such fire, General Anderson ... ordered a charge, before which our adversaries disappeared; some hiding in a wide ditch ... some fleeing to the Chickahominy."[39]

Col. Stockton, 16th Michigan, tells his side of the story. "[I] had faced my regiment to the rear for the purpose of falling back more under the hill and save being flanked, when Major Barnum of the 12th New York rode up to me and urged that I would hold a few minutes longer. Immediately afterwards Major Welch came and stated that if I remained there a minute longer we would be cut to pieces. I faced my regiment to the rear ... but I had no sooner given the command to march [when] ... most ran off to the bridge over the Chickahominy. Many sought the timberland along the river."[40]

Brigadier Anderson detached Col. Micah Jenkins, Palmetto Sharpshooters with the 5th South Carolina (Battle Group Jenkins), to move south, in case there were any Federals towards the Chickahominy.

Butterfield's Brigade

When the 1st Michigan collapsed, it allowed Battle Group Wilcox to attack Brigadier Butterfield's right flank. Butterfield ordered the 12th New York up to support it,[41] but the right wing of the 12th disintegrated in the confusion, as did the right flank of the 83rd Pennsylvania.[42] Brigadier Butterfield rallied the left wing of the 12th and 83rd, and sent the 16th Michigan to their support. These were the movements that Brigadier Hood espied. Brigadier Butterfield rode to the 44th New York, still in place along Boatswain's Creek, and exhorted them to stand fast, as the rest of the brigade was on its way. Lt. Col. Rice, 44th New York, was shocked when "the commanding officer [Col. Stephen W. Stryker] ... with the left wing of the regiment commenced to retreat, and at length to fly toward the Chickahominy. I was in command of the right wing, and as soon as I saw this conduct of the left wing I was fired with indignation and anger, for not a moment before the entire regiment had assured the general ... that he might depend upon its consistency. With such feelings I at once ordered the right wing to stand firm, and overtook the left before it reached the river. I halted the columns, seized the colors, rallied the battalion ... and in line of battle led it back under a murderous fire to its original position."[43] The 44th New York was back at Boatswain's Creek, facing west.

In the meantime, the right of the 83rd had formed a line in the woods behind Boatswain's Creek facing north.[44]

> The line had scarcely formed before the enemy ... opened on us.... The rebels advanced without order, and some of them came within 30 feet of our line and, taking shelter behind trees, poured a destructive fire into our ranks. In a moment more we had hurled a shower of bullets into their advancing columns, and given them a bloody check. They had intended to charge upon us and drive us out of the woods. Now the conflict became almost hand to hand, and the crash of musketry was absolutely appalling.... [N]ow [our men] began to fall thick and fast around us. One brave boy of 16 who was knocked down by a crushing wound in the head, was seen to grasp his musket and attempt repeatedly to rise, as if determined to fight while the ebb of his life lasted. A bullet piercing the breast of Col. McLane prostrated him upon the ground, and ... a moment more and Major Naghel fell, stricken with a fragment of a shell, and gave up the ghost.[45] Major von Vegesack ... came galloping up and ... ordered a retreat.[46]

The 16th led the 83rd, marching in column of fours, south though the dusky gloom. In this formation, they were almost defenseless.

Battle Group Jenkins

It was rapidly nearing night. Col. Jackson of the 5th South Carolina observed the 83rd coming out of the woods in column of fours, and alerted Col. Jenkins. Both regiments maneuvered to face west, the Sharpshooters on the left (south), and the 5th South Carolina on the right (north). "While these movements were being executed, a regiment with flag closely furled was observed [marching] in line about 75 yards in front. Not being able to distinguish the flag Col. [Jenkins] went to the front and repeatedly demanded the display of the flag, and the name of the regiment. Receiving no reply but 'friends' he retired to his lines...."[47] Pvt. Hoyt of the Sharpshooters continues, "Their column was not more than a 50 yards in our front ... while our men were at the ready.... The officer in command [of the 16th] commanded 'Halt! Front!' to which Jenkins replied 'Fire!'"[48] "A sheet of flame burst from his rifles, and the front rank of the 16th Michigan went down as if smitten with a scythe blade."[49] Jenkins ordered the charge.[50]

T.R. Lackie was in the 16th Michigan. "Maj. Welch's [portion of the 16th Michigan] on seeing a brigade advancing on our flank, gave the command, right face file right, march, ... and fronted. The confederate troops on our front halted within 30 paces. There were no shots fired between us. We were not quite certain that they were our enemy until their commander, who was in front and on foot, commanded us to surrender. Maj Welch replied 'Damned if we do,' when they immediately opened on us a withering volley by regiments, the first kneeling down. We replied with the best we had."[51]

The 5th South Carolina had been thrown off its guard by overtures to surrender on the part of a regiment which was deploying in its front and completely at its mercy. As soon as the deployment was complete, the Yankee officer gave the order to fire. Crippled and maddened, but not staggered, the 5th replied with a volley and a charge about the same time the Palmetto Sharpshooters made its charge.[52]

The 83rd Pennsylvania saw it differently:

> At that moment Von Vegesack, giving a white handkerchief to Lt. White, directed him to go out under a flag of truce and ascertain who they were. Placing the handkerchief on the point of his sword and holding it in the air, White started out boldly upon his perilous undertaking. He had advanced but half way between the two armies when he was met by the Colonel and Adjutant of the regiment, who asked him if he had come to surrender. "Who are you?" said White in return. "The [5th][53] South Carolina" was the reply. "The 83rd Pennsylvania never surrenders to South Carolinians," retorted White defiantly. "Then what do you want?" said the rebel commander. "I have come to demand that you surrender unconditionally to the forces of the United States."[54]

"This latter proposition that caused indignant mirth among us," a South Carolinian recalled.[55] "[H]ad the rebel forces been made up of old men and cripples, women and children, they would never have surrendered to such a handful of men...."[56] Lt. White and the Southern officer both ran back to their commands. "White had scarcely made it back half way, when he heard the click of a thousand muskets in his rear, and looking around and seeing they were about to fire, instantly threw himself on the ground. In a moment a storm of leaden hail whistled over him. In another moment another storm whistled over him from the opposite direction.... Capt. Campbell, observing too the motions of the enemy, had ordered the men to lie down and commence firing.[57] At once we fell flat on the ground, raising on one knee and returning the fire...."[58]

The 44th New York left its breastworks to support the 83rd Pennsylvania and the 16th Michigan. "The regiment was at once ordered to leap over the earthwork and pour its fire into the ranks of the enemy, now closing on us from the rear and right.[59] Capt. Judson relates what happened next: "The 16th ... began

The tattered National Color of the 44th New York (Library of Congress).

to waver and fall back pursued by the enemy. This left our right exposed to the attack of the regiment that was pursuing the 16th. We should then have been surrounded on all sides. Capt. Campbell ordered us to fall back into the woods, take position again behind their old line of defenses, and prepare for another attack. They fell back in good order, and on reaching the works found the 44th still holding their position, under command of Lt. Col. Rice."[60]

The 83rd, 16th and 44th were now formed behind the works, but facing now in the direction opposite to our line of battle in the morning. Scarcely had they taken position when the woods began to swarm with enemy pressing upon flank, front and rear, firing as they advanced. "'What is to be done?' said Campbell to Rice. 'Skedaddle is the word!' ... [T]he men began to scatter ... accordingly they broke, each man for himself...."[61]

Butterfield's command was wrecked. The 44th New York lost 15 percent, many more missing than wounded. Lt. Col. Stryker was "discharged" a week after the battle.[62] The 12th New York lost 21 percent, fewer missing than wounded. The 16th Michigan lost its flag to the Palmetto Sharpshooters,[63] 34 percent of its men, and had twice as many wounded as missing. The 83rd Pennsylvania lost 36 percent, with twice as many missing as wounded, Capt. Judson notwithstanding.

Battle Group Wilcox

In Battle Group Wilcox, a 2nd Florida staff officer overhead a captured Yankee bemoan, "God save our poor fellows, if there's more than one Florida regiment.... It is no use killing them for they won't run; and they seem to have only two commands, 'Fire at will,' and 'Charge!'"[64] Pryor's Brigade, who also broke the line and captured two sets of guns, was terribly devastated, losing 860 out of 1400 men, an instant rate of 61 percent.[65] Stragglers reduced that to 306. The 3rd Virginia lost 11 percent, the 14th Louisiana lost 21 percent, the 2nd Florida 22 percent, the 14th Alabama 23 percent. Coppen's Zouaves, though, lost 36 percent. Lt. Miller, 14th Louisiana, said after the battle, "I have got my fill of fighting, I want no more of it."[66]

J.R. Jones' Brigade, of the Valley Army, had followed Fulkerson's Brigade and had also wound up with Longstreet. He sent it forward to relieve Wilcox's Brigade.[67] Jones' men were the Confederates on the west side of the creek who menaced Butterfield's men who had jumped their own works. It had four men slightly wounded.[68]

24

It Was Death to Stay
and Cold Steel
Was the Next Thing

Near Old Cold Harbor

As Longstreet and Whiting were starting their attack on the Cold Harbor Road, the Rev. Major Dabney had rejoined Stonewall Jackson. "Cheek and brow were blazing with crimson blood, and beneath the vizor of his old drab cap, his eye glared with a fire, before which every other eye quailed."[1] J.E.B. Stuart was present, with an ostrich plume in his hat. Jackson said something to Stuart about a cavalry charge, to which Stuart replied, "No, General, too many cannons there." Jackson would have to look elsewhere for reinforcements.

A member of the 1st Maryland recalled:

General Jackson went to the front; we were left with our battery and the 12th Georgia. Col. Johnson, preferring to go in rather than wait in support of a battery, rode off to attract General Jackson's attention, hoping for orders. He found him with half a dozen of his staff in front, on a rise of ground to the right of the road. "Good evening, General," said he. "Good evening Colonel," was the curt reply. "If you want me I am there." "Very good, sir." His teeth were clenched, his lips clamped closer than ever, and the blaze of his eye alone betrayed excitement. Straight in the saddle, straighter than usual, for he stooped forward in riding, he sat, his head raised up, catching every sound. Then half a dozen horsemen appeared in a field, a quarter of a mile off, galloping wildly to and fro. Suddenly Jackson threw his horse's head toward them, jerked bolt upright in his saddle, and raised his right arm, horizontal to the elbow, thence perpendicular. "I'll bring them to you," said Col. Johnson, quickly, thinking he was beckoning to the horsemen. There was no reply, and looking round at his face, he saw the soldier was praying, abstracted, dead to the strife, and blind to all around, his soul communed alone with his God. Everyone observed a dead silence, until turning, he said in his calm, quick tone, "Colonel, send all the infantry in except a hundred to each battery; you cover them." "All right, sir," said the Colonel, and galloped off to make a circuit of the batteries. He found each supported by a small regiment, so reduced by the Valley Campaign as to admit of no further reduction.[2]

This was Battle Group Virginia that Brigadier Elzey had detailed as battery support, and the whole Stonewall Brigade, such as it was. The 2nd Virginia had 80 men; the 27th Virginia had 125, but the 33rd boasted 134. Arriving at New Cold Harbor, Powell Hill had ordered Brigadier Winder to detail two regiments to support the Purcell Artillery.[3] Winder sent the 2nd Virginia and the 5th Virginia.[4] The 4th, 27th and 33rd and 1st Virginia Battalion were halted "by Gen Winder near a house which I believe is called [Old] Cold Harbor tavern."[5]

The member of the 1st Maryland continues. "On his return, [Col. Johnson] met the General and his staff coming up the road at a trot, and reported the facts to him. Jackson's face was in a blaze of enthusiasm, his whole expression lighted with the fervor of his feelings. 'Take all the infantry in, colonel,' said he; 'I shall support the batteries with cavalry, and Johnson, make your men shoot like they are shooting at a mark, slow and low, hit them here and here.' Thrusting the colonel in the waist with his fore finger at the words. It was the first and last time the Colonel ever heard the General call anyone by name."[6] After Jackson gave Johnson his orders, the Rev. Major Dabney recollected, "But a half hour of sunlight remained…. He supposed that all his force had been put forth, and … the enemy was not crushed. It was then that he despatched messengers to all commanders of his division, with these words: 'Tell them this affair must hang in suspense no longer; *sweep the field with the bayonet!*'"[7]

11th U.S. Regulars, Supporting Martin's Battery

Major Floyd-Jones had been supporting Martin's Battery C, Massachusetts Light Artillery (6 Napoleons) and Voeglee's Battery, 1st New York Light Artillery (6 20-lb. Parrotts) all day.[8] They spent the day in the morass of Boatswain's Run. Capt. Robins wryly noted, "To lie still under a fire to which you can make no reply … taxes the courage and discipline of a regiment…." During the day, one private complained that this was a lousy place to locate the regiment; there were bees nearby, because he could hear them. A sergeant informed him that if he would just crest the hill he'd find a *hornet's nest indeed*, "which remark brought forth shouts of laughter." Capt. Robins watched a Confederate solid shot decapitate a gunner. Soon wounded came streaming by, and then more.[9] The 11th U.S. watched the 31st New York's charge, and how quickly Col. Pratt was carried back, with three wounds.[10] Ominously, Voeglee's Battery A, 1st New York Light Artillery limbered up their gigantic guns and retired.[11] The 11th was alone with Martin's Battery.

Hill's Division, at the Foot of Regulars' Hill

Most of Harvey Hill's men were still reorganizing after the fight with Reynolds' Brigade when Battle Group Georgia burst out of the woods on Zouave Hill and crossed their front, 1,300 men charging southwest, on a direct line at the McGehee House. Martin's Battery C, Massachusetts Light Artillery (6 Napoleons), just west of the McGehee House, concentrated its whole fire directly on them.[12] Capt. Robins, 11th U.S., near Martin's guns, described the scene: "[W]e are on the crest of the hill to the right of the battery, whose men are working with frantic energy, pouring into the advancing enemy double charges of canister. The plain in front of it was dotted with men, while far in front was a gray mass under a cloud of smoke."[13]

The dots included Lt. Park and a special detail from the 12th Alabama, Rodes' brigade. "I was placed in command of a detachment of four men from each company, and ordered to deploy in their front, and shoot the cannoneers who were doing fatal damage in our ranks. The cannon belched forth fire and smoke, and the bursting shells were hurtling among us."[14] Lt. Park's men passed behind Battle Group Georgia and entered Griffin's Woods to get on the battery's flank.

Part of that gray line was Battle Group McGowan. One of the double canister shots, at least, had good effect. When Battle Group McGowan was about halfway up the hill, a single 2-inch ball hit Col. McGowan in the chest, bruising him severely and knocking him out of the fight. Leaderless and exhausted, his men stopped and laid on their arms.[15] South Carolina's duty for the day was done.

Griffin's Woods

A few hundred yards to the southwest, Brigadier Lawton and his men passed over Pender's North Carolinians and "were all the time under a continuous fire of musketry and artillery."[16] They "advanced steadily forward ... the regiments occasionally disunited by the smoke, dust and confusion of the battle field, and then brought together again."[17] Once brought together, Taylor's two New Jersey regiments heard the "distinct command to 'aim' and 'fire' ... from the brigade's front, and a deadly shower of bullets poured into the unprepared Jerseyans."[18] Once again, the Confederates had managed to penetrate Griffin's Woods unseen in the smoke and were almost on top of the Northerners. This volley from about 2,000 rifles[19] stunned them, and according to a Union staff officer, "was the most withering I ever saw delivered. The New Jersey brigade broke all to pieces."[20] Lawton's men were disunited again, and so he called a halt.[21] A member of the regiment wrote, "While waiting here a regiment of the enemy, which proved to be the Third New Jersey, emerged from the woods on the right. Fire was immediately opened on it and it fled precipitately, and were nearly all captured by some regiment of our troops stationed to the right of our brigade. Major Birney of the 4th New Jersey, and several non-commissioned officers and privates fell into our hands. Pvt. Mack [13th Georgia], while unarmed, captured 1 lieutenant, 1 sergeant, and 2 privates of the 1st New Jersey, all armed."[22] Though Lawton's fire was severe, Battle Group Georgia was bearing down on the New Jersey right flank, and they had no choice but to break or suffer capture. Capt. Augustus Martin, whose battery was supporting the New Jerseyans, was forced to withdraw because "The left of our line of troops [Taylor's New Jersey Brigade] was entirely driven from the field...."[23]

"[Brigadier] Taylor, who had dismounted, scrambled through the woods for his horse and galloped after his men to prevent a rout."[24] He managed to do so near Hexamer's Battery, between the Adams House and the McGehee House, where parts of the 2nd New Jersey joined him. Capt. Frank Knight thereof had surrendered to a Confederate, who clobbered him with the butt of his musket; Knight drew his revolver, shot the Rebel, and then ran. The 2nd New Jersey's Col. Tucker had been shot dead. Major Ryerson had rallied them with the 1st and 3rd, but then was shot in the abdomen and the 2nd New Jersey retreated south beyond the Adams House.[25] The 2nd New Jersey lost almost 43 percent of its men, with slightly more missing than wounded.

Behind the 11th U.S. and Martin's Battery, Capt. Hexamer's guns were still in position supporting the New Jersey Brigade, about midway between McCall's Gunline on its left and the McGehee House on its right. Capt. Hexamer reported, "[O]ur infantry left the woods. At this moment I received an order to open fire with spherical case and canister...."[26] Twelve guns, four Parrott guns and eight murderous Howitzers and Napoleons, concentrated their fire on Battle Group Georgia.

Battle Group Georgia, West of the McGehee House

A member of the 38th Georgia, L.A.M., recalled:

In emerging from the wood, these two regiments found themselves in the hottest part of the field, where our friends were pressing the enemy toward the left, and joined them in the contest at that point under a murderous fire. As we emerged from the thicket and came in full view of the enemy, the order to double quick was given and the "Rebel yell" ringing over the field, we began to charge. It seemed as if they were expecting us for it was as if every cannon in the Yankee army was turned loose upon us. Shells burst in front of us and scattering, carried death and wounds in their track. Solid shot cut men in twain, solid shot shrieked overhead and scared us just as bad, solid shot struck the ground just in front of us and scattered dirt and gravel in our faces and would ricochet and go howling to our rear.[27]

In the first 150 yards up the hill, the 38th Georgia's Lt. Col. Parr had his arm sliced off, and then Major Matthews went down. Private Lumpkin, over six feet tall, was somehow unscathed, but many of the captains and "dozens" of lieutenants joined the 250 men who had already fallen.[28] Captain Battey reported, "[We] found ourselves in line of battle face to face with the enemy at the distance of about 300 yards. Thus we marched under a most terrific fire to within about 180 yards of a body of 4,000 to 5,000 regulars. It was here that our colonel and major were wounded and the command devolved upon me. In obedience to orders received from Captain Lawton I commanded my men to 'fire and load lying.'"[29] In fact, the 38th was wavering. L.A.M. continues: "The terrific fire we were under produced a demoralization that was fearful to witness. Men huddled up and became entangled with one another. Some lay down and seemed to spread out like adders, while some just turned their backs and went at a [racehorse] gait to the rear. What officers were left were nobly doing their duty, but did not seem to know what to do. Our color bearer, Sgt. … Wright … wildly and frantically waved the colors, but otherwise stood still. No one seemed to be in command. In fact there was no commander. Some of us could see plainly that this panic would get worse if not checked…."[30]

Next door in the 31st Georgia, Lt. William "Tip" Harrison remembered, "We marched up within 200 yards of the Yankees who were stationed behind a fence protected by cedar trees. Our line was formed in a cornfield down an inclined plane from the Yankees. They ought to have whipped 5 times their number with such advantages."[31] Pvt. Bradwell, 31st Georgia, remembered the action well:

[T]he 38th and 31st coming up last, were thrown forward and struck the enemy's extreme right in the vicinity of the McGehee House, where already desperate fighting had taken place. On an eminence to the [Union] right of the House was posted … [Martin's Battery C, Massachusetts Light Artillery (6 Napoleons)] … of six guns, with an open field in every direction. This Yankee battery was supported by infantry and was dealing death to the confederate lines in every direction, and especially in the 38th, when the 31st came up some distance to the left of that splendid command. As soon as the 38th came out into the open, armed only with smooth-bore muskets, its losses were so heavy from the enemy's infantry, armed with long range rifles, and the battery on the hill, that the men in the ranks called out to the colonel, Clement Evans, that we could not stand it and we must capture the battery and put a stop to the slaughter of our own regiment and the 38th.[32]

Another member of the 38th wrote, "Col. Evans, 31st marched up and asked 'What have you stopped for? 'We have no one to command us' was the reply. 'I'll lead you,' said the Col…."[33] "Col Evans, 31st Ga. … came over to order the charge, and went to our Color Bearer Sgt. James Wright, and asked him for the battle flag. Wright refused to give him the flag; told Col Evans that he would carry the flag as long as he was able, and all he

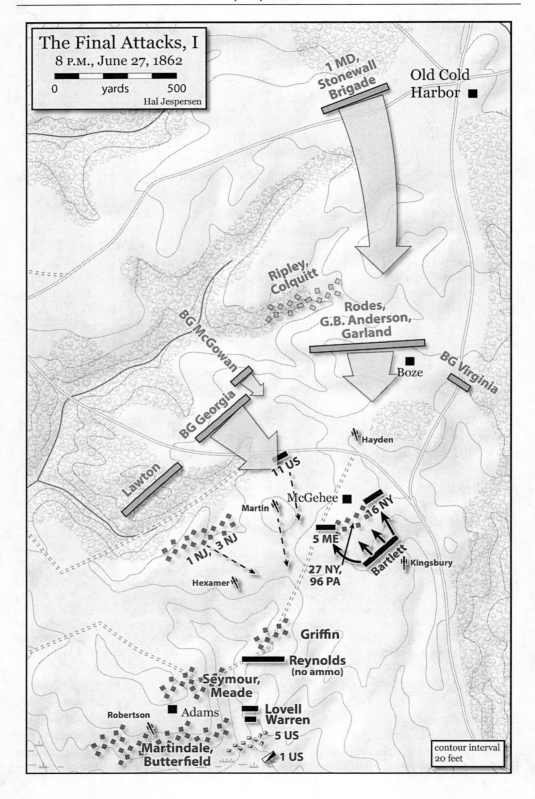

The Final Attacks, I
8 P.M., June 27, 1862

0   yards   500

Hal Jespersen

1 MD, Stonewall Brigade

Old Cold Harbor

Ripley, Colquitt

Rodes, G.B. Anderson, Garland

Boze

BG Virginia

BG McGowan

BG Georgia

Lawton

Hayden

11 US

McGehee

Martin

16 NY

5 ME

1 NJ, 3 NJ

27 NY, 96 PA

Bartlett

Kingsbury

Hexamer

Griffin

Reynolds
(no ammo)

Seymour, Meade

Robertson   Adams

Lovell Warren

5 US

Martindale, Butterfield

1 US

contour interval
20 feet

wanted Col. Evans to do was tell him where to take it and it would go to the cannon's mouth."[34] One Georgian recorded, "With a voice that was heard above the din and roar he shouted, 'Georgians, is this the way to meet the enemy? 38th rally to your colors!' His words, his fearlessness, and cool bearing and his commands acted like magic. Everyone caught the spirit, and though men were falling every second … our line was restored…. With his sword pointing to the front Col. Evans said, 'Carry them yonder, and quickly follow him boys!'"[35] Pvt. Bradwell continues, "[T]hey dashed forward in a trot for the battery and the enemy's lines, and when they came within their old musket range, they opened on them with buck and ball cartridges such a withering fire and yell that the enemy's line broke and fell back immediately toward the battery. Nor could the enemy be censured for this, for the noise made by our shooting and yelling, and the destruction wrought by our buck and ball cartridges was enough to frighten any man, however well disciplined."[36]

11th U.S., Supporting Martin's Battery

Capt. Robins continues, "We commenced firing, but were ordered to stop as there were some of our men in front (the Bucktails) [Reynolds' Brigade, Pennsylvania Reserves]. As they filed out the rear of us, we opened fire—the gray mass in front halted and poured into us a withering volley, which we returned."[37] The 11th U.S. survived the volley, but the fire decimated the horses of Martin's Battery.[38]

Martin's Battery C, Massachusetts Light Artillery

Twenty-nine years later Capt. Augustus Martin still vividly recalled, "The Confederates advanced in fine array…. I have seen nothing like it except, of course, at Gettysburg…. It was as though they were mown down in swaths as by a mighty scythe…. Stonewall Jackson had effected his junction, and it was his troops that were in front of us, and they advanced on my battery and were going to carry it with cold steel. Jackson had declared that his men would do it with the bayonet … and it was stated at the time that the charge was led by Jackson in person."[39] At the time, he sanguinely reported, "The battery remained in this position until late in the afternoon, when it was found that the enemy had broken the left of our line, and I was ordered to retire with my battery. My support had all retired except the 11th U.S. Infantry, who were immediately on the right of the battery. When the enemy arrived within 150 yards of the battery we poured a double charge of canister into the regiment in our front, which broke their lines and drove them to the rear in utter confusion, giving me the opportunity … to retire in safety…."[40] Martin had fired 30 rounds of canister,[41] five per gun, but the last shot was double canister, so his guns had time for only four shots, which took about two minutes. So many horses were down that Lt. Reed recalled that the men initially hauled the guns back by hand: "Prologs were attached, and they were drawn a few yards down the hill."[42] There Martin fired his last canister rounds, with a little extra. "I had a number of spare sponge staffs and so I told my boys to let those fly. We gave them a volley of sponges. Their execution was not that of double shotted canister, but they made up in noise what they lacked in other respects…."[43] After this shot, Martin's Battery beat a hasty retreat.

Lt. Reed noted, "It was at this time that Adjutant Boyer, [96th] Pennsylvania was riding to give an order to a regiment on his right, a piece of shell hit his horse on the head and neck, nearly cutting off the head."[44] Martin's battery lost so many horses that three caissons were left on the field. While crossing the river, one of his guns ran off a bridge and was lost.[45]

Capt. Robins continues, "Our battery continued to pour in charges of canister, and then, the troops on their left having gone, limbered up and left the field to us."[46] He was mesmerized by the closeness of the Rebels and the Rebel Yell but found his wits, and realized that he was all alone. He stopped to help a wounded man, gave the Rebels one shot, and "receiv[ed] a perfect shower in return—all fortunately going over my head."[47]

Harvey Hill's Division, in Front of the McGehee House

Utterly unmindful of Battle Group Georgia, Harvey Hill reported, "The temporary silence of the battery [Hayden's Section by the 20th North Carolina] enabled the division to move up in fine style and turn the tide of battle in our favor."[48] Another Carolinian more truthfully recollected, "On reaching the top of the ridge the enemy was seen lying in an old road, seeking shelter behind its banks and other objects that afforded him protection."[49]

These were the remnants of Sykes' men. With Martin's guns gone, Hexamer's guns alone were holding back Battle Group Georgia, but they were doing it well. The remnants of Sykes' infantry were trying to form a second line. The 11th U.S. was in the sunken part of the McGehee Road. The 14th U.S. had rallied its decimated ranks in the road, and the equally shot-up 12th U.S. was trying to do so.[50]

In the 31st Georgia, "The older men of the regiment called out to our field officers that we could not stand [it] and that we must take the battery on the hill in front of us, in full view except for the smoke around it. With this they dashed forward, without orders, with a hideous yell. We were within range of their infantry, and the whole regiment opened fire."[51] "The blue line broke immediately … shooting all the while."[52] "This was most unfortunate for us, for in front of the battery was a fence and a sunken road, which gave them a splendid position…. Here we suffered our greatest loss in all the battles through which we ever passed…. We remained there, loading and shooting our old muskets at the enemy, while their infantry and battery slaughtered the 31st and 38th."[53]

G.B. Anderson's men were on Battle Group Georgia's left (east). Said a man in the 4th North Carolina, "The order was given to charge, and the men responded with a shout, rushing across the field in the face of furious fire. The scene was terrific beyond description. The yells of our men, the roar of musketry, the thunder of artillery, the shrieks of the wounded and dying, the screaming of shells, with the loud commands of the officers, all combined to excite and stimulate the men."[54] The 2nd North Carolina advanced ahead of the line; after 2 volleys from Confederates behind them, they "sprang to the charge."[55]

Brigadier Garland's men were to G.B. Anderson's left (east).[56] A member of the 13th North Carolina recalled, "At the top of a steep hill, which was about 90 yards, there was a high new fence. General Hill ordered us not to climb it, but to tear it down, run over it and charge the enemy. We marched steadily up the bluff to the fence, every man seized the fence, and rushed against it and it fell as if a tornado had struck it. Down … we went, yelling and shooting like mad men. The enemy ran like sheep before a pack of dogs. We were pursuing them in a southerly course."[57] Col. McRae, 5th North Carolina, recounted, "At a point one or two hundred yards in front, a young man, Captain of a company … made an effort to rally his command, which was retiring. He had his sword drawn, and could be distinctly seen by us to appeal to his men to make a stand. He partially succeeded, and when his company halted and faced to our lines, he was in front, some ten or twenty paces, and was thrown between two fires. Our firing was very heavy, causing him to be wounded. I learned afterwards, by the men who carried him, that he died…."[58]

The 5th and 26th Alabama, Rodes' Brigade, arrived at the McGehee Road just to the east of the McGehee House. The 5th and 26th "continued the charge, and had successfully and almost alone beaten back two large bodies of the enemy on top of the hill, besides taking a battery of the enemy directly in our front."[59] The 5th Alabama retook Hayden's two Parrotts, and kept going.

The rallied 12th and 14th U.S. "broke and retreated, and made a second stand, which induced [us] to halt under cover of the road side and return their fire."[60] Major Floyd Jones, commanding the 11th U.S., reported drily that "two regiments of our troops which had reformed … broke and disappeared. Being thus entirely left alone with a handful of men and being in danger being cut off, the regiment retired."[61] "The 12th and 14th U.S. fell back to the 'second fence in McGehee's orchard.' Every post, bush and tree now cover[ed] a man who is blasting away as fast as he can load and fire."[62] Twice wounded, Major Clitz, 12th U.S., passed out from loss of blood and was taken to the McGehee House. "While lying there I witnessed the most desperate fighting of the day."[63]

Smelling victory, Battle Group Georgia and Harvey Hill's men charged across the McGehee Road. Sgt. Evans, 12th U.S., describes what he saw: "The enemy attempt to cross the road … our artillerymen are straining every nerve to keep back the enemy columns, who are rushing on in frantic masses and trying to sweep the whole crest. All the open space … is a sea of men. Column after column forms and charges up to the very muzzles of our guns, which belch forth grape and canister in a continual stream."[64]

Bartlett's Brigade, Southeast of the McGehee House

The stand of a few hundred Regulars at the McGehee House bought precious minutes for the last Federal troops to come to their rescue. When the 16th New York fell back from Hayden's guns, it panicked two of Bartlett's three remaining regiments, the 96th Pennsylvania and 27th New York,[65] who were trying to form a line behind the McGhee House. This forced Bartlett to call up his trail regiment.[66] The 5th Maine was to stop the Rebel charge so that Bartlett could establish his line behind it towards 16th New York. Hexamer's Battery A, New Jersey Light Artillery (4 Parrotts, 2 howitzers) was on the 5th Maine's left.[67] A member of the 96th Pennsylvania recalled, "Immediately the Fifth Maine, right next to us, formed, and ran up the bank into the battle, to make the same charge that the 16th New York failed to accomplish…. The 5th Maine was a magnificent body of men, tall, bronzed woodsmen, looking as though nothing could stop them. They went into the maelstrom, a thousand strong, they came back … by fives and tens, the remainder, wounded, crippled or dead, were left in God's hands…."[68] Pvt. Bicknell recalled, "So on we pressed to the position assigned us, led by Col. Jackson, and which was within a few rods of the enemy's line, but protected by the brow of a hill from their direct fire. Here we laid down for a few moments…. Just then the [27th New York[69]] who were upon our right, sent up a tremendous cheer, which attracted … the attention of a rebel battery, which sent a perfect broadside over into the ranks, and from which we did not escape."[70] General Stonewall Jackson's Grand Battery, about 30 guns, had opened fire at Col. Jackson of the 5th Maine.

Brigadier Bartlett was desperately trying to get his brigade on line "under the same scathing fire," about 200 yards behind the McGehee House.[71] The 27th New York went in on the right of the 5th Maine, with the 27th aligned on the McGehee House, "from which the enemy were firing."[72] The 96th Pennsylvania had finally sorted itself out. With "the left [5th Maine, 27th New York] and the right [16th New York] of my line … established, I ordered them … to the front, and most nobly did they respond.…"[73]

Bartlett's "brigade was immediately ordered to advance."[74] "Having advanced some fifteen rods perhaps [about 200 yards], the order came 'lie down.' … [A]lmost at the same moment a full volley from a brigade of the enemy was fired at our men, without the slightest effect. Now the fight grew terrific. The air was full of bullets. 'On,' came the order. Down dashed our Colonel, 'take such a position and hold it!' Col. Jackson fell with a bad wound, and Lt. Col Heath took over."[75] "A house proved an obstacle in our lines, and companies I, G, C, and H became disengaged from the rest of the regiment. 'Move these companies to the left and perfect the line,' was in substance the last order which … Lt. Col Heath gave…. Ten minutes had elapsed before he fell. Now here we were in a terrific fight, without a field officer to command. Comrade after comrade fell upon either side."[76] Lt. Col. Heath was shot through the head and died instantly.[77]

As the 27th New York advanced into the storm, "No rebel troops, however brave, could stand the unearthly yell that we had learned to give."[78] "When within about 50 yards [of the McGehee House] before delivering a shot … the line advanced at double quick…."[79] "A part of our line encountered a picket fence along a garden near the McGehee House. They quickly battered this down with the butt end of their muskets, and moved on and took possession of the dwelling and outbuildings."[80]

The 96th Pennsylvania charged "across the field … in fine style … cheering as they advanced. The firing was heavy in front, a shower of lead and iron falling around us."[81] " My God, but there the bullets flew, a perfect rain of them. Uncle [Israel's] cap was shot from his head, merely taking the skin a little. He fought without a cap…. I cannot see how so many escaped."[82] "We drove them back after we got across the field to the fence. We all dropped down behind the fence…."[83] "Massed behind a broken down rail fence, and lying flat on the ground, with the impossible protection of a rail or two, what looked like a long gray serpent trailing its length across the field about 50 yards in front of us, and spitting fire from every joint. Just as we started, the serpent seemed to rise up, and break into a fleeing mass of men, flying back to better cover than the broken fence."[84]

Battle Group Georgia and Harvey Hill's Division

When the 11th U.S. broke, Battle Group Georgia had had enough of Hexamer's fire and "determined to drive them from the field, capture the battery, and … put an end to the engagement. This we were doing very nicely when Col. Evans … fearing that in our enthusiasm and the confusion we would penetrate too far … and all be killed or captured, ordered us to halt."[85] "This we absolutely refused to do and continued our drive. Col. Evans succeeded in stopping Company E [31st Georgia] by threatening to strike them with his sword if they did not stop … and then the other companies did so. This was the most unfortunate thing that could have happened to us. The enemy, only a few yards in our front … had all the advantage of us, being well protected, while we were in the open and exposed. Here our loss was very heavy."[86]

The 5th Alabama reported, "As soon as the force in front gave way, we wheeled to the left and met at double quick the enemy who were advancing from that direction at the same pace."[87] The 5th Alabama had outdistanced the 26th and rest of the line and had smashed into Bartlett's counterattack. It was the serpent. It broke, taking the 26th Alabama with it.[88]

A member of the 13th North Carolina remembered:

> General Hill had come up where we had torn the fence down; there he saw the enemy on our left advancing and about to enfilade Garland's Brigade. General Garland ordered a change of front. Col. Scales rushed in front of the 13th Regiment, as cool as if we had been on drill; his voice rang clear. The old 13th swung like a door on its hinges. By the time we fronted our new position the enemy were within 150 yards of us at a large dwelling house and in position behind a fence along the road, with their guns poked through the fence. There we met the most galling storm of lead. We charged the fence up a long slant and poured lead back at them as fast as we could load, shoot and charge.[89]

Arriving at the 23rd North Carolina, "General Garland rode up to the short but firm line and said, 'There are not many of you boys, but you are a noble few.'"[90] "So down we swept and up the hill to their position. We pressed forward in the charge as part of an Alabama regiment rushed back upon our line. Its Colonel shouted that he was going

Battle of Friday on the Chickahominy, Alfred Waud, 1862 (Library of Congress).

back to reform. Capt. Young, then in command of the regiment, Col. Christie having just fallen severely wounded, exclaimed, 'Don't go back to reform, we are all needed to carry this line!' So the regiment turned and charged with us. Up the hill we pressed."[91] Harvey Hill's men were taking a beating; they fell back and continued to slug it out, but Battle Group Georgia was out of ammunition and was ordered to the rear.[92]

Along the Cold Harbor Road

Col. Johnson, 1st Maryland, stopped just north of Boatswain's Branch to inspire his men: "Men, we alone represent Maryland here; we are few in number, but for that reason our duty to our state is greater, we must do her honor."[93] After making it through Boatswain's Branch and advancing across the open to the McGehee Road, Johnson "found to my horror regiment after regiment rushing back in utter disorder. The 5th Alabama I tried in vain to rally with my sword and the rifles of men. The 12th Alabama reformed readily on my right...."[94] Col. Gayle of the 12th saw that "a new line of battle was now coming up from the rear with the same object in view. I found it to be a part of General Jackson's command."[95] Col. Johnson continues, "Directly two small groups came back around two battle flags. 'Who are you,' cried the colonel. 'The Fifth and [3rd] North Carolina,' said they. 'Col. McRae ordered us to take that orchard and house, but we can't stand it.' [Col Johnson said] 'For the love of the Old North State Forever, rally and charge!' [The North Carolinians responded,] 'Yes, for her, the Old North State forever!'"[96] The 5th and 3rd North Carolina rallied on Johnson's left, with two Virginia regiments.[97] These were the 5th and 2nd Virginia, of Brigadier Winder's Stonewall Brigade. Boatswain's Branch had played havoc with Winder's line, leaving "the line somewhat broken in consequence of the swamp...."[98] The Stonewall Brigade broke apart; the 4th, 27th, and 33rd Virginia went to the right; the 2nd Virginia and the 5th Virginia went to the left.

Griffin's Woods

Lt. Park's 12th Alabama gunner assassination detail was sneaking through strangely empty Griffin's Woods, when Hexamer's guns "turned their shot, shell grape and canister directly upon my small squad, and the limbs of trees and countless leaves fell upon us, cut down by the enemy's fire." "We marched ... near enough to one of the batteries to shoot the artillerymen. The men were not slow in doing execution, and very soon we silenced the battery in our immediate front."[99] Hexamer's Battery A, New Jersey Light Artillery (4 Parrotts, 2 howitzers) was the target of their 40 rifles. "Suddenly, we received a volley of musketry from our left, followed by an incessant firing of infantry."[100] Lawton's Brigade now came up. Pvt. Murray, 26th Georgia, recounted, "The brigade went a short distance, and advanced over the dead and wounded, friends and foes, and charged the enemy, and took their battery and captured these guns and some prisoners and horses before the 'Yankees' could kill the horses. The battery we captured was the Hoboken battery...."[101]

Capt. Hexamer continues, "Not being supported, I found it necessary to limber and retire. One driver of the left section was shot down, while two horses of the same piece ... were disabled. The [howitzer], the horses of which were shot could not be brought forward, and fell into the hands of the enemy." Hexamer had fired 165 rounds, lost five men wounded and five horses killed, and lost one gun.[102]

Along the McGehee Road

Capt. McHenry Howard, of Brigadier Winder's staff, was all over the field:

[J]ust before crossing the ... road I saw the flag of some regiment ... lying abandoned on the ground. I did not stop for it [and] continued to ride forward.... Seeing a large body of Confederates to the right (west) and a short distance in rear, I rode over there and found General Lawton with part of his brigade, General Garland with his, and perhaps other scattered bodies, massed or crowded together in some confusion and seemingly uncertain as what to do. I spoke to them and explained that General Winder was charging on the left and asked if they could not join with it. General Lawton asked, 'Where are the enemy?' I said in front, and that I had just ridden on them and that a movement in front would connect with General Winder. Nothing being immediately done, I was starting to go to look for General Winder when I came across several companies of our 33rd Virginia in the crowd, under Major F.W. Holliday, and undertook to show them the way. We presently crossed a little branch [Boatswain's Run] when we saw on the crest ... a shadowy line of men. Major Holliday and I rode forward until we were near enough to see two men, apparently officers.... 'What command is that?' The answer came back '[27th] New York, what do you belong to?' We made no reply and I looked anxiously back to see if our men were not coming up, but an inevitable straggler ... answered '33rd Virginia' ... where-upon they fired. I remember well the little ghostlike pillars of white dust that sprang up ... at least one under my horse's nose ... making him unmanageable for some moments. Before our men could form and return the fire, the New York regiment had melted away.[103]

Howard continues, "I rode back to Generals Lawton and Garland. General Garland said he had just received orders to rejoin his command, 'but,' said he, 'Captain, I will see what I can do for you,' and turning to General Lawton he asked, 'General Lawton, what is the date of your commission?' He replied, 'I am the oldest brigadier-general in the service.' 'That settles it,' said General Garland, [who] began to move [his men] off.'"[104] The remnants of Rodes' and G.B. Anderson's brigades would have to make do.

East of the Adams House

Lovell's Brigade and Warren's Brigade had been relieved hours earlier by Reynolds' Brigade of Pennsylvania Reserves and had fallen back far behind the line to a place just east of the Adams House. They were now just behind Brigadier Bartlett's line, the only useable troops, and marginal ones at that. Sgt. Wright, 5th New York Zouaves, wrote, "The regiment had now been under fire for four or five hours, and the men were so exhausted as to be scarcely able to stand—our pieces from constant use had become so foul that half of them were unfit for service."[105] Lovell's men were in about the same shape, but Major Andrews of the 10/17 U.S. had had a full ammunition resupply. Two companies of the 13th Pennsylvania Reserves joined them, as did the 2nd U.S., creating Battle Group Andrews.[106]

Battle Group Georgia

After crossing Boatswain's Branch, Col. Baylor, 5th Virginia, commanding the left of the Stonewall Brigade, found himself on the right of the 2nd Virginia, and some distance from it, where he "discovered a regiment lying down between the two, somewhat to their rear." These were the 31st and 38th Georgia Regiments,[107] Battle Group Georgia, out of ammunition. "I inquired if he had bayonets, and whether he would fill up the space between me and the Second [Virginia] in the charge. He replied that he would...."[108] With this addition, Battle Group Georgia now includes the 2nd and 5th Virginia. Capt. McHenry Howard arrived at Battle Group Georgia: "I had been busied for a while in getting forward some Virginia regiment of another command, which seemed to have no field officers and to be inclined to falter, and after getting it well started (by carrying its colors forward on horseback, which the color bearer gave me with reluctance and which I was glad to hand back to him as they seemed to draw a good deal of fire) I found myself again with the 2nd and 5th Virginia. It was the only field I had seen on which the smoke of battle rested, through which the setting sun shone red and dim."[109] This was probably the 52nd Virginia, of Elzey's Brigade, and later Battle Group Virginia.[110]

French's and Meagher's Brigades, Crossing the Grapevine Bridge

By the time French's two brigades arrived, most of Morell's and McCall's Divisions were in hot skedaddle for the river. "When the head of the column debouched into the meadow on the opposite bank a crowd of fugitives, encumbering the road and preventing the progress of the ambulances, were encountered."[111] "At this critical moment," reported Brigadier Meagher, "French ordered me to throw forward and deploy one company of the 69th, and with fixed bayonets to drive back the runaways. Captain Duffy's company was thrown forward and deployed ... driving the fugitives back."[112] It was not far enough, as Brigadier French ordered the heads of his regiments to force their way through the crowd through any openings they could find to get 'extricated' from the mob."[113]

Johnson's 1st Maryland Regiment

Passing the McGehee Road, Col. Johnson remarked:

The farther side [of the hill] was covered with a thick curtain of smoke, rolling backward and forward, in which only incessant, lurid flashes could be seen. Occasionally a small group would emerge, bearing a wounded man, or a frightened soldier would run back. Some distance to the left a large battery was sweeping the plateau. From the front came an incessant rain of bullets. Direct to the left the most tremendous roar of small arms announced a desperate struggle. "Up, men" was the order.... The regiment moved forward as it never moved on drill, as steady and straight as line. On it went, over that dreadful plain, strewed with the dead and dying, every officer in place.... Coming to a small rise which would shelter the men, they were halted.... Col Johnson went forward to reconnoiter and returning quickly commanded "Up men, and forward!" Just then Capt. McHenry Howard of Gen Winder's staff rode up and said "General Winder thinks you are not strong enough to take those batteries. He directs you to wait until he can bring up the Stonewall brigade to your support."[114]

"In a minute the Stonewall brigade [4th, 27th, and part of the 33rd Virginia] was found on the right, and General Winder ordered Col. Johnson to take direction of the line and charge. As they rose from the crest, the batteries became visible near the McGehee House, the orchard and sunken road between us and the McGehee house being filled with Yankees, who were covered by the road and a breastwork of knapsacks.... canister screamed above them."[115]

Goldsborough records:

The men of the First Maryland became unsteady for the first time as these fugitives crowded upon them and almost swept them off their feet. They began to tread upon each other's heels and the alignment was broken. Then was witnessed one of the most remarkable sights ever seen upon a battle-field. "Halt!" Cried out the gallant Johnson. "On the colors, dress!" With his line set, Col. Johnson put his men through the manual of arms. "Order Arms! Shoulder Arms! Present Arms! Shoulder Arms! Forward, March!" The effect was magical. The men recovered themselves, and the formation of the regiment was restored. But all this had its effect in another direction, for the brave men coming to the rear had observed it, and rallied on the regiment's flanks. The gallant color bearer of Hampton's Legion planted his colors on the left of the Marylanders and swore that it would go no farther to the rear. The men of the Legion rallied around it…. Then came fragments of the 12th Alabama, 52nd Virginia, and 38th Georgia, and in the time it takes to narrate it Col. Johnson had a small brigade around him that otherwise would have been lost.[116]

Col. Johnson, who never himself mentioned having his men perform the manual of arms in combat, continues, "[Brigadier] Winder brought the [Stonewall] Brigade into line on my right."[117]

It was pretty far to the right. The 27th and 33rd were so far to the right that they were in the union camp at Griffin's Woods that Brigadier Pender's men entered, and where Cpl. Brantley of the 5th Texas had terrified the Yankees with his fearsome sword bayonet. Col. Neff, 33rd Virginia, even met General Ewell here.[118] General Ewell was on foot, as his "splendid chestnut mare 'Maggie' had been killed. He was also limping … he was just pulling off his boot & emptying out the bullet, which had flattened against a tree before striking him."[119] The 27th Virginia did not fire a shot,[120] so it is doubtful if the 33rd did. These three regiments had only 10 casualties out of about 550 men.

Near the McGehee House, Col. Johnson led his mishmash of regiments (Battle Group Johnson) forward. "The charge was now made with an old time cheer"[121] on the left of Battle Group Georgia.

Battle Group Georgia

Brigadier Winder watched as the 2nd and 5th Virginia "got in advance of the line, receiving a heavy fire, which stunned their ranks…."[122] Lt. Col. Botts "found the fire from the enemy's batteries and their supports terrible."[123] McHenry Howard "saw Col. Allen's dead body, and also saw Major Jones on the ground … in a shattered nervous condition and did not wish me to come near him."[124] Botts was the only surviving field officer in the 2nd Virginia.[125] The 5th Virginia lost about 15 percent. The 2nd Virginia was almost wiped out, losing 27 men out of 80, about 34 percent; it had only 53 men left.

Union Lines, Near the McGehee House

After checking its fire to allow the 16th New York to make its ill-fated charge, Kingsbury's Battery, 5th U.S. Artillery (6 Parrotts), "directed the guns to the left, where there were crowds of Union fugitives and where the enemy were still gaining ground. At this juncture a remnant of the 12th U.S. passed, disorganized but walking." This remnant include their colors. Kingsbury fell back with them, and opened fire. His guns were now east and south of the McGehee house, "now in the open plain, with no infantry near my battery."[126]

In fact, Battle Group Virginia was still stalking Capt. Kingsbury,[127] and now had artillery support. Brockenbrough's Baltimore Artillery (1 ordnance rifle, 1 Blakeley, 1 Parrott, 1 howitzer)[128] had taken off down the Grapevine Road. "'We are not close enough,' said the brave Brockenbrough.' Limber to the front, forward, gallop!' rung out his sharp command and in an instant the battery was in position at point blank range. Fiercely those men worked, despite the iron hail that plowed the ground around them. In a few minutes Brockenbrough had the satisfaction of seeing the enemy retire precipitately...."[129] Capt. Goldsborough misidentified Kingsbury as French's Battery, probably because French's Brigade was not far away.

Sgt. Evans tells the Union side of the tale. "[Capt. Kingsbury] rides along and says, 'Men, this battery must not be taken. I will not abandon my guns. I cannot cover your retreat; you must cover mine.' And there we stand, the shot and shell plowing through us until darkness closes in. [We had] scarcely two companies left out of the battalion."[130] The 12th U.S. was ordered to retire to the river bottom when Kingsbury limbered up.[131] Tidball's Battery A, 2nd U.S. Artillery (6 Parrotts), fell back along Grapevine Road.[132] The 3rd and 4th U.S. stayed with Weed's Battery I, 5th U.S. Artillery (6 ordnance rifles), as they withdrew down the Grapevine Road. Two of its guns broke their carriages and were abandoned.[133] The 14th U.S. had joined the 11th U.S. below Adams House.[134]

The remnant of Lovell's Brigade, Battle Group Andrews, had to go back in to stop the Rebels. As Major Andrews moved up to the line, the 5th Maine broke, throwing Battle Group Andrews into confusion. It rallied and went in near the McGehee House.[135] Lt. Montgomery of the 10/17th U.S. charged the Rebel line with only 20 men. Montgomery was captured, shot in thigh and arm. Capt. John Poland of the 2nd U.S. was ordered to charge. Said Pvt. Myers, one of his men:

> [W]e rushed up the hill for a hundred yards or so, cheering and yelling like mad. It suddenly occurred to me that we were about to attack the enemy with bayonets. I had been instructed in bayonet drill, and practiced until I was considered proficient; but I ... had a secret wish that the adversary whom I might encounter would not be a bigger man than I.... [W]e reached the crest of the hill, when we suddenly received a staggering fire, from a Rebel regiment that seemed not more than 20 yards away. I do not know whether it was by word of command or by instinct that we halted and instantly began firing instead of rushing on with the bayonet. I dropped on one knee and commenced firing as fast as I could; I aimed at their colors which were almost opposite ours. We were so close together I could plainly distinguish the features and color of clothing of our opponents until the smoke obscured them. Suddenly their fire slackened...; they seemed to have melted away down their side of the hill. Suddenly we heard the Rebel yell and saw a mass of Rebel infantry rushing toward us. I had not fired many shots in the second encounter on the hill and was in the act of ramming a cartridge, when a command or shout caused me to look to the right and I saw that our right wing had broken.[136]

Another observer noted: "The fearless Lt. Parker received a volley, swayed in the saddle, and fell from his horse, dead. We lost more men in this last charge than at any time during the day."[137] Pvt. Myers shot 58 of the 60 cartridges he had been issued.[138]

Warren's Brigade was now utterly all that was left, and it was now desperately thrown in, joining Battle Group Andrews in McGehee's orchard.[139] Two rebel regiments approached "with colors flying, flushed with success...."[140] Cpl. Southwick of the 5th recalled, "The noise was terrific, shaking the hills and reverberating through the valley, but loud above all was the exultant, fiend like yell of the Confederate soldiers." Col. Duryea, 5th New York, thought that they were friendly troops and held fire, giving the Rebels the first strike. "They are not our men, blaze into them, boys!" shouted Col. Warren.[141] Pvt. Thurber, 5th NY, wrote of this day, "We will probably never be in a harder fight than this, and I never want to be."[142] He would be disappointed: Hood's Texans would annihilate his regiment two months later at 2nd Manassas. The 18th Georgia would repair a tear in its battle flag with a lock of a Zouave's hair.[143] Battle Group Andrews and the Zouaves stopped the Rebel charge.

Pvt. Bradwell of the 31st Georgia was one of the stopped. "Glancing to the north, we saw a sight never to be forgotten. Coming into the open and at right angles to the enemy's line in splendid formation were the 12th, 26th, 60th, and 61st Georgia … to fall on and crush the enemy's right."[144] During the course of the day, the 38th Georgia lost about 25 percent of its men. The 31st lost 31 percent. Brigadier Lawton's other regiments suffered little. The 60th Georgia lost only 3 percent, the 61st only 6 percent, and the 26th only 7 percent. The 13th Georgia, who had charged with Ewell's men, lost 11 percent.

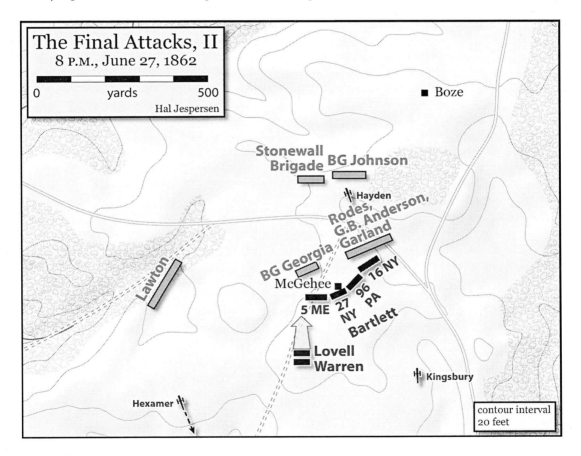

Battle Group Johnson

Battle Group Johnson pushed on beyond the McGehee House about 300 yards and then was stopped due to the darkness. It was barely scratched by the fight at McGehee's, despite the fact that the 96th Pennsylvania had brought up its Union repeating guns, firing from near Kingsbury's Battery D, 5th U.S. Artillery. Said Lt. Coiner, 52nd Virginia, "I only saw it as I passed by it stopping for a fraction of a second."[145] The 1st Maryland lost only 8 percent; the 12th Alabama lost only 6 percent. The 12th Georgia lost 4 percent. The 52nd Virginia, which Capt. Howard had rallied and whose flag he saw on the field, lost only 16 percent.

Union Brigadier French deployed his regiments in line of battle on the left, putting Meagher on the right, in two lines of battle[146] down in the river bottom. Brigadier French located General Porter, who directed him to form a line on the edge of the bluff about ¾ mile from Barker's Mill.[147] Meagher's men were posted between French and the Grapevine Road.[148] The two brigades covered the retreat of Porter's Fifth Corps until 4:00 a.m.[149]

Behind the McGehee House

The "two regiments with colors flying" that hit the Zouaves were actually Battle Group Johnson. The Hampton Legion Infantry was with it. "Finally they arrived at an open field, where they found posted Duryea's New York brigade of Zouaves—fancy but fierce looking fellows ... who were standing their ground with the most determined resolution. Lt. Col Gary ... at once ordered a fire to be opened.... The fighting took place at a distance of perhaps 300 yards, our boys cheering, loading and firing.... Finally [Lawton's] brigade of Confederates came in ... and with this onslaught they took to their heels."[150] The Legion was assisted by a few members of the 40th Virginia, Field's Brigade, Powell Hill's Division. "We ... poured a volley into the retiring Yankees, some of whom were Duryea's Zouaves with their flaming uniforms. It was then that we more than repaid them for the loss they had inflicted upon us."[151] Cpl. Myers, 2nd U.S. now part of Battle Group Andrews, was near the Zouaves. "Suddenly we heard the Rebel yell and saw a mass of Rebel infantry [Lawton's Brigade] rushing toward us.... We had been outflanked.... I yelled to my comrades of the color guard and started to run with them, not taking the time to withdraw the ramrod from the barrel of my gun.... For us the Battle of Gaines' Mill was over."[152]

25

I Have Got My Fill of Fighting

The Running

When the 13th Pennsylvania Reserves approached Woodbury's Bridge, Col. Berdan of the U.S. Sharpshooters and Col. Matheson of the 32nd New York were trying to rally the panicked men with threats of execution.[1] "Wagons, ambulances, guns and caissons were all in a jumble at the approach to the bridges. Walking wounded, stragglers from a score of regiments, remnants of detached units milled around in an unorganized mass of humanity."[2] Lew McKoy, 44th New York, Butterfield's Brigade took umbrage at reports that he had run away. "At the Battle of Gaines' Mill, June 27 it is reported that Col. Stryker and your humble servant ran away. I agree with the report, most emphatically. I saw Col Stryker run; the 44th ran; Butterfield's Brigade ran; and if any man can mention any regiment, brigade or division in that line that did not run, I would like to see it."[3] Capt. Judson, 83rd Pennsylvania, Butterfield's Brigade, Morell's Division ran toward Woodbury's Bridge. "Many of our boys ... ran towards the bridge, and, on arriving there, found the bridge partly destroyed. It was said that Martindale's brigade had passed over it before us, and ... had torn up the planks. Some rushed across the sleepers, some jumped into the stream attempting to swim or wade."[4]

Observing from Robertson's Battery B/L, 2nd U.S. Artillery (6 ordnance rifles), downslope from the Adams House, newspaperman George Townshend observed the rest of the line:

All at once there was a running hither and thither, a pause in the thunder, a quick consultation.... "They have flanked us again." In an instant I was overwhelmed with men. For a moment I thought the enemy had surrounded us.... I wheeled my horse, fell in with the stream of fugitives, and was born swiftly through field and lane.... I saw officers who had forgotten their regiments, or had been deserted by them, wending with the mass. The wounded fell and were trampled upon. As we approached the bridge, there was confusion and altercation ahead. "Go back! I'll blow you to hell if you don't go back! Not a man shall cross the bridge without orders!" [Townshend approached the voice.] "Colonel, may I pass out, I am a civilian!" "No!" said the Colonel, wrathfully. "This is no place for a civilian." "That's why I want to get away." I followed the winding of the woods to Woodbury's Bridge.[5]... The approaches were clogged with wagons and field-pieces, and I understand that some panic stricken people had pulled up the timbers.... At 9 o'clock we got underway—horsemen, batteries, ambulances, ammunition teams, infantry, and finally some great siege thirty twos [cannons] that had been hauled from Gaines' House. One of these pieces broke down the timbers again ... and was cast into the current. I made toward ... Trent's....[6]

Charles Henry Veil, 9th Pennsylvania Reserves, behind Sykes' line, had a similar experience. "[T]he sight was frightful. Men, wagons, ambulances and every individual that could move was in a run to the rear or toward Grapevine Bridge. Wounded men that had been carried to the rear when Jackson opened on our flank jumped to their feet and joined the party. Even one man, I recollect, who had lost one foot, jumped up and caught onto the step of an ambulance that was passing, loaded with a man hanging onto the step. He pulled him off and managed to get himself on and get away. It was one of the most demoralizing sights I ever saw."[7] Stopped by the jam, a private of Rush's Lancers crawled into a thicket for a snooze. Veil stole his horse and retreated with the others.[8]

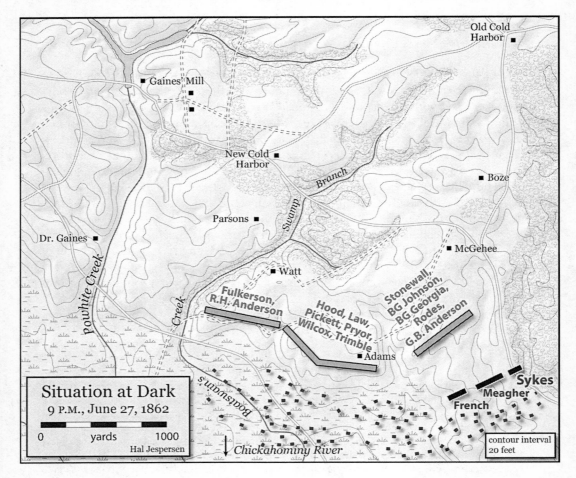

The Rallying

Not everyone ran. Pvt. Harrer, 14th New York, Griffin's Brigade, Morell's Division asserted, "I think the Pennsylvania Reserves were the only troops that held their formation and kept in the line of battle; but as we learned afterward, the most of them were out of ammunition."[9] This was Reynolds' Brigade. Private Urban, 1st Pennsylvania Reserves, Reynolds' Brigade, relates his experience after the collapse of Sykes' line at the McGehee Road:

Our regiment and the 8th Pennsylvania Reserves, which had been engaged on our right, and was also out of ammunition, were now ordered to march to the rear for the purpose of getting a new supply and a short rest. The two regiments marched to the rear stacked arms, and threw themselves on the ground. We had hardly more than done so, when a wild commotion in our front caused us to jump to our feet, when we discovered that a serious break had taken place in the line we had just vacated. The New York regiment which had relieved us broke and fled as soon as the rebels charged on them, and the enemy pouring through the gap thus created, flanked several regiments, which were also compelled to fall back. To add to the confusion, a body of cavalry ... charged the rebel line. Looking at the mass of rushing fugitives who came rushing toward us, I remarked to a comrade, "Now look out for a Bull Run stampede"; but it was not to be. Col. Roberts had formed his regiment in line, and to keep them steady commenced to drill.... [A]n officer, dashing up, exclaimed, "Colonel, fire into those men who are falling back!" The Colonel replied, "We are out of ammunition." In a moment after General Porter came riding up in haste, and exclaimed, "Col. Roberts, can't you take these two regiments and stop these men?" To which Roberts replied, "I will try, but get me some ammunition to stop the enemy." Col. Roberts formed the two regiments, [who] stood firm ... and presented a solid front of steel to the demoralized fugitives.... The two regiments succeeded in stopping most of them, but ... the rebels would soon be upon them.... Fortunately just at this time the cheering in our rear announced the fact that reinforcements were at hand ... the Irish Brigade ... came on the ground on the double quick....[10]

Though they maintained their order, that Reynolds' Brigade was "out of ammunition" for hours is a disgrace. The whole time they were "out of ammunition," the 2nd U.S., Lovell's Brigade, Sykes' Division, was resting nearby, and obtained more ammunition[11] before charging at the McGehee House. When it finally retreated near dark, the 2nd U.S. found mountains of ammunition just behind the Adams House; Augustus Myers was down to his last two Johnson & Dow cartridges. "We soon came to a place [on] the road ... on which were piled hundreds of boxes of infantry and artillery ammunition."[12] George Townshend observed, "At the foot of the hill ... the ammunition wagons lay in long lines, with the horses heads turned from the fight."[13] Even a civilian managed to find the ammunition depot.

The "solid front of steel" had some assistance that Pvt. Urban omitted. Capt. Woodward, 2nd Pennsylvania Reserves, Reynolds' Brigade, commented:

A dozen or fifteen horses cut loose from [Easton's] battery, dashed through our line followed closely by the enemy, and again driven, we slowly and sullenly ... retreated down over the fields ... under a murderous fire. Having reached a position whose sloping ground afforded some slight protection, Col. McCandless rallied the men and reformed the line, collecting a large number of stragglers. A squadron of Rush's Lancers and a squadron of [Illinois] cavalry now came up and formed in our rear. Soon after French's and Meagher's brigades came up.... About 8 o'clock, we were moved towards the rear ... near a field hospital [the Howe House].[14]

Other regiments claimed that they rallied. In Morell's Division, Martindale's Brigade, the 22nd Massachusetts claimed to be the last regiment to leave Morell's line before rallying at a battery.[15] The 2nd Maine also claims to have rallied near a battery.[16] More likely is that they were with the 1st Michigan; it rallied a mile behind the line.[17]

The 9th Massachusetts, Griffin's Brigade, which had been seen breaking three times by the other regiments in Griffin's Woods, claimed that it found its mettle after the collapse and repulsed no fewer than nine successive attacks while retreating.[18] Also according to it, the cheering at the arrival of French and especially Meagher's' *Irish* brigades caused the Confederates to "retreat" to the edge of the bluff overlooking the shattered remnants of the Fifth Corps, just as darkness fell.[19] M.H. McNamara, also of the 9th, tells a different story. They were asleep when Meagher arrived.[20]

The Lying

General Porter had about 29,000 men of all arms, excluding French and Meagher. Even assuming no casualties at all in Sykes' Division (4500) nor Reynolds' Brigade (3300), this leaves over 21,000 men to skedaddle. Col. Berdan's 12,000 figure was far too low. The disaster generated several tall tales. Brigadier Seymour's brigade of the Pennsylvania Reserves claimed that at Gaines' Mill it had "successfully protected the road on which the immense trains were moving."[21] Despite the capture of two whole regiments and the loss of over 20 guns, the 2nd Maine asserted, "There was a general retreat during the night, and all our men and guns were safely withdrawn to the opposite side of the river."[22] Even generals stretched the truth. While he was escaping the 4th Texas near the Adams House, according to his report, darkness found General McCall almost a mile away, on the Grapevine Road, gallantly saving the army single-handedly by ordering Capt. Weed and his Battery I, 5th U.S. Artillery (6 ordnance rifles), back into battle and stopping the stampede with the flashing sabers of the 8th Illinois Cavalry detachment. Col. Farnsworth of the 8th Illinois does not mention General McCall.[23] Despite the disintegration of his whole division, McCall's singular regret was the complete capture of the 11th Pennsylvania Reserves and 4th New Jersey.[24] One of the most mendacious stories came from the 14th New York. Pvt. Harrer vividly recounted an utter fantasy: "The Irish brigade made a bayonet charge I shall never forget. For a time it was now bayonet to bayonet, but the Irish drove the whole opposing army to the woods, where at noon the battle began."[25] To the cavalry must go the dubious honor of the biggest whopper. "In the battle of Gaines's Mill, [Rush's Lancers] charged, a little to the south of the old mill, upon an Alabama brigade, and handled the lance with terrible effect. The scene witnessed when this fine regiment charged, may well be historical; their long lances poised, their red pennants streaming, and the riders, like so many avengers, bending forward to the charge."[26]

The Groaning

Barry Benson, 1st South Carolina Volunteers, Gregg's Brigade, Powell Hill's Division, recalled, "[N]ow heard on all sides groans, and cries from the wounded of 'water, water!' We gave till our canteens were empty. Till late in the night men were calling for their regiments…. Not knowing where the command … was, we … lay together, a dead man at our feet, and dead men all about us."[27] A Tarheel noticed, "Hundreds of horses were lying around, some not dead, some with legs shot off, trying to get up, moaning and crying like children begging for help."[28] Col. Walker, 13th Virginia, Elzey's Brigade, Ewell's Division, wrote, "Even the dying men as they held my hand would say 'Colonel, how did the regiment behave? Did we do our duty?' There was not one unmanly word uttered by all these suffering and dying soldiers, not one tear was shed, nor was an expression of regret uttered by them."[29]

Pvt. Fulton, 5th Alabama Battalion, Archer's Brigade, Powell Hill's Division, was also attracted by a man's groaning. "I heard a fellow groaning and moaning terribly nearby … it was my old chum. I asked him what was the matter. 'Oh, I am shot plumb through.' He was evidently near death's door and I began to cut off his clothing…. As I got off his jacket and through his shirt I soon saw there was no hole and no blood, but a piece of exploded bombshell had … raised a great red blister. When I told him there was no hole and no ball had penetrated him, he sat up and straightened himself out, and drawing a long [happy] breath he exclaimed, 'Well! I thought I was dying!'"[30]

The Bleeding

The Confederates set up three field hospitals, one near Old Cold Harbor, one near New Cold Harbor, and one at the Gaines' Mansion. One soldier lamented, "The doctors do not stop day or night."[31] "At Cold Harbor at a little [Beulah] church near our line of battle converted into a field hospital I saw arms and legs and hands and feet that had been amputated and cast into a pile for burial which would have made a large wagon load."[32] Barry Benson went to the New Cold Harbor hospital. "Before leaving the hospital, I went in the garden and was shocked to see lying about it hands and arms and legs that had been amputated…."[33] A wounded man of Pickett's Brigade recalled, "[W]e were taken to a … field hospital [Dr. Gaines' Mansion], an elegant Southern home…. The spacious grounds had been converted into a huge operating hospital; and as the men were brought in, they were placed with their heads toward the fence and their faces toward the house. There were several operating tables, and amputations were constant…."[34] When the hospitals became full, the wounded were "carried to the surrounding shades, in the orchard and field."[35]

The Yankees fared no better. The Adams House, full of wounded, had been captured, so the Howe House became the hospital. *London Times* correspondent George Townshend wrote, "A mile or more from the Grapevine Bridge, on a hill-top, lay a frame farm house, with cherry trees encircling it, and along the declivity of the hill were some cabins, corn sheds, and corn bins. This house was now a surgeon's headquarters, and the wounded lay in the yard and lane, under the shade, waiting their turns to be hacked and maimed. I caught a glimpse through the door, of the butchers and their victims…."[36] Pvt. Roy of the 9th Pennsylvania Reserves had a visit from his captain at the Howe House Hospital. "[T]he captain said to me, 'Roy, McClellan has taken Richmond.'"[37]

The carnage outside the hospitals was even worse. Flies were everywhere.[38] Barry Benson, 1st South Carolina Volunteers, Gregg's Brigade, Powell Hill's Division, remembered, "Lt. Col. Hamilton made us a speech saying 'One more glorious day like [today] and our country is free!' … I also picked up on the field a bloody leaf, and placed it in my book. The leaf has been lost, but its imprint is left on the page, showing the dark stain of blood."[39] A member of the 17th Virginia, Kemper's Brigade, Longstreet's Division told of his experience. "Shortly after the battle ended, Alexander Hunter, 17th Virginia, went to a nearby stream to fill canteens…. After finishing his chore, he returned the first canteen to its owner. The man took one swig, spit the contents out of his mouth, and hollered, 'What did you put in my canteen?' Hunter replied, 'Water.' 'Water, hell,' the man exclaimed as he emptied his canteen. The contents were red."[40] The next day, a civilian noted, "The ground round the cannon was dyed purple."[41] In Griffin's Woods, "All of the undergrowth of the very thick timbers were mowed down in two like the end of snuff mop, at various heights, by the iron and leaden hailstorm which prevailed at that place…. And the other timbers being mangled or torn … and the pools of blood being so very thickly scattered about … caused a deep pensive or sad thought … exclaiming to myself what a lamentable evil war is…."[42]

The Burying

Many men did not have the luxury of groaning. A civilian wrote, "[T]he numbers of their dead, particularly in the woods, surpassed all belief. The timber was literally crowded with blue-jackets, and regiments which had won these positions could scarcely find sufficient ground on which to bivouac, without trampling on the poor creatures."[43] A Georgia soldier observed, "Dead men lie here in every conceivable position, and what is strange is that nearly every man is shot in the head. One Zouave only I saw who was shot through the heart, and he was struck in the back while running. I noticed their faces. The largest portion of them were regular Yankees, some few were foreign."[44] Pvt. McClendon of the 15th Alabama, Trimble's Brigade, Ewell's Division, reflected, "I actually thought, from the number of dead and wounded that I saw that evening, that the war was ended."[45] Capt. Morris, 37th North Carolina, Pender's Brigade, Powell Hill's Division found 800 dead in one pile.[46] Pvt. Collins recalled the burying. "Large trenches were dug and the dead unceremoniously placed within, to be covered with a little dirt."[47] Another civilian wrote, "I counted not less than ten Federal standard bearers who had been laid in a small ditch in one of their camps. I knew them to be such by the leathern belts used for carrying the colors, and could not remark but that several were shot in the head and body by numerous balls, as if an entire volley had been fired at them."[48] This is the effect of buck and ball. Chaplain Davis, 4th Texas, Hood's Brigade, Whiting's Division, was bitter. "And now *we* must give them graves in the very fields they pillaged."[49] As for the gallant young Union captain who had so heroically rallied his men, "Capt. Young [23rd North Carolina] assumed the task of examining the body.... I cannot be precise as to the articles found ... but I remember a watch was among them, and three letters.... These letters were read by Gen. Garland and myself, with a view to ascertain to whom his valuables might be sent ... and all the articles entrusted to Capt. Young, who charged himself with their transmission to the relatives of the deceased. About daybreak, the body of your son was buried, under my supervision, in the same manner in which our own officers were interred."[50] Pvt. Singleton, 9th Louisiana, Seymour's Brigade, Ewell's Division, walked the field where the 5th New York had been. At first sight he thought the area was a "field of blood," the Zouaves having worn red trousers.[51] Benjamin Jones, 44th Virginia, Elzey's Brigade, Ewell's Division, wrote, "I made an inspection of the field in front where we fought. There lay a dead and dying line of battle dressed in the garb of New York Zouaves."[52] By the next day, "The weather being very warm, the dead bodies which lay around were becoming very offensive...."[53]

The Carrying On

Despite the appalling scene, army business needed attending to. "Ammunition wagons were busily engaged in distributing cartridge for the morrow, while artillerymen were cleaning the captured guns, and the movements of couriers delivering orders, the tramp of troops and the rumble of artillery, bespoke active operations in the morning. Spades were everywhere in request for interring the dead; comrades, pipe in mouth, consigned their relations to the humble grave without tears or words...."[54] A member of the 21st Georgia "was kept busy until 2 o' clock in having the wounded taken care of and sending after a fresh supply of ammunition."[55] Pvt. Myers, 2nd U.S., was present at an absurd episode. "As we passed, a young and very indiscreet officer made frantic appeals for some of us to stop and help him set fire to the ammunition to prevent it from falling into the hands of the enemy. No attention was paid to him other than calling him a fool, for the road was crowded with retreating troop and wounded men.... An explosion of ammunition would have made havoc among them."[56]

Pvt. Fletcher, 4th Texas, Hood's Brigade, Whiting's Division, was sent to the rear for rations.

> When we arrived at the place there were a number of details with orders similar to ours and no effort being made to load up. I inquired what the trouble was and was told that we could get rations only with a written order, as there was a guard [from the Richmond Home Guard] over them. [We] went to where one guard was and I asked him why we could not get rations and he explained [that he was protecting captured stores]. I saw from the tone of expression of the [ration] details, that all was needed was a leader, so I backed off a short distance (it being dark) ... and spoke in a loud tone of voice commanding, "Fix bayonets and be ready to defend yourselves; take all the rations you want and leave the rest with the guard!" The guard raised no further objections.[57]

The Fatiguing

"I did not know how tired I was until the excitement of the battle was over," said Pvt. Barrett of the 9th Alabama, Wilcox's Brigade, Longstreet's Division.[58] The 38th North Carolina, Pender's Brigade, Powell Hill's Division "were by this time so exhausted by the fatigues of the day and the day previous that they were scarcely able to stand up."[59] The 23rd North Carolina, Garland's Brigade, Harvey Hill's Division, "bivouacked in a body of pines, too worn out to stand guard over prisoners, who seemed as tried and worn out as we were. They seemed well contented and showed no disposition to escape whole with us."[60] Some wrote letters. "This note is to inform you of the death of your brother Abe...."[61] Others, such as Pvt. Dobbins of the 16th Mississippi, Trimble's Brigade, Ewell's Division, just decompressed. "Exhausted, we rested, lighting fires to make coffee and stew apples we found in abandoned Yankee Haversacks, with many other good things (ham, soda and sweet crackers, cans of condensed milk, cheese, chocolate.... We feasted well, trying not to think of those who were no longer with us."[62]

The Weeping

Some of the officers were racked by survivor's guilt. Brigadier Gregg, Powell Hill's Division, who "really loved danger," was seen crying bitterly among his men.[63] Private Jones, 13th Virginia, Elzey's Brigade, Ewell's Division, recalled, "[W]hen our sturdy Colonel [Walker] saw so many of his brave fellows lying dead or wounded, his frame shook with emotion and he wept like a child."[64] While trying to sort out the scattered units of Harvey Hill's Division, Major Ratchford "came upon General Hood sitting on a cracker-box. As I approached, he looked up at me and I could see the tears streaming down his cheeks. His brigade had lost heavily, and all about him were the dead and wounded. I spoke to him and he replied brokenly, 'Just look here, Major, at all these dead and suffering men, and every one of them as good as I am, yet I am untouched.'"[65]

The Looting

Many of the men were still excited. "Friends walked and looked for friends, and brothers knew not the fate of each other, whether living or dead."[66] They found some interesting items. Harvey Hill's men captured some Union repeating guns, though the number is uncertain. Hill claimed three,[67] but McHenry Howard wrote, "We got ... two small revolving or repeating guns with hoppers on top of the breech...."[68] "At this battle we found some of the enemy were using breastplates," wrote Pvt. Coker of the 6th South Carolina, R.H. Anderson's Brigade, Longstreet's Division; "these are of steel, strapped on securely to protect the body from small arms."[69] A newspaperman wrote, "[O]ur men laid violent hands on whatever food or clothing they discovered.... I saw many of them attired in suits of Yankee clothing ... could not blame the poor fellows for securing clothing of some kind; the greater number were ragged and dirty, and wearing apparel could not be obtained at any price in Richmond. It was grotesque to see a tall, well developed Southerner attired in clothes much too small, but the men were delighted with the change, and strutted about with gold corded shoulder straps and striped pantaloons, often not sufficiently long to cover the ankle."[70] Capt. William Morris, 37th North Carolina, was delighted that "they left any amount of Camp Equipage ... we could pick up anything you would want, Napsacks, haversacks, guns & all kinds of clothing scattered for miles wide in the direction they went."[71] Barry Benson claimed that the "whole Confederate Army refitted itself with blankets, rubber cloths, tent flies ... so that in the middle of the war and later, to see equipment of Southern make was somewhat of a curiosity...."[72] Pvt. Pitt Callaway, 31st Georgia, Lawton's Brigade, "picked up a pair of gold rimmed glasses from a Union colonel."[73] In the 38th Georgia, "Every man in the regiment ... now cast aside his old gun and picked up a new Enfield or Springfield rifle, as the ground everywhere was strewn with rifles, and they were a menace, for most of them were loaded, cocked and capped ready to go off if struck by anybody passing over the battlefield."[74] "I never saw the like of destruction of clothing, blankets, guns, cartridge boxes, and knapsacks in my life. They are strewn everywhere, guns bent and cut up, wagons by the thousands drawn together and burned, commissaries in immense quantities burned, etc. etc.... I myself counted fifteen pieces magnificent brass and bronze field-pieces ... with caissons and horses and dozens of cannoniers, exactly as they were left by their vanquished owners."[75] Col. Grimes, 4th N.C., wrote, "Here I captured a fine St. Bernard dog, which was protecting the corpse of a Colonel of a Pennsylvania Regiment, who, upon inspection, was found to have on steel breast-plates...."[76] Private Coxe, of the Hampton Legion Infantry, captured an experience. He spent the night in "a very fine and in every way pleasant arboreal pavilion, which had been used by the French Officers as a dining saloon."[77]

The Capturing

Capt. Hunter of the 4th Texas captured five Yankees. "One of them was colonel of a Michigan regiment and the other a captain of a New York Regiment. The colonel was a big, portly middle aged man, weighing about 225.... The captain's sword was fine. I threw mine away and kept his...."[78]

A few Yankees earned a story for their grandchildren. According to Major T.O.

Chesney of Elzey's brigade, General Jackson "had come suddenly upon the bluecoats, with his characteristic impetuosity he charged among them and ordered them to surrender, which they made haste to do." Chesney had been wondering about that "squad of fifteen or twenty soldiers" he had encountered on their way to the rear, who had boasted that they had "been captured by Stonewall Jackson himself."[79] After marching from Pole Green Church at dawn and winning a battle, the allegedly dull, exhausted, and befuddled Stonewall Jackson personally captured a score of Yankees in personal combat. Let this be the death knell of that myth.

Major J.W. Ratchford of Harvey Hill's staff recounted:

> About 2 o'clock in the morning, as Hood was going over the field superintending the caring for the wounded … a man in the dress of a Federal Captain, raised himself painfully and asked if that were not Hood. He begged that he would be carried to Hood, that his old friend and fellow-soldier in the Second Cavalry, Captain Chambliss, was lying on the battlefield desperately wounded. The word was brought to Hood and he immediately sent a messenger to tell [Chambliss] that he would come as soon as possible.…[80]

Hunter concludes, "General Hood told Sgt. McAnery to take three men and carry Chambliss to the temporary hospital and see that he had medical attention…."[81]

The French princes dining in their arbor before the battle (Library of Congress).

Major Ratchford recounted that Harvey Hill himself had a poignant encounter:

> The night after the victory at Gaines' Mill, General Hill retired with his brigade commanders to a house on the battlefield (the [Boze][82] House, I think) where they could have a light while he gave instructions for the night and the next day. The little house only had one room and was bare of furniture save for a table and some chairs. Around this table General Hill sat with Generals Rodes, Anderson, Garland and Colquitt, while I dozed in the corner. The generals were so intent upon their maps that they did not notice the entrance of three men, a Confederate soldier and a Union soldier supporting between them a wounded Union officer. They reported to me and waited patiently until General Hill turned. At the sight of the prisoner he sprang forward exclaiming "Clitz!" Colonel Clitz reached out to Hill with the words, "Hill, old fellow, how are you?" They stood there for a moment grasping hands in silence and I suspect I saw tears in the eyes of both men. General Anderson came over and freed Col. Clitz with almost as much emotion. I learned that General Garland's [late] wife had been the ward of Col. Clitz. Hill and Clitz had served together in the Mexican War and had become very close friends. Col. Clitz had been Superintendent of the Military Academy at West Point when Anderson had been a cadet, and one of Clitz' favorite students. General Hill expressed his regret that he could offer the wounded man no relief…. To this apology Col. Clitz replied, "Don't you worry about that, Hill, there are lots of fellows that need attention worse than I do." Next morning, [Hill] helped Col. Clitz into an ambulance and gave him Mrs. Hill's address, telling him to draw on her for any money he might need while a prisoner….[83]

Ratchford continues, "Clitz told me that this house had been his headquarters during the battle, and that he had put a pair of spurs, inlaid with gold, under the edge of the house at the beginning of the fight, and begged that I would find them and accept them as a gift from him. This quest was … unsuccessful…."[84]

The 4th Texas was also less successful.

> That night, some of the men heard the tramping of horses and the clanking of sabers coming toward us from the direction of our own lines. We … halted them and demanded who they were, supposing them to be a scouting party of our own cavalry. A voice rang out clear and distinct, "Major General McCall of the Grand Army of the Potomac," which evidently came from one who had straightened himself up in his stirrups so as to get the answer out strong and forcibly. Our surprise can scarcely be imagined, as we had head that Gen. McCall was in command of the Federal forces the previous day at the battle of Mechanicsville. We at once demanded their surrender, but instead of doing so they put spurs to their horses and dashed by us down the hill toward their own lines, followed by a volley from us.[85]

General McCall's freedom would be short; he was captured under similar circumstances at Frayser's Farm 3 days later.[86]

The next day, Harvey Hill met an old friend. General Reynolds had last been seen at 6:00 Friday evening somewhere behind Sykes' front. After that, Reynolds had gotten lost in the dark and entangled in Boatswain's Branch, where he had slept until morning. Pvt. William Singleton was walking the battlefield early, when "he was accosted from a clump of bushes by a major general in a blue uniform, who told Singleton that he was General Reynolds. Reynolds said that in the retreat the evening before he had been cut off from his men and that he wanted to surrender for fear that some Confederate would shoot him…." Singleton took charge of Reynolds, brought him to brigade headquarters, and turned him over to the commanding officer.[87] Singleton apparently found the 4th Virginia, who turned Reynolds over to Brigadier Winder, who took him to Harvey Hill's headquarters at the Boze House,[88] as all claimed to have captured Brigadier Reynolds. General Hill continues, "The next morning General John F. Reynolds was brought in as a prisoner. He had been my messmate in the old army for more than a year, and for half that time my tent-mate. General Reynolds seemed confused and mortified at his position.

He sat down and covered his face with his hands, and at length said, 'Hill, we ought not to be enemies.' I told him that there was no bad feeling on my part, and he ought not to fret at the fortunes of war, which were notoriously fickle. He was placed in my ambulance and sent over to Richmond...."[89] Capt. McHenry Howard and Brigadier Winder were also present. "Brigadier-General John F. Reynolds [was] an old friend of General Winder in the United States Army. He asked General Winder, 'Have you seen Buchanan?'" Col. Buchanan, Sykes' Division, was Brigadier Winder's brother-in-law.[90]

The Sleeping

About midnight, General Ewell and Campbell Brown sat on the ground to eat, and were joined by Brigadier Roswell Ripley, Harvey Hill's Division. Brown's horse needed attention. When he left, Brigadier Ripley ate his lunch and Brown went without.[91] Powell Hill spent the night in the federal works along Boatswain's Creek.[92] General Stonewall Jackson was out and about, and visited the 4th North Carolina. Col. Grimes, 4th North Carolina recalled, "Here, for the first time, I had the honor of being introduced to the great Jackson, and I now have the mess-chest upon which he joined us at dinner, dining from the contents of a sutler's wagon captured the day previous."[93] Longstreet's aide, Major Moxley Sorrel, was sent to fetch General Jackson shortly after the battle: "Longstreet had sent me after [the battle] to find him and establish connections and communications. He was cheerful and pleasant. 'Explain, Major, to General Longstreet where I am and how my troops are lying, and say, with my compliments, I am ready to obey any orders he may send me.' Longstreet's immediate order was to repair to the Hogan House for a meeting with General Lee. After conferring with Longstreet and Jackson, Lee spent the night at the Hogan House."[94] Longstreet probably stayed there, too, as Dr. Gaines' Mansion was full of wounded, and no place for rest. Jackson retired to a farmhouse near Old Cold Harbor, which had a bed, bread, and milk for Jackson.[95]

The Intriguing

Lt. Booth, of the 1st Maryland, vividly recalled, "One very singular incident at this point was the finding of General Lee's order detailing the entire movement for the attack on McClellan."[96] The order was found on a prisoner captured at Gaines' Mill.[97] "At this time the organization of the army was in divisions, and the order set forth the instructions to each Division commander, from the crossing at Mechanicsville and on. This particular order found at the McGehee House was addressed to General D.H. Hill. How it came there in the enemy's lines, Heaven only knows, but it is a fact that one of our men found it ... and he permitted me to read it that night. I remember distinctly that in reading the order I was impressed with the fidelity to which, to that time, the instructions had been carried out...."[98]

Was this General Order 75, or was it the June 23 Dabbs House Memorandum, written by a staff officer? How did a copy of either wind up in the McGehee House on the night of June 27, 1862?

General Order 75 was created, at the earliest, at 7:00 p.m. on the night of June 23, 1862. Harvey Hill, Longstreet, Jackson, and Powell Hill would each get his own copy;

Lee's Headquarters would also keep a copy, creating, at minimum, one original and five copies. President Davis probably received another copy; he clearly knew where and when to be overlooking the Chickahominy on June 26, with a coterie of others.

From the troop movements, everyone in Richmond knew something was up, including the servants. Mary, who collected the bread for the Davis household, was in reality Mary Richards Bowser, a slave belonging to Elizabeth Van Lew. Mary Bowser had been educated at Van Lew's expense in the North.[99] Bowser probably found Jefferson Davis' copy of General Order 75, or perhaps the Dabbs House Memorandum, and passed it to McNiven's bakery wagon on the morning of June 26.[100] McNiven passed it to Van Lew. Years later, McNiven specifically remembered meeting with her on or about July 6, 1862.[101] Despite General Lee's June 1862 crackdown on civilians within army lines, and thousands of men marching towards Mechanicsville, Van Lew somehow, within hours, obtained an unobtainable pass to drive her carriage through the middle of a top secret military operation. According to McNiven, General John H. Winder, Provost Marshal of Richmond, issued these passes to Van Lew because she knew that Winder frequented the charms of a prostitute, Clara A., codename "Belle."[102] McNiven himself had used passes obtained by Van Lew "to go up and down … the Mechanicsville roads…."[103] While Van Lew was obtaining a pass, Elizabeth Carrington probably encoded the purloined document. The spy ring certainly used a cipher later in the war.[104]

With an otherwise unobtainable pass in hand, Van Lew and the bohemian Eliza Carrington traveled for hours to traitor John Minor Botts' Half Sink Farm, a mere mile away from Col. Farnsworth's Union cavalry outpost at Hughes' Store, and just too providentially the jumping-off point for Branch's Brigade to start Operation Chickahominy. Judson Knight, 2nd New Jersey, Taylor's Brigade, Slocum's Division was only one of the "army scouts." Sergeant Patton, 12th Alabama, captured another in Griffin's Woods, which had just been vacated by the New Jersey Brigade. "[W]e searched the young man and found a dispatch in cipher from General Kearny to General McClellan. We could not read it, and I sent the horse and its rider to Col. Gayle, … who sent the dispatch to General D.H. Hill. The Richmond papers next day gave an account of the capture, and stated that the dispatch was important, giving valuable information…."[105] Clearly, it had been quickly deciphered, allowing Lt. Booth read it before the Richmond papers did.

In the end, the phantom order made no difference. McClellan had seen the writing on the wall days earlier, knew his supply line was in danger, and had ordered Porter to stand at Gaines' Mill against all comers, which orders General Porter certainly complied with, though at terrible cost.

The Numbering

General Lee fielded about 41,984 men, with roughly 112 guns,[106] consisting of 124 infantry units in 26 brigades and 10 engaged batteries of about 55 guns. Of these, he lost about 10,057 (24 percent) and no guns.

General Porter had about 29,281 men on the field, excluding French's and Meagher's Brigades, with 98 guns,[107] excluding the Union repeating guns, consisting of 44 infantry regiments in 12 brigades and 16 engaged artillery batteries of 82 guns. Of these, he lost about 4,797 infantry (16 percent), and 22 guns (27 percent).

For more information, please refer to the orders of battle in the appendices.

The Inhabitants

Clinton Sydnor, who had seen his brother from the barn and dined with a general, continued to be a boy. "We boys gathered bullets from the battlefield and moulded them into shot to hunt with. Uncle Tom and Uncle Moses remained with us, sharing our joys and sorrows."[108]

Fannie Tinsley made it to the Wicker house, then occupied by Mrs. Glass, by sundown.[109] Glass had given all her food to the Confederates and only had a few peanuts left. The soldiers had used all of her drinking vessels and left them at the well, all broken. Fannie sent a note to the Johnsons asking to come there, and had dinner when she did. The wounded began arriving at the Johnsons' just before 9:00. Fannie's arms were black and blue from briars and branches, she had lost her shoes, and her baby was sick again. She could hear gunfire still going on at 9:00 when she went to bed.

The next morning, Fannie arose to wash diapers, only to find a wounded soldier asking to have his wound rebandaged. Fannie explained to him that she fainted at sight of blood, and enlisted Mrs. Gaines. About 8:30 a.m., Dr. Gaines, with the ailing Dr. Curtis, arrived; the former sent the latter on to Richmond. At about noon, Mr. Tinsley arrived; he had obtained General Lee's permission to search for family. He stayed with the family at the Johnsons' that night.

On June 29, Mr. Tinsley got Dr. Curtis' buggy and took Fannie to Richmond, stopping by Dr. Curtis' house on the way. All of Fannie's clothes had been used for bandages. Confederates had stolen her wedding dress, presents, and silver; she heard later that a Texas soldier had sold her jewelry in Lynchburg. Heading on to Richmond, the dead and wounded were strewn on every side, making her keep eyes closed. Dr. Gaines and Mrs. Gaines went back to their mansion that day to find a dead Yankee at the door. His officer had told him not to quit his post, and he had given his life in obedience to orders. The Gaines family buried him in their orchard.

When the armies came back in 1864,[110] Dr. and Mrs. Gaines had left Powhite and moved to Richmond. "Everything on the place was destroyed, and all the Negroes left except some old ones who could not get away." In early 1865, they moved to Amelia County, just southwest of Richmond, where they rented a farm. Mr. Tinsley surrendered at Appomattox,[111] after which he and Fannie had six more children.[112]

Mary Jane Haw wrote of her last trip to Mrs. Watt's House:

Once more I visited my grandmother's former home. It was September, two months after the battle. As we emerged from the wood into the open, what a scene of desolation! There was not a trace of any inclosures, and where there had been green fields of swaying corn and dun meadows dotted with haystacks, was a wide expanse of seeds dotted with patches of yellow clay. As we drew nearer, a sickening odor pervaded the air. The Confederates … had given slight burial to either friend or foe. Many open graves from which their own dead had been emptied, were not more than two feet deep and upon the corpses of the enemy, they had simply thrown up mounds of earth. Everywhere were dead horses, dried away in their skins like mummies. What prolonged stillness and mournful silence brooded over the scene! In the tall weeds, the bushes and trees, there was not a twitter nor the flutter of a wing. For it is a well-known fact that the sulphurous smoke and the noise of the guns drive every bird far away from the battlefield.

As we wandered over the fields, we found graves everywhere. For some of these, the rain had washed away much of the earth, disclosing grinning skulls and protruding hands upon which the skin had dried away like a glove. Into others wild animals had burrowed, scattering the bones around. Through a tangle of wild pea vines, we climbed the Pea Mount, where a battery had been placed to rake the valley over which the Confederates had to advance. On its crest were several dead horses, and around its base and sides many graves.

We strolled through the orchards, and along the woods bordering them, through which led the path to Parson's Spring. Here had been the fiercest fighting of the day, when Hood's Texans charged down one hill, across the brook, and up another hill, and over a barricade of bales of hay and the branches of trees, driving the enemy before them. Where the peach orchard joined the apple orchard, a battery had been posted; and here were four dead horses lying almost in a heap. Along the lane in the shade of the trees and among the weeds and wild flowers were not only single graves, but trenches of the dead. Last of all, we visited the house. Rank weeds had sprung up even to the doors, except where the yellow clay glared in the sunlight. Even in the corners of the yard there were graves. The garden was another trench said to contain forty dead.

The house was a wreck! The walls and roof were torn by shot and shell, the weather-boarding honeycombed by minnie balls, and every pane of glass shattered. And the floors! Grandmother's immaculate floors! In the summer they had always been kept bare, and the first sound heard in the morning would be the maid plying the dry-rubbing brush in the hall, while at almost any hour of the day, a couple of half grown girls might have been seen on their knees with an old slipper and a cracked plate of fine white sand rubbing up spots invisible to any eye but Grandmother's. Now from garret to cellar there was scarcely a space of flooring as large as a man's hand that did not bear the dark purple stain of blood.

What a harrowing spectacle this, of a once neat and comfortable home now a tenantless, foul and battered wreck—the household furnishings accumulated and carefully preserved through many years— the contents of the loving and the cherished mementos of the dead, all scattered and destroyed! I thought of Aunt Sarah's little white dresses, and dimity petticoats torn up to bandage wounds....[113]

Mary Jane went on to publish two novels, *The Beechwood Tragedy: A Tale of the Chickahominy*, and *The Rivals: A Chickahominy Story*, both filled with handsome gentlemen in gray dashing about on mighty steeds.

The Remembering

After the battle, many Confederate units added the honor of "Gaines' Farm," "Gaines' Mill," or "Cold Harbor" to their battle flags.

A year hence, General Longstreet would discuss a huge charge at Gettysburg with General Lee. Longstreet claims to have said that no 15,000 men could take Meade's position.[114] Lee's response is lost to history, but he might well have said, "General Longstreet, need I remember to you that 18,000 men under your own command did so at Gaines' Mill?"

After the war, Capt. Young, 23rd North Carolina, sent the watch he had been entrusted with to the widow of Capt. Theodore Rogers, 18th New York.[115]

Two and a half years after the battle, a member of the 16th Michigan again called out, "'What regiment is that?' The response was 'Palmetto Sharpshooters!' And the Michigan boys broke ranks again, but it was to rush across the line that was no longer to divide them and press hands with the South Carolinians." The question first posed at Gaines Mill had finally been answered—at Appomattox.[116]

Afterword

The 12th U.S. Infantry Regiment is now based at Ft. Carson, Colorado. On its regimental colors are two Moline crosses, commemorating its losses at Gaines' Mill.[1] The 14th U.S. Infantry's regimental colors contain a large white Maltese cross, the color of Sykes' Regular Brigade, and the cross of the Fifth Corps.

The National Regiment is a Union reenacting umbrella organization. Its member units honor many of the regiments at Gaines' Mill, including the 1st Pennsylvania Reserves, the 7th Pennsylvania Reserves, the 9th Pennsylvania Reserves, the 96th Pennsylvania, the 2d U.S., and the 5th New York Zouaves.

Longstreet's Corps is a Confederate reenacting umbrella organization. Its member units include the 1st Texas, 6th and 22nd North Carolina, and the 5th, 8th, 18th, 21st, 28th, 42d, 44th, 47th, 55th and 56th Virginia Regiments.

The Richmond National Battlefield Park, U.S. Park Service, Department of the Interior, owns and maintains the Watt House and periodically hosts living histories to further bring the battle alive.

APPENDIX I

Confederate Order of Battle

	Present	Casualties	%
LEE'S COMMAND	**41,984***	**9,002**	**21%**
*(sum of divisions)			
Powell Hill's Division	***10,496[1]***	***3,095***	***29%***
Field	**1,138**	**159**	**14%**
40 Va.	239[2]	59[3]	24
47 Va.	175[4]	35[5]	20
55 Va.	350[6]	25[7]	5
60 Va.	284*	40*	14

*No information available. Figure is an average of the other three regiments in the brigade.

	Present	Casualties	%
Gregg	**2,313**	**854**	**37%**
1 SC	500[8]	145[9]	
1 SCR	537[10]	315[11]	
12 SC	400[12]	138[13]	
13 SC	413[14]	48[15]	
14 SC	463*	208[16]	

*No information available. Figure is the brigade average.

	Present	Casualties	%
J.R. Anderson	**2,500[17]**	**627**	**25%**
14 Ga.	642*	160	25
35 Ga.	642*	160	25
45 Ga.	250[18]	61	24
49 Ga.	642*	160	25
3 La. Bn.	321*	80	25

*No information available. Figure is the brigade number divided by three and a half regiments.

	Present	Casualties	%
Branch	**1,946***	**560**	**29%**
7 NC	450[19]	207[20]	
18 NC	389*	68[21]	
28 NC	480[22]	91[23]	
33 NC	389*	75[24]	
37 NC	238[25]	119[26]	

*No information available. The brigade number is that sum of the regimental numbers. The regimental numbers are average of the rest of the regiments of the brigade.

Archer	**1,114**[27]	**320**[28]	**28%**
5AlBn	350[29]	64[30]	
19 Ga.	261*	64[31]	
1 Tn.	261*	64[32]	
7 Tn.	261*	64[33]	
14 Tn.	261*	64	Smoothbores[34]

*No information available. Regimental numbers are the brigade number divided by four regiments.

Pender	**1,918**[35]	**575**[36]	**39%**
16 NC	428*	127	
22 NC	428*	127	
34 NC	428*	127	
38 NC	420[37]	127	
22 Va. Bn.	214*	63	

*No information available. Figures are brigade number less 38 NC number divided by three and a half regiments.

Artillery
Crenshaw's Virginia Battery
Andrews 1st Md. Artillery
Bachman's Charleston German Battery
Braxton's Fredericksburg Arty
Davidson's Letcher arty
Richmond Batty (Crenshaw/Marmaduke Johnson)
Pee Dee South Carolina Artillery
Pegram's Purcell Artillery

Longstreet's Division	***9,501***[38]	***1773***	***19%***
Kemper	**1,469***		
1 Va.	45[39]		
7 Va.	367*		
11 Va.	367*		
17 Va.	367*		
24 Va.	367*		

*No information available. Brigade number is sum of regimental figures. Regimental figures were derived from the balance of division divided by number of unaccounted for regiments.

R.H. Anderson	**1,729***	**125**	
2 SC	389[40]	7[41]	
4 SC	70	7[42]	
5 SC	256	7[43]	
6 SC	279	4[44]	
Palmetto SS	735	100[45]	
*Sum of units			

Pickett	**2,400**[46]	**426#**	**18%**
8 Va.	219[47]	53[48]	24%
18 Va.	437[49]	118	27%
19 Va.	581*	92	16%
28 Va.	581*	88	15%
56 Va.	581*	75	13%

*No information available. Figures are based on balance of brigade number divided by number of regiments.
Sum of regimental figures

Wilcox	**1,850**[50]	**584**[51]	**32%**
8 Al.	400[52]	149[53]	
9 Al.	483*	145[54]	
10 Al.	483*	145[55]	
11 Al.	483*	145[56]	

*No information available. Figures are based on balance of brigade number divided by number of regiments.

Pryor	**1,400**[57]	**306#**	**22%**
14 Al.	262*	61[58]	23
2 Fla.	300[59]	65[60]	22
14 La.	474[61]	100[62]	21
1La. Zouave Bn.	140[63]	51[64]	36
3 Va.	262*	29[65]	11

*No information available. Figures are based on balance of brigade number divided by number of regiments.
Sum of regimental figures.

Featherston	**917***	**332**[66]	**36%**
12 Miss.	367*	133	
19 Miss.	367*	133	
2 Miss. Bn.	183*	66	

*No information available. Brigade number is sum of regimental figures. Regimental figures were derived from the balance of division divided by number of unaccounted for regiments.

Artillery

Rogers' Loudon Artillery
Anderson's Thomas Artillery
Maurin's Donaldsonville La arty
3d Co. Richmond Howitzers

Harvey Hill's Division	*10,000*[67]	*1672*	*17%*
Rodes	**1,460**[68]	**153**	**10%**
3 Al.	333[69]	17[70]	
5 Al.	309*	73[71]	
6 Al.	309*	16	
12 Al.	200[72]	12	
26 Al.	309*	32	

*No information available. Regimental numbers are the balance of brigade numbers divided by the number of regiments.

G.B. Anderson	**1,307***	**497**[73]	**38%**
2 NC	150[74]	30	
4 NC	80[75]	58[76]	
14 NC	409*	155	
30 NC	409*	155	

*No information available. Figure is based on balance of division divided by number of regiments.

Garland	**1,857***	**599**[77]	**32%**
5 NC	409*	81	
12 NC	480[78]	81	
13 NC	409*	81	

20 NC	800[79]	274[80]	
23 NC	150[81]	81	

*No information available. Figure is based on balance of division divided by number of regiments. Brigade figure is sum of regiments.

Colquitt	**1,711***	**354**	**21%**
13 Al.	409*	44	
6 Ga.	312[82]	156	
23 Ga.	409*	29	
27 Ga.	172[83]	86	
28 Ga.	409*	39	

*No information available. Figure is based on balance of division divided by number of regiments. Brigade figure is sum of regiments.

Ripley	**1,831[84]**	**69**	**4%**
44 Ga.	159[85]	0	
48 Ga.	896*	33	
1 NC	190[86]	20	
3 NC	586[87]	16	

*No information available. Figure is based on balance of brigade.

Artillery

Bondurant's Jeff Davis Artillery
Clark's Long Island (Virginia) Artillery
Fry's Orange Artillery
Rhett's South Carolina Artillery
Carter's King William Artillery
Hardaway's Alabama Battery

	Present	Casualties	%
VALLEY ARMY	**12,495**	**2,462**	**20%**
JACKSON			
Whiting's Division	*4,000[88]*	*948*	*24%*
Hood	**2,100[89]**	**501**	
1 Tx	440[90]	77[91]	
4 Tx	546[92]	195[93]	
5 Tx	474[94]	64[95]	
18 Ga.	429*	145[96]	
Hampton Legion	211[97]	20[98]	

*No information available. Figure based on balance of brigade.

Law	**1,900***	**447**	**24%**
6 NC	512*	52[99]	10%
4 Al.	512*	132[100]	26%
11 Miss.	363[101]	163[102]	45%
2 Miss.	512*	100[103]	20%

Artillery

Balthis' Staunton Artillery (Va.)
Reilly's Rowan Artillery (N.C.)

*No information available. Brigade number is balance of division. Regimental numbers are brigade number divided by number of regiments.

Jackson's Division	**4,000**[104]	***697***[105]	***17%***
Winder	**1,135**[106]	**79**[107]	**7%**
2 Va.	80[108]*	27[109]	
4 Va.	292*	4[110]	
5 Va.	292*	42[111]	
27 Va.	125[112]	2[113]	
33 Va.	134[114]	4[115]	

*No information available. Regimental numbers are based on balance of brigade divided by number of regiments.

Cunningham	**1,540**	**8**
21 Va.	440*	0[116]
42 Va.	440*	4[117]
48 Va.	440*	0[118]
1 Va. Bn.	220*	4[119]

*No information available. Figures are based on balance of division divided by number of regiments.

Fulkerson	**1,320**	**1**[120]
10 Va.	440*	0
23 Va.	440*	0
37 Va.	440*	0

*No information available. Figures are based on balance of division divided by number of regiments.

Lawton	**3,500**[121]	**492**	**14%**
13 Ga.	560*	60[122]	Enfield, no bayonets[123]
26 Ga.	560*	40	Enfield[124]
31 Ga.	560*	172	Smoothbores[125]
38 Ga.	700[126]	170	Enfield[127]
60 Ga.	560*	14	Enfield[128]
61 Ga.	560*	36	Enfield[129]

Artillery

Poague's 1st Rockbridge Artillery (Va.)
Caskie's Hampden Artillery (Va.)
Wooding's Danville Artillery (Va.)
Carpenter's Alleghany (Va.)

*No information available. Regimental numbers are based on the balance of the brigade figure divided by number of regiments.

Ewell's Division	**3,987**[130]	**817**[131]	***16%***
1Md	250**	8	Miss rifles[132]

Elzey	**1,293**[133]	**243**	**19%**
12 Ga.	178*	7	
13 Va.	250[134]	111	
25 Va.	178*	3	
31 Va.	214[135]	22	
44 Va.	44[136]	17	
52Va	178*	29	
58Va	250[137]	54	

*No information available. Regimental numbers are based on the balance of the brigade number divided by the number of regiments.

Trimble	**1,244**[138]	**400**	**32%**
15 Al.	255*	150	66
21 Ga.	350[139]	111	32
16 Miss.	255*	85	33
21 NC	255*	45	18
1 NC Bn.	127*	9	

*No information available. Regimental numbers are based on the balance of the brigade number divided by the number of regiments.

Seymour[140]	**1304**[141]	**173**	**13%**
6 La.	156	47	
7 La.	316	41	
8 La.	316	44	
9 La.	316	19	
1 La. Sp. Bn.	200[142]	22	

Artillery

Courtney's Henrico Artillery (Va.)
Carrington's Charlottesville Artillery (Va.)
Brockenbrough's Baltimore Artillery (Va.)

Disclaimer: Information on unit strengths is sparse. Many units reported only casualties for the campaign and not each individual engagement. Accordingly, strengths and casualties are based on incomplete information and highly questionable yet expedient assumptions. The figures are guidelines only.

Union Order of Battle

	Present	Casualties[1]	%
PORTER'S COMMAND	29281*	6,772	23.1%

*Sum of V Corps plus part
 of Slocum's Division.

V Corps	*21,281*	*4797*	*22.54%*

Sum of organic divisions plus artillery at 100 men per battery, cavalry, and U.S.
Sharpshooters.

Cavalry	**716***	**103**	**14.3%**
5 U.S. Cav.	220[2]	55	
1 U.S. Cav.	125[3]	25	
6 Pa. Cav. Lcrs.	250[4]	15	
4 Pa. Cav.	82[5]	2	
Provost	39[6]	6	

*Sum of units

Morell's Division	*7,414***	*19,04*	*25.5%*
U.S. Sharpshooters	100	11	11%

*Sum of brigades + USSS
 and arty

Griffin's Brigade	**2,338***	**583**	**23.0%**
9 Mass.	584*	231	Smoothbore[7]
14 NY	584*	100	Rifles[8]
62 Pa.	584*	164	muskets[9]
4 Mich.	584*	88	Smoothbores[10]

*No information available. Brigade number is derived from average of other brigades.
Regimental numbers are average of brigade number.

Martindale	**2,500**[11]	**688**	**27.5%**
1 Mich.	836[112]	151	
25 NY	338*	45	
13 NY	338*	120	M 1855 Sprngfields[13]
2 Me.	338	89	Smoothbore[14]
22 Mass.	650[15]	491	

!Roberts reports that 209 were ¼ of his men, so his total engaged is 836.
*The 22d Mass and 1 Mich account for all but 1,014 of Martindale's men. Accordingly,
his other three regiments had about 338 men each.

Butterfield	**2,176***	**596**		**27.3%**
44 NY	380[16]	55	smoothbores[17]	15%
12 NY	623	131	M1842, Enf.[18]	21%
16 Mich.	623	214	Spr., Enfields[19]	34%
83 Pa.	550[20]	196	smoothbores[21]	36%

*No information available. Regimental numbers are average of two known regiments, and brigade number is the sum of all four.

Artillery	**300**	**26**	
Weeden C RI	100	15	6 Ordnance Rifles
Martin, C Ma.	100	3	6 Napoleons
Hyde, E Ma	100	8	6 Ordnance Rifles

Sykes' Division	*4,500*[22]	*1,181*		*26.2%*
Buchanan	**1,884**	**516**		**27.3%**
3 U.S.	471*	45	1855 Spr.	
4 U.S.	471*	19	M1855 Spr.	
12 U.S.	471*	212	M1855 Spr.	
14 U.S.	471*	240	M1855 Spr.	
Lovell	**1,571**	**337**		**21.4%**
2 U.S.	471*	139		
6 U.S. 8 Cos.	380*	99		
10 U.S.	200#	22		
11 U.S.	270[23]	43		
17 U.S.	250#	34		
Warren	**1,025**	**284**		**27.7%**
5 NYZ	450[24]	162	Spr. rifle[25]	
10 NY	575[26]	122		

#10 and 17 were less than half regiments, so numbers assigned arbitrarily as 200 and 250, respectively.
*4500 men less above leaves 2,755 men, in 5 regiments of 10 cos and 1 regiment of 8 cos, a total of 58 cos. Each co. therefore had 47 men in it. Each 10 co. rgt. had about 471, and the 6th U.S. 380.

Artillery	**500**	**44**		**8%**
Tidball A, 2 U.S.	100	7	6 Ordnance Rifles	
Edwards L/M, 3 U.S.	100	10	6 Parrotts	
Weed I, 5 U.S.	100	7	6 Ordnance Rifles	
Kingsbury D, 5 U.S.	100	6	6 Parrotts	
Voeglee B, NYL	100	8	6 20 lb. Parrotts	

McCall's Division	*8,651*[27]	*1,609*		*18.5%*
Reynolds	**3,310***	**335**		**10.%**
1 PR	790*	45	Blg .69 rifles, smoothbores	
2 PR	321[28]*	35		
5 PR	790*	36	Springfield, smoothbores	
8 PR	790*	149	Rifles, smoothbores[29]	
13 PR	150[30]	26[31]	Sharps Infantry Rifles[32]	
Meade	**2,970***	**1,012**		**34%**
3 PR	790*	98	rifles, smoothbores[33]	
4 PR	600[34]	62	rifles, smoothbores[35]	
7 PR	336[36]	168	rifles,[37] smoothbores[38]	
11 PR	790	684	rifles, smoothbores[39]	

Seymour	**2,370***	**215**	**9.0%**
9 PR	790*	55	1 co Spr.[40] 1 co Sharps IR smoothbores[41]
10 PR	790*	134	rifles, smoothbores[42]
12 PR	790*	26	minie, smoothbores[43]

*McCall had 8,651 men, less 750 in 8 and 4 pares, for a total of 7,901 unaccounted for in 10 regiments. Each regiment had approx. 790 men in it. Brigade numbers are sums of regiments.

Artillery	**600**	**47**	**7.8%**
Easton A, PLA	100	13	4 Napoleons[44]
Cooper B, PLA	100	0	6 Parrotts[45]
Kerns G, PLA	100	19	6 Howitzers,[4647]
Dehart C, 5 U.S.	100	14	6 Napoleons[48]
Robertson B/L, 2US	100	1	6 Ordnance Rifles
Smead K, 5 U.S.	100	0	4 Napoleons
Slocum's Division*	***8,000***[49]	***1,975***	***24.6%***
Taylor	**2,800**[50]	**1,072**	**38.2%**
1 NJ	876*	159	
2 NJ	261[51]	113	
3 NJ	645![52]	215	
4 NJ	627[53]	585	

*2,3,4 add up to where 1 NJ would have 1200 men, so clearly wrong. Total of 2,800 must be all of 2 NJ included. If 261 = 4 cos, then 5 cos is 326 and 2x that is 652. Subtracting all of 2, 3 and 4 from 2800 gives 876 for 1NJ.
! losses are ⅓, so × 3 is 645

Newton	**2,692**	**382**	**14.1%**
18 NY	673*	110	16%
31 NY	673*	104	15%
32 NY	673*	56	7%
95 Pa.	673*	112	17%
Bartlett	**2,504***	**505**	**20.1%**
16 NY	485[54]	201	
27 NY	673*	151	
5 Me.	673*	66	
96 Pa.	673*	87	13%

*Slocum 8,000 less Taylor's 2,800 and 485 in the 16 NY leaves 4,715 men in division. Newton had 4 regiments and Bartlett 3 unaccounted, so 7 all told. This means each of 7 regiments had 673 men.

Artillery	**300**	**16**	**5.3%**
Hexamer A, NJL	100	5	4 Parrots, 2 Howitzers[55]
Porter, C MaL	100	5	4 Parrotts, 2 Howitzers[56]
Upton D 2, U.S.	100	6	4 Parrotts, 2 Howitzers[57]
NJ MG Co.			7 Union Repeating Guns
Bartlett MG Co.			3 Union Repeating Guns

*sum of units
28,565 infantry shooting an average of 40 rounds each fired 1,142,600 rounds.

Artillery Losses (Official) OR Ser. I Vol. 11 P. 419 Barry

Morell's Division
    C, Rhode Island (Waterman)   4 Ord. rifles

E Mass (Hyde)	4 Ord. rifles
C Mass (Martin)	1 Napoleons

Sykes
L/M 5th U.S. (Edwards)	2 Parrotts
I, 5 U.S. (Weed*)	3 Ord. rifles

McCall
C 5 U.S. Dehart	2 Napoleons
A Penna. (Easton)	4 Napoleons
C Penna. (Kerns)	2 Howitzers

Slocum
A NJ Hexamer	1 Howitzer
NJ MG Co.	2 URG
Mg Co.	3 URG

*Weed says that 2 were lost.

Chapter Notes

Preface

1. *Lee's Lieutenants*, Vol. I, 489–537.
2. Schenck, 362, citing St. Maur.
3. Schmutz, Location 2578.

Prologue

1. "Henry David Thoreau," Wikipedia.
2. McNiven.
3. These were horsemen armed with Austrian lances, with a small red flag at the end.
4. At the grocery store, the whole bacon section is about three hundred pounds.
5. Judith McGuire, Location 2369-Location 2621.
6. This was probably Major Carlisle Boyd, 5th New York Infantry.
7. Sydnor, 105–106.
8. http://thaddeuslowe.name/CWDispatches2.htm; accessed 5/21/17.
9. Joseph Haw, 8.
10. Mary Jane Haw.

Chapter 1

1. J.B. Jones, *Rebel War Clerk Diary*, 133. This policy started June 4.
2. Generally, at what is now Richmond International Airport.
3. It also violates Sun Tzu's maxim of attacking the enemy where he is weak, not strong.
4. "White House Landing," Wikipedia.
5. Kilblaine.
6. Kilblaine.
7. Kilblaine.
8. Townshend, 127.
9. Dowdey, 183. Lee letter to Jefferson Davis, June 5, 1861.
10. Ibid., 185. Lt. John M. Brooks, CSN, designed it, and had it completed by June 14, 1862. It mounted a 32-pound gun on a naval carriage. The railroad iron-clad weighed 60 tons, and had cotton-clad flatcars behind it for sharpshooters. It went into action near Fair Oaks and Savage Station. American Civil War Armored Rail Cars, http://www.firstmdus.net/Rail%20cars.htm.
11. Dowdey, 185.
12. Dowdey, 185.

13. Dowdey, 187. Lee's letter to Jackson of June 8, 1862. This is the first official mention of the "unite near Richmond" idea.
14. Fox III. The digital edition does not have page numbers. Fox implies that Stuart's personal scouting expedition on the night of June 8 was the genesis of the idea to attack White House Landing, but this is not the case. Lee already had the idea; Stuart was just checking it out later that day.
15. OR Ser. I, Vol. 11, Pt. 3, 590.
16. Fox III.
17. Fox III.
18. "Union Balloon Corps," Wikipedia. Thaddeus Lowe, Chief Aeronaut, had three balloons based at White House Landing by May of 1862, and by May 18 the balloon *Intrepid* was stationed at mansion of Dr. W.F. Gaines, who also owned a mill nearby. The site of the balloon base has recently been found, on Powhite Creek about halfway between the Gaines' Mill site and Dr. Gaines' Mansion site.
19. Technically, because the Union Army had torn up the Virginia Central's rails east of Ashland, it was somewhat easier to move the Valley Army to White House Landing than to Richmond. See "Virginia Central Railroad," Wikipedia.
20. "Peninsula Campaign," Wikipedia.
21. Porter Alexander, 111.
22. Dowdey, 189.
23. Garber, Location 243, says that the 7,000-man Valley Army had 160 wagons. These are approximate numbers. See also Kilblaine.
24. Dowdey, 191.
25. OR Ser. I, Vol. 14, 589.
26. Csa-railroads.com, NA, VC 9/10/1862.
27. Csa-railroads.com, NA, VC 9/10/1862.
28. Robertson, *Stonewall*, 458.
29. Howard, 135. This would account for the paucity of information about this movement.
30. Howard, 462.
31. Jackson's brother-in-law.
32. Robertson, *Stonewall*, 463.
33. This is the other Hill. He is referred to as Powell Hill. He contracted gonorrhea shortly after West Point, so it is a good thing his girlfriend rejected him. She married McClellan instead. He was killed in 1865 while attending a call of nature.
34. Hereinafter, "Dabbs House Memorandum." The tone of the memorandum indicates that is it a staff officer's notes, as shown by the references to "Maj. Genl," and

the specific records that a communication is to be in duplicate. Without any map, references the "first road" and
the "second road" from the Chickahominy are meaning-
less.

35. Freeman, *Lee's Lieutenants*, 500. This document
is in the Hotchkiss papers, marked "Mrs. Jackson." Freeman delves into whether this is in Jackson's hand, which
it is probably not. It appears to be Chilton's notes for
writing General Order 75.

36. OR Ser. I, Vol. 11, 515–523.
37. Freeman, *REL*, 138.
38. Robertson, *Stonewall*, 465.
39. Robertson, *Stonewall*, 467.
40. Dabney, 198–200.
41. Harvey Hill, *Battles and Leaders*, 361.
42. OR Ser. I, Vol. 11, 513.
43. Robertson, *Stonewall*, 468.
44. Joe Ryan, "What happened in January 1862?" The
George McClellan Papers, http://joeryancivilwar.com/
Sesquicentennial-Monthly-Articles/June-1862/Papers-
George-McClellan-June-1862.html.
45. OR Ser. III, Vol. 3, 252.
46. Tsouras, xi.
47. Hill, *Our Boys*, 277–278. This was the night of a
great storm, so bad it was reported in the New York papers. While 30 miles is quite a distance, trains were still
running to Ashland in safety; John Boteler, an aide to
Jackson, was on detached duty and remarked that Virginia Governor Letcher had taken the cars from Ashland to Richmond on the 26th. Boteler, *SHSP* 40.
48. *The Life Story and Narrations of Private Charles
Rean.*
49. Alexander, 114.
50. Kilblaine.
51. Fox III.
52. This raises the question of why McClellan located
his base at White House in the first place. In March,
when the Peninsula Campaign started, the ironclad CSS
Virginia guarded the James River. The Yankees captured
White House Landing on May 10, 1862. The James was
not opened to Union shipping until May 11, 1862, when
the CSS *Virginia* was destroyed to prevent its capture.
On May 15, the Union fleet steamed up the James to
Drewry's Bluff, seven miles from Richmond, only to
find that the bluff was very heavily fortified and high
enough so that the rebels could shoot down through
their decks. Any supply point on the James had to be
south of Drewry's Bluff.
53. Robertson, 467.
54. Howard, 135.
55. Association for the Preservation of Beaver Dam
Depot.
56. Robertson, *Stonewall*, 467.
57. Robertson, *Stonewall*, 467. Fontaine's is a mile
west of Beaver Dam Depot and on the road down which
the Valley Army was marching, which was probably not
conducive to restful sleep. Howard Carter's was about a
mile north of the Depot.
58. Douglas, 99.
59. *New York Herald*, 6/25/62.
60. Brown, 45–46.
61. Daniel, *Richmond Howitzers*, 40.
62. Potter, 33.

Chapter 2

1. Comte de Paris, 87.
2. Among these were the Jeff Davis Legion of Mis-

sissippi and the Cobb Legion of Georgia. The most famous, though fictitious, member of the Cobb Legion
was Major Ashley Wilkes.
3. OR Ser. I, Vol. 11, 528.
4. Gilmer Map 548; the 8th Illinois OR Report begins on June 26.
5. OR Ser. I, Vol. 11, 528.
6. OR Ser. I, Vol. 11, 116–117.
7. On the Gilmer Map, it is "Mrs. Daub's." It still exists on Creighton Road, which leads to Dr. Gaines' Mansion site.
8. OR Ser. I, Vol. 11, 834. Powell Hill says he concentrated his Division "Wednesday night."
9. Herndon, 173.
10. Howard, 135.
11. Murray, 52.
12. Dabney, 439, says the Federals had destroyed the
bridge, but there is no record of that. There is some
question as to whether this was over the Little River or
the New Found River. According to uglybridges.com,
the Teman Road/Little River bridge spans almost 70
feet, while the Coatesville Road/New Found River bridge
spans only 30 feet, so it was probably the Little River.
Note that this is the major road bridge over the Chickahominy at Mechanicsville, on the Telegraph Road,
which led to Washington, i.e., the Interstate 95 of the
day. One can only imagine what the New Found River
bridge, far away from civilization, was like.
13. Garber, Location 349.
14. "Claiborne R. Mason"; "Re: Stonewall Jackson's
Black Confederates."
15. Howard, 135.
16. "Pioneers" were as skilled as modern-day "engineer" troops are.
17. Howard, 135.
18. Page, 80–81.
19. Howe, *History of Hanover County*. As of 1840, legend had it that a master left his children with a trusted
slave, and the slave killed the children. The slave's pun-
ishment was to be torn apart by horses, and this area of
the county is where they found his foot. Howard, 134–
135, laments that he could not remember much about
this part of the march, but he remembers Negrofoot.
20. OR Ser. I, Vol. 11, 592.
21. Gilmer Map 548.
22. Dabney, 439.
23. Robertson, *Stonewall*, 468.
24. OR Ser. I, Vol. 11, 528.
25. Brown, 46.
26. Driver, 25.
27. "Ashland during the Civil War, 1861–1865," http://
ashlandmuseum.org/explore-online/civil-war/ashland-
during-the-civil-war-1861-1865. Railroad Avenue is a
modern road, alongside the railroad tracks. The HQ
would have been in the northern part of the town.
28. OR Ser. I, Vol. 11, 614.
29. Alexander, 115.
30. Robertson, 873.
31. OR Ser. I, Vol. 11, 552.
32. OR Ser. I, Vol. 11, 491.
33. Now "Poor House Park," Hanover County.
34. "Ashland during the Civil War, 1861–1865," http://
ashlandmuseum.org/explore-online/civil-war/ashland-
during-the-civil-war-1861-1865.
35. Alexander, 115. In the very next sentence, Alexander asserts that the Virginia Central is 25 miles away from
Ashland at "Stark Church." In fact, it is only 5.6 miles
from the RF&P in Ashland to Slash Church.

36. Hanover County 186? Map.
37. Brown, 46, says they were in communication with Lee at Ashland.
38. Robertson, *Stonewall*, 469.
39. Robertson, 469; Dabney, 440 as to the time reference.
40. Von Borcke, 52. He has the date wrong; it was the 25th.
41. OR Ser. I, Vol. 11, 513–514; Stuart Report; 186? Map of Hanover County; OR Ser. 1, Vol. 11, Part 2, 523 concerning the attachment of the "Map of the Operations of the Cavalry Brigade": http://digitalcollections.baylor.edu/cdm/singleitem/collection/tx-wotr/id/1063/rec/259
42. OR Ser. I, Vol. 11 p. 513.
43. Robertson, *Stonewall*, 477.
44. Gilmer Map 544.
45. Hanover's History.
46. For unknown reasons, many writers have claimed that Jackson was to simultaneously support Powell Hill, and at the same time Powell Hill, Longstreet and Harvey Hill were to support Jackson.
47. One greatly respected historian claimed that Slash Church was 25 miles from Ashland; it is only 6. Another claimed that the Valley Army made only 5 miles on June 25; in fact, they made 18 miles. Another claimed that the red lines on the Gilmer maps were troop movements, not roads.
48. The speed of a march is determined by many things, foremost of which is the possibility of attack. The modern U.S. army uses a speed of one mile per hour for men on foot; this has not changed in 155 years. Whitman, 47, says that they retreated from the Beaver Dam Creek Line at a rate of 1 mile per hour. When an attack is feared, the march rate is closer to half a mile per hour, as the lead formation must look out for ambushes, obstructions, land mines, and the like; a modern analogy would be moving through the Bocage in Normandy in the summer of 1944. A better cavalry screen allows the infantry to move faster by its looking out for the enemy.
49. Without cavalry, the lead division must use its lead brigade to watch out for ambushes by putting out skirmishers. For example, in the movie *Gettysburg*, when Chamberlain (Jeff Daniels) is told to march to Gettysburg, he is told he is the lead regiment and to put out skirmishers. He is shocked, because he did not think the enemy was that close.
50. OR Ser. I, Vol. 11, 528.
51. Sears, McLellan Papers, 309.
52. Dowdey, 198.
53. "John Minor Botts," Wikipedia.
54. Gilmer Map 526.
55. Gilmer Map 548.
56. Robertson, 471.
57. OR Ser. I, Vol. 12, 881.
58. OR Ser. I, Vol. 11, 894.
59. OR Ser. I, Vol. 11, 835, Powell says that he had about 14,000. The 10,000 figure excludes artillery and is from other period sources.
60. OR Ser. I, Vol. 11, 834.
61. OR Ser. I, Vol. 11, 877.
62. Usually referred to as D.H. Hill. Since there is also a Powell Hill at this battle, and a few underlings by that name, he will be referred to as Harvey Hill.
63. Usually referred to as G.B. Anderson, but referred to here as George, because, of course, this battle includes Brigadier R.H. "Dick" Anderson (Longstreet's Division) and numerous others.

64. OR Ser. I, Vol. 11, 623.
65. A "battalion" is any organization larger than one company and smaller than 10 companies. The number of men in a battalion varied, but it was always smaller than a regiment. A battalion does not carry a flag; only regiments carry flags, called "colors." Union regiments had two, a national flag and a state flag. Confederate regiments carried one. Union flags were about six feet by six feet and square, not rectangular. Confederate flags were about four feet square. Capturing the enemy's regimental colors symbolized the annihilation of that regiment, and brought shame onto the remnants of it.
66. OR Ser. I, Vol. 11, 657.
67. OR Ser. I, Vol. 22, 756.

Chapter 3

1. Tinsley, 398.
2. Jackson was technically the head of the Valley Army, one division of it (Jackson's), and also of one brigade of that division (the Stonewall Brigade). Jackson's Division was actually commanded by General Sidney Winder, who also commanded the Stonewall Brigade. In this work, it will be Winder's Division and the Stonewall Brigade.
3. The Valley Army was a big division on the Richmond Confederate Army scale. Longstreet, Powell Hill and Harvey Hill each had roughly 10,000 men.
4. The Yankees' "front" was towards Richmond. Therefore, their "right" was facing south at Mechanicsville, The Yankees' "left" was east of Richmond.
5. Kilblaine.
6. Kilblaine.
7. "Berkley Plantation," Wikipedia.
8. McNiven.
9. SHSP 10, 149.
10. OR Ser. I, Vol. 11, 514.
11. Brown, 46.
12. Richard Taylor was sick, and so command devolved on Col Isaac Seymour. Since Union Col. Seymour commanded a brigade in the Pennsylvania Reserves, Taylor's Louisiana brigade will remain Taylor's, not Seymour's.
13. OR, Ser. I, Vol. 11, 621.
14. Andrews, *Memoir*, 40.
15. Douglas, 100.
16. Also known as Leach's Steam Mill. At 10 p.m., Jackson sent a message to Branch that the head of his column, i.e., Ewell's division, was 2 miles away from where he crossed the Virginia Central, and on the Mechanicsville—Shady Grove Church road. This is about right for Ewell at this time, who was in camp at Hundley's Corner, near Pole Green Church. If the Valley Army had crossed the Virginia Central at Peake's Turnout, in two miles it would be at Slaughter's House, 8 miles from Pole Green Church.
17. OR Ser. I, Vol. 11, 552; see OR Ser. I, Vol. 11, 620 for a text version of the note.
18. OR Ser. I, Vol. 11, 562, 657. Note that a 4,000-man Valley Army Division only takes an hour to pass a given point, a march speed of 1 mile per hour.
19. OR Ser. I, Vol. 11, 882.
20. A "vidette" is a cavalryman on picket. Men on horseback can see further than a man on the ground, so there would be more space between them, and hence fewer men watching a larger area.
21. OR Ser. I, Vol. 11, 232.

22. Ent, Location 2322.

23. Kelsey, 71.

24. SHSP 10, 149.

25. OR Ser. I, Vol. 11, 232; Ent, Location 2322.

26. Hereinafter the Virginia Central.

27. Pennsylvania mustered too many men at the beginning of the war. Those who went early were the Pennsylvania Volunteers, and were numbered as such, viz., 62d Pennsylvania. The rest were kept in service but remained in Pennsylvania until later in the war, and were called the Pennsylvania Reserves, and numbered separately. Wikipedia.

28. A company is supposed to be 98 men plus officers. Ten of them make a regiment. Neither were at full strength very often.

29. To cover a large area, a company would place a man every ten, twenty, or 50 yards, depending on the size of the area to be watched. These were called "pickets." If the enemy were very close or shooting, these companies would shoot and then retreat to the reserve.

30. When the shooting started, the reserve, usually off duty, would "form up," that is, go into a formation of two ranks of men standing shoulder to shoulder; this maximized firepower to cover the returning pickets.

31. OR Ser. I, Vol. 11, 414. "Skirmishers" are one rank of men, each about 5 yards apart. These were sent out to explore the country ahead and to make sure that the reserve did not walk into an ambush.

32. OR Ser. I, Vol. 11, 882.

33. OR Ser. I, Vol. 11, 886.

34. OR Ser. I, Vol. 11, 414.

35. OR Ser. I, Vol. 11, 414. This was Col. Simmons of the 5th Pennsylvania Reserves.

36. OR Ser. I, Vol. 11, 414.

37. OR Ser. I, Vol. 11, 882. A "guidon" is a small flag used by soldiers to align its troops and identify themselves. It's the little flag that the cavalry in western movies always have when attacking the Indians.

38. OR Ser. I, Vol. 11, 837.

39. OR Ser. I, Vol. 11, 894.

40. OR Ser. I, Vol. 11, 414.

41. Sears, McClellan Papers, 312.

42. OR Ser. I, Vol. 11, 330.

43. OR Ser. 1, Vol. 11, 298.

44. SHSP 10, 149.

45. OR Ser. I, Vol. 11, 605.

46. Page, 79.

47. Robertson, *Stonewall*, 471.

48. SHSP 10, 149.

49. Adams, Jr., 208. The letter says "Ashland, 10 miles this side."

50. OR Ser. I, Vol. 11, 514. This is a crossroads. Overton's is on one corner, Dr. Shelton's on the opposite.

51. OR Ser. I, Vol. 11, 562.

52. Stuart says it was torn up: OR Ser. I, Vol. 11, 514. Dabney, 440, says it was "destroyed."

53. Boat howitzers are designed for use after assembly by naval landing parties, use an iron carriage, and have a large loop at the bottom of the barrel for mounting, rather than trunnions. These were captured from the 71st New York at 1st Manassas.

54. Dabney, 441. Dabney was apparently with Whiting and the rest of the Valley Army on the Pole Green Church Road.

55. Robson, 59.

56. OR Ser. I, Vol. 11, 233.

57. OR Ser. I, Vol. 11, 514.

58. Dabney, 440–441.

59. Sears, McClellan Papers, 313.

60. R. Jones, 149–150.

61. OR Ser. I, Vol. 11, 233.

62. SHSP 10, 150.

63. Woodward, 118. The 2nd thought that the 1st Maryland had crossed the Chickahominy with Branch.

64. Two Napoleons, two: The Second Maryland, U.S., and Maryland in the Civil War website.

65. SHSP 10, 150.

66. Dowdey, 198–199.

67. OR Ser. I, Vol. 11, 835.

68. Bigbee, 357.

69. OR Ser. I, Vol. 11, 835, 841. Powell Hill and Field both say they went without orders because they had not heard from Branch nor Jackson, but this would mean that Branch did not tell Powell Hill that he had crossed at 10.00 a.m., which is hard to believe. Additionally, Powell Hill ordered Field to cross when Branch should appear. Branch was fully deployed at Atlee's Station, and the 7th N.C. was in a fight south of there. It's also hard to believe that no one heard this. Powell probably moved when he heard this, despite what his report says. Additionally, the Baltimore Artillery of Ewell's division was booming away at Farnsworth's 8th Illinois Cavalry over at Shady Grove Church about this time.

70. McGuire, Location 2154.

71. OR Ser. I, Vol. 11, 414.

72. OR Ser. I, Vol. 11, 841.

73. OR Ser. I, Vol. 11, 841.

74. OR Ser. I, Vol. 11, 863.

75. OR Ser. I, Vol. 11, 271.

76. OR Ser. I, Vol. 11, 289.

77. Sears, McClellan Papers, 314.

78. Brown, 48. "Column of regiments" means regiments deployed in successive lines, each one following the one before.

79. Wood, 69–70.

80. OR Ser. I, Vol. 11, 882.

81. Clark, *N.C. Troops*, Vol. 1, 180–181.

82. Brent.

83. Freeman, *LL*, 122.

84. OR Ser. I, Vol. 11, 117.

85. McGuire, Location 2139.

86. Katherine Jones, 120.

87. Varon, Location 184.

88. Gilmer Map 548.

89. Botts, 293.

90. Varon, Location 1045–1047.

91. Jones, *Rebel War Clerk*, 138.

Chapter 4

1. OR Ser. I, Vol. 11, 386.

2. Landers Map, Beaver Dam Creek.

3. Gilmer Map 548.

4. A "Parrott" rifle is an iron cannon with a rifled barrel that shoots a 10-pound bullet-shaped projectile. It has a distinctive casing or band around the breech. Rifling the barrel gives it accuracy at maximum range, 1800 yards, a little over a mile. As with most Union Civil War field artillery, each gun had a crew of 8. A "limber" with an ammunition chest on it pulled the gun itself. This was accompanied by two more limbers attached together, creating a caisson. Each gun and each caisson weighed about 4,000 pounds, and was pulled by six horses.

5. A "howitzer" is a bronze non-rifled cannon with

short barrel but a high angle of fire so it could theoretically shoot over hills. Range: 1,100 yards, about ¾ mile.

6. A "Napoleon" is the nickname given to a non-rifled bronze cannon that fired a 12-pound round projectile in a more-or-less straight line. Range: 1,600 yards, just under a mile. It has a slightly different appearance from a howitzer.

7. A 3" ordnance rifle was an iron rifled cannon without the breech casing that a Parrott had. It had about the same range, 1800 yards.

8. Landers Map, Beaver Dam Creek.

9. Landers Map, Beaver Dam Creek.

10. Cannon count from Landers Beaver Dam Creek Map; infantry count from U.S. Appendix.

11. Freeman, 112.

12. Sydnor, 105.

13. OR Ser. I, Vol. 11, 835.

14. OR Ser. I, Vol. 11, 841.

15. The Confederates used the same cannons as the Federals, usually in four-gun, rather than six-gun, groups called "batteries." The Confederates pulled each vehicle with four horses rather than six.

16. OR Ser. I, Vol. 11, 841.

17. OR Ser. I, Vol. 11, 835.

18. OR Ser. I, Vol. 11, 897.

19. The 6-lb. smoothbore fired a six-pound projectile, half that of the Napoleon. It did not have the range of a Napoleon, but was about as accurate. These guns were almost obsolete.

20. OR Ser. I, Vol. 11, 898.

21. OR Ser. I, Vol. 11, 835.

22. OR Ser. I, Vol. 11, 835–6.

23. OR Ser. I, Vol. 11, 841.

24. OR Ser. I, Vol. 11, 841.

25. OR Ser. I, Vol. 11, 897.

26. OR Ser. I, Vol. 11, 899.

27. OR Supplement, 455, 457–8.

28. OR Ser. I, Vol. 11, 899.

29. OR Ser. I, Vol. 11, 648–649.

30. Jackson, 15–16.

31. Freeman, *LL*, 131–132.

32. OR Ser. I, Vol. 11, 409.

33. OR Ser. I, Vol. 11, 424.

34. OR Ser. I, Vol. 11, 426; Griffin, OR Ser. I, Vol. 11, 313, does not mention that the 9th Massachusetts was engaged but had two wounded.

35. OR Ser. I, Vol. 11, 877–8.

36. *History of the 4th Michigan*, Chapter 7.

37. *History of the 4th Michigan*, Chapter 7.

38. OR Ser. I, Vol. 11, 312; pp. 877–8.

39. OR Ser. I, Vol. 11, 835.

40. OR Ser. I, Vol. 11, 835.

41. OR Ser. I, Vol. 11, 623.

42. OR Ser. I, Vol. 11, 623.

43. OR Ser. I, Vol. 11, 835.

44. Varon, Location 1037–1040.

45. OR Ser. I, Vol. 1, 514.

46. SHSP 10, 148; OR Ser. I, Vol. 11, 621 says it was one artillery piece.

47. OR Ser. I, Vol. 11, Part 3, 620.

48. OR Ser. I, Vol. 11, 624.

49. Marshall, ch. 4.

50. OR Ser. I, Vol. 11, 605.

51. Hotchkiss to Henderson letter, April 6, 1896, Hotchkiss papers.

52. OR Ser. I, Vol. 11, 553.

53. Matison, 161.

54. McClandon, 70.

55. Tinsley, 398.

56. Robertson, *SJ*, 477; Dabney letter to Henderson.

57. There were three Sydnors in the 4th Virginia Cavalry, according to the National Park Service Solders and Sailor Database. It is unclear whether this is the same Sydnor who found his younger brother in Mechanicsville. Neither Longstreet nor his entourage mention any Lt. Sydnor.

58. OR Ser. I, Vol. 11, 625.

59. Marshall, ch. 4.

60. Dabney to Henderson letter.

61. None of the Gilmer Maps name Powhite Creek, nor Boatswain's Creek.

62. Dabney Letter to Henderson.

63. OR Ser. I, Vol. 11, 756.

64. Marshal, ch. 4.

65. Dabney to Henderson letter; Dabney says he slept in a different house than Jackson.

66. OR Ser. I, Vol. 11, 118.

67. Sears, McClellan Papers, 317.

68. Dabney, 442. Even one of Dr. Gaines' servants mentioned that Stonewall Jackson was near.

Chapter 5

1. OR Ser. I, Vol. 11, 290.

2. OR Ser. I, Vol. 11, 298.

3. OR Ser. I, Vol. 11, 419.

4. OR Ser. I, Vol. 11, 358, 356.

5. OR Ser. I, Vol. 11, 116, 315; Barnard says there were 6 heavy guns.

6. OR Ser. I, Vol. 51, 112.

7. OR Ser. I, Vol. 11, 271.

8. OR Ser. I, Vol. 11, Part 1, 286.

9. OR Ser. I, Vol. 11, 411.

10. OR Ser. I, Vol. 11, 242.

11. Roberts; OR Ser. I, Vol. 51, Part 1, 110 (1st Pennsylvania Reserves, Reynolds' Brigade); OR Ser. I, Vol. 11, 424 (Seymour's Brigade).

12. OR Ser. I, Vol. 11, 261, 357, 422.

13. OR Ser. I, Vol. 11, 408.

14. OR Ser. I, Vol. 11, 836, 885.

15. Marshall, ch. 4.

16. OR Ser. I, Vol. 11, 640.

17. Landers Map.

18. OR Ser. I, Vol. 11, 389, 781, 398.

19. OR Ser. I, Vol. 11, 836.

20. OR Ser. I, Vol. 11, 781.

21. OR Ser. I, Vol. 11, 779.

22. OR Ser. I, Vol. 11, 781.

23. OR Ser. I, Vol. 11, 781, 899.

24. OR Ser. I, Vol. 11, 899.

25. OR Ser. I, Vol. 11, 899.

26. OR Ser. I, Vol. 11, 422.

27. OR Ser. I, Vol. 11, 426.

28. Stevens, 102.

29. Called the "Bucktails" because each man had lashed a deer tail to his cap.

30. OR Ser. I, Vol. 11, 899.

31. OR Ser. I, Vol. 11, 836. This flag would be recaptured by the Yankees after Gaines' Mill.

32. Stevens, 105.

33. Known since World War II as a foxhole.

34. OR Ser. I, Vol. 11, 866.

35. Mattison, 161.

36. OR Ser. I, Vol. 11, 836.

37. OR Ser. I, Vol. 11, 756, 783. Longstreet mentions this in a disapproving tone.

38. OR Ser. I, Vol. 11, 783.
39. OR Ser. I, Vol. 11, 272.
40. Whitman, 47.
41. OR Ser. I, Vol. 11, 301.
42. OR Ser. I, Vol. 11, 272.
43. Now known as "corned" beef; whole peppercorns are added as flavoring, hence the more appetizing name.
44. Harrer, 43.
45. At the beginning of the war, field artillery was designated in two kinds, Horse (or Flying) Artillery, and everything else. Horse artillerymen were trained to mount and ride the limbers, allowing them to move at a horse's speed, rather than at the speed of a man walking. The walkers soon learned to ride the limbers.
46. OR Ser. I, Vol. 11, 244.
47. OR Ser. I, Vol. 11, 316.
48. OR Ser. I, Vol. 11, 338.
49. These monstrosities were designed to sink ships as seacoast defense guns. Weighing over 7,200 pounds, they fired a 32-pound projectile from a bore of 6.25 inches, over twice the size of Napoleons, Parrotts, and ordnance rifles. http://moultrie.battlefieldsinmotion.com/Artillery-32-pounder.html.
50. OR Ser. I, Vol. 11, 322.
51. OR Ser. I, Vol. 11, 361.
52. Reese, 75.
53. OR Ser. I, Vol. 11, 358.
54. Evans, 42.
55. Evans, 42.
56. Evans, 41; Meyers, 227.
57. Davenport, 202.
58. Davenport, 202–203.
59. OR Ser. I, Vol. 11, 244.
60. Robertson, *Stonewall*, 469.
61. OR Ser. I, Vol. 11, 515, 528.
62. OR Ser. I, Vol. 11, 570.
63. Howard, 136.
64. OR, Ser. I, Vol. 11, 553.
65. SHSP 10, 150; Dabney, 442.
66. Dabney, 442; OR Ser. I, Vol. 11, 621; Johnston says the 6th Louisiana replaced the 1st Maryland. Jones, SHSP 10, 150, says it was the 9th Louisiana.
67. OR Ser. I, Vol. 11, 553.
68. Robertson, *Stonewall*, 475.
69. OR Ser. I, Vol. 11, 553.
70. OR Ser. I, Vol. 11, 233, 289–299.
71. OR Ser. I, Vol. 11, 299.
72. There are two 1st South Carolinas in Gregg's Brigade. One is the 1st Volunteers, and the other is the First Rifles. They are two different regiments.
73. Caldwell, 39.
74. OR Ser. I, Vol. 11, 855.
75. Caldwell, 39.
76. OR Ser. I, Vol. 11, 855.
77. Caldwell, 39.
78. Goldsborough, MD Archive Edition, 59.
79. Goldsborough, MD Archive Edition, 59. The original says "Mahone's." Of course, Powell Hill was not out of position at all.
80. Edwards, 866.
81. Douglas, 101.
82. Robertson, *SJ*, 475.
83. Sherrill, 21st North Carolina Location. 2174, 2178, citing Major Wharton, 1 NCSS.
84. J. William Jones, 557–8.
85. Robertson, *Stonewall*, 477.
86. Tinsley, 403.
87. Mattison, 161.

88. OR Ser. I, Vol. 11, 853.
89. Marshall, ch. 4.
90. Dabney, 443.
91. Krick, "Maxcy Gregg," 11.
92. OR Ser. I, Vol. 11, 853. Jackson. Campbell Brown precisely alludes to this, but gets it confused with another, later incident, even drawing a precise map. Brown, 48.
93. OR Atlas, Map of the Operations of the Cavalry Brigade.
94. Blackford, 72.
95. Von Borcke, 54.
96. Blackford, 72; von Borcke, 54, says they "turned tail and fled in disorder."
97. OR Ser. I, Vol. 11, 528.
98. OR Ser. I, Vol. 11, 528.
99. OR Ser. I, Vol. 11, 330.
100. OR Ser. I, Vol. 11, 528.
101. Sydnor, 105. Henry Clinton Sydnor says that he was taken to Longstreet. However, Harvey Hill's guide was a Lt. Thomas Sydnor. OR Ser. I, Vol. 11, 630.
102. OR Ser. I, Vol. 11, 771.
103. Wilcox, OR Ser. I, Vol. 11, 771, says they came to a house about a mile from Beaver Dam Creek; on the Gilmer map, this is W.B. Sydnor's.
104. Sydnor, 105; he had 12 living siblings. Sydnor pp. 106–107. The boys were in the Confederate Army, and all but one girl were sent away, leaving Mr. and Mrs. Sydnor, the sister and young Henry in the house.
105. OR Ser. I, Vol. 11, 771.
106. OR Ser. I, Vol. 11, 772.
107. OR Ser. I, Vol. 11, 771.
108. OR Ser. I, Vol. 11, 855; Bouge, 16.
109. OR Ser. I, Vol. 11, 249.
110. OR Ser. I, Vol. 11, 244, 249.
111. Mattison, 161; OR Ser. I, Vol. 11, 854.
112. OR Ser. I, Vol. 11, 300.
113. "Pontoon Bridges."
114. OR Ser. I, Vol. 11, 855.
115. St. Maur, 331.
116. St. Maur, 332.
117. St. Maur, 333–334.
118. Freeman, *REL*, 141–2.
119. St. Maur, 332. St. Maur says the target was a mile from Hogan's. Powhite Creek is about a mile east of Hogan's. Boatswain's Creek is about a mile and a half.
120. Dowdey, *Wartime Papers*, 203.
121. Hinsdale Diary.
122. Tinsley, 393–398.
123. Tinsley, 399.
124. Pohanka, "Charge Bayonets," 32.
125. This is the area on the Gilmer Map near Gaines' Mill, not half a mile west where the main force of the Yankees were.
126. Tinsley, 333–398.

Chapter 6

1. OR Atlas.
2. The Reverend Dabney, Jackson's chief of staff, copyrighted his book in 1865 and published it in 1866.
3. "Southern Historical Society: Its Origin and History," Wikisource, https://en.wikisource.org/wiki/Southern_Historical_Society:_Its_Origin_and_History.
4. "*The Century* Magazine," Wikipedia,
5. "United Confederate Veterans," Wikipedia. The Yankees had the Grand Army of the Republic, but they mostly just erected monuments at Gettysburg.

6. Dabney, 447.
7. Elmer Woodard, "The Watt House Road."
8. Haw.
9. OR Atlas, Plate 77.
10. OR Atlas, Plate 63.
11. Gilmer Map 548.
12. It goes on to Raleigh Tavern, which is the "Old Raleigh" mentioned in Lee's Merry Oaks Communique.
13. Gilmer Map 548.
14. Watt House, LOC.
15. 186? Hanover County Map.
16. Woodard, "The Watt House Road."
17. Gilmer Map 548.
18. OR Ser. I, Vol. 11, 249.
19. OR Ser. I, Vol. 11, 118; unfortunately, the map referred to is lost.
20. 186? Hanover County Map.
21. 186? Hanover County Map.
22. Green.
23. Map of the Battlefield of Gaines' Mill, *B&L*.
24. Reese, 79.
25. OR Ser. I, Vol. 11, 348, 349, 580, 600, 601, 625, 638, 856, 869.

Chapter 7

1. Porter, *B&L*, 335.
2. OR Ser. I, Vol. 11, 117.
3. Hager Letter.
4. Lowe, 1.
5. OR Ser. I, Vol. 11, 348.
6. OR Ser. I, Vol. 11, 358.
7. OR Ser. I, Vol. 11, 348, 358.
8. OR Ser. I, Vol. 11, 356.
9. OR Ser. I, Vol. 11, 243, 348, 354.
10. OR Ser. I, Vol. 11, 364, 348.
11. Google Earth reveals that 1,003 yards from Old Cold Harbor is a short ridge where the elevation is slightly higher than that of Old Cold Harbor. It was to the north of the Boze House and about midway between the Grapevine Road and Boatswain's Branch.
12. OR Ser. I, Vol. 11, 348.
13. OR Ser. I, Vol. 11, 366, 367.
14. OR Ser. I, Vol. 11, 358.
15. Cowtan, 82.
16. Cowtan, 89; OR Ser. I, Vol. 11, 376.
17. Davenport, 204–6; OR Ser. I, Vol. 11, 381, 376.
18. OR Ser. I, Vol. 11, 370.
19. OR Ser. I, Vol. 11, 228, 372.
20. OR Ser. I, Vol. 11, 373, 370.
21. Seyburn; Chubb. The 17th U.S. had 5 companies with the Army of the Potomac, two of which (B and D) were General McClellan's Headquarters Guard. The 10th U.S. had three companies with McClellan, E, G and I. later in the war, Companies C, E, F and I, 81 men, would be consolidated; apparently when a company consisted of about 25 men it suffered this fate. The 10/17 U.S. probably contained about 150 men.
22. OR Ser. I, Vol. 11, 376.
23. OR Ser. I, Vol. 11, 374; Ames Papers; Lowe Papers.
24. OR Ser. I, Vol. 11, 237. This is the sole reference to Voeglee in all of the official reports. Pyne, 6th U.S., does mention that they supported a German battery. The exact location of Voeglee is debatable, but someone was shelling the woods on the Cariton Road, according to Fannie Gaines Tinsley, and only Voeglee's guns had

that range. McHenry Howard, 137, also says that shells were hitting the woods on the north side of the Carleton Road at about the same time and about the same place. Hunt reports that Voeglee lost 28 horses to musket fire, so he must have been within about 100 yards of many Confederates at some point. Since these were heavy and slow long-range rifles, they would have been placed behind the infantry lines in the first place.
25. Woodward, 90.
26. Harper, 118.
27. Woodward, 93.
28. Ent, Location 1995.
29. Pa-roots.com.
30. Sauers, 31.
31. Sauers, 31.
32. OR Ser. I, Vol. 11, 400.
33. Ent, Location 1928.
34. OR Ser. I, Vol. 11, 114, 260, 249, 367, 408, 411; p. 114; Landers Gaines' Mill Map concerning the 1st position of these units.
35. OR Ser. I, Vol. 11, 261–262.
36. The line of battle formation was two men deep and several hundred men wide, depending on the size of the regiment or battalion. The first line of men, one man deep and several hundred men wide, was called the "front rank." The other was the "rear rank."
37. OR Ser. I, Vol. 11, 361. Butterfield
38. *Franklin (New York) Visitor.*
39. OR Ser. I, Vol. 11, 338.
40. OR Ser. I, Vol. 11, 232.
41. Pennsylvania regiments that were actually mustered into Federal service early in the war before the Pennsylvania Reserves carried the normal state appellations, e.g., 83d Pennsylvania, 62d Pennsylvania.
42. OR Ser. I, Vol. 11, 344.
43. Norton, 90.
44. OR Ser. I, Vol. 11, 344.
45. Judson, 59.
46. OR Ser. I, Vol. 11, 316; p. 344 says that the 83d Pennsylvania sent Cos. A and B.
47. OR Ser. I Vol. 11, 290.
48. OR Ser. I Vol. 11, 290.
49. OR Ser. I, Vol. 11, 290.
50. OR Ser. I, Vol. 11, 290, 304; Parker, 119.
51. Bennett, 56.
52. OR Ser. I. Vol. 11, 301.
53. Bennett, 56.
54. OR Ser. I, Vol. 11, 290.
55. OR Ser. I, Vol. 11, 307, 311.
56. Betera, "Dear Thad."
57. Mahaffy, 66.
58. Harrer, 49.
59. Harrer, 49.
60. In the coming battle, brigades and even regiments would split apart, but usually join others in a temporary fighting formation. In this work, these are called "battle groups," and generally identified by who was in charge, e.g., Battle Group McQuade.
61. OR Ser. I, Vol. 11, 313.
62. Mahaffy, 66.
63. Fifth Mass. Battery, 323, OR Ser. I, Vol. 11, 285.
64. OR Ser. I, Vol. 11, 284.
65. OR Ser. I, Vol. 11, 282.
66. OR Ser. I, Vol. 11, 281.
67. A "troop" is roughly equivalent to two infantry companies, e.g., "F Troop."
68. Arnold, 356–7.
69. OR Ser. I, Vol. 11, 430.

70. OR Ser. I, Vol. 11, 406.
71. OR Ser. I, Vol. 11, 406.
72. OR Ser. I, Vol. 11, 237.
73. OR Ser. I, Vol. 11, 249.
74. OR Ser. I, Vol. 11, 291.
75. OR Ser. I, Vol. 11, 318; Sykes says that the McGehee House was the "commanding point" of the position.
76. Stevens, 111.
77. Bertera, "Letter from Recruit No. 14."

Chapter 8

1. OR Ser. I, Vol. 11, 853; Benson, 9; Caldwell; p. 39; Barnes, OR p. 862; Mattison, 161.
2. Mattison, 161.
3. Hinsdale diary.
4. OR Supp., Vol. 11, 457.
5. Hinsdale Diary.
6. Jones, Campbell Brown, 47.
7. Fletcher, 19.
8. Coles, *Huntsville*, 46.
9. Nabours, *CV* 24, 69.
10. Brent, 170.
11. OR Ser. I Vol. 11, 780.
12. Hurst, 11.
13. OR Ser. I, Vol. 11, 780.
14. OR Ser. I, Vol. 11, 772.
15. OR Ser. I, Vol. 11, 307.
16. OR Ser. I, Vol. 11, 301.
17. OR Ser. I, Vol. 11, 304.
18. Marshall, *Gallant Creoles*, 70.
19. OR Ser. I, Vol. 11, 773.
20. Marshall, *Gallant Creoles*, 70.
21. OR Ser. I, Vol. 11, 306.
22. OR Ser. I, Vol. 11, 311.
23. OR Ser. I, Vol. 11, 316.
24. The 2nd Maine only noted the Confederate shelling and firing to their left. The regiments in the gorge don't even mention this attack.
25. OR Ser. I, Vol. 11, 304.
26. Hurst, 11.
27. OR Ser. I, Vol. 11, 772.
28. Pollard, 11.
29. OR Ser. I, Vol. 11, 772.
30. OR Ser. I, Vol. 11, 783.
31. OR Ser. I, Vol. 11, 757.
32. Stevens, 112.
33. Tinsley, 399.
34. Stevens, 113.
35. Stevens, 113.
36. Benson, 9; Krick, 11.
37. Benson, 9.
38. Benson, 9.
39. OR Ser. I, Vol. 11, 313.
40. Daniel MacNamara, 117.
41. Michael MacNamara, 97.
42. Michael MacNamara, 95.
43. OR Ser. I, Vol. 11, 244.
44. OR Ser. I. Vol. 11, 244, 249; Map of Mechanicsville and Gaines' Mill, OR Atlas, Plate 63, position "z."
45. Daniel MacNamara, 118.
46. Bougue, 16; Stevens, 41.
47. OR Ser. I, Vol. 11, 273; Stevens, 113.
48. OR Ser. I, Vol. 11, 856, 890; Kelley, *1st Md. Arty*, 22.
49. Caldwell, 40.
50. OR Ser. I, Vol. 11, 854.
51. Caldwell, 40; OR Ser. I, Vol. 11, 863.

52. Caldwell, 40.
53. Mattison, 161.
54. OR Ser. I, Vol. 11, 854.
55. Robins, 4.
56. Caldwell, 40.
57. Daniel MacNamara, 118.
58. Caldwell, 40; Mattison, 161.
59. OR Ser. I, Vol. 11, 890; Mills, 17.
60. Stevens, 113.
61. OR Ser. I, Vol. 11, 836, 890.
62. OR Ser. I, Vol. 11, 890.
63. OR Ser. I, Vol. 11, 890.
64. Daniel MacNamara, 117.
65. Daniel MacNamara, 117.
66. OR Ser. I, Vol. 11, 836.
67. OR Ser. I, Vol. 11, 804.
68. Mattison, 162.
69. Mattison, 162.
70. OR Ser. I, Vol. 11, 356.
71. Mattison, 162.
72. Daniel MacNamara, 118.
73. "Pard" is a term the soldiers used to describe he relationship with their closest buddy, which could include tentmate, messmate, and pal. Author's experience.
74. Daniel MacNamara, 118–119.
75. Caldwell, 41.
76. Mattison, 162.
77. Mattison, 162.
78. OR Ser. I, Vol. 11, 862.
79. Benson, 10.
80. OR Ser. I, Vol. 11, 836, 854.
81. OR Ser. I, Vol. 11, 836.
82. OR Ser. I, Vol. 11, 886.
83. OR Ser. I, Vol. 11, 886.
84. Michael MacNamara, 95.
85. Michael MacNamara, 118.
86. J.R. Anderson was the owner of Tredegar Iron Works, the largest armaments producer of the Confederacy. "Joseph R. Anderson," Wikipedia.
87. OR Ser. I, Vol. 11, 879.
88. OR Ser. I, Vol. 11, 879.
89. Scharf, 21–22.
90. Hodges, 38.
91. "Bellona Arsenal" Registration Form. The site still exists. In 1962, an unfinished rifled cannon casting and the flask it was cast in were recovered from the James River.
92. Hodges, 38.
93. OR Ser. I, Vol. 11, 836; Field only had about 1,000 men in 5.5 regiments.
94. OR Ser. I, Vol. 11, 890.
95. OR Ser. I, Vol. 11, 772–3.
96. OR Ser. I, Vol. 11, 836.
97. Sears, 319; Porter, *B&L*, 333–335.
98. OR Ser. I, Vol. 11, 432.
99. "The 95th Pennsylvania Uniform in the Field," 53d Pennsylvania Volunteer Infantry, http://www.53rd pvi.org/95th-pennsylvania-volunteer-infantry/the-95th-pennsylvania-uniform-in-the-field/.
100. 32NY and California.
101. Westervelt, 15.
102. OR Ser. I, Vol. 11, 432.
103. OR Ser. I, Vol. 11, 433.
104. Bennett, 45.
105. OR Ser. I, Vol. 11, 433.
106. Bennett, 45.
107. OR Ser. I, Vol. 11, 432; Slocum says he was ordered to move Taylor and Bartlett at 2:30 and they

crossed at 3:00. Bartlett, 447, says he was ordered across at 2:30 and arrived about 4:00.

108. Crenshaw, Andrews, and Braxton.
109. Tinsley, 401.

Chapter 9

1. There is a dearth of information on Hill's exact route. The SHSP map says that he followed Jackson's route, but this is impossible. It is only 2⅛ miles from Beulah Church to the intersection of the Carleton Road with the Walnut Grove Church–Bethesda Church Road. Jackson had 15,000 men plus artillery. Dabney's map, 447, shows that Lawton's 3,500-man brigade and Winder's whole division marched off the Walnut Grove Church–Bethesda Church Road cross-country. Only Whiting's 4,000-man division and Ewell's 4,000-man division were actually on the Carleton Road, Ewell in front. A column of 4,000 men takes up about a mile of road, and the Carleton Road is about 2⅛ mile long, so it was long enough to hold both Ewell and Whiting. If Harvey Hill went down the Carleton Road, his whole 10,000-man army would have been crammed into the one mile between Beulah Church and Old Cold Harbor.

2. OR Ser. I, Vol. 11, 514, 528.
3. OR Ser. I, Vol. 11, 853.
4. Dabney, 443.
5. Gilmer Map 548.
6. Gilmer 544, and the scale of miles thereon.
7. Kyle Duffer.
8. Kyle Duffer.
9. Dabney, 443–444.
10. Campbell Brown, 47. A map accompanied Brown's writing. Point A is the intersection of the Foster Road and the Carlton Road. Point X is the intersection of the Foster Road with the Walnut Grove Church–Bethesda Church Road. Brown's map has been augmented by a later author with the erroneous notation that Point X is the intersection of the Pole Green Church Road and the *Mechanicsville*–Bethesda Church Road, i.e., Hundley's Corner.
11. Dabney, 444.
12. Units usually marched "right in front." In other words, when deploying from column of fours into line of battle, the right end would deploy first, and the rest would follow it. This rule applied to formations of soldiers ranging in size from companies all the way to armies. When "reversed," the left/rear end of the unit was now in front, and the men needed to know about that change to follow the correct end of the unit.
13. Robertson, *Stonewall*, 477, erroneously places the reversal on the Walnut Grove Church–Bethesda Church Road. This is impossible; the whole Valley Army took up at least 2.5 miles of road, so when Ewell's men were at Fosters, Winder's men were near Walnut Grove Church. Robertson then erroneously claims that the whole Valley Army backtracked to Walnut Grove Church, and somehow from there miracled itself to Old Cold Harbor, wasting two hours in the process, arriving at 3:00 p.m. Dabney, 444, and Brown, 49, place Jackson himself and the head of Ewell's Division (Elzey's Brigade) at Old Cold Harbor at 2:00. Harvey Hill also places Jackson at Old Cold Harbor about 2:00. Hill, *B&L*, 355.
14. Dabney, 444.
15. "Foot cavalry," Wikipedia.
16. Kyle Duffer.

17. Jones, Campbell Brown, 47.
18. Dabney to Henderson letter.
19. OR Ser. I, Vol. 11, 614. Trimble says that at 3:30, he was passing an unnamed church, 1.5 miles away from "Cold Harbor." Google Earth shows that it is almost exactly 1.5 miles to the intersection of the Carleton Road and the Grapevine Road north of Beulah Church.
20. The most famous fictional member of the Cobb Legion was, of course, Ashley Wilkes, "friend" of Scarlett O'Hara.
21. OR Ser. I, Vol. 11, 528.
22. OR Ser. I Vol. 11, 515.
23. OR Ser. I Vol. 11, 515.
24. Harvey Hill, *B&L*, 354; Campbell Brown, 49; Dabney, 444.
25. Douglas, 101.
26. Dabney, 444.
27. Hotchkiss Papers, Dabney to Henderson letter.
28. Reese, 79. Captain Weed, Battery I, 5th U.S. Artillery, says he arrived in position about noon. OR Ser. I, Vol. 11, 353; Reese, 79, says that Weed opened on Confederate cavalry shortly after that. Stuart, OR Ser. I, Vol. 11, 515, says that he found General Jackson at Old Cold Harbor and put his men in the woods east of there, subject only to a "raking artillery fire." W.W. Blackford says that Stuart's staff was under artillery fire. Blackford, 78. Von Borcke, 55, says that he was under cannon fire all day. None mention riding dangerously close to any guns.
29. Hotchkiss Papers, Dabney to Henderson letter.
30. Hotchkiss Papers, Dabney to Henderson letter.
31. Campbell Brown, 49.
32. Laboda, 34.
33. Laboda, 35; Landers places them to the left of the road, for unknown reasons.
34. OR Ser. I, Vol. 11, 365.
35. OR Ser. I, Vol. 11, 353.
36. Laboda, 37.
37. Laboda, 37.
38. Laboda, 37.
39. OR Ser. I, Vol. 11, 245.
40. Laboda, 37.
41. OR Ser. I, Vol. 11, 624.
42. "Jeff. Davis Artillery," Alabama Dept. of Archives and History.
43. Laboda, 38.
44. Douglas, 103.
45. Douglas, 103.
46. Douglas, 103.
47. OR Ser. I, Vol. 11, 631.
48. OR Ser. I, Vol. 11, 640.
49. OR Ser. I, Vol. 11, 640.
50. OR Supp., 437.
51. OR Ser. I, Vol. 11, 631.
52. Dabney, 444–445.
53. Dabney to Henderson letter.
54. Kyle Duffer; 15,000 men take up about 2.5 miles of road; the Valley Army stretched roughly from the Beulah Church northwest on the Carleton Road, while Harvey Hill's men were roughly northeast on the road from Old Raleigh.
55. Dabney to Henderson letter.
56. Campbell Brown, 49.
57. The American Civil War, Virginia Charlottesville Artillery Battery.
58. Herndon, *CV* 30, 173.
59. OR Ser. I, Vol. 11, 614. Trimble was last in Ewell's order of march, and he received the order to advance at about 3:30.

60. Campbell Brown, 49.
61. Campbell Brown, 49.
62. Campbell Brown, 49–50.
63. Dabney to Henderson letter.
64. See, e.g., Robertson, *Stonewall*, 479 "anything but simple."
65. Dabney to Henderson letter.
66. Dabney to Henderson letter.
67. Campbell Brown, 50.
68. Dufour, 193.
69. Kyd Douglas, 102.
70. Cooke, *REL*, 83. Cooke himself was not present for this conversation. In *Wearing of the Gray*, 1867, on page 46, Cook reveals that it was at or near Old Cold Harbor, not New Cold Harbor, that he saw Jackson three times that day.
71. See, e.g., Porter Alexander's misapprehension of the Merry Oaks order and Beaver Dam Creek, *Military Memoirs*, 115–116, "practically a whole day late"; "lost opportunity"; "excuses of biographers," etc. See also p. 128, blaming Jackson for not engaging when he reached Cold Harbor (in contradiction to Lee's orders at that time); Longstreet, *B&L*, 399, "Jackson was missing again"; Dowdey, *Seven Days*, 217–218: "uninspired reasoning"; "failure to communicate with Lee"; "failure to assume active command"; "Jackson did nothing"; p. 220: "possible that Jackson knew nothing of his two divisions' employment in the Battle around New Cold Harbor"; Freeman, *Lee's Lieutenants*, 524: "Jackson was late"; Robertson, *Stonewall*, 478: "Major Taylor's two visits were Jackson's only long range contact with Lee"; p. 479: "a blanketing fatigue limited his range and depth of thinking."
72. Dabney, 444.
73. Powell Hill did not reach Gaines' Mill at 2:30, but before that. Hill heard back from Longstreet and gave the attack order at 2:30. OR Ser. I, Vol. 11, 836. Gregg says that his men had attacked the Union skirmishers, rebuilt the bridge, and were on the eastern side of Powhite Creek by 2:00. OR Ser. I, Vol. 11, 854. Col. Edwards, 13th South Carolina, says that he formed line of battle at noon, and waited for the bridge to be repaired. OR Ser. I, Vol. 11, 866. Accordingly, Powell Hill reached Gaines' Mill by something between 12 noon and 2:00.
74. St. Maur, 332, says Hogan's was Lee's headquarters, and that General Longstreet and Brigadier Gregg were there. Gregg had passed through Walnut Grove Church while Lee was meeting with Generals Powell Hill, Harvey Hill, and Jackson, about 10:30, and had been accosted by General Lee after that, putting Lee at Hogan's around noon.

Chapter 10

1. OR Ser. I, Vol. 11, 836; Powell.
2. See, e.g., Sears, *Gates of Richmond*, 224; Robertson, *SJ*, 477, which claims that Powell Hill *and* Longstreet actually attacked at 2:00.
3. At the 140th anniversary reenactment of Gettysburg, it took 4 hours for experienced commanders to march 10,000 veteran Union infantry half a mile, and no one was actually shooting. Author's experience.
4. OR Ser. I Vol. 11, 854.
5. OR Ser. I Vol. 11, 873, 863.
6. OR Ser. I Vol. 11, 887.
7. OR Ser. I Vol. 11, 891.
8. The Union sources disagree completely. See, e.g., OR Ser. I, Vol. 11, 348. Brigadier Sykes says the fighting started at 11:00 a.m. and raged until 2:00 p.m., during which time the Confederate enemy "made repeated attempts on the flanks and center of my line and was as often driven back to his lair."
9. OR Ser. I, Vol. 11, 836.
10. OR Ser. I, Vol. 11, 854.
11. OR Ser. I, Vol. 11, 356.
12. Pyne Letter.
13. Caldwell, 41.
14. OR Ser. I, Vol. 11, 903.
15. OR Ser. I, Vol. 11, 356.
16. OR Ser. I, Vol. 11, 367.
17. OR Ser. I, Vol. 11, 903.
18. OR Ser. I, Vol. 11, 378.
19. Bogue, 40.
20. OR Ser. I, Vol. 11, 871. Gregg, 854, says his regiments were two up and two back, with the 1st Rifles on the left of the 13th, but this does not make sense in light of later movements. The First Rifles headed off to the right after Kelly's and Brownson's combined sections of Edwards Battery L/M 3rd U.S. (6 Parrotts). It makes no sense to send the First Rifles from the 13th's left, around behind them, to the right, when Gregg could have just sent the 13th to the right.
21. OR Ser. I, Vol. 11, 863.
22. OR Ser. I, Vol. 11, 369.
23. OR Ser. I, Vol. 11, 382.
24. Davenport, 208.
25. Davenport, 208.
26. Hager Diary.
27. Myers, 229.
28. OR Ser. I, Vol. 11, 382.
29. OR Ser. I, Vol. 11, 358.
30. OR Ser. I, Vol. 11, 378.
31. When in line of battle, each half of the regiment is called a "wing," so there is a right wing and a left wing. Warrant stacked his right wing behind the left wing. This makes the regiment's line of battle shorter but twice as thick, but the rear two ranks cannot fire without kiting the front rank.
32. Woodward, 125.
33. SHSP 31, 277.
34. Timing of the combat is difficult. Gregg and Marshall (1SCR) say they did not move until 4:00, but Sykes says (OR Ser. I, Vol. 11, 348–9) that Confederates made one attack after 3:00 and that the big attack came at about 5:30.
35. OR Ser. I, Vol. 11, 346.
36. OR Ser. I, Vol. 11, 346.
37. OR Ser. I, Vol. 11, 872.
38. OR Ser. I, Vol. 11, 861.
39. A "battalion volley" occurs when a regiment fires all of its rifles or muskets at once. A regiment with 450 men would therefore fire 450 bullets all at the same time. The effectiveness of a battalion volley increases the closer one is to the target. At 100 yards, one can expect about 25 percent hits; at 75 yards, about 40 percent hits; at 50 yards, 50 percent hits. A battalion could theoretically fire about once a minute. Sykes' men carried 60 cartridges per man. At that rate, they would run out of ammunition in 60 minutes. As the battalion fired more, fouling in the barrels made the weapons slower to load. After 35 shots, loading is slow indeed. Author's experience.
40. Caldwell, 43.
41. "Changing front" is a maneuver whereby a regiment faces in another direction. One company takes up the new direction, and then the other companies move to conform to it. It's not just everyone facing in another

direction, as this would not allow many to fire, which is the whole point of the line of battle. Wheeling (moving like a gate) a 150-yard-long line of battle under fire is almost impossible, and hence a maneuver that does the same thing.

42. OR Ser. I, Vol. 11, 359, 361.
43. OR Ser. I, Vol. 11, 362.
44. "Canister," with one "n," was an artillery projectile used against infantry at short range. It was a tin can filled with 27 iron balls, each 1.5" in diameter, and was devastating at 400 yards. Single canister from one gun would take out about a dozen men at each shot. When the enemy moved closer, double and even triple canister was used. For a video demonstration, see https://civil wartalk.com/threads/canister-shot-video.78404/.
45. Meyer, 230.
46. OR Ser. I, Vol. 11, 367, 378.
47. OR Ser. I, Vol. 11, 834.
48. Bogue, 82.
49. McCrady, 238; OR Ser. I, Vol. 11, 861; Bogue, 82.
50. OR Ser. I, Vol. 11, 856.
51. Hager Diary.
52. Pohanka, *Vortex*, 259.
53. Pohanka, *Vortex*, 261.
54. Pohanka, *Vortex*, 261.
55. Pohanka, *Vortex*, 259.
56. Pohanka, *Vortex*, 262.
57. Wikipedia informs us that "fuze" is the proper spelling for fuses that explode artillery shells.
58. Pohanka, *Vortex*, 262.
59. Pohanka, *Vortex*, 263.
60. OR Ser. I, Vol. 11, 873; Marshall was more or less correct, viz.: the 10th New York, 9th Massachusetts, 62d Pennsylvania, 14th New York, 1st U.S. Sharpshooters, 9th Pennsylvania Reserves, and 10th Pennsylvania Reserves, the 2d Pennsylvania Reserves, and the 6th U.S. were all in the vicinity.
61. OR Ser. I, Vol. 11, 873.
62. Cowtan, 92.
63. Mattison, 162.
64. Cowtan, 92.
65. OR Ser. I, Vol. 11, 873.
66. Martin, *Adirondack*, 67.
67. Cowtan, 92.
68. Mattison, 162–164.
69. Davenport, 211.
70. "Charge Bayonets" is a command that starts a bayonet charge. The weapon is held by the right side, with the bayonet forward, and the whole line advances, first at a walk, and then at the double-quick, maintaining, at all costs, the line. It is not a boiling gaggle of screaming soldiers, but a controlled assault, and absolutely terrifying.
71. Davenport, 212.
72. OR Ser. I, Vol. 11, 874.
73. Davenport, 212.
74. Davenport, 212.
75. OR Ser. I, Vol. 11, 874; Davenport, 212.
76. Marshall, OR Ser. I, Vol. 11, 874.
77. OR Ser. I, Vol. 11, 359, 855.

Chapter 11

1. OR Ser. I, Vol. 11, 883.
2. OR Ser. I, Vol. 11, 883.
3. Clarke, Vol. 1, 367.
4. OR Ser. I, Vol. 11, 887.

5. OR Ser. I, Vol. 11, 888.
6. Cowtan, 92.
7. Cowtan, 92.
8. Cowtan, 93.
9. Cowtan, 93.
10. OR Ser. I, Vol. 11, 893.
11. OR Ser. I, Vol. 11, 893.
12. OR Ser. I, Vol. 11, 313.
13. Boatswain's Branch turns into Boatswain's Swamp at Boatswain's Run.
14. Harrer, 49.
15. Ripley, 42.
16. Coffin, 135.
17. OR Ser. I, Vol. 11, 891.
18. OR Ser. I, Vol. 11, 893, 897.
19. OR Ser. I, Vol. 11, 893. Lane says he marched his men out, and was ordered back in by one of Powell Hill's staff, but this is an odd maneuver in the face of the enemy.
20. OR Ser. I, Vol. 11, 605.
21. OR Ser. I, Vol. 11, 605; Harding, 50.
22. Harding, 30.
23. OR Ser. I, Vol. 11, 888. Lt. Col. Haywood says that General Ewell moved Campbell and his men "about a quarter mile" to a position south of the road. This puts the 7th near the Parsons House.
24. Buck, 41. Buck says that he fought Federals behind breastworks, which ended at Boatswain's Run, so the 13th had to be south of Boatswain's Run.
25. Hardy, 71.
26. Hardy, 71.
27. Thomas, 67.
28. Hardy, 71.
29. Its members shot and mortally wounded Stonewall Jackson at Chancellorsville in May of 1863.
30. OR Ser. I, Vol. 11, 891.
31. OR Ser. I, Vol. 11, 278; Thomas, 61–62.
32. OR Ser. I, Vol. 11, 313.
33. The 11th U.S. was supporting Martin's battery; theoretically they could have done the same.
34. Powell, *5 AC*, 79.
35. Woodward, 125.
36. Woodward, 125–126.
37. Woodward, 125.
38. Several regiments in Griffin's Woods claim to have witnessed this ruse. There is no record of any Confederate units wearing blue uniforms.
39. Woodward, 126.
40. Woodward, 126. The text says from "fragments of other regiments."
41. Martin, *Adirondack*, 67; Woodward, 125.
42. Woodward, 127.
43. Pluskat, 30.
44. Harrer, 49.
45. Thomas, 66.
46. Harrer, 50.
47. Thomas, 61–62.
48. Ripley, 42.
49. Hoke's OR Report says he lost 75 men during the whole campaign.
50. OR Ser. I, Vol. 11, 891.
51. 40 percent of his campaign losses.

Chapter 12

1. OR Ser. I, Vol. 11, 772.
2. Lemmon, *CV 8*, 66. There may have been some

tension between Hood and Archer. One of Archer's men met Hood in Boatswain's Creek, but Hood never even mentions Archer's participation in the fight or the breakthrough.

3. OR Ser. I, Vol. 11, 697.

4. OR Ser. I, Vol. 11, 757, 772, 780. Wilcox says it was only one regiment with the brigade in close support. See also York, OR Supp., Vol. 11, 445.

5. OR Ser. I, Vol. 11, 577.

6. OR Ser. I, Vol. 11, 849. Starke says the 60th was in close column of companies, a non-combat formation. A lieutenant of the 40th Virginia picked up the 55th's flag, so they were probably near each other. At Frazier's Farm, according to Field, the 55th and 60th operated together and the 40th, 47th and 22nd Virginia Battalion together. The 47th says it was in Field's first line in Mayo's OR Report, 845.

7. Carmichael, 16. Four of Pegram's guns were unserviceable after Beaver Dam Creek, and he had lost almost two-thirds of his men. Carmichael says he replaced them overnight with four "captured Yankee Napoleons," citing SHSP 21, 364, which erroneously claims that the four guns were captured at Beaver Dam Creek. No guns were captured at that place; Pegram most probably rendered his guns serviceable during the night.

8. Hodges, 38.

9. M'Comb, CV 23, 161.

10. Kelley, 22.

11. Fulton, 37.

12. Benton, CV 15, 507.

13. Hodges, 38.

14. Fulton, 37.

15. Fulton, War Reminiscences, 37; the 2nd Maine took the 5th Alabama Battalion's flag. The 13th New York was immediately south of the 2nd Maine and took the 1st Tennessee's flag, so the 1st had to be to the right of the 5th. The 14th Tennessee later would be in the area of the artillery behind the line, indicating that they too were usually on the right of the 5th.

16. Bertera, "Dear Thad."

17. OR Ser. I, Vol. 11, 301.

18. OR Ser. I, Vol. 11, 304.

19. OR Ser. I, Vol. 11, 309.

20. OR Ser. I, Vol. 11, 879.

21. OR Ser. I, Vol. 11, 879.

22. OR Ser. I, Vol. 11, 845.

23. Dewberry, 19.

24. Stone, Rhode Island, 113.

25. Shell is a hollow iron ball filled with explosive and fused to explode after a set number of seconds. Shrapnel, or spherical case, is more or less the same thing, but is filled with round lead balls and a smaller bursting charge. The difference is that shell spreads large chunks of iron widely, due to the large bursting charge, causing horrific tearing wounds. Shrapnel sends more, but smaller, chunks, plus the lead balls, into a smaller area due to the smaller bursting charge.

26. SHSP 29, 417.

27. O'Sullivan, 28; OR Ser. I, Vol. 11, 849.

28. SHSP 29, 417.

29. OR Ser. I, Vol. 11, 282, 879. This is one of the few instances where both sides actually agree on what happened.

30. OR Ser. I, Vol. 51, Part 1, 118.

31. Lemmon, CV, 66; M'Comb, 161; Ledbetter, SHSP, 353.

32. Ledbetter, CV 1, 245.

33. OR Ser. I, Vol. 11, 849.

34. M'Comb, CV 23, 161.

35. Fulton, 37.

36. Ledbetter, CV 29, 252.

37. OR Ser. I, Vol. 11, 842.

38. M'Comb, CV 23, 161.

39. Ledbetter, CV 29, 352.

40. Tolley, CV 11, 54.

41. Ledbetter, CV 29, 352.

42. OR Ser. I, Vol. 11, 309.

43. OR Ser. I, Vol. 11, 897.

44. OR Ser. I, Vol. 11, 845; O'Sullivan, 28.

45. OR Ser. I, Vol. 11, 772–773.

46. OR Ser. I, Vol. 11, 781.

47. OR Ser. I, Vol. 11, 781.

48. OR Ser. I, Vol. 11, 316.

49. 5th Mass. Battery, 331.

50. OR Ser. I, Vol. 11, 316, 339, 344.

51. OR Ser. I, Vol. 11, 291.

52. OR Ser. I, Vol. 11, 301.

53. OR Ser. I, Vol. 11, 304.

54. OR Ser. I, Vol. 11, 316–317.

55. O'Sullivan, 28.

Chapter 13

1. OR Ser. I Vol. 11, 605.

2. Coles, 46.

3. Tinsley, 401.

4. Hotchkiss Papers, Dabney to Henderson letter. This makes sense; Jackson gave Harman the order about 1:30.

5. OR Ser. I, Vol. 11, 362.

6. OR Ser. I, Vol. 11, 568.

7. Evander Law, B&L, 362.

8. Named for Wade Hampton III, and a South Carolina politician, who raised it. According to Wikipedia, in his youth, Hampton is said to have killed bears with just a knife. He was one of the largest slaveholders in the South. Hampton himself was off with the cavalry of the Legion.

9. Ares Diary.

10. Kyle Duffer. "Double-quick" is a jog, not a sprint; the point is to move faster but still be able to fight at the end of the run.

11. As to Hood, Laswell, 110; as to Law, Chambers, 510.

12. Hunter, CV 31, 112.

13. Hamby, CV 14, 183.

14. Laswell, 110.

15. Hamby, CV 14, 183; Crozier, CV 25, 556; Fields, HL; Laswell, 110.

16. Coles, Huntsville, 46.

17. Hankins, CV 20, 571.

18. Coles, Huntsville, 47.

19. Crozier, CV 25, 556.

20. Lane, 169.

21. Fletcher, RP, 23.

22. Chambers CV 19, 510.

23. McClendon, 72.

24. Cooke, REL, 83.

25. Cooke, 46.

26. Cooke, REL, 84.

27. Hotchkiss Papers, Dabney to Henderson letter.

28. OR Ser. I, Vol. 11, 492.

29. The flu and inflammation of the testicles, respectively.

30. , J.J. Woodward, 31.
31. OR, Ser. I, Vol. 11, 492.
32. Civil war infantry did not fight much after night-fall. Since targets could not be identified in the dark, fratricide was a great danger, even if maneuvering thousands of men in the dark was successful.
33. Dobbins, 87; Lightsey.
34. Law, *B&L*, 363.
35. Maurin's Donaldsonville Artillery was behind Battle Groups Pickett and Wilcox, too far south for Law to pass. Braxton's Fredericksburg artillery was in the area, but lost no men and only a few horses, which is not "badly cut up." Andrews' 1st Maryland Artillery was on Powhite Creek firing away. It had to be Crenshaw's Battery; it was the only Confederate battery that had been damaged severely.
36. OR Ser. I, Vol. 11, 563.
37. OR Ser. I, Vol. 11, 614.
38. OR Ser. I, Vol. 11, 563.
39. Hamby, *CV* 14, 183.
40. Hood, *A&R*, 25.
41. Crozier *CV* 25, 557.
42. Stevens, 28–29.
43. Hamby, *CV* 14, 183.
44. Jones, *Campbell Brown*, 51.
45. OR Ser. I, Vol. 11, 595. Lawton says he was 1.5 miles away from the fighting when he got the word. This places him near the intersection of the two roads; as to finding Lawton, *Campbell Brown*, 51.
46. Bradwell, SHSP 24, 22.
47. OR Ser. I, Vol. 11, 595; Bradwell, 22.
48. White, *31st Georgia*, 24.
49. OR Ser. I, Vol. 11, 495.
50. White, *31st Georgia*, 26.
51. White, *31st Georgia*, 26.
52. Bradwell, SHSP 24, 21.
53. Murray, 50.
54. Bradwell, SHSP 24, 21.
55. OR Ser. I, Vol. 11, 505.
56. OR Ser. I, Vol. 11, 602.
57. OR Ser. I, Vol. 11, 603.
58. OR Ser. I, Vol. 11, 599.
59. OR Ser. I, Vol. 11, 504.
60. Bradwell, SHSP 24, 22.
61. Nichols, *Soldier's Story*, 41.
62. OR Ser. I, Vol. 11, 595.
63. Jones, *Campbell Brown*, 51.
64. Nichols, Dale, 16.
65. OR Ser. I, Vol. 11, 495.
66. Howard, 137, says he saw Harman as Winder's brigades changed front and wondered what he was doing there; Howard never saw Harmon giving Winder any orders. Howard denied ever seeing Dabney.
67. Howard, 137.
68. OR Ser. I, Vol. 11, 570.
69. Howard, 138.
70. OR Ser. I, Vol. 11, 614–615.
71. Dabney Map p. 447; OR Ser. I, Vol. 11, 570.
72. OR Ser. I, Vol. 11, 590.
73. OR Ser. I, Vol. 11, 624.
74. OR Ser. I, Vol. 11, 624.
75. OR Ser. I, Vol. 11, 649.
76. OR Ser. I, Vol. 11, 624.
77. OR Ser. I, Vol. 11, 349.
78. OR Ser. I, Vol. 11, 869.
79. OR Ser. I, Vol. 11, 867.
80. OR Ser. I, Vol. 11, 864.
81. OR Ser. I, Vol. 11, 624–625.

82. OR Ser. I, Vol. 11, 631.
83. OR Ser. I, Vol. 11, 631.
84. OR Supplement, 167.
85. OR Ser. I, Vol. 11, 631.
86. OR Ser. I, Vol. 11, 638.
87. Longstreet, *B&L*, 399.
88. Goree, 93.
89. OR Ser. I, Vol. 11, 756.
90. Hinsdale, 38.
91. OR Ser. I, Vol. 11, 780.
92. OR Ser. I, Vol. 11, 316.
93. OR Ser. I, Vol. 11, 780.
94. Walker, 84.
95. Longstreet, *B&L*, 399.
96. OR Ser. I, Vol. 11, 772.
97. Harrison, 28; OR Ser. I, Vol. 11, 757.
98. OR Ser. I, Vol. 11, 317, 327, 344.
99. OR Ser. I, Vol. 11, 780.
100. OR Ser. I, Vol. 11, 773.
101. Ingle, 337.
102. OR Ser. I, Vol. 11, 757.
103. All of the accounts from Pryor's brigade mention the horrendous first blast, indicating they were in one line. Featherston's reinforcement of Pryor also indicates this.
104. Coppens' Zouaves were another Zouave battalion from Louisiana, and were not Wheat's Battalion of Zouaves. They were consolidated with the St. Paul Chasseurs a Pied and lost 50 percent casualties at Seven Pines. They may have been wearing bits and pieces of their Zouave or Chasseur uniforms, which were at this time almost a year old. 1st Louisiana Battalion.
105. Hodges, 39–40.
106. OR Ser. I, Vol. 11, 757.
107. OR Ser. I, Vol. 11, 773.
108. OR Ser. I, Vol. 11, 772.
109. OR Ser. I, Vol. 11, 757; Longstreet, *B&L*, 399.
110. Walker, 84.
111. Govan, 31.
112. Hartwell, 2. The ground where Bucklin's guns were goes down from north to south. The 7th Pennsylvania Reserves said that the battery horses' blood was running downhill into their position. Accordingly, the 7th had to be to the south of Bucklin's guns.

Chapter 14

1. Reese, 83.
2. Harrer, 50; Thomas, 67. Both the 14th New York and 9th Massachusetts mention seeing hundreds of Zouaves on the ground; this could only have been from the northern part of Griffin's Woods.
3. OR Ser. I, Vol. 11, 373–374.
4. OR Ser. I, Vol. 11, 349.
5. OR Ser. I, Vol. 11, 349.
6. OR Ser. I, Vol. 11, 387.
7. OR Ser. I, Vol. 11, 387.
8. OR Ser. I, Vol. 11, 856.
9. OR Ser. I, Vol. 11, 867.
10. OR Ser. I, Vol. 11, 856, 869.
11. OR Ser. I, Vol. 11, 868.
12. OR Ser. I, Vol. 11, 382.
13. Davenport, 214; Pohanka, "Charge Bayonet," 36.
14. Lane, 146.
15. Harding, 51.
16. Davenport, 214; Woodward, 222.
17. OR Ser. I, Vol. 11, 378.

18. Urban, 119.
19. OR Ser. I, Vol. 11, 383.
20. OR Ser. I, Vol. 11, 371, 372, 376.
21. Myers, 231.
22. Myers, 231.
23. Myers, 332.
24. Myers, 233.
25. Hill, *Our Boys*, 304.
26. Myers, 234.
27. Author's experience.
28. Myers, 234; OR Ser. I Vol. 11, 379; Pohanka, "Charge Bayonets," 38.
29. Evans, 43.
30. OR Ser. I, Vol. 11, 377.
31. The 13th Pennsylvania Reserves only contained about 150 men. Glover, 92. It attached itself to the 5th Pennsylvania Reserves. Glover, 93.
32. The 2nd Pennsylvania Reserves had been sent to Griffin's Woods.
33. The 5th New York fez is not like that of a Shriner, but rather crushed down to form a skullcap. Author's experience.
34. Pohanka, "Charge Bayonets," 39.
35. Urban, 119.
36. Urban, 120.
37. Hill, *Our Boys*, 303.
38. OR Ser. I, Vol. 11, 358, 362.
39. OR Ser. I, Vol. 11, 358.
40. OR Ser. I, Vol. 11, 286.
41. Hassler, 38.
42. OR Ser. I, Vol. 11, 515.
43. Hassler, 38.
44. OR Ser. I, Vol. 11, 286.
45. Evans, 43. Since Evans was in the 12th U.S., he was only two regiments removed from the right end of the entire Corps' line, making the "left" almost anyone.
46. OR Ser. I, Vol. 11, 625.
47. Clark, *NC Regiments*, Vol. 1, 165.
48. The 4th North Carolina mustered only 150 men.
49. OR Ser. I, Vol. 11, 631.
50. Clark, *NC Regiments*, Vol. 1, 243.
51. Taylor, *Drive*, 189.
52. Evans, 44.
53. Evans, 43.
54. Evans, 44.
55. OR Ser. I Vol. 11, 286.
56. Evans, 44.
57. Hager Diary.
58. Being "flanked" is what happened when the enemy is to the left or right of your unit, and you can't shoot back without maneuvering to bring your firepower to bear on him. You get slaughtered until you change front or "skedaddle."
59. Hager Diary.
60. Evans, 44.
61. Evans, 44.
62. Evans, 44.
63. Hill, *B&L*, 360.
64. Evans, 44.
65. OR Ser. I, Vol. 11, 245. Tidball claims that he retired because his "caissons were endangered" when the Confederates were at the top of the hill, and that he was almost out of ammunition. Collins 4th U.S., OR Ser. I, Vol. 11, 364, confirms the ammunition issue, but says they all retired when they discerned that the infantry on their left had fallen back.
66. "In the air" is a military term of art. It means that the end of your line is vulnerable for flanking, and is a

situation to be avoided if at all possible. For example, McClellan's right flank was "in the air" north of the Chickahominy on June 25, which is why Lee attacked it.
67. "Daniel Harvey Hill," Wikipedia.
68. OR Ser. I, Vol. 11, 625.
69. Pohanka, "Charge Bayonet," 33.
70. OR Ser. I, Vol. 11, 447.
71. OR Ser. I, Vol. 11, 70, 75.
72. OR Ser. I, Vol. 11, 54.
73. OR Ser. I, Vol. 11, 75.
74. Gilmer Map. Fair Oaks is 3 miles from the Grapevine Bridge, which is a mile from Barker's Mill. French says his line was ¾ mile from Barker's Mill. Even if French cut the corner after the Grapevine Bridge, at 1 mile per hour, it was still about a 3.5-hour trip.
75. OR Ser. I, Vol. 11, 641. Garland says he was ordered to the support of the rest of the division, so he moved last.
76. OR Ser. I, Vol. 11, 625.
77. The 12th Georgia claimed vaguely to have captured artillery: Adams, *Post of Honor*, 210. The 52nd Virginia was with the Stonewall Brigade and not only captured cannons, but also Union repeating guns, which were with Bartlett's Brigade, Slocum's Division; Driver, 35. Armstrong, 36, describes the 25th Virginia as going with a guide to attack guns from the side while 3 North Carolina regiments attacked in front. The targeted guns were certainly Hayden's section of Edward's Battery. The 25th Virginia mission account is unique to the three regiments. The other four regiments of Elzey's Brigade were either with Ewell at the Parsons House or with the 31st Virginia near New Cold Harbor.
78. OR Ser. I, Vol. 11, 625.
79. Driver, 35.
80. OR Ser. I, Vol. 11, 625.
81. OR Ser. I, Vol. 11, 641.
82. OR Ser. I, Vol. 11, 864, 867, 869.
83. OR Ser. I, Vol. 11, 883.
84. Douglas, 103–104.
85. *CV* 1, 19.
86. Antietam on the Web.
87. The American Civil War, Virginia Charlottesville Artillery Battery.
88. Nicholas, 123.
89. OR Ser. I, Vol. 11, 556.
90. Nicholas, 125.
91. OR Ser. I, Vol. 11, 652.
92. OR Ser. I, Vol. 11, 556.
93. The exact number of men is impossible to calculate, but in rough numbers, Garland, 1,500 men; George Anderson, 1,000 men; Rodes, 1,000 men; Gregg, 1,500 men; Branch, 1,200 men; Elzey, 1,000 men.
94. Townshend, 132–133.

Chapter 15

1. OR Ser. I, Vol. 11, 890.
2. Dula, 3.
3. OR Ser. I, Vol. 11, 898. Pender says the 16th and 22nd entered the Union camps. Lt. Col Franklin of the 38th says that he was in support. OR Supplement, 457.
4. OR Ser. I, Vol. 11, 890. Pender says he found a "fragment" of a regiment. Berdan, OR Ser. I, Vol. 11, 278, says that this second attack also occurred on his left, where the 18th was. Cowan, 18th North Carolina, OR Ser. I, Vol. 11, 891, says: "Again and again was that posi-

tion assaulted, and again and again we were repulsed by vastly superior numbers." The "vast numbers" were the U.S. Sharpshooters with Sharps Infantry Rifles.

5. OR Ser. I, Vol. 11, 278.
6. OR Ser. I, Vol. 11, 890.
7. "Truman Seymour," Wikipedia.
8. OR Ser. I, Vol. 11, 890.
9. Ent, location 2755.
10. Hinsdale Diary.
11. OR Ser. I, Vol. 11, 898.
12. OR Ser. I, Vol. 11, 422.
13. Veil, 15.
14. Veil, 16.
15. OR Ser. I, Vol. 11, 90, 422.
16. OR Ser. I, Vol. 11, 373–4.
17. OR Ser. I, Vol. 11, 422.
18. OR Ser. I, Vol. 11, 890.
19. Miller, 21.
20. OR Ser. I, Vol. 11, 424.
21. Miller, 21.
22. Young, SHSP 31 p. 277.
23. These are the guns that Johnson had at Antietam, two months later. Much of the artillery present at Gaines' Mill was rearmed with one or more of the 22 guns captured by the Confederates that day.
24. OR Ser. I, Vol. 11, 903.
25. OR Ser. I, Vol. 11, 456.
26. The other three (12th Georgia, 25th Virginia, and 52nd Virginia) had been tasked with battery support back at Old Cold Harbor.
27. OR Ser. I, Vol. 11, 888.
28. "James A. Walker," Wikipedia. *General* Walker was awarded an honorary degree by VMI after the war.
29. Buck, 41.
30. Jones, SHSP 9. observed that one man from the 13th Virginia fell in later with the "56th" Virginia. Elzey had the 52nd and 58th Virginia. The 58th's casualties are more reflective of close fighting.
31. Caldwell, *Stonewall Jim*, 52.
32. Buck, 41.
33. Caldwell, 50, says "knoll." A member of Trimble's Brigade said a house disrupted their line.
34. Buck, 41.
35. Caldwall, *Stonewall Jim*, 52.
36. It is unclear whether the Louisiana brigade arrived before Trimble, or vice versa. Since no Louisiana source mentions Trimble, Louisiana probably arrived first.
37. OR Ser. I, Vol. 11, 614. These were probably from Field's Brigade. Later references refer to Field's men refusing to join the last attack.
38. OR Ser. I, Vol. 11, 605.
39. Jones, *Campbell Brown*, 52, says Cantey and two companies came out of the woods with the 7th, 8th, and 9th Louisiana regiments. Cantey and his remnant would wind up with the12th South Carolina of Gregg's Brigade. OR Ser. I, Vol. 11, 985.
40. United States Military Academy, 1854; mentioned for gallantry, Gettysburg, 1863; killed in action at the Battle of Plymouth, April 18, 1864. https://www.findagrave.com/cgi-bin/fg.cgi?page=gr&GRid=10901303
41. Nisbett, 64.
42. McClendon, 72.
43. OR Ser. I, Vol. 11, 605.
44. OR Ser. I, Vol. 11, 605.
45. Roby says it was Brigadier Hays, but he was a colonel in the 7th Louisiana at the time; Seymour was a colonel in the 9th but was commanding the brigade,

and it seems more likely that Seymour was addressing the "Louisianans."

46. Roby, *CV*, 548.
47. Caldwell, *Stonewall Jim*, 52.
48. OR Ser. I, Vol. 11, 420.
49. OR Ser. I, Vol. 11, 421.
50. Ent, Location 2907.
51. Caldwell, 54.
52. Caldwell, 54.
53. Walshe, *CV*, 54.
54. Walshe, *CV*, 54.
55. Handerson, 45.
56. Handerson, 45.
57. Walshe *CV*, 54.
58. Handerson, 48.
59. Jones, *Lee's Tigers*, 104.
60. Handerson, 45–46.
61. Walshe *CV*, 54.
62. OR Ser. I, Vol. 11, 605.
63. McClendon, 73, says that Lt. Col. Trentlen had command of the "left wing," which was at least Companies K, B, and one other.
64. McClendon says these were New York Zouaves, but Gosline's Zouaves, Newton's Brigade, were in the area and closer. However, the 5th New York was retiring at the time behind the Adams House.
65. The rear rank in a line of battle is required to maintain a close distance from the front rank, so that the concussion of the rear ranker's gun does not "ring the bell" of the front rank, nor spray him with burnt powder from the muzzle blast. Failing to do this is always the rear ranker's fault.
66. McClendon, 74–76.
67. McClendon, 76–77.
68. Nisbett, 64.
69. Lane, 172.
70. OR Ser. I, Vol. 11, 114, 420.
71. Lane, 172.
72. Nisbett, 64.
73. Martin, *Road to Glory*, 109.
74. Martin, *Road to Glory*, 109.
75. Jones, *Campbell Brown*, 52–53. Panicked troops can indeed carry their supports with them. At a reenactment at McDowell, Virginia, ca. 2004, the author saw this exact phenomenon. We were lined up in column of companies on the main street of the town; the Confederates swarmed forward at the lead company, which broke, panicking two other companies behind them.
76. OR Ser. I, Vol. 11, 291.

Chapter 16

1. Veil, 16.
2. Dabney to Hotchkiss.
3. OR Ser. I, Vol. 11, 495.
4. OR Ser. I, Vol. 11, 495.
5. OR Ser. I, Vol. 11, 599.
6. OR Ser. I, Vol. 11, 502. The 5 right companies were directed by an aide to Gen. Ewell, probably Campbell Brown, as was the 13th Georgia.
7. OR Ser. I, Vol. 11, 505. Berry says that he was near the capture of the 4th New Jersey, which puts him near the intersection of the Boatswain's Run and Boatswain's Creek, and that General Lawton was present with them at times. Nichols says the 61st was on the right of the brigade, after being moved to the right, and was little engaged. Accordingly, the 61st was ahead of the 60th,

went in to its left, and then was moved to the right behind the 60th. These are the regiments with Enfields. The 13th Georgia had Mississippi rifles.

   8. OR Ser. I, Vol. 11, 502, 504.

   9. OR Ser. I, Vol. 11, 225.

  10. OR Ser. I, Vol. 11, 456.

  11. The 95th wore a "Pennsylvania" style Zouave uniform: blue pants, blue jacket waist-length with a swallowtail front, red piping, and many buttons.

  12. NYSMM, 31st Regiment.

  13. 32nd Regiment NYSMM; The incomplete Empire City Regiment and equally incomplete Cerro Gordo Legion were merged to form the 32nd. California State Military Museum.

  14. OR Ser. I, Vol. 11, 456.

  15. OR Ser. I, Vol. 11, 461.

  16. OR Ser. I, Vol. 11, 458.

  17. Conklin, Location 228.

  18. Conklin, 215, Pluskat, 30.

  19. OR Ser. I, Vol. 11, 313.

  20. Harrer, 50.

  21. OR Ser. I, Vol. 11, 460.

  22. OR Ser. I, Vol. 11, 461.

  23. Nichols, 42.

  24. OR Ser. I, Vol. 11, 458.

  25. It might also have been Voeglee; troops in the sunken part of the McGehee Road had been hit by friendly fire all day, viz., 5th New York, 2nd U.S.

  26. OR Ser. I, Vol. 11, 458.

  27. OR Ser. I, Vol. 11, 457, 458.

  28. Conklin, Location 216.

  29. Conklin, Location 216.

  30. Conklin, Location 218.

  31. Conklin, Location 219.

  32. Conklin, Location 220.

  33. Conklin, Location 221.

  34. Conklin, Location 220.

  35. OR Ser. I, Vol. 11, 459.

  36. Harding, 51.

  37. Pollard, Major General Arnold Elzey.

  38. Hale, *CV* 30, 252.

  39. Conklin, Location 222.

  40. Conklin, Location 222.

  41. Conklin, Location 220.

  42. Conklin, Location 228.

  43. OR Ser. I, Vol. 11, 460.

  44. Robins, 7.

  45. Conklin, Location 220.

  46. OR Ser. I, Vol. 11, 460.

  47. OR Ser. I, Vol. 11, 458.

  48. Conklin, Location 225.

  49. Conklin, Location 225.

  50. Conklin, Location 227.

  51. Conklin, Location 227.

  52. Bilby, "Some of Us," 12.

  53. Bilby, "Some of Us," 12.

  54. Bilby, "Some of Us," 12.

  55. Bilby, "Some of Us," 13.

  56. OR Ser. I, Vol. 11, 510.

  57. "Agar Gun," Wikipedia.

  58. Bilby, "Load the Hopper."

  59. Daniel Russ, "The 'Army in a Box.'"

  60. Hill, Harvey, *Bethel to Sharpsburg*, 123.

  61. 96th Infantry Regiment Pennsylvania Volunteers, pa-roots.com; schulylkillcountymilitary history.blogspot.com.

  62. https://www.inmemoryglobal.com/remembrance/2015/11/edward-burd-grubb-jr/.

  63. Bilby, "Load the Hopper."

  64. Bilby, "Some of Us," 13.

  65. Bilby, "Some of Us," 12.

  66. OR Ser. I, Vol. 11, 438.

  67. Martin, *Hexamer*, 2.

  68. Bilby, "Some of Us," 12.

  69. OR Ser. I, Vol. 11, 444, 445.

  70. Woodward, *History of the Third*, 89.

  71. 11th Pennsylvania Reserves, pa.roots.com.

  72. OR Ser. I, Vol. 11, 282, 291.

  73. Bilby and the 2nd's OR Report say a Michigan regiment. The 4th Michigan at the time had just been relieved by the 4th New Jersey and the 11th Pennsylvania Reserves, so they did not need any more support. These two latter were both captured, but the 2nd was not, so they were not with them. Martindale had the 1st Michigan as his southmost regiment. Butterfield had the 16th Michigan, as his leftmost up-top regiment, but they had barely been engaged all day, and had little need for relief; Butterfield had two more of his own regiments to do that, and had sent the 7th Pennsylvania Reserves away as unneeded. The 1st Michigan is the best candidate.

  74. Bilby, "Some of Us," 12.

  75. Dale Nichols, 16.

  76. Dale Nichols, 16.

Chapter 17

   1. Walton, 159.

   2. Pohanka, "Charge Bayonets," 39.

   3. OR Ser. I, Vol. 11, 379; Cowtan, 95.

   4. Davenport, 217.

   5. Davenport, 217.

   6. OR Ser. I, Vol. 11, 370.

   7. Evans, 44.

   8. Ronan, 56.

   9. OR Ser. I, Vol. 11, 376.

  10. Pyne Letter.

  11. OR Ser. I, Vol. 11, 370.

  12. The Sharpshooters probably attached themselves to the 13th Pennsylvania Reserves because the latter had an ammunition supply for the Sharpshooters' Sharps Infantry Rifles.

  13. OR Ser. I, Vol. 11, 417.

  14. Ripley, 116.

  15. Krick, *14th South Carolina*, 8.

  16. OR Ser. I, Vol. 11, 638.

  17. Hobson Papers, LoV.

  18. Urban, 120.

  19. Urban, 120–124.

  20. OR Ser. I, Vol. 11, 413.

  21. Eberly, 81–82.

  22. Urban, 122; Hill, *Our Boys*, 305–307.

  23. Brandt, 80–81.

  24. Smith, *Anson Guards*, 103.

  25. Taylor, *Drive the Enemy*, 189.

  26. Smith, *Anson Guards*, 103.

  27. OR Ser. I, Vol. 11, 869.

  28. Smith, *Anson Guards*, 103.

  29. Brandt, 81.

  30. OR Supp., 437.

  31. OR Supp., 437.

  32. OR Ser. I, Vol. 11, 631.

  33. Armstrong, *52d Virginia*, 36.

  34. OR Ser. I, Vol. 11, 286.

  35. OR Ser. I, Vol. 11, 427.

  36. Paroots.com, 12th Reserves.

37. OR Ser. I, Vol. 11, 287.
38. OR Supp., Vol. 11, 437.
39. Clark, *NC Troops*, Vol. 1, 616.
40. Clark, *NC Troops*, Vol. 1, 211.
41. OR Ser. I, Vol. 11, 644.
42. Hager Diary.
43. OR Ser. I, Vol. 11, 356–7; Hager Diary.
44. Curtis, p. 121.
45. OR Ser. I, Vol. 11, 356–7.
46. OR Ser. I,Vol. 11, 356–7. Edwards reports that 8 out of 16 horses in this section fell. Dead or wounded horses must be cut out of the harnesses so that the survivors can haul the gun away.
47. OR Supp., 437.
48. Curtis, 122–123.
49. Edwards' report is unclear as to whether any of Brownson's guns were actually lost. By focusing on the horse problems with one gun, it implies that the other was lost. However, it is also possible that the other gun successfully retired. In his report, General Barry, Chief of Ordnance, OR Ser. I, Vol. 11, 282, says that 23 guns were lost, but his data only sums to 22. According to Barry, Edwards lost only the two guns of Hayden's section, making the 23rd gun a mystery, unless Edwards lost three, not two guns. The battery was at Antietam in September with 4 guns. http://antietam.aotw.org/officers.php?unit_id=516, but one could have been replaced. Col. Hunt, Chief of the Artillery Reserve, deftly omits any mention of lost guns in his report. OR Ser. I, Vol. 11, 236. Edwards is frank about losing Hayden's section; Brownson probably saved both guns.
50. OR Ser. I, Vol. 11, 356.
51. OR Ser. I, Vol. 11, 287.
52. Curtis, 125.
53. OR Ser. I, Vol. 11, 447.
54. Hager Letter.
55. Curtis, 124.
56. Curtis, 125.
57. OR Ser. I, Vol. 11, 449.
58. Curtin, 123.
59. OR Ser. I, Vol. 11, 644.
60. Curtin, 123.
61. Curtis, 124.
62. Hager Letter.
63. *Richmond Daily Whig*, July 8, 1862.
64. John Saylor.
65. Curtis, 127.
66. Foard Papers.
67. OR Supp., 437.
68. Bradwell, *CV* 24, 23.
69. OR Ser. I, Vol. 11, 869.
70. OR Ser. I, Vol. 11, 893.
71. Krick, *14th South Carolina*, 8; OR Ser. I, Vol. 11, 893, 887.
72. OR Supp., 437.

Chapter 18

1. Glasgow, 123.
2. Longstreet, *B&L*, 399.
3. Longstreet's Division

Longstreet's Division	9,501
Less Kemper	1,469
Plus Whiting	4,000
Plus Archer	1,000
Plus BG Douglas	840
Plus BG Trimble	952
Total	17,762

Longstreet's divisional numbers would be diminished by rear echelon troops and artillerymen not engaged, but unorganized stragglers from Powell Hill's Division would augment the lower number.

4. Easton's Battery A, Pennsylvania Light Artillery (4 Napoleons)
   Cooper's Battery B, Pennsylvania Light Artillery (4 Parrotts)
   Kerns' Battery G, Pennsylvania Light Artillery (6 howitzers)
   DeHart's Battery C, 5th U.S. Artillery (6 Napoleons)
5. Davis, 55.
6. OR Ser. I, Vol. 11, 420.
7. Bertera, Dear Thad, 2.
8. OR Ser. I, Vol. 11, 420.
9. Woodward, 90.
10. Harper, 119.
11. OR Ser. I, Vol. 11, 443.
12. Bennett, 57, who says that the relatively unengaged 13th New York was resupplied with ammunition. If Martindale was bright enough to resupply one regiment, he probably resupplied the rest.
13. Hartwell, 2; PaRoots.com, 7th Reserves.
14. OR Ser. I, Vol. 11, 316.
15. 5th Mass. Battery, 324.
16. McClendon, 77.
17. Buck, 41.
18. 13thva.com.
19. OR Ser. I, Vol. 11, 606.
20. Caldwell, 51.
21. Jones, *Campbell Brown*, 53.
22. Jones, *Campbell Brown*, 53.
23. OR Ser. I, Vol. 11, 599.
24. Murray, 61.
25. OR Ser. I, Vol. 11, 614.
26. Sherrill, Location 4227.
27. Sherrill, Location 4227.
28. Dobbins, 87.
29. Walker, 84.
30. OR Ser. I, Vol. 11, 773.
31. Bigbee, 357.
32. Simpson, unreferenced notes, 8.
33. Law, 363.
34. Law, 352.
35. OR Ser. I, Vol. 11, 568.
36. OR Ser. I, Vol. 11, 568.
37. Davis, 50, citing "Chickahominie."
38. OR Supp., Vol. 11, 433.
39. Todd, *CV* 6, 565; 1st Texas was to the left and rear of 4th Texas; Glover, 18, and Todd, First Texas Regiment, make clear that their experience was unique.
40. These two companies are what several have referred to as the left wing of the 18th Georgia. Since their experience is closer to that of the 5th Texas, they are included here, rather than with the other eight. The separation of these two parts of is probably what caused Hood to overestimate the number of guns his men had taken.
41. NP, 20.
42. Brantley, 9.
43. Brantley, 9.
44. Bigbee, *CV* 7, 357.
45. Stevens, 28.
46. OR Supp., Vol. 11, 433.
47. Brantley, 9.
48. OR Supp., Vol. 11, 433.
49. Simpson, unreferenced notes, 8.

50. Govan, 31.
51. Glover, 18.
52. Schardt, *CV* 7, 55.
53. Chambers, *CV* 19, 511.
54. Clark, *NC Troops*, Vol. 1, 304.
55. Hankins, *CV* 20, 572.
56. NP, 19.
57. Coles, 47.
58. Law, 363.
59. Schmutz, 2709.
60. Coles, 47; Shardt, *CV* 7, 55.
61. Coles, 47.
62. Chambers, *CV* 19, 511.
63. Davis, 55.
64. 2nd Mississippi, S&S Database.
65. Hankins, *CV* 20, 572.
66. Davis, 55.
67. Davis, 55.
68. Davis, 55.
69. Hamby, *CV* 14, 184.
70. Hamby, *CV* 14, 184.
71. Davis, 55.
72. Crozier, *CV* 25, 556.
73. Crozier, *CV* 25, 556.
74. As soldiers in the line fall, gaps form; all the men in the line edge towards the flag in the center as they march, to "close" these gaps.
75. Hood, *A&R*, 27.
76. Hamby, *CV* 14, 184.
77. Hamby, *CV* 14, 184.
78. Davis, 55.
79. Polley, 46.
80. Hamby, *CV* 14, 184; Polley, *HTB*, 55.
81. Law, 363.
82. Coles, 48.
83. Coles, 47.
84. Hankins, 572.
85. Law, 363.
86. Law, 363.
87. OR Ser. I, Vol. 11, 896.
88. Cross, 31.
89. M'Comb, *CV* 3, 161.
90. M'Comb, *CV* 3, 161.
91. Musselman, 23.
92. O'Sullivan, 28.
93. Lemmon, *CV* 8, 66.
94. Tolley, *CV* 7, 54.
95. M'Comb, *CV* 3, 161.
96. None of these four commanders mention Archer's second attack. Longstreet says that the attack was made by Whiting and BG Pickett in *B&L*, 399. Law says R.H. Anderson's Brigade was on the right (*B&L*, 364) while Hood says that Jenkins was on the right (*A&R*, 28). Whiting, OR, 563, says the unit on the right of his division was Pickett's Brigade.
97. Govan, 32.
98. Longacre, 85.
99. Walker, *Life of Anderson*, 89.
100. Walker, 84.
101. Hunton, *CV* 7, 224.
102. Hunton, *CV* 7, 223.
103. Evander Law would ask for support and get R.H. Anderson's brigade. It crossed Boatswain's Creek where Pickett did, when the Yankees were long gone, deployed on both sides of Boatswain's Creek, and headed south-southeast, getting into a fight with the 16th New York and the 83rd Pennsylvania. This is covered in more detail later.

104. Woodward, Jr., 58.
105. Harrison, 28.
106. Cooper, *CV* 6, 472.
107. Harrison, *PM*, 29.
108. Wiley, *Big I*, 23.
109. Longacre, 86.
110. Harrison, *PM*, 29.
111. Longacre, 86.
112. Hunton, *CV* 7, 223.
113. Cooper, *CV* 6, 472.
114. Edwards, *Confederate Soldier*, 88.
115. Robertson, *18th Virginia*, 14.
116. Robertson, *18th Virginia*, 14.
117. Thos. M. Fowler papers, MOC.
118. Hamilton, *Shotwell*, 345–6.
119. Clarke, *CV* 7, 227.
120. Hunton, *CV* 7, 223.
122. Govan, 33.
123. Govan, 32.
124. Govan, 32. The identity of the officer is unknown, but Haskell's overall story is consistent with the northern end of Archer's men in the creek bottom. Perhaps it is a coincidence, but the 19th Georgia filed no report of this battle. Archer, OR p. 898, says that the Colonel of the 19th Georgia was killed at Mechanicsville and that the rest of the field officers of that regiment fell at Gaines' Mill. In fairness, the same thing can be said about the 1th and 7th Tennessee.
125. Govan, 32–33. This is too bizarre an incident to be fabricated. The identity of the skedaddling officer is an enigma.
126. Hamilton, *Shotwell*, 246.
127. OR Ser. I, Vol. 11, 735.
128. OR Ser. I, Vol. 11, 773.
129. OR Ser. I, Vol. 11, 773.
130. Hogan, *CV* 6, 568.
131. OR Ser. I, Vol. 11, 773.
132. OR Ser. I, Vol. 11, 780; Polley, 45, says, "Law's Brigade, it is likely, had by this time found its place and been repulsed. The only attack that was 'repulsed' was Pryor's."
133. OR Ser. I, Vol. 11, 757; Lemmon, 66.
134. OR Ser. I, Vol. 11, 780.
135. OR Ser. I, Vol. 11, 780.
136. Hurst, 11–12.
137. Jones, *Lee's Tigers*, 99–100.
138. Jones, *Lee's Tigers*, 99–100.
139. Hurst, 11–12.
140. OR Supp., Vol. 11, 446–7.
141. Wallace, 28.
142. Cooper, *CV* 6, 472.
143. OR Ser. I, Vol. 11, 780.
144. Williams, *CV* 7, 443–444.
145. Barrett, *Yankee Rebel*, 32–35.
146. Williams, *CV* 7, 443–444.
147. OR Ser. I, Vol. 11, 773.
148. OR Ser. I, Vol. 11, 773.
149. Burress, *CV* 7, 111.
150. OR Ser. I, Vol. 11, 781.

Chapter 19

1. OR Ser. I, Vol. 11, 599.
2. OR Ser. I, Vol. 11, 599.
3. Murray, 61.
4. Foster, 75.
5. OR Ser. I, Vol. 11, 602.

6. OR Ser. I, Vol. 11, 442–443.
7. OR Ser. I, Vol. 11, 614.
8. OR Ser. I, Vol. 11, 538.
9. OR Ser. I, Vol. 11, 614.
10. Riggs, p. 15.
11. OR Ser. I, Vol. 11, 614.
12. OR Ser. I, Vol. 11, 614.
13. Brantley, 10; Stevens, 28.
14. Simpson, unreferenced notes, 8.
15. Brantley, 9.
16. Schmutz, Location 2665.
17. Brantley, 15.
18. Simpson, unreferenced notes, 8.
19. NP, 20–21.
20. Brantley, 10.
21. Brantley, 9.
22. Schmutz, Location 2644.
23. Gibbs, 116.
24. Bilby, "Some of Us," 13.
25. Pa-roots, 11th Reserves.
26. Hamby, *CV* 14, 184.
27. Tolley, 54; M'Comb, 161.
28. Simpson, *HTB*, 120.
29. Polley, p. 47.
30. Davis, p. 55.
31. Hunter, *CV* 26, 112.
32. *Richmond Daily Whig*, August 8, 1862.
33. Lasswell, p. 110.
34. Davis, "Chickahominie," 51; Hankins, 572; Ares, 26; Polley, 45; Davis, 55.
35. Chambers, *CV* 19, 511.
36. Coles, 47–48.
37. Harper, 119.
38. OR Ser. I, Vol. 11, 296–7.
39. OR Ser. I, Vol. 11, 421.
40. Lemmon, *CV* 8, 66.
41. M'Comb, *CV* 3, 161.
42. M'Comb, *CV* 3, 161.
43. Lemmon, *CV* 8, 66.
44. M'Comb, *CV* 3, 161.
45. M'Comb, *CV* 3, 161.
46. Lemmon, *CV* 8, 66.
47. Tolley, *CV* 7, 54.
48. OR Ser. I, Vol. 11, 309.
49. Christiancy Diary, 4a.
50. OR Ser. I, Vol. 11, 309.
51. Wood, 23.
52. Clarke, *CV* 7, 227.
53. Wiley, *Big I*, 24.
54. Clarke, *CV* 7, 227.
55. Irby, 19.
56. Hamilton, *Shotwell*, 345–346.
57. Govan, 33.
58. OR Ser. I, Vol. 11, 611.
59. OR Ser. I, Vol. 11, 307.
60. Jones, *Lee's Tigers*, 99–100.
61. Barrett, 32.
62. Herbert, 10.
63. Williams, *CV* 7, 443–444.
64. Hogan, *CV* 6, 568.
65. Hurst, 11–12.
66. Barrett, 33.
67. OR Ser. I, Vol. 11, 344.
68. "Daniel Butterfield," Wikipedia.
69. Judson, 61.
70. Judson, 62.
71. Judson, 62.
72. Barrett, 32.
73. Barrett, 32.
74. Williams, *CV* 7, 443–444.
75. Herbert, 10.
76. OR Ser. I, Vol. 11, 339.
77. Corydon Warner Papers.

Chapter 20

1. OR Ser. I, Vol. 11, 602.
2. OR Ser. I, Vol. 11, 442.
3. Brantley, 10.
4. Brantley, 10.
5. Schmutz Location 2669.
6. NP, 20–21.
7. Coles, 47–48.
8. Hamby, 184; Davis, 55.
9. Polley, *CN*, 55; Polley, *HTB*, quoting "a member" of the 4th Texas, 47; Polley, *HTB*, 55; *Richmond Whig*, 2; Brantley, 1–12.
10. Polley, 47.
11. Polley, *HTB*, 47.
12. Polley, *HTB*, 47.
13. Polley, *CN*, 55.
14. Hood, *A&R*, 27; Hamby, 183; Davis, 56.
15. Davis, 56.
16. Davis, "Chickahomine," 51.
17. M'Comb, *CV* 23, 161.
18. OR Ser. I, Vol. 11, 282.
19. M'Comb, *CV* 23, 161.
20. OR Ser. I, Vol. 11, 282.
21. Benton, *CV* 11, 507.
22. O'Sullivan, 28.
23. Cooper, 472.
24. OR Ser. I, Vol. 11, 768.
25. Williams, 444.
26. The guns currently at the Watt House, Richmond National Battlefield Park, mark Hyde's location, though Hyde had ordnance rifles and the markers are Napoleons.
27. 5th Mass. Battery, 339; Lt. Scott says the road to his right was choked with fleeing infantry and artillery.
28. OR Ser. I, Vol. 11, 291.
29. OR Ser. I, Vol. 11, 301.
30. Parker, 120.
31. OR Ser. I, Vol. 11, 301.
32. Bennett, *M&S*, 57–58.
33. OR Ser. I, Vol. 11, 304–305.
34. Parker, 120.
35. OR Ser. I, Vol. 11, pp. 304–305.
36. OR Ser. I, Vol. 11, pp. 304–305.
37. Pa roots, 7th Reserves.
38. Ent, Location 2850.
39. Ent, Location 2870–71.
40. Ent, Location 2870–71.
41. Ent, Location. 2889.
42. Ent, Location 2889.
43. Ent, Location 2889.
44. Pa roots, 7th Reserves.
45. 5th Mass. Battery, 347.
46. 5th Mass. Battery, 342.
47. 5th Mass. Battery, 347.
48. 5th Mass. Battery, 334.
49. 5th Mass. Battery, 349.
50. 5th Mass. Battery, 340.
51. Edwards, 85–86.
52. Clark, *CV* 7, 227.
53. 5th Mass. Battery, 330.

54. 5th Mass. Battery, 331.
55. 5th Mass. Battery, 337.
56. 5th Mass. Battery, 344.
57. 5th Mass. Battery, 338.
58. 5th Mass. Battery, 324.
59. 5th Mass. Battery, 346.
60. 5th Mass. Battery, 324.
61. 5th Mass. Battery, 324.
62. 5th Mass. Battery, 325.
63. 5th Mass. Battery, 338.
64. 5th Mass. Battery, 333.
65. 5th Mass. Battery, 326.
66. 5th Mass. Battery, 327.
67. 5th Mass Battery, 337.
68. Cooper, *CV* 6, 472.
69. OR Ser. I, Vol. 11, 767.
70. Hogan, *CV* 6, 568.
71. J.H. Williams, *CV* 7, 443–444.
72. Hogan, *CV* 6, 568.
73. OR Ser. I, Vol. 11, 781.
74. Lackie, *CV*.
75. OR Ser. I, Vol. 11, 324.

Chapter 21

1. OR Ser. I, Vol. 11, 282.
2. Gibbs, 118.
3. Polley, 49.
4. Lasswell, 111–112.
5. *Richmond Daily Whig*, August 8, 1862.
6. Polley, *HTB*, 49; Davis, "Chickahominie," 52.
7. Polley, *HTB*, 49.
8. Polley, *HTB*, 54; Hood, *A&R*, 27.
9. Davis, 56.
10. Davis, "Chickahominie," 52; Polley, 50; Hood, *A&R*, 27.
11. Davis, 50.
12. Davis, 56.
13. OR Ser. I, Vol. 11, 317, 324, 327; OR, 340.
14. Hood, *A&R*, 27; Davis, 56; Brantley, 14.
15. Govan, 34.
16. Davis, 49.
17. Cooper, 472; Hamilton, *Shotwell*, 246; James, 2; Hunton, 223.
18. Hurst, 12.
19. OR Ser. I, Vol. 11, 774; Patterson, 33; Hogan, 568.
20. C.F. James Papers, 8th Virginia CV papers, Battles Box 1, letter of January 3, 1899.
21. Hoyt, *CV* 7, 225.
22. In October of 1867, Brigadier R.H. Anderson was asked about his memories of Gaines' Mill. In response, he offered some generalities, and included, "What troops these were, I can no more now remember than I can who … commanded the Second Cohort, First Legion at the battle of Pharsalus."

Chapter 22

1. McClendon, 77.
2. McClendon, 77.
3. McClendon, 77.
4. McClendon, 77.
5. McClendon, 77.
6. OR Supp., Vol. 11, 433.
7. Kerns later lost the fewest guns, but 18 men and 10 horses, reflecting an infantry attack. He also does not mention the later cavalry charge that disorganized the other three batteries in the gunline.
8. OR Ser. I, Vol. 11, 538.
9. Clark, *NC Regiments*, Vol. 1, 368.
10. Nisbett, 64–65.
11. Pa-roots.com, 1st Light Artillery 43rd Regiment Pennsylvania Volunteers Kerns.
12. OR Ser. I, Vol. 11, 411.
13. Pa-roots.com, 1st Light Artillery 43rd Regiment Pennsylvania Volunteers Kerns.
14. OR Ser. I, Vol. 11, 408.
15. OR Ser. I, Vol. 11, 282.
16. Davis, 52.
17. Merritt, p. 91.
18. Gibbs, 118.
19. Gibbs, 118.
20. Davis, "Chickahominie," 52.
21. Hunton, *CV* 7, 223–234.
22. Polley, *HTB*, 50.
23. Davis, "Chickahominie," 52.
24. Polley, *HTB*, 50.
25. Hunton, *CV* 7, 233–234.
26. C.F. James Papers.
27. Polley, *HTB*, 50.
28. Davis, "Chickahominie," 52.
29. *Richmond Daily Whig*, August 4, 1862.
30. Polley, 50.
31. OR Ser. I, Vol. 11, 41.
32. Merritt, 90.
33. Gracey, 66.
34. Merritt, 90.
35. Pa-roots, Easton.
36. OR Ser. I, Vol. 11, 46.
37. McConnell, Hard Duty.
38. "Horse," speedofanimals.com.
39. OR Ser. I, Vol. 11, 41.
40. OR Ser. I, Vol. 11, 46.
41. OR Ser. I, Vol. 11, 46.
42. Hogan, *CV* 6, 568.
43. Hamby, *CV* 14, 184.
44. Hamby, *CV* 14, 184.
45. C.F. James Papers.
46. *Richmond Daily Whig*, August 4, 1862.
47. Hamby, *CV* 14, 184.
48. Davis, "Chickahominie," 53.
49. Davis, 57.
50. *Richmond Daily Whig*, August 4, 1862.
51. Hunter, *CV* 51, 113.
52. Todd, *CV* 6, 565.
53. Hogan, *CV* 6, 568.
54. Pa-Roots, Easton.
55. Gracey, 63.
56. Davis, 56.
57. Sherrill, Location 4264.
58. Lane, 172.
59. Sherrill, Location 4271.
60. OR Ser. I, Vol. 11, 616.
61. Kerns was captured before, or outside the area of, the cavalry charge and retreat, as neither the Federals nor the Confederates involved mention the cavalry. The mention that the 18th Georgia, of Battle Group Hood, arrived just after the guns were taken indicates the former.
62. OR Ser. I, Vol. 11, 412.
63. OR Ser. I, Vol. 11, 412.
64. Davis, "Chickahominie," 53.
65. Cannons were fired by friction primers, not with flaming torches. The primer was put into a small hole

in the rear of the gun above the gunpowder and projectile. The primer was two small perpendicular brass tubes, one filled with fine gunpowder and the other with a match and abrasive. A strong pull on a lanyard hooked to the match would ignite the match, which would ignite the gunpowder in the other tube, which ignited the main charge, sending the projectile downrange.

66. Hill, *Our Boys*, 309.
67. Govan, 34.
68. Stevens, 28–29.
69. Davis, "Chickahominie," 53.
70. OR Ser. I, Vol. 11, 408.
71. Hamby, *CV* 14, 184.
72. OR Ser. I, Vol. 11, 282.
73. C.F. James Papers.
74. Edwards, 90.
75. OR Supp., Vol. 11, 445.
76. Hoole, 12; Drane, 521.
77. Barrett, 33.
78. Hoole, 12.
79. Cooper, *CV* 6, 472; C.F. James Papers.
80. OR Ser. I, Vol. 11, 115.
81. OR Supp., Vol. 11, 419.
82. OR Ser. I, Vol. 11, 283.
83. OR Ser. I, Vol. 11, 115.
84. OR Ser. I, Vol. 11, 41, 115, 282, 408.
85. OR Ser. I, Vol. 11, 225–226.
86. *Encyclopedia Virginia*.
87. Merritt, 91.
88. Harrer, 51–52.
89. Berdan, OR 278.
90. Townshend, 135.
91. OR Ser. I, Vol. 11, 249–250.
92. Gracey, 64.
93. Gracey, 64.

Chapter 23

1. Nisbett, 65.
2. OR Ser. I, Vol. 11, 615.
3. Nisbett, 65.
4. Nisbett, 65.
5. Schmutz, Location 2678.
6. OR Supp., Vol. 11, 433.
7. NP, 20–21.
8. Nabors, *CV* 24, 69.
9. Nabors, *CV* 24, 69.
10. Fletcher, 25.
11. Bilby, "Some of Us," 13.
12. Pa-roots.com, 11th Reserves.
13. Bilby, "Some of Us," 13.
14. Schmutz, Location 2714.
15. Brantley, 13.
16. Brantley, 12.
17. OR Supp., Vol. 11, 419.
18. Hood, *A&R*, 28–29.
19. *Richmond Daily Whig*, August 8, 1862.
20. Hunter, *CV* 24, 113.
21. Hamby, *CV* 14, 184.
22. Brown, 29.
23. Coles, 48; the text says 8th U.S., but they surrendered as a body in 1861 in Texas. McLemore had also been in the 6th U.S.
24. Alphonso Ames Papers.
25. Brown, 29.
26. Hankins, *CV* 20, 572.

27. OR Ser. I, Vol. 11, 896.
28. McBrien, 30.
29. Lemmon, *CV* 8, 66.
30. M'Comb, *CV* 3, 161.
31. OR. Ser. I, Vol. 11, 592.
32. OR. Ser. I, Vol. 11, 592–593.
33. Wood, *The War*, 74.
34. Edwards, *CS*, 88.
35. Wise, *CV* 6, 568.
36. Fields, 15–16.
37. OR Supp., Vol. 11, 429.
38. OR Ser. I, Vol. 11, 322–323, 327.
39. Peter McDavid, *CV* 37, 263.
40. OR Ser. I, Vol. 11, 322–323.
41. OR Ser. I, Vol. 11, 327.
42. OR Ser. I, Vol. 11, 339.
43. OR Ser. I, Vol. 11, 339.
44. Judson, 65.
45. Judson, 65.
46. Judson, 63–68.
47. OR Supp., Vol. 11, 440–441.
48. Hoyt, *CV* 27, 226.
49. OR Supp., Vol. 11, 440–441.
50. Hoyt, *CV* 27, 226.
51. Lackie, CV.
52. OR Supp. Vol. 11, 441.
53. The text says "Eleventh South Carolina," but they were in South Carolina at the time. http://www.research online.net/sccw/unit142.htm.
54. Judson, 63–68.
55. OR Ser. I, Vol. 11, 344.
56. Judson, 63–68.
57. Judson, 63–68.
58. OR Ser. I, Vol. 11, 344.
59. OR Ser. I, Vol. 11, 339.
60. Judson, 63–68.
61. Judson, 63–68.
62. 1st Lt. Stephen W. Stryker, 11th Infantry Regiment Civil War, DMNA.
63. Hoyt, *CV* 27, 226.
64. Waters, 21.
65. Jones, *Lee's Tigers*, 100.
66. Jones, *Lee's Tigers*, 99–100.
67. Chapla, *42nd Virginia*, 15.
68. Chapla, *48th Virginia*, 26.

Chapter 24

1. Dabney, 455–456.
2. Johnson, Memoir, SHSP 10, 151–152.
3. OR Ser. I, Vol. 11, 570.
4. OR Ser. I, Vol. 11, 570.
5. OR Ser. I, Vol. 11, 577.
6. Johnson, Memoir, SHSP 10, 151–152.
7. Dabney, 455–456.
8. OR Ser. I Vol. 11, 375.
9. Robins, 5.
10. Robins, 7.
11. OR Ser. I, Vol. 11, 375. These were the 20-lb. Parrott guns.
12. Robins, 8.
13. Robins, 8.
14. Park, 37–39.
15. OR Ser. I, Vol. 11, 856, 869.
16. OR Ser. I, Vol. 11, 495.
17. OR Ser. I, Vol. 11, 495.
18. Bilby, "Some of Us," 12–13.

19. The 60th, 61st, and about half of the 26th Georgia Regiments.
20. Robertson, *Stonewall Brigade*, 353.
21. OR Ser. I, Vol. 11, 605.
22. OR Ser. I, Vol. 11, 605.
23. Coffin, 133–124.
24. Bilby, "Some of Us," 12–13.
25. Bilby, "Some of Us," 12–13.
26. OR Ser. I Vol. 11, 437.
27. Dale Nichols, 17.
28. Dale Nichols, 18.
29. OR Ser. I, Vol. 11, 503.
30. Dale Nichols, 19.
31. White, "31st Georgia," 30.
32. Bradwell, *CV* 33, 382.
33. White, "31st Georgia," 30.
34. Stephens, 107.
35. Dale Nichols, 19.
36. Bradwell, *CV* 33, 382.
37. Robins, 8.
38. OR Ser. I, Vol. 11, 284.
39. Coffin, 133–124.
40. OR Ser. I, Vol. 11, 284.
41. OR Ser. I, Vol. 11, 284.
42. Coffin, 136.
43. Coffin, 124.
44. Coffin, 136.
45. OR Ser. I, Vol. 11, 284.
46. Robins, 8.
47. Robins, 9.
48. OR Ser. I, Vol. 11, 626.
49. Clark, Vol. 1, 242–243.
50. OR Ser. I, Vol. 11, 367.
51. Bradwell, *CV* 33, 383.
52. Bradwell, *CV* 24, 23.
53. Bradwell, *CV* 33, 383.
54. Clark, *NC Troops*, Vol. 1, 242–3.
55. Clark, *NC Troops*, Vol. 1, 165.
56. Clark, *NC Troops*, Vol. 1, 660.
57. Clark, *NC Troops*, Vol. 1, 661.
58. Clark, Patriot-Martyrs.
59. OR Ser. I, Vol. 11, 632.
60. OR Ser. I, Vol. 11, 642.
61. OR Ser. I, Vol. 11, 375.
62. Evans, 44.
63. OR Ser. I, Vol. 11, 367–368.
64. Evans, 44.
65. OR Ser. I, Vol. 11, 447–448; *Richmond Daily Whig*, July 8, 1862.
66. OR Ser. I, Vol. 11, 448.
67. Whitman, 117.
68. Saylor.
69. OR Ser. I, Vol. 11, 448.
70. Bicknell, 101.
71. OR Ser. I, Vol. 11, 448.
72. OR Ser. I, Vol. 11, 453.
73. OR Ser. I, Vol. 11, 448.
74. Whitman, 101–103.
75. Whitman, 118.
76. Whitman, 101–103.
77. Whitman, 118.
78. Fairchild, 53.
79. OR Ser. I, Vol. 11, 453.
80. Fairchild, 53.
81. OR Ser. I, Vol. 11, 455.
82. Reed Papers.
83. Luckinbill Diary.
84. Saylor.
85. The brigade did precisely this at Fredericksburg in December 1862 with disastrous results. See Dale Nichols, *Hurrah for Georgia!*
86. Bradwell, *CV* 24, 23.
87. Hobson Papers.
88. Clark, 210.
89. Clark, *NC Troops*, Vol. 1, 661.
90. OR Ser. I, Vol. 11, 647.
91. Clark, *NC Troops*, Vol. 1, 210.
92. Bradwell, *CV* 24, 23.
93. SHSP 10, 153.
94. OR Ser. I, Vol. 11, 620.
95. OR Ser. I, Vol. 11, 639.
96. Johnson, Memoir, SHSP 10, 153.
97. OR Ser. I, Vol. 11, 620.
98. OR Ser. I, Vol. 11, 570.
99. Park, 37–39.
100. OR Ser. I, Vol. 11, 437.
101. Murray, 61.
102. OR Ser. I, Vol. 11, 437.
103. Howard, 143.
104. Howard, 144.
105. Pohanka, *Vortex*, 277.
106. Reece, 89.
107. White, *31st Georgia*, 30.
108. OR Ser. I, Vol. 11, 580.
109. Howard, 143.
110. OR Ser. I, Vol. 11, 570.
111. OR Ser. I, Vol. 11, 75.
112. OR Ser. I, Vol. 11, 70.
113. OR Ser. I, Vol. 11, 76.
114. Johnson, *CMH*, Vol. 2, 84–85.
115. Johnson, *CMH*, Vol. 2, 85–86.
116. Goldsborough.
117. OR Ser. I, Vol. 11, 620.
118. OR Ser. I, Vol. 11, 583.
119. Campbell Brown, 54.
120. OR Ser. I, Vol. 11, 582.
121. Johnson, *CMH*, Vol. 2, 84–87.
122. OR Ser. I, Vol. 11, 570.
123. OR Ser. I, Vol. 11, 575.
124. Howard p. 140.
125. Frye, *2nd Virginia*, 32.
126. OR Ser. I, Vol. 11, 286–7.
127. OR Ser. I, Vol. 11, 365.
128. Antietam on the Web.
129. Goldsborough, 421.
130. Evans, 45.
131. Evans, 45.
132. OR Ser. I, Vol. 11, 245.
133. OR Ser. I, Vol. 11, 362.
134. OR Ser. I, Vol. 11, 372.
135. Reece, 88–89.
136. Myers, 236.
137. Reece, 89.
138. Myers, 238.
139. Pohanka, *Vortex*, 279.
140. Pohanka, *Vortex*, 279.
141. Pohanka, *Vortex*, 279.
142. Pohanka, *Vortex*, 281.
143. Pohanka, *Vortex*, 336.
144. Bradwell, *CV* 33, 383.
145. Driver, 28.
146. OR Ser. I, Vol. 11, 71.
147. OR Ser. I, Vol. 11, 76.
148. OR Ser. I, Vol. 11, 71.
149. OR Ser. I, Vol. 11, 76.
150. Field, Hampton Legion.

151. Dunaway, 30.
152. Reece, 90.

Chapter 25

1. Stevens, *Berdan's USSS*, 117.
2. Glover, 94.
3. McKoy.
4. Judson, 69.
5. About ¼ mile upstream from the Grapevine Bridge.
6. Townshend, 135–141.
7. Veil, 16.
8. Veil, 17.
9. Harrer, 51–52.
10. Urban, 123–124.
11. Myers, 235.
12. Myers, 239.
13. Townshend, 135.
14. Woodward, *2 PR*, 127.
15. Parker, 122.
16. Mundy, 164.
17. Christiancy Papers.
18. Daniel McNamara, 127.
19. Daniel McNamara, 129.
20. M.H. McNamara, 101.
21. Pa-roots.com, Ninth Reserves.
22. Whitman, 48.
23. OR Ser. I, Vol. 11, 233.
24. OR Ser. I, Vol. 11, 388.
25. Harrer, 51–52.
26. Gracey, 65–66.
27. Benson, 11.
28. Robertson, *Warrior*, 86.
29. Caldwell, *Stonewall Jim*, 56.
30. Fulton, 39–40.
31. Allen, *Old Stonewall*, 116.
32. Foard Papers.
33. Benson, 11–12.
34. Walshe, *CV* 7, 55.
35. Davis, *Texas to Maryland*, 59.
36. Townshend, 134.
37. Roy, 24.
38. Glasgow, 125.
39. Benson, 11–12.
40. Glasgow, 125.
41. St. Maur, 342.
42. Kelsey, 77.
43. St. Maur, 343.
44. Lane, 146.
45. McClendon, 79.
46. Hardy, 73.
47. Hardy, 73.
48. St. Maur, 344.
49. Davis, *Texas to Maryland*, 58.
50. Clark, *Patriot-Martyrs*.
51. Jacobs, *Cry Heart*, 164.
52. Benjamin Anderson Jones.
53. McHenry Howard, 146.
54. St. Maur, 343.
55. Lane, 172.
56. Myers, 239.
57. Fletcher, 25.
58. Barrett, 34.
59. OR Supp., Vol. 11, 459.
60. Clark, *NC Troops*, Vol. 1, 211.
61. Wills, 59.
62. Dobbins, 88.
63. Krick, *Gregg*, 13.
64. Jones, SHSP 9, 561.
65. Ratchford, *Some Reminiscences*, 19.
66. Davis, *Texas to Maryland*, 59.
67. Hill, *B&L*, 123.
68. McHenry Howard, 145.
69. Coker, 74–75.
70. St. Maur, 345.
71. Robertson, *Warrior*, 86.
72. Benson, 11–12.
73. White, *31st Georgia*, 32.
74. Bradwell, *CV* 23, 383.
75. St. Maur, 342.
76. Cowper, 17.
77. Field.
78. Hunter, *CV* 31, 113.
79. Hill, *B&L*, 359.
80. Ratchford, *Some Reminiscences*, 26.
81. Hunter, *CV* 31, 113.
82. The McGehee house had a stable, a garden, an orchard, and at least two fences. It was General Sykes' headquarters during the battle. A bare room with only a table and some chairs seems too low a status for the McGehee House, so this was probably the Boze House, which is consistent with Col. Clitz using it as his headquarters. Buchanan's Brigade was just to the west of it, with Weed and Tidball's guns just to the north. Both houses were between the lines in the 1864 Battle of Cold Harbor, and were probably destroyed at that time.
83. Ratchford, *Some Reminiscences*, 18.
84. Ratchford, *Some Reminiscences*, 24.
85. Hamby, *CV* 14, 184–185.
86. "George A. McCall," Wikipedia.
87. Jacobs, *Cry Heart*, 164.
88. Nichols, *Toward Gettysburg*, 97.
89. Hill, *B&L*, 360.
90. McHenry Howard, 145.
91. Jones, *Campbell Brown*, 54.
92. Robertson, *Warrior*, 86.
93. Cowper, 17.
94. Freeman, *REL*, Vol. 2, 158–189.
95. Dabney to Hotchkiss handwritten letter.
96. Booth, 47.
97. Ross, 44.
98. Booth, 47.
99. Varon, Location 2180, 2213.
100. Given the limitations of hand copying and delivery by army courier, G.O. 75 probably arrived at the divisional headquarters during the daylight hours of June 24, after the morning bread deliveries.
101. McNiven.
102. Sutton.
103. McNiven.
104. Varon, 1478.
105. Park, 38.
106. This number is approximate, as the Confederates used both 4-gun and six-gun batteries, and had 112 guns present. Only five batteries (Maurin, Braxton, Andrews, Johnson, Crenshaw, perhaps 25 guns) were engaged before Jackson generated his Grand Battery of 30 guns in the evening; in all, only 55 guns were engaged.
107. General Barry, McClellan's Chief of Ordnance, claims only 62 were engaged, a difference of 36 guns. OR Supp., Vol. 11, 418. The batteries of Smead, Porter, and Upton, 16 guns, were not much engaged, so this accounts for 16, leaving 20 unaccounted for. Barry also

says that 22 guns were lost, but his information does not match with the battery commander's reports.

108. Sydnor, *CV* 20, 107.

109. 186? Hanover map.

110. Fannie says 1863, but the armies arrived again in June of 1864 for the Battle of Cold Harbor.

111. Tinsley, 402–404.

112. http://www.suddenlink.net/pages/fpreston/sgtinsl.htm.

113. Haw.

114. Wert.

115. Clark, *Patriot-Martyrs*.

116. Hoyt, *CV* 7, 226.

Afterword

1. https://www.25thida.org/units/infantry/12th-infantry-regiment/.

Appendix I

1. This number is the sum of the brigade numbers below. SHSP 1, 421 claims 12,628 including artillery, etc. Powell himself claimed 14,000 before Mechanicsville.

2. Brockenbrough, OR Ser. I, Vol. 11, 844, says about half of the regiment were casualties. Based on this figure, the 40th entered the Mechanicsville fight with 360, and lost 121 there. The 40th Virginia lost 59 at Gaines' Mill. Accordingly, it entered the fight of the 27th with but 239 men.

3. Krick, *40th Virginia Infantry*, 13.

4. Mayo, OR Ser. I, Vol. 11, 845.

5. Mayo, OR Ser. I, Vol. 11, 845.

6. O'Sullivan, 29, says that they had about 350 men.

7. O'Sullivan, 29.

8. America's Civil War Commands, 82.

9. Caldwell, 45.

10. Gregg, OR Ser. I, Vol. 11, 855.

11. Caldwell, 45.

12. Barnes, OR Ser. I, Vol. 11, 865.

13. Caldwell, 45.

14. Edwards, OR Ser. I, Vol. 11, 866.

15. Caldwell, 45.

16. Caldwell, 45.

17. SHSP 1, 421. There are no accurate casualty figures for this battle alone. Fitzpatrick says that the 45th Georgia lost 61 men, or 25 percent, so that figure is used for the entire brigade.

18. Fitzpatrick says his company of the 45th Georgia had only 25 men left. Assuming ten companies, the 45th Georgia had 250 men. Fitzpatrick also says that the 45th lost 61 men, almost 25 percent. The other figures are based on this percentage, which seems high.

19. Haywood, OR Ser. I, Vol. 11, 890.

20. Haywood, OR Ser. I, Vol. 11, 884, says that 11 officers fell at Gaines' Mill, and two at Malvern Hill. His campaign casualties were 253, if the men fell at the same rate as the officers, 82 percent of the casualties were at Gaines' Mill.

21. Cowan, OR Ser. I, Vol. 11, 891.

22. Lane, OR Ser. I, Vol. 11, 892.

23. Lane, OR Ser. I, Vol. 11, 893.

24. Hoke, OR Ser. I, Vol. 11, 897.

25. Barbour, OR Ser. I, Vol. 11, 896, says that they had 138 casualties for the campaign. The William Groves Morris Papers, SHC-CH, say that they had 100 men left after Malvern Hill. This gives a figure of 238 for Gaines' Mill.

26. Barbour, OR Ser. I, Vol. 11, 897, says that his campaign losses were 138. The 37th lost one officer each at Gaines' Mill and thereafter. If the enlisted men fell at the same rate, then half of his campaign casualties were at Gaines' Mill.

27. Archer, OR Ser. I, Vol. 11, 897, says that before Mechanicsville the brigade was 1,228 strong. He also reports 114 casualties at Mechanicsville, for a Gaines' Mill total of 1,114. However, he opines on the same page that at Gaines' Mill the brigade was fewer than 1,000 men.

28. Archer, OR Ser. I, Vol. 11, 897.

29. Fulton, *CV* p. 300, says there were 70 in his company. Since the 5th Alabama Battalion lost it flag, it had at least five companies, for a total of 350 men.

30. Figure is 320 divided by four and a half regiments.

31. Ibid.

32. Ibid.

33. CW Centennial Commission, Tennesseans in the Civil War, 189.

34. Cross, *Ordeal by Fire*, 32.

35. Pender, OR Ser. I, Vol. 11, 891. The 16th N.C. lost 200 at Meadow Bridge (p. 894), bringing their number down to 2,150. According to Hoke, OR Supp, 454, the 38th N.C. lost 125 out of 420 at Mechanicsville, or 29 percent. Pender also reports a brigade loss of 800 for the two fights. If Mechanicsville cost him 29 percent of his casualties, he showed up at Gaines' Mill with but 1,918 men.

36. Dula, 3, says that his company lost 4 of 13 men, which is 30 percent. The casualty figures are 30 percent of the brigade divided by 4.5 regiments.

37. Hoke, OR Supp., 454.

38. SHSP 1, 419.

39. Loehr, 25.

40. Jenkins? OR Supp., 443–444, gives his numbers before Frazier's Farm and his casualties thereat.

41. Unsigned, OR Supp., 441, says the loss was trifling in the rest of the brigade.

42. Ibid.

43. OR Supp., 441.

44. Coker, 74.

45. SC Regimental Series, 15.

46. Fields, *28th Virginia Infantry*, 15.

47. Divine, *8th Virginia Infantry*, 11.

48. All casualties are from Strange's report, OR Ser. I, Vol. 11, 769.

49. Robertson, *18th Virginia Infantry*, 13.

50. Wilcox, OR Ser. I, Vol. 11, 774.

51. Wilcox, OR Ser. I, Vol. 11, 774–5.

52. Herbert, 10.

53. Herbert, 10.

54. Brigade casualties less the 8 Alabama divided by three.

55. Ibid.

56. Ibid.

57. Pryor, OR Ser. I, Vol. 11, 780.

58. Average of other losses.

59. Waters, 20.

60. Ingle, 337.

61. York, OR Supp., 448.

62. York, OR Supp., 447.

63. Jones, *Lee's Tigers*, 100.

64. Jones, *Lee's Tigers*, 100.

65. Wallace, Jr., *3rd Virginia Infantry*, 28.

66. Longstreet's casualty table, OR Ser. I, Vol. 11, 761, indicates that Featherston had 664 casualties for the

campaign. Based on the ratios from Pryor and Wilcox's brigades, half of these were at Gaines' Mill.

67. D.H. Hill, OR Ser. I, Vol. 11, 629.

68. Rodes, OR Ser. I, Vol. 11, 631.

69. Battle, OR Supp., 165, says that he had 333 men left after 7 Pines.

70. Battle, OR Supp., 176.

71. Hobson Papers, 1.

72. Gayle, OR Ser. I, Vol. 11, 639.

73. G.B. Anderson never reported his casualties for this fight, as he was killed in September. The 2NC apparently lost 38 percent, so this ratio is used for the brigade casualties. The regiments are the balance divided by the number thereof.

74. Osborne, 1.

75. Osborne, 1.

76. Cowper, 14.

77. Garland did not break out his losses at each battle, and there are few references from his regiments. The 20th N.C. lost 71 percent of its campaign casualties at Gaines' Mill, so that number is used. The regimental numbers are that figure less the 274 that the 20th N.C. lost divided by the number of regiments.

78. Collins, SHC, 3, says that 1 company began the 7 Days with 48 men. With 10 companies in a regiment, this gives the 12th N.C. 480 men.

79. Foard Papers.

80. Toon, OR Supp., 439.

81. Wall, *Pee Dee Guards*, 30. His company had but 15 men, so the regiment had 150.

82. D.H. Hill, OR Ser. I, Vol. 11, 527, says that this regiment lost 50 percent. Its losses on the original of the return in the MoC claim 156 total casualties.

83. D.H. Hill says that this regiment lost half its number: OR Ser. I, Vol. 11, 527.

84. SHSP 1, 416. The 44th Georgia lost 355 men at Mechanicsville, bringing the figure down to 2,011. The 1st N.C. lost 133 there, so only 1878 remained. The 3rd N.C. lost 47, so 1,831 survived. The 48th Georgia was also badly hurt at Mechanicsville.

85. Sauers, 29.

86. Ripley, OR Ser. I, Vol. 11, 648.

87. DeRosset, OR Ser. I, Vol. 11, 358, says he left camp with 645 men and lost 47 at Mechanicsville.

88. SHSP 1, 421.

89. ORS, 431.

90. Simpson, *Touched with Valor*, 69.

91. Simpson, *TWV*, 70.

92. Simpson, *TWV*, 82.

93. Simpson, *TWV*, 82.

94. Simpson, *TWV*, 87.

95. Simpson, *TWV*, 87.

96. Hood, OR Ser. I, Vol. 11, 569.

97. Field, 18.

98. Hood, OR Ser. I, Vol. 11, 569.

99. Whiting, OR Ser. I, Vol. 11, 565.

100. Coles, 48.

101. Davis, *CWR*, 281.

102. Davis, *CWR*, 281.

103. Whiting, OR Ser. I, Vol. 11, 565.

104. SHSP 1, 421, estimates Jackson's Division at 4,000, exclusive of Lawton.

105. Jackson, OR Ser. I, Vol. 11, 559.

106. SHSP 1, 419.

107. Robertson, *SB*, 120.

108. Botts, OR Ser. I, Vol. 11, 575.

109. Botts, OR Ser. I, Vol. 11, 576–577.

110. Ronald, OR Ser. I, Vol. 11, 579.

111. Balance of casualties.

112. Smith, OR Ser. I, Vol. 11, 583.

113. Smith, OR Ser. I, Vol. 11, 583.

114. Neff, OR Ser. I, Vol. 11, 585, says that they had 130 men at Malvern and 4 casualties at Gaines' Mill, for a total of 134.

115. Neff, OR Ser. I, Vol. 11, 585.

116. Cunningham, OR Ser. I, Vol. 11, 587.

117. Vermillion, OR Ser. I, Vol. 11, 598.

118. Cunningham, OR Ser. I, Vol. 11, 588.

119. Leigh, OR Ser. I, Vol. 11, 591.

120. Warren, OR Ser. I, Vol. 11, 592–593 reports that their loss was slight, except for Brigadier Fulkerson himself.

121. Lawton, OR Ser. I, Vol. 11, 595.

122. Lawton, OR Ser. I, Vol. 11, 597, has a casualty table for this battle.

123. Lawton OR Ser. I, Vol. 11, 597.

124. Brantley, *CV* 33, 397.

125. Brantley, *CV* 33, 382.

126. Nichols, 78.

127. Brantley, *CV* 33, 397.

128. Brantley, *CV* 33, 397.

129. Brantley, *CV* 33, 397.

130. Sum of brigade numbers.

131. OR Ser. I, Vol. 11, 508, contains the casualty returns for GM of Ewell's Division.

132. Andrews, *Memoir*, 40.

133. Early, OR Ser. I, Vol. 11, 671. Elzey lost 243 at Gaines' Mill, so these added to Early's figure total 1293.

134. Walker, OR Ser. I, Vol. 11, 611.

135. *31th Va. Reg. Hist.*, 31.

136. *44th Va. Reg. Hist.*, 26.

137. Turner, Allen Family Papers, 15.

138. Trimble, OR Ser. I, Vol. 11, 616. Trimble cites his brigade as having almost 3,000 men, a mistake pointed out in SHSP 1, 419. The lower figure is probably more correct.

139. Lane, 172.

140. The 6 Louisiana lost 156 men, 50 percent at Port Republic. That means that before that fight, it had 316 men. No other Louisiana unit size information is available. Assuming each regiment was about the same size, the 7th, 8th, and 9th Louisiana would total 948 men. Wheat's Battalion was about 150, and the 6th Louisiana 156, for a total of 1254 men.

141. Brigade number is based on SHSP 1, 419, wherein Ewell says brigades were about equal. Regimental numbers are the balance of this figure divided by number of regiments.

142. DuFour, 199.

Appendix II

1. The casualty figures are taken from those appearing in OR Ser. I, Vol. 11, 39–40. In the actual reports and eyewitness accounts, the figures reported are close enough to these to make further comparison useless.

2. Arnold, 357.

3. Arnold, 357.

4. Arnold, 357.

5. Childs, OR Ser. I, Vol. 11, 406, does not give the number of men in the 4th Pennsylvania Cavalry, but says there were at least two companies. The 6th Pennsylvania Cavalry had 250 men in six companies, for an average of 41 men per company.

6. Arnold, 357.

7. McNamara, 115, buck and ball.

8. Harrer, 49.

9. 62d Pennsylvania, Location 536.

10. http://www.4thmichigan.com/4th_Michigan_History.htm.

11. Martindale, OR Ser. I, Vol. 11, 291.

12. Roberts, OR Ser. I, Vol. 11, 307.

13. http://theminiaturespage.com/boards/msg.mv?id=193653.

14. Whitman, 39.

15. Parker, 122.

16. DMNA 44th NY.

17. Eugene Nash.

18. https://dmna.ny.gov/historic/reghist/civil/infantry/12thInf/12thInfBMSHistSketch.htm.

19. Wayne Abernathy. Springfield rifles and Enfield rifles, 4 percent.

20. Smith, *CW* 22, 40.

21. 83d Pennsylvania Harpers Ferry Muskets. http://www.pa-roots.com/pacw/infantry/83rd/83dorg.html. "Springfield muskets."

22. Sykes, OR Ser. I, Vol. 11, 349.

23. Floyd-Jones, OR Ser. I, Vol. 11, 375.

24. Warren, OR Ser. I, Vol. 11, 377.

25. Warren, OR Ser. I, Vol. 11, 377.

26. Rare Presentation Model, 1861 Springfield.

27. Nichols, *Toward Gettysburg*, 98, reports that McCall had fewer than 7,000 at New Market. Add to this the Gaines' Mill losses for a total engaged in the battle of 8651.

28. McCandless, OR Ser. I, Vol. 11, 111.

29. Ent, Location 897.

30. Stone, OR Ser. I, Vol. 11, 416.

31. Stone, OR Ser. I, Vol. 11, 417.

32. Ent, Location 897.

33. Woodward, *Third Pennsylvania Reserves*, 55; Ent, Location 897.

34. Magilton, OR Ser. I, Vol. 11, 421.

35. Ent, Location 897.

36. Pa-roots: "half its strength."

37. Ent, Location 897.

38. http://7thpares.org/history.html.

39. Ent, Location 897.

40. http://www.9thpareserves.org/9th1.htm.

41. Ent, Location 897.

42. Ent, Location 897.

43. Ent, Location 897.

44. Ent, Location 3204.

45. Ent, Location 3189.

46. Ent, Location 3200.

47. Pa-roots.

48. Ent, Location 3200.

49. Slocum, OR Ser. I, Vol. 11, 433.

50. Foster, NJ in Rebellion, 77.

51. Bishop, OR Ser. I, Vol. 11, 442.

52. Taylor, OR Ser. I, Vol. 11, 438.

53. Foster, *New Jersey and the Rebellion*, quoting Simpson letter of 7/22/62, 77.

54. Curtis, *Bull Run to Chancellorsville*, 127.

55. Bennett, 45.

56. Bennett, 21.

57. Bennett, 45.

Bibliography

Commonly used abbreviations:
CV: Confederate Veteran
SHSP: Southern Historical Society Papers
OR: Official Record of the War of the Rebellion
NYSMM: New York State Military Museum
USAMHI: Unites States Army Military History Institute
RNBP: Richmond National Battlefield Park

Abernathy, Wayne. "Arms for Brady's Sharpshooters," http://www.bradyssharpshooters.org/bradys/ssrifles. htm; accessed 7/23/17. [1USSS]

Adams, Charles R., Jr. *A Post of Honor.* Fort Valley, GA: Garrett Publications, 1989. {12Ga}

"Agar Gun." Wikipedia.

Alexander, E. Porter. *Military Memoirs of a Confederate.* Bloomington, IL: Indiana University Press, 1962.

Allen, Randall, ed. *Campaigning with Old Stonewall.* Baton Rouge: Louisiana State University Press, 1998. {21 Georgia}

American Civil War Armored Rail Cars. http://www.firstmdus.net/Rail%20cars.htm; accessed 7/23/17.

Ames, John. W. Capt. Letter of 6/28/62, USAMHI. {11US}

Anderson, Benjamin. *Memoir,* USAMHI. {44Va}

Anderson, Joseph R., Jr., "Anderson's Brigade in the Battles Around Richmond." *Confederate Veteran* 31 (1991): 448. {14Ga} {35GA} {45GA} {49GA} {3LABN}

Andrews, Richard Snowden, *Richard Snowden Andrews: A Memoir.* Baltimore: Sun Job Printing Press, 1910.

Andrus, Michael J. *The Brooke, Fauquier, Loudon and Alexandria Artillery.* Lynchburg, VA: H.E. Howard, 1990. {Brooke} {Loudon} {Alexandria}

Anonymous Texas Officer. "Graphic Description of the Battle of Gaines' Mill," *Richmond Daily Whig,* August 4, 1862, courtesy Richmond National Battlefield Park. {4TX}

Ares, Alphonso. *Diary.* Perkins Library, Duke University. {6NC}

Armstrong, E.H. Letter of 6/29/62, Armstrong Family Papers, SHC.

Armstrong, Richard L. *25th Virginia and 9th Battalion Virginia Infantry.* Lynchburg, VA: H.E. Howard, 1990. {25VA}

Ashcraft, John M. *31st Virginia Infantry.* Lynchburg, VA: H.E. Howard, 1988. {31VA}

"Ashland during the Civil War, 1861–1865." http://ashlandmuseum.org/explore-online/civil-war/ashland-during-the-civil-war-1861–1865; accessed 5/3/17.

Association for the Preservation of Beaver Dam Depot. www.beaverdamdepot.org; accessed 7/23/17.

Averell, William W. "With the Cavalry on the Peninsula." *Battles and Leaders of the Civil War,* vol. 3.

Baltimore (MD) Artillery, Antietam on the Web. http://antietam.aotw.org/officers.php?unit_id=737, accessed 8/6/17.

Baquet, Camille. *History of the First Brigade, New Jersey Volunteers from 1861 to 1865.* Gaithersburg, MD: Van-Sickle, 1910. www.archinve.org; accessed 7/23/17.

Barnes, Joseph K. *The Medical and Surgical History of the War of the Rebellion, Part 1,* vol. I. Washington, DC: Government Printing Office, 1870.

Barrett, O.S. *Reminiscences, Incidents, Battles, Marches, and Camp Life of the 4th Michigan Infantry.* Detroit: W.S. Ostler, 1888. Courtesy 4th Michigan Volunteer Infantry, Martin Bertera. {4MI}

Bates, Samuel *History of Pennsylvania Volunteers.* Harrisburg: B. Singerly, State Printer, 1869.

Battery D (Rowan Artillery or Reilly's Battery) 10th North Carolina State Troops (1st Regiment North Carolina Artillery). http://reillysbattery.org/Reillys History.htm; accessed 7/23/17.

Beall, John Bramblett. *In Barrack and Field: Poems and Sketches of Army Life.* Nashville: M.E. Church, 1906. {19 Ga}

Bean, W.G. *Stonewall's Man Sandie Pendleton.* UNC Press, 1959.

Bellona Arsenal Historic Place registration form. http://www.dhr.virginia.gov/registers/Counties/Chesterfield/020-0006_Bellona_Arsenal_1971_Final_Nomination.pdf; accessed 7/23/17.

Bellona Arsenal video. https://www.youtube.com/watch?v=8FwtlAbziHE; accessed 7/23/17.

Bennett, A.J. *The Story of the First Massachusetts Light Battery.* Boston: Press of Deland and Barte, 1886. {A, MA}

Bennett, Edwin C. *Musket and Sword.* Boston: Coburn, 1900. {22MA}

Benson, Susan Williams, ed. *Berry Benson's Civil War Book.* Athens, GA: U. of Ga. Press, 1962. {1SCV}

Benton, T.H. "A Tennessee Private in Virginia." *Confederate Veteran* 15 (1991): 507. {14TN}

"Berkley Plantation." Wikipedia.

Bertera, Marty E. *The History of the 4th Michigan Infantry*. Unpublished manuscript. {4MI}

Bicknell, George W. *History of the Fifth Regiment, Maine Volunteers*. Portland, ME: Hall L. Davis, 1871. {5ME}

Bigbee, T.M. Untitled article. *Confederate Veteran* 7 (1991): 357. {5TX}

Bilby, Joseph G. "Load the Hopper and Turn the Crank: Rapid Fire Guns of the Civil War." http://www.history net.com/civil-war-guns; accessed 8/10/17.

_____. "Some of Us Will Never Come Out." *Military Images* 14, No. 3 (Nov.-Dec. 1992): 10. {1NJ} {2NJ} {3NJ} {4NJ}

Blackford, W.W. "Map of the Operations of the Cavalry Brigade." http://digitalcollections.baylor.edu/cdm/singleitem/collection/tx-wotr/id/1063/rec/259; accessed 7/23/17.

_____. *War Years with Jeb Stuart*. New York: Scribner's, 1946.

Borcke, Heros von. *Memoirs of the Confederate War for Independence*. New York: Peter Smith, 1938.

Boteler, John. *Southern Historical Society Papers* 40, Number 2 (September 1915).

"Botts, John Minor." Wikipedia.

Bowen, James L. *Massachusetts in the War*. Springfield, MA: Clark W. Bryan, 1889. {C, MA} {22MA}

Bradwell, I.G. "First Lesson in War." *Confederate Veteran* 33 (1991): 382. {31GA}

_____. "Soldier Life in the Confederate Army." *Confederate Veteran* 24 (1991): 20. {31GA}

Brant, Nat. *Mr. Tubbs' Civil War*. Syracuse: Syracuse University Press, 1996. {PR}

Brantley, R.A. *The Fifth Texas: Seven Days Around Richmond*. Unpublished manuscript, Simpson Center, Hillsboro College, Hillsboro, Texas.{5TX}

Brent, Joseph Lancaster. *Memoirs of the War Between the States*. New Orleans: Fontana, 1940. Courtesy Robert Krick, Jr., Richmond National Battlefield Park.

"Brig. Gen. James J. Archer." *Confederate Veteran* 7 (1991): 65. {1TN} {7TN} {14TH} {19GA}

Brock, R.A., ed. "General Joseph R. Anderson." *Southern Historical Society Papers*, vol. 19. Wilmington, NC: Broadfoot Morningside, 1991. {14Ga} {35GA} {45GA} {49GA} {3LABN}

_____. "Life and Character of Lt. Gen. D.H. Hill." *Southern Historical Society Papers*. Wilmington, NC: Broadfoot Morningside, 1991.

_____. "Strength of General Lee's Army in the Seven Days around Richmond." *Southern Historical Society Papers*, vol. 1. Wilmington, NC: Broadfoot Morningside, 1991.

_____. "William Chase Whiting," *Southern Historical Society Papers*, vol. 26. Wilmington, NC: Broadfoot Morningside, 1991.

Brown, Maud Morrison. *The University Grays*. Richmond, VA: Garrett & Massie, 1940. {11MISS}

Buchanan, G.G. Untitled article. *Confederate Veteran* 7 (1991): 216. {PSS}

Buck, Samuel D. *With the Old Confeds*. Baltimore: H.F. Houck, 1925. {13VA}

Burress, L.R. "Brave Mississippians in Virginia." *Confederate Veteran* (1991): 111. {19MISS}

Burton, Brian K. *Extraordinary Circumstances: The Seven Days Battles*. Bloomington: Indiana University Press, 2001.

Caldwell, J.F.J. *History of a Brigade of South Carolinians*. Dayton, OH: Morningside Press, 1992. {1SCV}

California State Military Museum. "California and the Civil War 32nd Regiment of Infantry, New York Volunteers." http://www.militarymuseum.org/32dNY.html; accessed 7/23/17.

"Canister Shot Video." https://civilwartalk.com/threads/canister-shot-video.78404/; accessed 7/23/17.

Capron, Horace, Jr. "Regimental History." http://8thillinois cavalry.org/regimental-history.html; accessed 7/23/17. {8thIllCav}

Carmichael, Peter S. *The Purcell, Crenshaw, and Letcher Artillery*. Lynchburg, VA: H.E. Howard, 1990.

Chambers, C.C. "Mississippians at Gaines' Mill." *Confederate Veteran* 19 (1991): 510. {12MISS} {19MISS}

Chapla, John D. *42nd Virginia Infantry*. Lynchburg, VA: H.E. Howard, 1983. {42VA}

_____. *48nd Virginia Infantry*. Lynchburg, VA: H.E. Howard, 1989. {48VA}

Charlotte Observer. Untitled article of 3/23/1900, in NC Collection Clipping file through 1975, UNC Library, Chapel Hill, NC. {4NC}

Charlottesville Artillery Battery. The American Civil War, Virginia: http://antietam.aotw.org/officers.php?unit_id=737, accessed 8/6/17

Cheshire, James. "Re: Lt. Col. Franklin J. Faison, CSA," by James Cheshire. http://www.genealogy.com/forum/surnames/topics/faison/241; accessed 7/23/17.

Christiancy, Henry Clay. *Diary, 1862–64*. Bentley Historical Library, University of Michigan, Ann Arbor. {1MI}

Chubb, C. St. J. "The Seventeenth Regiment of Infantry." http://www.history.army.mil/books/R&H/R&H-17IN.htm accessed 7/11/17

Civil War Centennial Commission. *Tennesseans in the Civil War*. Nashville: 1964. {1TN} {7TN} {14TN}

"Claiborne R. Mason." Waddell's Annals of Augusta County, Virginia, from 1726 to 1871. http://www.roanetnhistory.org/bookread.php?loc=WaddellsAnnals&pgid=518; accessed 5/6/17. {African Pioneers}

Clark, Rufus W. *Heroes of Albany*. Albany: S.R. Gray, 1867.

Clark, Walter, ed. *Histories of the Several Regiments and Battalions from North Carolina*. Raleigh: E.M. Uzzell, Printer, 1901. https://archive.org/details/historiesofsever03clar; accessed 7/4/17.

Clover, Edwin A. *Bucktailed Wildcats*. New York: Thomas Yoseloff, 1960. {13PR}

Coatsville Road over New Found River. http://ugly bridges.com; accessed 7/23/17.

Coffin, Charles. *Stories of Our Soldiers*. Boston: Journal Publishing, 1892. {Martin's Battery}

Coker, James Lida. *History of Company G, Ninth South Carolina Regiment Infantry* ... Greenwood, SC: Attic Press, 1979. {9SC} {6SC}

Cole, James Reid. *Miscellany*. Dallas: Press of Ewing B. Bedford, 1897. {23NC}

Coles, R.T. *From Huntsville to Appomattox*. Ed. Jeffery T. Stocker. Knoxville: University of Tennessee Press, 1996. {4AL}

Collins, Benjamin M. Papers. SHC. {12NC}

Company A, 27th Regiment, Georgia Volunteers, CSA. http://www.thegagenweb.com/marion/military/civilwar/a27th.htm; accessed 7/23/17.

Conklin, Ryan A. *The 18th New York Infantry in the Civil War*. Jefferson, NC: McFarland, 2017.

Conway, Alan. "Welshmen in the Union Armies." Civil War History, Iowa State University, June 1958. {5NY}

Cooke, James Dell. *A History of the 31st Virginia Infantry*

Regiment Volunteers C.S.A. Roy Bird Cook Collection, West Virginia History Online Digital Collections, 1955.

Cooke, John Esten, *War Diary of John Esten Cooke*. SHSP 40 (1915).

"Cooke, Philip St. George." Encyclopedia Virginia, https://www.encyclopediavirginia.org/Cooke_Philip_St_George_1809-1895#start_entry; accessed 8/26/17

Cooper, J. "Pickett's Brigade at Gaines' Mill." *Confederate Veteran* 6 (1991): 472. {8VA} {18VA} {19VA} {56VA} {28VA}

Coppée, Henry, ed. *History of the Civil War in America*, vol. 2. Philadelphia: Jos. H. Coates, 1876.

Cowles, Calvin P., ed. *The Official Military Atlas of the Civil War*. New York: Fairfax Press, 1983.

Cowles, Luther. *History of the Fifth Massachusetts Battery*. Boston: L.E. Cowles, 1902.

Cowper, Pulaski, comp. *Extracts of Letters of Major General Bryan Grimes to his Wife*. Ed. Gary W. Gallagher. Wilmington, NC: Broadfoot Publishing, 1986. {4NC}

Cowtan, Charles W. *Services of the Tenth New York Volunteers*. New York: Charles H. Ludwig, 1882. {10NY}

Crawford, Mark J. "I'll Live Yet to Dance on that Foot." *Civil War Times Illustrated* 32, No. 2 (May-June 1993). {13NC} {23NC}

Croom, Wendell D. *The War-History of Company "C" (Beauregard Volunteers), Sixth Georgia Regiment (infantry) with a graphic account of each member*. Fort Valley, GA: printed at the *Advertiser* office, 1879. https://archive.org/details/warhistoryofcomp00croo; accessed 7/19/17.

Cross, C. Wallace. *Ordeal by Fire*. Clarksville, TN: Clarksville Montgomery County Museum, 1990. {1TN}{7TN} {14TN}

Crozier, Granville H. "A Private with General Hood." *Confederate Veteran* 25 (1991): 556. {4TX}

Curtis, Martin. *From Bull Run to Chancellorsville*. New York: Knickerbocker Press, 1906. {16NY}

Cutrer, Thomas E., ed. *Longstreet's Aide*. Charlottesville: University Press of Virginia, 1995.

Dabney, R.L. *Life and Campaigns of Lieut.-Gen. Thomas J. Jackson*. New York: Blelock, 1866.

"Daniel Butterfield." Wikipedia.

Daniel, Frederick. *The Richmond Howitzers in the War*. Richmond, 1891.

"Daniel Harvey Hill." Wikipedia.

Davenport, Alfred. *Camp and Field Life of the Fifth New York Volunteer Infantry*. New York: Dick and Fitzgerald, 1879. {5NY}

Davidson, J. Wood. "Horrors of the Battlefield." *Confederate Veteran* 14 (1991): 305. {1SCV} {1SCR} {13SC} {14SC}{12SC}

Davis, Jefferson. *The Rise and Fall of the Confederate Government*. New York: T. Yoseloff, 1958. https://archive.org/details/riseandfallconf01davigoog; accessed 7/23/17.

Davis, Nicholas A. *The Campaign from Texas to Maryland*. Austin, TX: Steck, 1961. {4TX}

Davis, Varina. *Jefferson Davis: Ex-President of the Confederate States of America: A Memoir*. New York: Belford, 1890. https://archive.org/stream/jeffersondavisex02davi#page/n7/mode/2up; accessed 7/23/17.

Dewberry, Ray. *History of the 14th Georgia Infantry Regiment*. Berwyn Heights, MD: Heritage Books, 2008.

Divine, John E. *8th Virginia Infantry*. Lynchburg, VA: H.E. Howard, 1987. {8VA}

Dobbins, Austin C. *Grandfather's Journal*. Dayton, OH: Morningside, 1988. {16MISS}

Douglas, Henry Kyd. *I Rode with Stonewall*. Chapel Hill: UNC Press, 1940.

Dowdey, Clifford. *The Seven Days*. Boston: Little, Brown, 1964.

_____, ed. *The Wartime Papers of R.E. Lee*. Boston: Little, Brown, 1967.

Drane, J.W. "Louisiana Tigers at Fair Oaks, Va." *Confederate Veteran* 14, 521. {1LZB}

Driver, Robert J., Jr. *52nd Virginia Infantry*. Lynchburg, VA: H.E. Howard, 1986. {52VA}

_____. *58th Virginia Infantry*. Lynchburg, VA: H.E. Howard, 1990. {58VA}

Duffer, Kyle, Major. Virginia National Guard: Sgt. 18th Virginian Infantry Co B. Danville Greys. {March Order; Road Space; Trains}

Dufour, Charles L. *Gentle Tiger*. Baton Rouge: LSU Press, 1957. {WHEAT}

Dula, A.J. "Civil War Incidents." Perkins Library, Duke University, Durham, NC. {22NC}

Dunaway, Wayland Fuller. *Reminiscences of a Rebel*. New York: Neale, 1913. {40VA}

Eberly, Robert E., Jr. *Bouquets from the Cannon's Mouth*. Shippensburg, PA: White Mane Books, 2005. {8 PR}

Edwards, John E. *The Confederate Soldier*. New York: Blelock, 1868. {19VA}

"83d Regiment Pennsylvania Volunteers." http://www.pa-roots.com/pacw/infantry/83rd/83dorg.html; accessed 7/23/17.

Ent, Uzal. *The Pennsylvania Reserves in the Civil War*. Jefferson, NC: McFarland, 2014.

Evans, Clement, ed. *Confederate Military History*: Atlanta: Confederate Publishing, 1899.

Evans, Thomas H. "There is no use in trying to dodge shot." *Civil War Times Illustrated* 6 (August 1967).

Everett, Donald E., ed. *Chaplain Davis and Hood's Texas Brigade*. San Antonio: Principia Press of Trinity University, 1962. {4Tx}

Fairchild, C.B. *History of the 27th Regiment, New York Volunteers*. Binghamton, NY: Carl & Matthews, 1888. {27NY}

Farwell, Byron. *Stonewall*. New York: W.W. Norton, 1992.

Fields, Frank E., Jr. *28th Virginia Infantry*. Lynchburg, VA: H.E. Howard, 1985. {28VA}

Fields, Ron. *The Hampton Legion*. Gloucestershire, UK: Design Folio, 1994. {HL}

1st Army Corps (Union), Wikipedia.

"1st Lt. Stephen W. Stryker, 11th Infantry Regiment Civil War." http://dmna.ny.gov/historic/reghist/civil/infantry/11thInf/11thInfPersonStryker.htm; accessed 7/24/17.

1st Louisiana Battalion, Coppens' Zouaves. http://www.angelfire.com/rebellion2/coppenszouaves/history.htm, accessed 8/14/17.

"First South Carolina Volunteers." *America's Civil War* 5, No. 5 (1992). {1SCV}

Fletcher, William Andrew. *Rebel Private Front and Rear*. Austin: University of Texas Press, 1954. {5TX}

Foard, Fred C. Papers. NC Dept. of Archives and History, Raleigh, NC. {20NC}

"Foot Cavalry." Wikipedia.

Foote, Keith. *Mark the Lines of Your Weary Marches*. CreateSpace, 2014

Fortin, Maurice S., ed. "Col. Henry A. Herbert's History of the Sixth Alabama Volunteer Regiment, CSA." *Alabama Historical Quarterly* 29, Nos. 1, 2, 3, & 4 (1977). {6AL}

Foster, John Y. *New Jersey and the Rebellion*. Newark: Martin R. Dennis, 1868. {1NJ} {2NJ} {3NJ} {4NJ}

14th Brooklyn Regiment. Wikipedia.

14th Infantry Regiment. https://www.25thida.org/units/infantry/14th-infantry-regiment/ accessed 7/23/17.

Fourth Michigan Letters and Diaries. Marty Bertera and the 4th Michigan Volunteer Infantry. {4MI}

Fowler, Thos. M. Papers, Letter mentioning George Pickett. Museum of the Confederacy, Richmond, VA.

Fox, John J., III. *Stuart's Ride*. El Dorado, CA: Savas, 2014.

Franklin Visitor, newspaper article, 7/22/62 Richmond Nat'l Battlefield Park. {44NY}

Freeman, Douglas Southall. *Lee's Lieutenants: A Study in Command*. New York: Scribner's, 1942.

_____. *R.E. Lee*. New York: Scribner's, 1935. http://penelope.uchicago.edu/Thayer/E/Gazetteer/People/Robert_E_Lee/FREREL/home.html; accessed 5/1/17.

Frye, Dennis E. *2nd Virginia Infantry*. Lynchburg, VA: H.E. Howard, 1984. {2VA}

Fry's Peyton Orange (Virginia) Artillery. http://www.americancivilwar101.com/units/csa-va/va-art-lt-batt-richmondorange.html; accessed 7/23/17.

Fulton, W.F. "Archer's Brigade at Cold Harbor." *Confederate Veteran* 31 (1991): 300. {5ALBN}

_____. *The War Reminiscences of William Frierson Fulton II*. Gaithersburg, MD: Butternut Press, 1986. {5ALBN}

Galloway, George Norton. *The 95th Pennsylvania Volunteers (Gosline's Zouaves) in the Sixth Corps*. Collins, PA: 1884. (Kindle Edition)

Garber, Alexander M., Jr. *Stonewall Jackson's Way: A Sketch of the Life and Services of Major John A. Harman*. Kindle Edition, 2014.

Garrison, Webb. *Civil War Curiosities*. Nashville: Rutledge Hill Press, 1994.

Gayley, Alice J. "Great Battle on the Chickahominy." http://www.pa-roots.com/pacw/infantry/105th/battlesevenpines105th.html; accessed 7/3/17

General Micah Jenkins and the Palmetto Sharpshooters. South Carolina Regimental Series. Germantown, TN: Guild Bindery Press, 1994. {PSS}

"George A. McCall." Wikipedia.

Gibbs, Joseph. *Three Years in the Bloody Eleventh*. University Park: Pennsylvania State University Press, 2002.

Gilmer, Jeremy Francis. Papers #276. Southern Historical Collection, Wilson Library, University of North Carolina at Chapel Hill.

Glasgow, William M. *Northern Virginia's Own*. Alexandria, VA: Gobill Press, 1989. {17VA}

Glover, Robert W., ed. *Tyler to Sharpsburg*. Waco, TX: W.H. Morrison, Bookseller, 1960. {1TX}

Goldsborough, W.W. *The Maryland Line in the Confederate States Army*. Baltimore: Kelly, Piet & Co., 1869. {1MD}

Green, Dr. James L. "Civil War Ballooning During the Seven Days Campaign." http://www.civilwar.org/education/history/civil-war-ballooning/ballooning-during-the-seven.html; accessed 7/23/17. {Lowe Balloon}

Guiney, Patrick R. *Commanding the Irish Ninth*. Ed. Christian G, Samito. Oxford University Press, 1958.

Hale, G.W.B. "At Gaines' Mill and Malvern Hill." *Confederate Veteran* 30 (1991): 252.

Hamby, William R. "Fourth Texas in Battle of Gaines' Mill." *Confederate Veteran* 14 (1991): 183. {4TX}

_____. "Historical Sketch of Hood's Texas Brigade." *Confederate Veteran* 18 (1991): 565. {HL} {1TX} {4TX} {5TX} {18GA}

Hamilton, J.G. de Roulhac, ed. *The Papers of Randolph Abbott Shotwell*. Raleigh: The North Carolina Historical Commission, 1929. {8VA}

Hamilton, John A. *Confederate Veteran* 1, 72.

Hankins, Samuel. "Simple Story of a Soldier IV." *Confederate Veteran* 20 (1991): 571. {11MISS} {4AL} {6NC} {2MISS}

Hanover County Historical Society. *Old Homes of Hanover County, Virginia*. Hanover County, 1983.

Hanover's History. www.hanovercounty.gov; accessed 7/23/17. {Merry Oaks Tavern}

Hardy, Michael C. *The 37th North Carolina Troops*. Jefferson, NC: McFarland, 2003.

Harding, Ro. Resume of a Manuscript by Major Joseph Harding. Brockenbrough Library, Museum of the Confederacy, Richmond, VA. {Elzey}

Harris, J.S. *Historical Sketches, Seventh Regiment North Carolina Troops*. Mooresville, NC, 1893. {7NC}

Harrison, Walter. *Pickett's Men: A Fragment of War History*. New York: D. van Nostrand, 1870. {8VA} {18VA} {28VA} {19VA} {56VA}

Harper, Douglas R. *If Thee Must Fight*. West Chester, PA: Charter County Historical Society, 1990. {4PR}

Harrer, William. *With Drum and Gun in '61*. Greenville, PA: Beaver Printing Company, 1908. Reprint edition, 1982. {14NY}

Hartwell, Richard H., donator. "Pennsylvania Reserves" USAMHI. {7PR}

Haskell, John Cheves. *The Haskell Memoirs*. Eds. Gilbert Govan and James W. Livingood. New York: G.P. Putnam's Sons, 1960.

Hassler, William W., ed. *The General to His Lady*. Chapel Hill, NC: University of North Carolina Press, 1960. {16NC} {22NC} {34NC} {38NC} {22VABN}

Haw, Joseph. "In the Battle of First Cold Harbor." *Confederate Veteran* 34.

Haw, Mary Jane. "My Visits to Grandmother." *Charlotte Christian Observer*, May 18, 1910.

"Hdqrtrs 5th Regt Ala, [?] Farm, July 19th, 1862." Hobson Papers, Virginia Historical Society, Richmond, VA.

Hewett, Janet, et al., ed. *Supplement to the Official Records of the Union and Confederate Armies*. Wilmington, NC: Broadfoot Publishing, 1994.

Hill, A.F. *Our Boys*. Philadelphia: Keystone, 1889. {8PR}

Hill, Daniel Harvey. *Bethel to Sharpsburg*. Raleigh, NC: Edwards & Broughton, 1926.

_____. "Lee's Attacks North of the Chickahominy." *Battles and Leaders of the Civil War*, vol. 2.

_____. Report of Casualties. Eleanor Brockenbrough Library, Museum of the Confederacy, Richmond, VA.

Hinsdale Diary. Perkins Library, Duke University. {16NC} {22NC} {34NC} {38NC} {22VABN}

"History of the Third Light Artillery." http://www.oocities.org/pentagon/3622/battery1.html; accessed 7/23/17.

"A History of the 12th Georgia Infantry." http://twelvega.tripod.com/id17.html; accessed 7/3/17.

"History of the 13th Virginia Infantry Flag," http://cw13thvirginiacoe.tripod.com/id8.html; accessed 7/3/17. {13th Va.}

"A History of the [95th] Regiment, 1861–1862." http://www.53rdpvi.org/95th-pennsylvania-volunteer-infantry/a-history-of-the-regiment-1861-1862/; accessed 7/23/17, courtesy 53d Pennsylvania Volunteer Infantry.

Hitchcock, W.H. "Recollections of a Participant in the Charge." *Battles and Leaders of the Civil War*.

Hobson Papers. Virginia Historical Society, Richmond, VA. {5AL}

Hodges, Elizabeth M. *C.B. Fleet: The Man and his Company*. No publishing information.

Holloway, Eleanor S. Diary. Brockenbrough Library, Museum of the Confederacy, Richmond, VA. {4Tx}

Holt, John Lee. *I Wrote You Word*. Ed. James Mumper. Lynchburg, VA: H.E. Howard, 1993. {56VA}

Hood, John Bell. *Advance and Retreat*. Bloomington: Indiana University Press, 1959. {18GA} {1TX} {4TX} {5TX} {HL}

Hoole, William Stanley, ed. *History of the Fourteenth Regiment Alabama Volunteers*. Dayton, OH: Morningside House, 1982. {14AL}

_____. *Pee Dee Light Artillery*, University, AL: Confederate Publishing, 1983.

Hopper, George. Letter of 10/19/62, USAMHI. {10NY}

"Horse (*Equus ferus caballus*)." http://speedofanimals.com/animals/horse; accessed 8/25/17.

Howard, McHenry. *Recollections of a Maryland Confederate Soldier & Staff Officer*. Ed. James I. Robertson. Dayton, OH: Morningside Bookshop, 1975. {1MD}

Howard, McHenry. *Recollections of a Maryland Confederate Soldier and Staff Officer Under Johnston, Jackson and Lee*. Baltimore: Williams & Wilkins, 1914 Book digitized by Google from the library of Harvard University and uploaded to the Internet Archive by user tpb; accessed 7/23/17.

Howard, Wiley C. *Sketch of Cobb Legion*. {Cobb Legion}

Howe, Henry. *History of Hanover County*. 1845.

Howerton, Bryan R. "Second Arkansas Infantry Battalion: A Brief History." http://cpouchgenweb.com/civilwar/2bdbnhis.html; accessed 7/23/17.

Hoyt, James A. "Anderson's Brigade at Gaines' Mill." *Confederate Veteran* 7 (1991): v24. {PSS}

Hunter, J.T. "At Yorktown in 1862 and What Followed." *Confederate Veteran* 26 (1991): 112. {Whiting's Staff}

_____. "Lieut. Gen. John B. Hood." *Confederate Veteran* 24 (1991): 257.

Hunton, Eppa. "Gaines' Mill." *Confederate Veteran* 7 (1991): 223. {8VA}

Hunts, George T. *A Touch of History*. Fincastle, VA: Botetourt County Historical Society, 1995. {28Va}

Hurst, M.E. *History of the 14th Alabama*. Dayton, OH: Morningside House, 1982.

Hutton, A.W. "Bury Me on the Field, Boys." *Confederate Veteran* 17 (1991): 168. {WHEAT}

Ingle, John P., Jr. "Soldiering with the Second Florida Infantry Regiment." *Florida Historical Quarterly* 59, No. 3 (January 1981). {2FLA}

Iobst, Richard W., and Louis H. Manarin. *The Bloody Sixth*. Raleigh, NC: North Carolina Historical Commission, 1965. {6NC}

Irby, Richard. *Historical Sketch of the Nottoway Grays*. Richmond, VA: J.W. Ferguson & Son, 1878. {18VA}

Jackson, Edgar Allen. *Letters of Edgar Allen Jackson*. Privately published, no date. {1NC}

Jackson, Mary Ann. *Memoirs of Stonewall Jackson*. Louisville, KY: Prentiss Press, 1895, https://archive.org/details/memoirsofstonewall00jack, accessed 7/14/17.

Jacobs, Lee. *Cry Heart*. Camden, SC: John Culler & Sons, 1995.

"James A. Walker." Wikipedia.

James, C.F. Letter of unknown date. Confederate Veteran Papers, Perkins Library, Duke University.

_____. Papers, 8th Va. CV papers, Battles Box 1, letter of Jan. 3, 1899.

Jeff Davis Artillery, Alabama Dept. of Archives and History. http://www.archives.alabama.gov/referenc/alamilor/jef-artl.html; accessed 7/23/17.

"John M. Jones." Wikipedia.

"John Thomas Mercer," https://www.findagrave.com/cgi-bin/fg.cgi?page=gr&GRid=10901303; accessed 7/23/17.

Johnson, Sid. *Texans Who Wore the Gray*. Tyler, TX: privately printed, 1907.

Jones, Benjamin. Memoirs. USAMHI, CWTI COLL. {44VA}

Jones, The Rev. J. William, ed. "History of the Crenshaw Battery." *Southern Historical Society Papers* 31.

_____. "Reminiscences of the Army of Northern Virginia," *SHSP* 9.

_____. *SHSP* 10 (Jan. to Dec. 1882).

_____. Untitled article. *Confederate Veteran* 1 (1991): 72. {13VA}

Jones, Terry L. *Lee's Tigers*. Baton Rouge: LSU Press, 1987. {LA}

___, ed. *Memoirs of George Campbell Brown*. Provided by the editor. {Ewell's Staff}

_____. "Wheat's Tigers," *Civil War Times Illustrated* 33, No. 1 (March-April 1994). {WHEAT}

Jordan, Ervin L., Jr., and Herbert A. Thomas, Jr. *19th Virginia Infantry*. Lynchburg, VA: H.E. Howard, 1987. {19VA}

"Joseph R. Anderson." Wikipedia.

Judson, Amos M. *History of the Eighty-Third Regiment Pennsylvania Volunteers*. Dayton, OH: Morningside, 1986. {83PA}

Kelley, Tom, ed. *The Personal Memoirs of Jonathan Thomas Schaf of the First Maryland Artillery*. Baltimore: Butternut & Blue, 1992.

Kilblaine, Richard E., Transportation Corps Historian. "White House Landing—Sustaining the Army of the Potomac During the Peninsula Campaign." http://www.transchool.lee.army.mil/historian/documents/White%20House%20Landing%20paper.pdf; accessed 5/1/17.

Kilpatrick, Marion Hall. *Letters to Amanda*. Nashville: Champion Resources, no date. {45GA}

Kirkland, Joseph. "The Story of Chicago." http://8thillinoiscavalry.org/biographies.html#WilliamMedill; accessed 7/23/17. {8thIllCav}

Krick, Robert L. *40th Virginia Infantry*. Lynchburg, VA: H.E. Howard, 1985. {40VA}

_____. "Maxcy Gregg." Reprinted from *Civil War History* 19, No. 4 (1973). Kent State University Press.

Laboda, Lawrence. *From Selma to Appomattox*. New York: Oxford University Press, 1994.

Lackie, T.R. "Report of the Gaines' Mill affair by a Federal." *Confederate Veteran*.

Laine, J. Gary, and Morris M. Penny. *Law's Alabama Brigade*. Shippensburg, PA: White Mane Books, 1996.

Lane, Mills, ed. *Dear Mother: Don't Grieve about Me…* Savannah, GA: Beehive Press, 1977. {18GA} {21GA} {COLQUITT} {44GA}

Laswell, Mary L., ed. *Rags and Hope*. New York: Coward-McCann, 1961. {4TX}

Lattimore, T.D. 34th North Carolina Infantry. http://34nc.com/pdfs/History34NC-Lattimore.pdf; accessed 7/23/17.

Law, Evander. "On the Confederate Right at Gaines' Mill." *Battles and Leaders of the Civil War*, 3 vols. New York: Thomas Yoseloff, 1956.

Ledbetter, M.T. "Mechanicsville and Gaines' Mill." *Confederate Veteran* 1 (1991): 244. {5ALBN}

_____. "Wants His Old Flag—Likes the Veteran." *Confederate Veteran* 1 (1991): 185. {5ALBN}

_____. "With Archer's Brigade." *SHSP* 29, 1898. {5ALBN}

Ledford, Preston Lafayette. *Reminiscences of the Civil War, 1861–1865.* https://archive.org/details/reminiscences ofc00ledf, accessed 7/14/17 {14NC}

"The Leon Rifles, Second Florida Volunteer Infantry Regiment Company D: The Actual Unit History of the Real 2nd Florida Volunteer Infantry." http://www. leonrifles.com/History.html; accessed 7/23/17.

"The Life Story and Narrations of Private Charles Rean." http://civilwardailygazette.com/the-life-story-and-narrations-of-private-charles-rean-prisoner-blind-or-tocsin/; accessed 7/23/17.

Lightsey, Ada Christine, "The Jasper Grays." http//www. rootsweb.ancestry.com~msjasper/military/gras2 html; accessed 7/24/17

Loftin, John T. "6th Georgia Infantry." http://196thovi. tripod.com/23rdgeorgiainfantry/id38.html; accessed 7/3/17.

Longacre, Edward G. *Pickett: Leader of the Charge.* Shippensburg, PA: White Mane, 1995.

Longstreet, James. *From Manassas to Appomattox.* New York: Da Capo Press, 1992.

Lowe, William B. Letter of 7/5/62, CW MISC COLL US-AMHI. {11US}

Lowen, James W. *Lies Across America,* Touchstone Books, 2007.

Lubbock, F.R. Untitled article. *Confederate Veteran* 7 (1991): 485.

Lubock, Francis Richard. *Six Decades in Texas.* Austin: B.C. Jones, 1900.

Luckenbill, Lewis. Diary. NW Corner CWTI Collection, USAMHI. {96PA}

McAfoos, Joanie Quairoli. "95th Infantry Regiment Pennsylvania Volunteers." http://www.pa-roots.com/ pacw/infantry/95th/95threg.html; accessed 7/23/17.

McBrien, Joe Bennett. *The Tennessee Brigade.* Chattanooga: Hudson Printing and Litho., 1977. {1TN} {7TN} {14TN} {19GA}

McClandon, William Augustus. *Recollections of War Times:* Montgomery: Paragon, 1909. {15AL}

McComb, William. "The Battles in Front of Richmond, 1862." *Confederate Veteran* 23 (1991): 161. {14TN}

McCrady, Edward. "Boy Heroes of Cold Harbor." *SHSP* 25 (1991): 235. {1SCV}

McDaid, William Kelsey. *Four Years of Arduous Service.* Ann Arbor: University Manuscripts, Inc. {7NC {18NC} {28NC} {33NC} {37NC}

McDavid, Peter. "With the Palmetto Riflemen." *Confederate Veteran* 37 (1991): 262. {2d SC Rifles}

McGuire, Judith. *Diary of a Southern Refugee During the War.* New York: E.J. Hale & Sons, 1867.

_____. *Diary of a Southern Refugee During the War.* Richmond, VA: J.W. Randolph & English, 1889. Kindle Edition.

McIlvane, William, Letter of 7/27/62, Richmond Nat'l. Battlefield Park. {5NY}

McKoy, Lew. Letter of Sept. 13, 1862 to the *Armenia Times.*

MacNamara, Daniel George. *The History of the Ninth Regiment Massachusetts Volunteer Infantry.* Boston: E.B. Stallings, 1899. {9MA} Courtesy 9th Mass Reenactors.

MacNamara, Michael H. *The Irish 9th in Bivouac and Battle.* Boston: Lee & Shepherd, 1867. {9MA} Courtesy 9th Mass Reenactors.

McNiven, Thomas. "Recollections of Thomas McNiven." Civil War Richmond. www.mdgorman.com, accessed 9/9/17.

"Major Chatham Roberdeau Wheat." *Confederate Veteran* 49, 425. {WHEAT}

Manly, Matt, "Second Regiment." http://www.civilwar index.com/armync/reghist/2nd_nc_infantry_ rehist>pdf; accessed 7/23/17. {2NC}

_____. "4th Regiment." http://www.civilwarindex.com/ armync/reghist/4th_nc_infantry_reghist.pdf; accessed 7/23/17. {4 NC}

Map of Louisa County. https://www.loc.gov/resource/ gvhs01.vhs00361/, Confederate States of America. Army. Dept. of Northern Virginia. Chief Engineer's Office. Blackford, B. L. (Benjamin Lewis), 1835–1908. Campbell, Albert H. (Albert Henry), 1826–1899. O'Connor, James. 1863 Map from the Confederate Engineer Bureau in Richmond, Va. General J.F. Gilmer, Chief Engineer. "Presented to the Virginia Historical Society by his only daughter, Mrs. J.F. Minis, Savannah, Ga."—Note on map.

Marshall, Charles. *An Aide-de Camp of General Lee.* Boston: Little, Brown, 1927. Leefamilyarchives.org; accessed 5/14/17.

Marshall, Michael. *Gallant Creoles.* Lafayette: University of Louisiana at Lafayette Press, 2013.

Martin, David G., ed., *Hexamer's First New Jersey Battery in the Civil War.* Hightstown, NJ: Longstreet House, 1992.

Martin, Samuel J. *Road to Glory.* Indianapolis: Guild Press of Indiana, 1991. {Ewell}

"Mary Crenshaw." http://www.afaoa.org/db_files/William _Wilson_Austin_VA/Individuals/I82.html; accessed 5/24/17.

Mattison, J.W. "Orr's South Carolina Rifles." *SHSP* 27 (1991): 157. {1SCR}

Merritt, Wesley. "Life and Services of General Phillip St. George Cooke, U.S. Army." *Journal of the U.S. Cavalry Association* 8, No. 29 (June 1895): 79.

Miller, Francis Trevelyan, and Robert S. Lanier. *The Photographic History of The Civil War in Ten Volumes: Volume 5, Forts and Artillery.* New York: Review of Reviews, 1911. http://digitalcollections.baylor.edu/ cdm/landingpage/collection/tx-wotr; accessed 7/ 23/17.

Mills, George Henry. *History of the 16th North Carolina Regiment.* Hamilton, NY: Edmonston, 1992. {16NC}

Minnigh, H.M. *History of Company K.* "Home Print" Publisher, no date, located in USAMHI. {1PR}

Mitchell, Joseph B. *The Badge of Gallantry.* Shippensburg, PA: White Mane Books, 1997. {83 Pa}

Moore, Edward A. *The Story of a Cannoneer under Stonewall Jackson.* New York: Neale, 1907. {Rockbridge}

Moore, James Orville. "The Men of the Bayou City Guards." Master's thesis, University of Houston at Clear Lake City, 1988. {5TX}

Moore, Robert H., II. *The Charlottesville, Lee Lynchburg and Johnson's Bedford Artillery.* Lynchburg, VA: H.E. Howard, 1990. {Carrington Charlottesville Artillery}

Morgan, W.H. *Personal Reminiscences of the War of 1861–1865.* Lynchburg, VA: J.P. Bell, 1911. {11VA}

Morris, William Groves. Letters of 7/3/62, 7/6/62. Southern Historical Collection, University of North Carolina. {37NC}

Mundy, James H. *Second to None.* Scarborough, ME: Harp, 1992. {2ME}

Murray, Alton J. *South Georgia Rebels.* St. Mary's, GA: privately published, 1976. {26GA} {61GA}

Musselman, Homer D. *47th Virginia Infantry.* Lynchburg, VA: H.E. Howard, 1991. {47VA}

Muth, Chaz. "U.S. Army Chaplain Sets Marching Speed Record, Inspiring Troops." https://www.nwcatholic.

org/news/national/us-army-chaplain-sets-marching-speed-record; accessed 7/23/17.

Myers, Augustus. *Ten Years in the Ranks*. New York: Arno Press, 1979. {2US}

Nabours, W.A. "Service of a Texas Command." *Confederate Veteran* 24 (1991): 69. {5TX}

Naisawald, L. VanLoan. *Grape and Canister*. New York: Oxford University Press, 1960.

Nash, Eugene Arus. *A History of the Forty-Fourth Regiment New York Volunteer Infantry*. Chicago: R.R. Donnelly & Sons, 1911. {44NY}

National Park Service, Soldiers' and Sailors' Database. https://www.nps.gov/civilwar/soldiers-and-sailors-database.htm; accessed 7/23/17.

Newton, Steven H. *The Battle of Seven Pines*. Lynchburg, VA: H.E. Howard, 1993.

Nicholas, Richard L. *Powhatan, Salem and Courtney Henrico Artillery*. Lynchburg, VA: H.E. Howard, 1997. {Courtney Henrico Artillery}

Nichols, Dale Gary. *Hurrah for Georgia!* A15 Publishing, 2017.

Nichols, Edward J. *Toward Gettysburg*. University Park: Pennsylvania State University Press, 1958.

Nichols, G.W. *A Soldier's Story of his Regiment*. Kennesaw, GA: Continental, 1961. {61GA}

"The 95th Pennsylvania Uniform in the Field." 53d Pennsylvania Volunteer Infantry, http://www.53rdpvi.org/95th-pennsylvania-volunteer-infantry/the-95th-pennsylvania-uniform-in-the-field/; accessed 7/23/17.

96th Infantry Regiment Pennsylvania Volunteers. paroots.com; schulylkillcountymilitary history.blogspot.com; accessed 7/23/17.

Nisbet, James Cooper. *Four Years on the Firing Line*. Jackson, TN: McCowat-Mercer, 1962. {21Ga}

Norton, Oliver. *Army Letters, 1861–1865*. Dayton, OH: Morningside, 1990. {83PA}

N.P. "The Battle of Gaines' Mill June 27, 1862." Monograph at the Simpson Center for Confederate History, Hillsboro, TX.

Oates, William C. *The War Between the Union and the Confederacy*. New York: Neale, 1905. {15AL}

O'Farrell, John. Letter. Brockenbrough Library, Museum of the Confederacy, Richmond, VA.

Osborne, C.A. "The Battle of Mechanicsville." *Charlotte Semi Weekly Observer*, March 23, 1900, North Carolina Collection Clipping File through 1975, Civil War Regimental Histories, 4th Regt., UNC Library, Chapel Hill, NC. {4 NC}

O'Sullivan, Richard. *55th Virginia Infantry*. Lynchburg, VA: H.E. Howard, 1989. {55VA}

Owen, Samuel Tine. "Letters of a Teen-Age Soldier." Newspaper clipping at the Simpson Center for Confederate History, Hillsboro, TX.

Page, Rosewell. *Hanover County: Its History and Legends*. Richmond, VA: Unknown binding, 1926.

Paris, Comte de. *History of the Civil War in America*, vol. 2. Philadelphia: Porter & Coates, 1875. https://archive.org/details/historyofcivilwa22pari accessed 5/5/17.

Park, Robert Emory. *Sketch of the Twelfth Alabama Infantry*. Richmond, VA: Wm. Ellis Jones, 1906. {12AL}

Parker, John L. *History of the Twenty-Second Massachusetts Infantry*. Boston: Rand Avery, 1887. {22MA}

Patterson, Edmund DeWitt. *Yankee Rebel*. Ed. John G. Barrett. UNC Press, 1966. {9AL}

Patton, William R. *Drums and Guns Around Petersburg*. Bowie, MD: Heritage Books, 1995. {8PR, 11PR}

Peacock, William H. Letter of 7/5/62. CWMISC, US-AMHI.

"Peninsula Campaign." Wikipedia.

Penn, Greenville B. Letter of 6/27/62 in Papers, Perkins Library, Duke University. {42VA}

"Pennsylvania Reserves." Wikipedia.

Personal Reminiscences of a Maryland Soldier in the War Between the States. Baltimore: Privately published, 1898. {1MD}

"Pickett's Charge" Wikipedia

Pluskat, Ken. "On to Prison." *Civil War Times Illustrated* 29, No. 2 (May-June 1990). {9MA}

Poague, William Thomas. *Gunner with Stonewall*. Pickle Partners Publishing, 2014. Kindle Edition. {Rockbridge Artillery}

Pohanka, Brian C. "Charge Bayonets." *Civil War Times Illustrated* 33, No. 2 (May-June 1994). {5NY}

_____. *Vortex of Hell: History of the 5th New York Volunteer Infantry*. Farmville, VA: Schroeder, 2012. {5NY}

Pollard, Edward A. *Lee and his Lieutenants*. New York: E.B. Treat, 1867. https://archive.org/details/leeandhislieute00pollgoog; accessed 7/23/17.

Polley, J.B. *Hood's Texas Brigade*. New York: Neale, 1910. {18GA} {1TX} {4TX} {5TX} {HL}

_____. *A Soldier's Letters to Charming Nellie*. New York: Neale, 1908. {5TX}

"Pontoon Bridges." DaveBrt. https://www.civilwartalk.com/threads/details-of-pontoon-bridges.110008/ accessed 5/20/17

Potter, William, and John Michael Priest, eds. *One Surgeon's Private War*. Shippensburg, PA: White Mane, 1996.

Powell, William H. *The Fifth Army Corps*. Dayton, OH: Morningside Bookshop, 1984.

_____. "Footnote to 'The Charge of Cooke's Cavalry at Gaines' Mill.'" *Battles and Leaders of the Civil War*, vol. 2.

Pyne, C.M. Letter to Mother, July 7, 1862. Courtesy Brian Pohanka.

Rankin, Thomas M. *23rd Virginia Infantry*. Lynchburg, VA: H.E. Howard, 1985. {23VA}

_____. *37th Virginia Infantry*. Lynchburg, VA: H.E. Howard, 1987. {37VA}

Rare Presentation Model 1861 Springfield Rifle Musket Dated 1861, "10TH NEW YORK ZOUAVES." https://jamesdjulia.com/item/lot-812-rare-presentation-model-1861-springfield-rifle-musket-dated-1861-10th-new-york-zouaves-51218/; accessed 7/23/17.

Ratchford, J.W. *Some Reminiscences of Persons and Incidents of the Civil War*. Richmond, VA: Whittet & Shepperson, 1909.

"Re: Stonewall Jackson's Black Confederates." http://history-sites.com/cgi-bin/bbs62x/nvcwmb/webbbs_config.pl?md=read;id=72968. Citations to Robertson, Mary Ann Jackson, and others are included there. {African Pioneers}

Reed, Erasmus W. Letter of 7/6/62. Sesquicentennial Hist. Proj. Coll., Indiana Hist. Soc. {96PA}

Reese, Timothy J. *Sykes' Regular Infantry Division, 1861–1865*. Jefferson, NC: McFarland, 1990.

Rhett's Brooks South Carolina Artillery. http://wade-hamptoncamp.org/brooks-unit-ba.html; accessed 7/23/17.

Richmond Daily Whig, article of 7/8/62 RNBP. {27NY}

Riedenbaugh, Lowell. *27th Virginia Infantry*. Lynchburg, VA: H.E. Howard, 1993. {27VA}

_____. *33rd Virginia Infantry*. Lynchburg, VA: H.E. Howard, 1987. {33VA}

Rigdon, John C. *Historical Sketch & Roster of the Alabama 6th Infantry Regiment.* CreateSpace, 2015.

Riggs, David F. *13th Virginia Infantry.* Lynchburg, VA: H.E. Howard, 1988. {13VA}

Riggs, Susan A. *21st Virginia Infantry.* Lynchburg, VA: H.E. Howard, 1991. {21VA}

Ripley, William Y.W. *Vermont Riflemen in the War for the Union.* Rutland, VT: Tuttle, 1883. {1USSS}

Robertson, James I., Jr. *4th Virginia Infantry.* Lynchburg, VA: H.E. Howard, 1982. {4VA}

_____. *18th Virginia Infantry.* Lynchburg, VA: H.E. Howard, 1984. {18VA}

_____. *General A.P. Hill: The Story of a Confederate Warrior.* New York: Random House, 1987.

_____. *The Stonewall Brigade.* Baton Rouge: LSU Press, 1963. {2VA} {4VA} {5VA} {27VA} {33VA}

_____. *Stonewall Jackson: The Man, the Soldier, the Legend.* New York: Macmillan, 1997.

Robins, Richard. "With Sykes' Regulars in the Seven Days' Battles." Monograph, Military Historical Society of Massachusetts Collection, Boston Univ. Courtesy Richmond National Battlefield Park.

Robson, John S. *How a One-Legged Rebel Lives.* Charlottesville, VA: Chronicle Steam, 1881. {52VA}

Roby, T.K. "Reminiscences of a Private." *Confederate Veteran* 23 (1991): 548. {9LA}

Roddy, Ray. *The Georgia Volunteer Infantry 1861–1865.* Kearny, NE: Monroe.

Rodgers, Thomas G. "Third Alabama." *America's Civil War* 3, No. 2 (1990). {3AL}

Ronan, James B., II. "Regulars to the Rescue at Gaines' Mill." *America's Civil War* (November 1994).

Rosengarten, J.G. *The German Soldier in the Wars of the United States.* Philadelphia: J.B. Lippincott, 1890.

Ross, Fitzgerald. *Cities and Camps of the Confederate States.* Urbana: Illinois University Press, 1958.

Roy, Andrew, and William J. Miller, eds. *Fallen Soldier.* Montgomery, AL: Elliott & Clark, 1996. {10PR}

Ruffner, Kevin C. *44th Virginia Infantry.* Lynchburg, VA: H.E. Howard, 1987. {44VA}

Russ, Daniel. "The 'Army in a Box.'" https://civilianmilitaryintelligencegroup.com/20471/the-the-army-in-a-box, accessed 8/10/17.

Ryan, Joe. "What happened in January 1862?" The George McClellan Papers. http://joeryancivilwar.com/Sesquicentennial-Monthly-Articles/June-1862/Papers-George-McClellan-June-1862.html; accessed 7/23/17.

St. Lawrence Republican. Odensburgh, New York. Article of 7/22/62, RMBP. {16NY}

Sauers, Richard A. "The Pennsylvania Reserves..." In *The Peninsular Campaign.* Ed. William J. Miller. Campbell, CA: Savas Woodbury, 1993.

Saylor, John. Monograph belonging to Mrs. John Potts donated to RNBP by Michael T. Snyder. {96PA}

Scaife, William R. *The Georgia Brigade.* Atlanta, GA: Self-published, 1988. {LAWTON}

Schardt, W., and Charles Neder. "What the Texans Did at Gaines' Mill." *Confederate Veteran* 7 (1991): 55. {11NC}

Schenk, Robert. "Hallowed Air—Rediscovering Lowe's Gaines' Mill Balloon Camp." http://www.civilwar.org/education/history/civil-war-ballooning/hallowed-air.html; accessed 7/23/17.

Schmutz, George. "The Bloody Fifth." *Civil War Times Illustrated* 30, No. 5 (Nov.-Dec. 1991). {5TX}

Schock, George W. "Grand Army Paper." Schock Collection USAMHI. RNBP. {5PR}

Scott, J.L. *60th Virginia Infantry.* Lynchburg, VA: H.E. Howard, 1997.

Seage, Henry S. Diary in possession of Steve Roberts, courtesy 4th Michigan Reenactors.

Sears, Stephen B. *To the Gates of Richmond.* New York: Ticknor & Fields, 1992.

_____. *The Wartime Papers of George B. McClellan.* New York: Ticknor & Fields, 1989.

"The Second Maryland Infantry: US and Maryland in the Civil War." http://www.2ndmdinfantryus.org/csart2.html; accessed 5/2/17.

"7th Regiment, Virginia Cavalry (Ashby's) (Confederate)." Wikipedia.

Seyburn, Lt. S.Y. "The Tenth Regiment of Infantry." http://www.history.army.mil/books/R&H/R&H-10IN.htm; accessed 7/11/17.

Shaw, Maurice F. *Stonewall Jackson's Surgeon.* Lynchburg, VA: H.E. Howard, 1993.

Shenck, Martin. *Up Came Hill.* Harrisburg, PA: Stackpole, 1958.

Sheppard, W. L. "Jackson of the Chickahominy." *Civil War Times Illustrated* 27, No. 2 (April 1968).

Sherrill, Lee W., Jr. *The 21st North Carolina Infantry: A Civil War History, with a Roster of Officers.* Jefferson, NC: McFarland, 2015.

Shiels, Daman. "Before the Reaper's Sickle." Irish in the Civil War. civilhttps://irishamericancivilwar.com/2011/05/02/before-the-reapers-sickle-the-9th-massachusetts-at-gaines-mill/; accessed 6/30/17

Shober, Mary Wheat. Untitled article. *Confederate Veteran* 19 (1991): 520. {WHEAT}

Simpson, Harold B. *Gaines' Mill to Appomattox.* Waco, TX: Texian Press, 1963. {4TX}

_____. *Hood's Texas Brigade: Lee's Grenadier Guard.* Waco, TX: Texian Press, 1970. {18GA} {1TX} {4TX} {5TX} {HL}

_____, ed. *Touched with Valor.* Hillsboro, TX: Hill Junior College Press, 1964. {1TX} {4TX} {5TX}

_____. Unreferenced notes at the Simpson Center of Confederate History, Hillsboro, TX. These notes were from the writings of Robert Campbell, later published as George Skoch's *Lone Star Confederate,* first ed. College Station: Texas A&M University Press, 2003.

Smith, Fred. *Samuel Duncan Oliphant: The Indomitable Campaigner.* New York: Exposition Press, 1967.

Smith, W.A. *The Anson Guards.* Charlotte, NC: Stone, 1914. {14NC}

Smith, Wayne. "Redemption of the 83d Pennsylvania." *Civil War Magazine* 22, 38. {83PA}

Sorrel, Moxley. *Recollections of a Confederate Staff Officer.* New York: Neale, 1905.

Spisak, Ernest D. *Pittsburgh's Forgotten Civil War Regiment: A History of the 62nd Pennsylvania Volunteer Infantry,* first ed. Tarentum, PA: Word Association, 2013.

Stephens, Robert Grier, Jr. *Intrepid Warrior.* Dayton, OH: Morningside, 1992. {31GA}

Stevens, C.A. *Berdan's United States Sharpshooters in the Army of the Potomac.* St. Paul, MN: Price-McGill, 1892. {1USSS}

Stevens, Jno. W. *Reminiscences of the Civil War.* Powhatan, VA: Derwent Books, 1982.

Stone, Edwin W. *Rhode Island in the Rebellion.* Providence: Knowles, Anthony & Co., 1864.

Sutton, Tiffany. "Prostitution in the Civil War." https://prezi.com/lltsxfxu_g7x/prostitution-in-the-civil-war/; accessed 8/13/17.

Swift, Eben. *History of the 5th U.S. Cavalry from 1855 to 1927.* Ft. Clark, TX: N.p., 1927

Swisher, James K. *Prince of Edisto*. Berryville, VA: Rockbridge, 1996.

Sword, Wiley. *Sharpshooter: Hiram Berdan, his Famous Sharpshooters and their Sharps Rifles*. Lincoln, RI: Andrew Mowbray, 1988.

Sydnor, Henry Clinton. "A Virginia Boy in the Sixties." *Confederate Veteran* 20 (1991): 105.

Sypher, J.R. *History of the Pennsylvania Reserve Corps*. Lancaster, PA: Elias Barr, 1865.

Taylor, Doyle. "2nd Battalion, Arkansas Infantry, CSA." http://www.history-sites.co/cgi-bin/bbs62x/arcwmb/webbbs_config.pl?md=read;id=15169; accessed 7/23/17.

Taylor, Edward Henry. Letter of 7/14/62. Bentley Historical Collection, University of Michigan, Ann Arbor. Courtesy of 4th Michigan Reenactors.

Taylor, Michael W. *To Drive the Enemy from Southern Soil*. Dayton, OH: Morningside, 1998. {30 NC}

Teman Road over Little River. http://uglybridges.com.

"They Couldn't Hit an Elephant Optional Rule." fatwally.com; accessed 7/23/17.

Thacker, Victor L. *French Harding Civil War Memoirs*. Parsons, WV: McClain, 2002. {31 VA}

31st Infantry Regiment. NYSMM, http://dmna.ny.gov/historic/reghist/civil/infantry/31stInf/31stInfMain.htm#photos; accessed 7/23/17.

31st New York Infantry. NY Dept. of Military and Naval Archives. http://dmna.ny.gov/historic/reghist/civil/infantry/31stInf/31stInfBMSHistSketch.htm; accessed 7/23/17.

32nd Infantry Regiment. NYSMM, https://dmna.ny.gov/historic/reghist/civil/infantry/32ndInf/32ndInfMain.htm; accessed 7/23/17.

32nd New York. https://dmna.ny.gov/historic/reghist/civil/infantry/32ndInf/32ndInfMain.htm; accessed 7/23/17.

"32 Pounder Guns." http://moultrie.battlefieldsinmotion.com/Artillery-32-pounder.html; accessed 7/23/17.

Thomas, Howard. *Boys in Blue from the Adirondack Foothills*. Prospect, NY: Prospect Books, 1960. {14NY}

Thomas, John *Career and Character of General Micah Jenkins, CSA*. Columbia, SC: State, 1908.

Tilney, Robert. *My Life in the Army*. Philadelphia: Parris & Leach, 1912. [12 NY]

Timberlake envelope. https://www.worthpoint.com/worthopedia/confederate-civil-war-cover-csa-11-77473587;accessed 7/2/17.

Tinsley, Fannie. "Mrs. Tinsley's War Recollections." *Virginia Magazine of History and Biography* 35 (1927).

Todd, George T. *First Texas Regiment*. Waco, TX: Texian Press, 1963. {1TX}

_____. "Gaines' Mill-Pickett and Hood." *Confederate Veteran* 6 (1991): 565. {1TX}

Tolley, William "That Gaines' Mill Affair." *Confederate Veteran* 7 (1991): 54. {4TX}

Townshend, George. *Battlefields of the South*. New York: John Bradburn, 1864.

Townshend, George Alfred. *Rustics in Rebellion*. Chapel Hill: UNC Press, 1950.

"Truman Seymour." Wikipedia.

Tsouras, Peter G. *Scouting for Grant and Meade*. New York: Skyhorse, 2014.

Turner, Charles E., ed. *The Allen Family of Amherst County, Virginia: Civil War Letters*. Berryville, VA: Rockbridge, 1995.

12th Infantry Regiment. https://www.25thida.org/units/infantry/12th-infantry-regiment/; accessed 7/23/17.

22nd Mass / USSC Boston Branch Reenactors, History of the 22nd MVI, https://www.22ndmass.org/history; accessed 7/23/17.

22d Massachusetts Infantry. http://www.oocities.org/pentagon/3622/history.html#pen; accessed 7/23/17.

"Union Balloon Corps." Wikipedia.

Urban, John W. *Battlefield and Prison Pen*. Edgewood, 1882. {1PR}

Varon, Elizabeth. *Southern Lady, Yankee Spy: The True Story of Elizabeth Van Lew*. New York: Oxford University Press, 2003. Kindle Edition.

Veil, Charles Henry. *The Memoirs of Charles Henry Veil*. Ed. Herman S. Vida. New York: Orion, 1993. {9PR}

"Virginia Central Railroad." Wikipedia.

Vreeland, M.J. Letter of 7/4/62. Courtesy 4th Mich. reenactors. {4MI}

Waddell, A.M. "Memorial Address, General George Burgwyn Anderson." *SHSP* 14. 387.

Walker, C. Irvine. *The Life of Lt. Gen. Richard Heron Anderson*. Charleston, SC: Art, 1917.

Wall, H.C. *Historical Sketch of the Pee Dee Guards*. Raleigh, NC: Edwards, Broughton & Co., 1876. {23NC}

Wallace, Lee A., Jr. *3rd Virginia Infantry*. Lynchburg, VA: H.E. Howard, 1986. {3VA}

_____. *5th Virginia Infantry*. Lynchburg, VA: H.E. Howard, 1988. {5VA}

_____. *The Richmond Howitzers*. Lynchburg, VA: H.E. Howard, 1993.

Walling, William Henry. Letter of 7/4/62. Transcript of letters donated to RNBP by Richard S. Walling, E. Brunswick, N.J. {16NY}

Walshe, B.T. "Recollections of Gaines' Mill." *Confederate Veteran* 7 (1991): 54. {6LA}

The War of the Rebellion: A Compilation of the Official Records of the Union and Confederate Armies. Washington, DC: Government Printing Office, 1901. Republished by the National Historical Society, 1972.

Warner, A.J. Typescript in "Save the Flags" Collection, USAMHI. {10PR}

Warner, Corydon O. Warner Family Reunion, Set 2, Corydon O. Warner Collection, 44th Regiment. http://dmna.ny.gov/historic/reghist/civil/infantry/44thInf/44thInf_Warner_set2.htm; accessed 6/30/17.

Warner, Ezra J. *Generals in Gray*. Baton Rouge: LSU Press, 1959.

Waters, Zack, and James C. Edmonds. *A Small but Spartan Band*. Tuscaloosa: University of Alabama Press, 2010.

Welch, Spencer Glasgow. *A Confederate Surgeon's Letters to his Wife*. Marietta, GA: Continental, 1954. {13SC}

Wellman, Manly Wade. *Rebel Boast*. New York: Henry Holt, 1956.

Wert, Jeffry D. *General James Longstreet: The Confederacy's Most Controversial Soldier: A Biography*. New York: Simon & Schuster, 1993.

Westervelt, William B. *Lights and Shadows of Army Life*. Marlboro, NY: C.H. Cochrane, 1886. {27NY}

Wheeler, Richard. *Sword Over Richmond*. New York: Harper Perennial, 1986.

White, Gregory C. *A History of the 31st Georgia Volunteer Infantry*. Baltimore: Butternut and Blue, 1997.

"White House Landing." Wikipedia.

Whitman, William E.S., and Charles H. True. *Maine in the War for the Union*. Lewiston, ME: Nelson Dingley, Jr., 1865.

Wilcox, Cadmus. "Four Years with General Lee." *Southern Historical Society Papers* 6 (1990): 77. {8AL} {9AL} {10AL} {11AL} {12AL}

Williams, Geo F. *Bullet and Shell*. New York: Fords, Howard and Hulbert, no date. {5NY}

Williams, J.H. "Wilcox's Brigade at Gaines' Mill." *Confederate Veteran* 7 (1991): 443. {8AL} {9AL} {10AL} {11AL} {12AL}

Wills, Ridley II. *Old Enough to Die.* Franklin, TN: Hillsboro Press, 1996. {1TN} {7TN} {14TN}

Wise, George. *History of the Seventeenth Virginia Infantry.* Baltimore: Kelly, Piet & Co., 1870. {17Va}

Wise, Jennings Cropper, *The Long Arm of Lee.* Lynchburg, VA: J.P. Bell, 1915.

Wood, H.E. "A Typical Confederate—Jesse Barber." *Confederate Veteran* 16 (1991): 114. {18VA}

Wood, James H. *The War.* Gaithersburg, MD: Butternut Press, 1984. {37Va}

Wood, William Nathaniel. *Reminiscences of Big I.* Wilmington, NC: Broadfoot, 1987. {19Va}

Woodard, Elmer. "Mystery Ammunition of the 5th New York Infantry, Duryea's Zouaves." *Military Collector & Historian* 58, No. 4.

Woodward, E.M. *History of the Third Pennsylvania Reserves.* Trenton, NJ: MacRellish & Quigley, 1883. {3PR}

_____. *Our Campaigns.* Ed. Stanley W. Zamonski. Burd Street Press, 1995. {2PR}

Woodward, Harold R., Jr. *The Confederacy's Forgotten Son.* Natural Bridge Station, VA: Rockbridge, 1993.

Woodward, J.J. *Medical and Surgical History of the War of the Rebellion.* Washington, DC: Government Printing Office, 1870.

Young, William A., Jr., and Patricia C. Young. *56th Virginia Infantry.* Lynchburg, VA: H.E. Howard, 1990. {56VA}

Index